Design of CMOS Millimeter-Wave and Terahertz Integrated Circuits with Metamaterials

Design of CMOS Millimeter-Wave and Terahertz Integrated Circuits with Metamaterials

Hao Yu
Yang Shang

CRC Press
Taylor & Francis Group
Boca Raton London New York

CRC Press is an imprint of the
Taylor & Francis Group, an **informa** business

First published in paperback 2024

Published 2016 by CRC Press
2385 NW Executive Center Drive, Suite 320, Boca Raton FL 33431

and by CRC Press
4 Park Square, Milton Park, Abingdon, Oxon, OX14 4RN

CRC Press is an imprint of Taylor & Francis Group, LLC

Version Date: 20150806

Publisher's Note
The publisher has gone to great lengths to ensure the quality of this reprint but points out that some imperfections in the original copies may be apparent.

ISBN: 978-1-4822-3815-0 (hbk)
ISBN: 978-1-138-89412-9 (pbk)
ISBN: 978-0-429-07608-4 (ebk)

DOI: 10.1201/b19373

Contents

SECTION IV: CMOS THZ SIGNAL DETECTION 211

SECTION V: APPLICATIONS 259

List of Figures

List of Tables

Preface

Terahertz (THz) radiation ($0.1 \sim 30$ THz) fills the gap between electronics and photonics with unique spectroscopic and communication properties. A great deal of attention has been paid to THz electronic and photonics recently due to their moderate wavelengths to leverage advantages of both microwave and optics, such as good bandwidth, spatial resolution, and penetration depth with no harmful ionization. However, the current optics-based THz systems are bulky, expensive, lack portability, and have low detection capability by electro-optic sampling techniques.

With the rapid scaling of CMOS technology, it has become feasible to realize integrated circuits with the standard CMOS process in millimeter-wave (mm-wave) and even the THz frequency region toward low-cost, portable and large-arrayed systems on a chip. However, it is still challenging to deal with generation, amplification, transmission and detection of THz signals by a single CMOS transistor due to the huge substrate and path propagation loss as well as low device gain. Instead, one needs to figure out how to have a coherent design of arrayed CMOS transistors with high output power, high gain, and high sensitivity. The main point here is how to manipulate the phase of EM waves.

As such, this book shows that with the use of metamaterials, one can have coherent THz signal generation, amplification, transmission, and detection for arrayed CMOS transistors with significantly improved performance. New metamaterial-based THz imaging and communication systems have been demonstrated in CMOS as well.

- For CMOS THz signal generation, the target is to improve the output power and power efficiency with a wide frequency tuning range (FTR) in a compact size. By coupling N oscillators in-phase, the coupled oscillator network (CON) can effectively achieve an N times higher output power but also N times less phase noise. The conventional on-chip coupling network by a length of $\lambda/2$ or λ transmission-line

(T-line) is too bulky and lossy with difficulty for the same purpose as phase synchronization. Non-resonant-type metamaterials such as the magnetic plasmon waveguide (MPW) with zero-phase-shift property can be applied to achieve an in-phase and low-loss coupling between oscillators with compact size, which enables the design of a THz signal source with high power density and high efficiency.

- For CMOS THz signal amplification, the target is to improve the output power density and bandwidth. With the use of non-resonant-type metamaterials, composite right-/left-handed (CRLH) T-line, a new 2D distributed in-phase power-combining network can be developed to provide distributed amplification and power combining within a compact area simultaneously. As such, one can achieve high output power, high output power density and wide-band performance for a power amplifier (PA).
- For CMOS THz signal transmission, the target is to design wide-band, high-gain on-chip antennas within a compact area. Substrate integrated waveguides (SIW) have been recently explored for the design of high quality factor (Q) passive devices from mm-wave to THz, which enables an on-chip antenna design that can leverage the advantages of both planar T-line and non-planar waveguides with low loss and wide band performance in a miniaturized cavity. Moreover, a non-resonant-type metamaterial such as CRLH T-line with a nonlinear phase-to-length relationship enables more compact antenna design toward even higher gain and efficiency.
- For CMOS THz signal detection, the target is to improve receiver sensitivity within a compact size. The use of resonant-type metamaterial, transmission line (T-line) loaded with a split ring resonator (TL-SRR) or complementary split ring resonator (TL-CSRR), can significantly improve both high-Q oscillation and oscillatory amplification within a compact area. As such, one can achieve high sensitivity for a super-regenerative receiver (SRX) with quench control. Moreover, with the use of zero-phase coupling, one can further improve sensitivity.

Finally, with the proposed coherent component designs, both narrow and wide-band THz transceivers can be demonstrated at 135 GHz and 280 GHz, respectively. In summary, the coherent CMOS THz transceiver by metamaterials is explored in this book with significantly improved performance for signal generation, transmission, and detection. For signal generation, non-resonant-type metamaterials such as MPW can be applied for high-power signal source designs; for signal amplification, non-resonant-type metamaterials such as CRLH T-line can be applied for high PAE and compact power amplifier designs; for signal transmission, non-resonant-type metamaterials such as CRLH T-line can be applied for high-gain antenna designs; for signal detection, resonant-type metamaterials such as DTL-SRR or DTL-CSRR can be applied in high-sensitivity receiver designs. The component designs are supported by chip demonstrations with measurement results. The system performance is also evaluated after CMOS-based system-on-chip integration. It has shown great potential for metamaterial-based coherent designs for CMOS THz electronics with wide applications in next-generation communication and imaging systems.

Acknowledgments

The authors of the book would like to acknowledge all the staff of the School of Electrical and Electronic Engineering and VIRTUS IC Design Centre of Excellence at Nanyang Technological University, who have provided a lot of guidance during the research period and endless support in using the lab facilities. In particular, we thank all the wonderful and talented students and staff in the NTU CMOS Emerging Technology Group, such as Wei Fei, Chang Yang, Yuan Liang, Nan Li, Deyun Cai, Haipeng Fu, Shunli Ma and Wei Meng Lim, who have given us lot of valuable support in the process of the research work. We thank them for all their help, interest and valuable hints. Moreover, we appreciate the fruitful comments and measurement support from the staff at the Institute of Microelectronics, A*STAR in Singapore, such as Sanming Hu, Xiaojun Bi, Minkyu Ge and Muthukumaraswamy Annamalai Arasu. In addition, we appreciate the technical discussion and collaboration from our colleagues such as Prof. Junyan Ren, Prof. Tiejun Cui, Prof. Kiat Seng Yeo, Prof. Howard Luong, Prof. Yueping Zhang, Prof. Qun Gu, Prof. Baoyong Chi, Prof. Qijie Wang, Prof. Linlin Sun and Prof. Zhihua Wang. Finally, we should give great appreciation to our family members for their love and endless support. This book would never have been possible without their devotion and sacrifice. We also appreciate funding support from Singapore-MOE, Singapore-NRF and Huawei, the EMX simulation tool from Integrand Software, and CMOS 65 nm tapeout support from MediaTek and Global Foundries.

FUNDAMENTAL I

Chapter 1

Introduction

1.1 Overview of Terahertz Technology

The terahertz (THz) radiation (0.1 $\sim$ 30 THz) is categorized between millimeter-wave (mm-wave) and infrared light wave [16]. Recently, a great deal of attention has been paid to the THz spectroscopy and imaging system due to the moderate wavelength of the THz wave that can leverage the advantages of both millimeter-waves (mm-waves) and light waves [17, 16, 18]. Like mm-wave, THz wave has deep penetration to dielectric substances such as ceramics, plastics, powders and food; like light wave, THz images with high spatial resolution can be obtained by a 2-dimensional (2D) detection with THz sensor array [19]. On the other hand, high-data-rate THz wireless communications have also come into view due to the abundance of undeveloped bandwidth resources [20].

1.1.1 Terahertz Applications

1.1.1.1 Terahertz Spectroscopy and Imaging

Spectroscopy is a very mature method to identify substance composition by fingerprint analysis in physical and analytical chemistry. A comparison of general spectroscopy and imaging technologies is shown in Table 1.1. The commonly used spectroscopy methods are Fourier transform infrared spectroscopy (FTIR), non-dispersive infrared spectroscopy (NDIR), Ramen spectroscopy, and X-ray spectroscopy. THz spectroscopy not only shows the unique spectral fingerprints for many substances [21], but also has several distinct advantages when compared to these conventional spectroscopy methods. Firstly, unlike X-ray, THz radiation is safe to the tissue under test as well as the people

Table 1.1: Comparison of General Spectroscopy and Imaging Technologies

Specifications	Ultrasound	MRI	THz	FTIR, NDIR, Ramen	CM, OCT	X-rays
Applications	Imaging	Imaging	Spectroscopy & Imaging	Spectroscopy	Imaging	Spectroscopy & Imaging
Radiation	Mechanical wave	Magnetic field	EM wave (Non-ionizing)	EM wave (Non-ionizing)	EM wave (Non-ionizing)	EM wave (Ionizing)
Frequency (Hz)	10^6-10^7	10^7-10^8	10^{11}-10^{13}	10^{13}-10^{15}	$\sim 10^{15}$	10^{16}-10^{19}
Molecular interactions	No	No	Yes	No	No	No
Image resolution	~2mm	~1mm	~200μm	—	0.1-10μm	~15nm
Penetration depth to human body	200-300mm	>1m	1-3mm	0.5-5μm	0.2-0.8μm	>1m

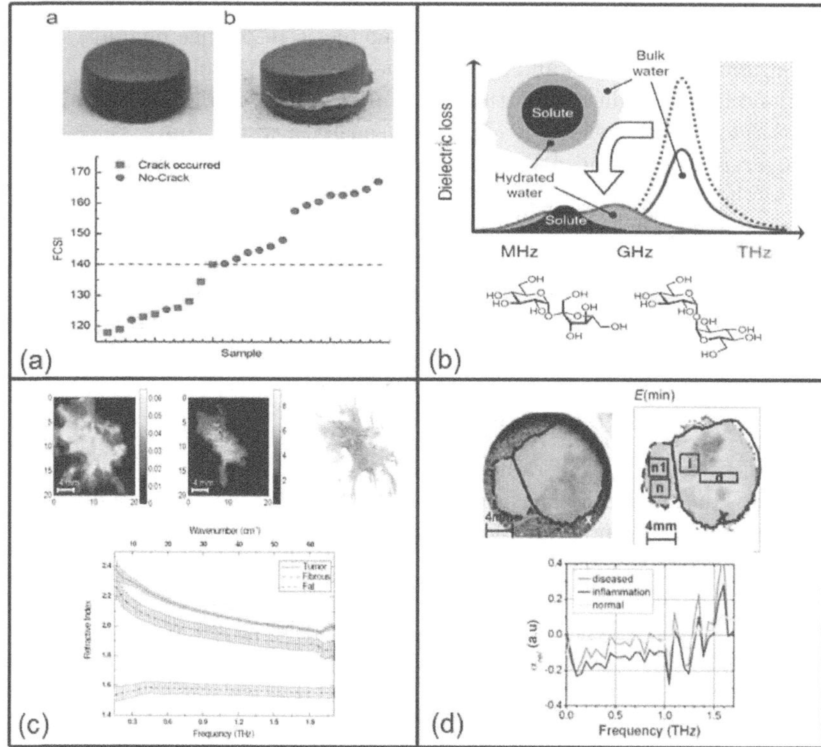

Figure 1.1: Application examples of THz spectroscopy and imaging. (a) non-destructive detection of crack initiation in a film-coated layer on a swelling tablet [1], (b) hydration state characterization in solution [2], (c) *in-vitro* breast cancer diagnosis [3], and (d) *in-vivo* skin cancer diagnosis [4].

who are conducting the measurement due to its longer wavelength and non-ionizing nature [16]. Secondly, many materials that cannot be penetrated by infrared are transparent to THz, which enables a non-destructive analysis to the coated substance. For example, THz-based inner layer reflectance analysis can be applied in the thin-film coating analysis of drug tablets as shown in Figure 1.1(a) [1]. Thirdly, THz radiation is highly sensitive to the water hydration state, which can be utilized in the concentration analysis of disaccharide water solutions as shown in Figure 1.1(b) [2]. Finally, THz radiation is more sensitive to the vibration and interaction of molecules such as protein or polymer. Therefore, it can be utilized for the in-vitro cancer diagnosis (Figure 1.1(c)) [3] as well as explosive detection [22].

THz imaging also has several distinct advantages compared to other imaging techniques, such as ultrasound scan, magnetic resonance imaging (MRI), confocal microscopy (CM) and optical coherence tomography (OCT). Firstly, THz imaging has higher resolution than ultrasound scan or MRI due to its much shorter wavelength. It is also more sensitive to the thin tissues due to a stronger reflection and attenuation in the water content. Secondly, compared to the existing optics-based imaging methods such as CM and OCT, even though the THz imaging system has lower resolution, it has much higher penetration depth due to its much longer wavelength. Recently, with remarkable contrast in skin and breast cancer demonstrated in THz images as shown in Figure 1.1(d) [3, 4], the THz imaging system has been used as an intra-operative tool during breast cancer surgery in Guys hospital in London [23].

1.1.1.2 Terahertz High-Data-Rate Wireless Communication

Ever since the invention of radio in the late 1800s, the pace of development of wireless communication has never stopped. In the past half century, the carrier frequency of communication systems has rapidly increased from several megahertz (MHz) into multi-gigahertz (GHz) ranges to satisfy the growing bandwidth requirement. The recently developed 60GHz systems with 5 $\sim$ 9GHz license-free band are able to provide a transfer speed up to 10 Gb/s for short distance data communication [5]. In order to further enhance the data transfer speed to multiple tens or hundreds of Gb/s for various applications such as ultra-high definition TV in the near future, we have to develop the communication systems in THz regime with abundant bandwidth resources. The application of THz communication systems can be mainly categorized into in-door data-links and system level data-transfer as shown in Figure 1.2.

For the in-door data-links application, one THz wireless data transmission was initially demonstrated in 2009 at 300GHz with a photonics-based transmitter; this system is able to achieve a data rate of 12.5 Gb/s over 0.5-m distance [24]. The lab scale communication was also demonstrated at 625 GHz with a data rate of 2.5Gb/s in 2011 [25]. Most recent developments in semiconductor technologies have demonstrated a very clear potential of higher-level integration with wireless I/Os for inter-chip or intra-chip communication [26], which is very likely to be achieved in THz. Recently, an integrated millimeter-wave integrated circuits (MMICs) THz transceiver has been demonstrated in 50nm mHEMT technology with a data rate of 25 Gb/s at 220 GHz [27]. Potentially, it is very promising for inter-chip or intra-chip communication in THz regime with high data rate and energy efficiency [28, 29].

1.1.2 Optics-Based Terahertz System

The current optics-based THz imaging system is developed by the well-known electro-optic sampling technique [30] as shown in Figure 1.3. When an ultra-short optical pulse ($\sim$50 femtoseconds) illuminates a non-linear semiconductor

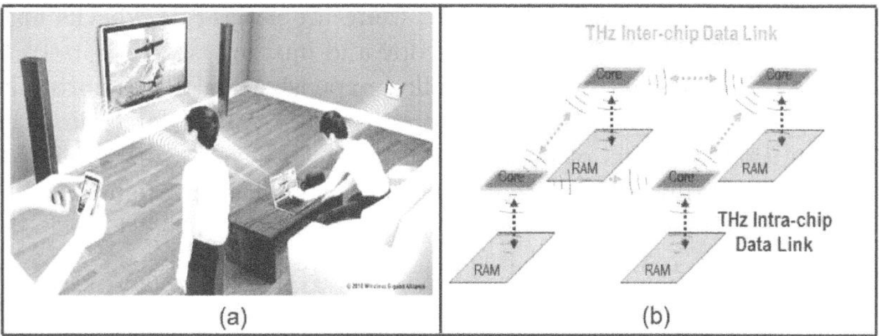

Figure 1.2: Application examples of THz communication. (a) high-definition multimedia interface (HDMI) provided by WiGiga and Wireless-HD [5], and (b) THz intra-chip high speed data link between core and memory, and THz inter-chip high speed data link between core and core.

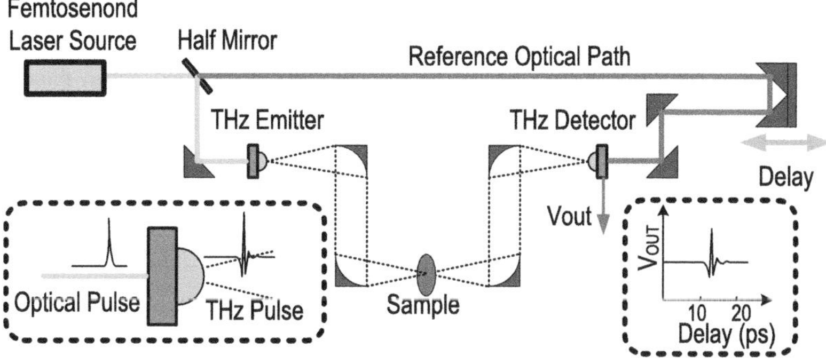

Figure 1.3: Schematic of a THz spectroscopy and imaging system by electro-optic sampling technique in transmission type.

material such as Zinc Telluride (ZnTe), a very short electric pulse is generated at the input of the dipole antenna with THz power spectrum. The average power level of the THz signal generated in this way is in the order of nanowatts, The resulting THz pulse usually has a very wide bandwidth, of which the upper and lower frequency boundaries are determined by the charge carrier's acceleration in the semiconductor material and the antenna cut-off frequency, respectively. After penetrating through the sample under test, the resulting THz radiation is coherently detected in the time domain with both intensity and phase information, which can be further utilized in the non-destructive testing as well as 3D imaging. However, there are several drawbacks in the optics-based time domain THz spectroscopy and imaging system. Firstly, the optics-based THz system is usually bulky, expensive and lacks portability. For example, a Ti:Sapphire laser source is usually required for femtosecond pulse generation, and lots of mirrors and lenses are needed for optical path adjustment. Secondly, the detection resolution and efficiency are limited. The absorption and reflection properties of tissues are usually spectral specific. As such, low spectrum resolution in frequency domain results.

1.2 CMOS THz Electronics

The THz imaging system can be potentially implemented by electronic approaches. With the rapid scaling of CMOS technology, it has become feasible to realize integrated circuits with standard CMOS process in THz regime towards a low-cost, portable and large-arrayed THz imaging system on a chip. Recently, several CMOS-based transmitting and receiving components have been developed in THz [31, 32, 33, 34, 35]. As shown in Fig. 1.4(a) from [6], when the size of transistors is scaling down, the gap between CMOS transistors and three five-group transistors is getting smaller and smaller. The ITRS (International Technology Roadmap for Semiconductors) projected roadmap of f_t and f_{max} for NMOS transistors is shown in Figure 1.4(b). By the year 2020, the f_{max} of CMOS transistors will be higher than 1THz. Compared to the other semiconductor fabrication processes like SiGe, InP or GaAs, stan-

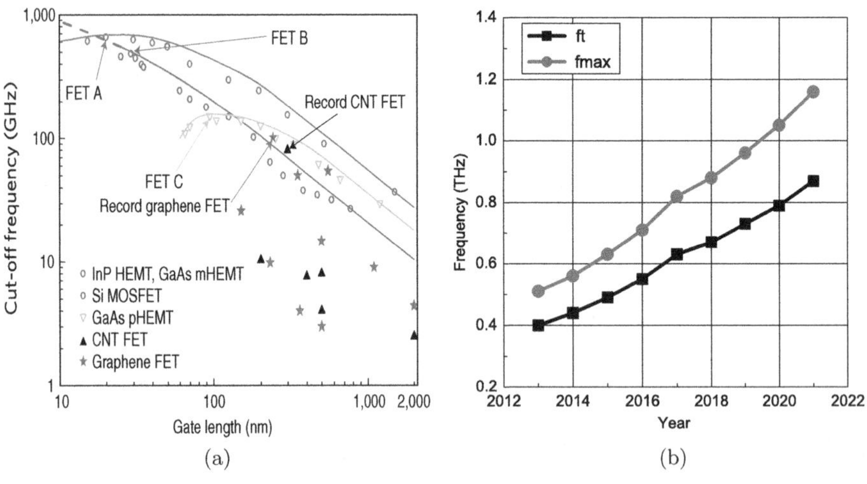

Figure 1.4: (a) Comparing cut-off frequencies for different FETs [6]; (b) ITRS projected f_{max} and f_t of NMOS transistors.

dard CMOS technology is always considered as the most cost effective solution to combine all digital, analog and RF system designs. Moreover, CMOS-based transmitter and receiver designs provide much higher flexibility in the power amplification and frequency control. As such, the THz imaging can be directly performed in frequency domain with improved detection resolution and efficiency. Therefore, it is of great interest to develop a CMOS-based THz imaging system with high resolution, low cost and high portability.

1.3 CMOS THz Applications

1.3.1 THz CMOS Imaging

As shown in Figure 1.5, THz waves suffer great loss when propagating inside free space. As a result, the major challenges in the CMOS imaging system design are to deal with the generation, transmission and detection of THz signals. Take 300GHz signal for example, assuming the power generated by the signal source is -15 dBm and it suffers a free space path loss of about 80~ 90 dB for 1 meter distance, if the antennas on both transmitter and receiver side can both provide 20dB gain, the sensitivity of receiver must be better than -85 dBm to detect the signal. Usually in a standard CMOS process, the transmitting power is limited by the maximum source drain voltage and the current, the receiver sensitivity is limited by the noise figure and bandwidth of receiver frontend, the gain and radiation efficiency of antennas are limited

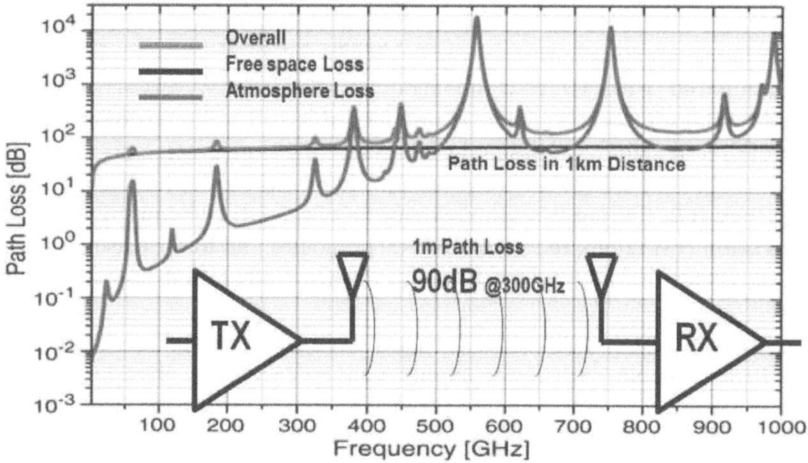

Figure 1.5: Design challenges of THz imaging system to overcome the huge path.

by the loss of metal and substrate and antenna size, respectively. In order to overcome the above difficulties and design a high-performance THz imaging system in CMOS process, the design of a high-Q passive structure is required in every part of the imaging system to replace the conversional transmission lines (T-line) or LC-tank resonators, which usually suffer from large size and low quality factor in THz and greatly limit the system performance.

1.3.2 THz CMOS Communication

The ever-expanding data size in various applications and associated increasing processing capability and memory size in mobile devices call for high-data-rate communication systems which can handle multi-Gbps data rate with compact size and low power consumption at the order of hundreds of mW or less. For example, the 5$\sim$9GHz license-free band at 60 GHz is attractive to meet these requirements.

For short distance communication with lower power consumption, normally line-of-sight set-up is used due to the high attenuation from passing through (around 40$\sim$50 dB) and reflection from (around 10$\sim$20 dB) a wall. As a result, the distance is normally targeted around ten meters or below to cover the distance within a room.

Recently, there has been extensive research on short distance THz communication systems [36, 37, 38, 39, 40, 41, 42, 43, 44, 45]. The potential applications are the wireless High Definition Media Interface (HDMI) where you can have an uncompressed high-definition movie transferred from laptop and displayed on TV in real time; and Personal Area Network (PAN), where a wireless link could be used to replace various cables used in home, and connect all electronic devices together with high-data-rate routers to provide smart house applications.

Compared with III-V technologies, CMOS shows various advantages. Firstly, a high integration can be provided due to the lower power consumption of digital signal processing in CMOS. A high integration also lowers cost from multi-die package and improves performance with elimination of high-frequency IOs. Secondly, a low cost can be obtained. In addition to the lower fabrication cost compared with III-V technologies and lower package cost, the testing cost can also be largely reduced with built-in-self-test (BIST) integrated on chip.

However, CMOS also brings various design challenges. For example, scaled CMOS transistors with lower supply voltage in advanced technologies can largely reduce size and dynamic power for digital processing. Unfortunately, many Figure-of-Merits (FOMs) in the frontend such as output power, linearity, and noise all degrades along with reduced supply voltage. Furthermore, large Process-Voltage-Temperature (PVT) variation tends to occur with advanced CMOS technologies, which makes RF design less accurate and poses requirement on extra bandwidth to cover. These design challenges motivate

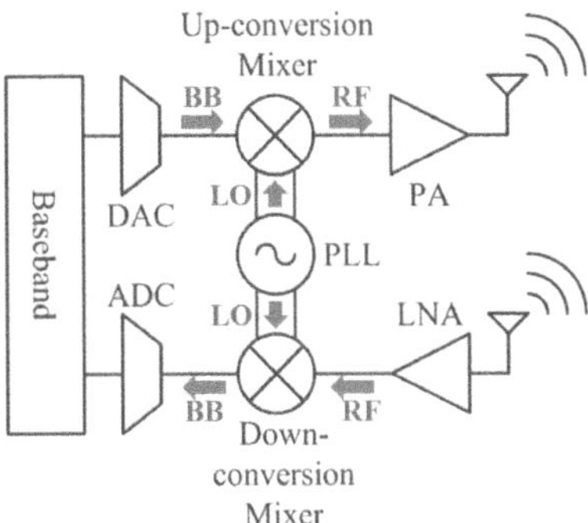

Figure 1.6: Simplified block diagram for a 60 GHz CMOS direct-conversion transceiver front end.

extensive researches on circuit and system innovations for 60GHz applications in CMOS [36, 37, 38, 39, 40, 46, 47].

Direct conversion architecture has the advantage of energy efficiency and was used for THz CMOS transceiver design in [48]. One simplified block diagram is shown in Figure 1.6. On the transmitter side, baseband digital signal is first converted to analog signal through a digital-to-analog convertor (DAC) and then up-converted to RF signal by mixing with the carrier (LO) generated by PLL through a mixer. The resulted RF signal is then amplified by a power amplifier (PA) and radiated out through the antenna. On the receiver side, the received RF signal from the antenna is first amplified by a low-noise amplifier (LNA) and then down-converted to baseband signal by mixing the corresponding LO generated by PLL through a mixer, which is further converted to digital signal through an analog-to-digital convertor (ADC).

As THz waves suffer great path propagation in free space, the primary challenge for THz communication system is to compensate the propagation loss with consideration of multi-path effect of channel. Usually, one needs to design a high-output power transmitter together with a high-sensitivity receiver to compensate the path loss. The present THz wireless systems are mainly single-input single-output (SISO) designs [49]. A wide-band and high-gain horn antenna is applied and is focused by aspherical Plano-convex lens to compensate high path loss in point-to-point link. This approach is hard to be integrated with the transceiver design. Recently, phase-arrayed multiple-input multiple-output (MIMO) design [50] can be developed to overcome the high path loss of the channel with a reasonable budget in the THz band.

In the phase-array MIMO architecture, a beam is formed in a desired direction by varying the relative delay in each element to compensate for the difference in propagation delays for signals from different elements. From a THz wireless system perspective, both the EIPR (the effective isotropic

Table 1.2: The Link Budget for THz Wireless Transmission System at 0.3 THz

	Norse floor (20 GHz bandwidth)	-70.8 dBm
	QPSK modulation (with 20G bps)	Eb/No=10dB @ BER=10^{-5}
Tx	Unit transmitter output power	-8 dBm
	Effective antenna gain	36 dBi
	EIPR	28 dBm
	Implementation loss	8 dB
Rx	Effective antenna gain	36 dBi
	Noise figure	10dB
	Demodulation loss	10 dB
	Implementation loss	8 dB
	Maximum allowed path loss	88.8 dB
	Maximum available distance (for amount link margin)	Around 5 m

radiated power) of the transmitter and sensitivity of the receiver can be improved in this MIMO architecture. For an n-element massive array, the antenna element is designed with a gain of 5dBi at 280GHz (estimated from our previous design [51]), the effective antenna gain is increased by $20\log_{10} n$. For example, if output power of each transmitter of a 100-element array is -8dBm for 280GHz modulated signal (estimated from our previous work [52]), the maximum permitted EIRP of 28dBm can be achieved. For the receiver side, the maximum antenna gain incensement of 36dB (for n = 64) can be achieved; this gain enhancement improves the signal strength (SNR) at the receiver side. Exemplary link budget for 64-element phase-arrayed MIMO transmission link at 300GHz can be seen in Table 1.2, which shows an enough link margin for implementing a near-field (~1m) THz wireless communication system by massive THz MIMO architecture.

Note that phase-arrayed MIMO can be used in two different modes: spatial diversity and spatial multiplexing. In spatial diversity mode, the same information is encoded into all transmit streams in such a way as to improve range of coverage. For low-frequency cellular network, diversity is often applied at receiving side of base station, because it is up-link limited in that scenario. An example of receiver spatial diversity is Maximal Ratio Combining (MRC); the signals from all receiver antennas are combined after first re-aligning their phases [53]. In spatial multiplexing mode, on the other hand, the transmission antennas simultaneously transmit independent signals over the same frequency channel, resulting in an increased spectral efficiency. In low-frequency applications, such as WLAN and cellular network, spatial multiplexing is widely applied in line-of-sight environment to support higher data rate with improved system capacity. For short-range THz high-speed wireless communication, phase-arrayed MIMO technique is more attractive. However,

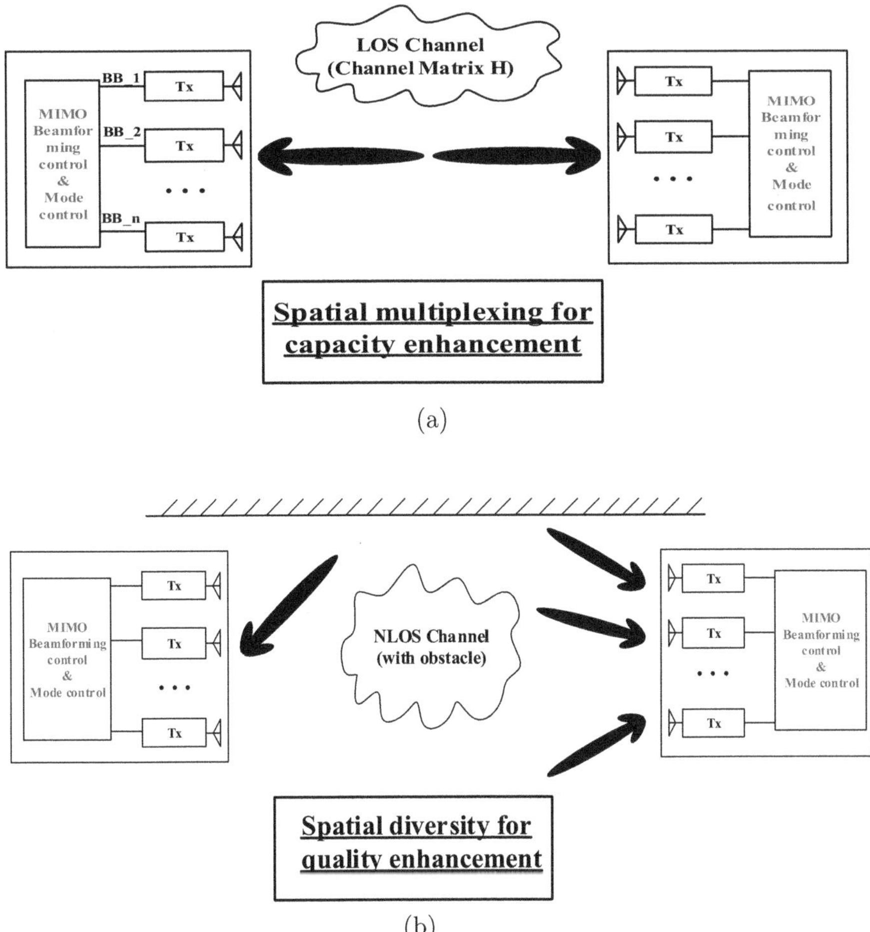

Figure 1.7: Two massive MIMO modes proposed for THz wireless link. (a) Spatial multiplexing mode in LOS scenario; (b) Spatial diversity mode in NLOS scenario.

different transmission scenarios are faced and have shown different characteristics compared to that in the low-frequency band. These differences inspire novel massive MIMO mechanism for THz wireless link. For different transmission scenarios, the following can be applied for performance enhancement.

- For LOS (Line-of-Sight) transmission, spatial multiplexing mode MIMO is applied as shown in Fig 1.7(a). Data of multiple users are transmitted simultaneously by each transmitter; and each receiver receives all transmitted data and separates (decode) them correctly for each user. For $M \times N$ MIMO, as given in (1.1), where M is the number of transmitter antennas, N is the number of receiver antennas. The relationship between the channel capacity and the SNR is logarithmic. This implies that trying to increase the data rate (capacity) by simply transmitting more power is not efficient. However, due to MIMO setup, as we can see from (1.1), a linear increase in capacity is obtained with respect to the number of transmitting antennas. Thus, it is more beneficial to transmit data using many different low-powered channels than by using one single, high-powered channel, which is a benefit of CMOS implementation as described previously.

$$C \approx M \times B \times log_2(1 + \frac{M}{N} SNR) \tag{1.1}$$

- For NLOS (Non-line-of-sight) transmission, some obstacles appeared between transmitter and receiver, and the spatial diversity mode MIMO is applied. Different from low-frequency band diversity where diversity is only deployed at the receiving side, both transmitter and receiver multiple-antenna structure is deployed for THz link, as shown in Figure 1.7(b). For the transmit side, the beam-forming operation is applied to concentrate all transmitters into one direction with largest radiation power. For the receiver side, spatial diversity is applied, where each receiver antenna captures the signal which experiences a different and independent fading environment. Then these received signals are combined based on an optimal algorithm for signal strength enhancement. As seen from (1.2), in a system with M transmitters and N receivers, the same signal is transmitted by each antenna. It is possible to achieve approximately an MN-fold increase in the SNR and then maintain a high data rate in a multipath environment with low error rate.

$$C \approx B \times Log_2(1 + M \cdot N \cdot SNR) \tag{1.2}$$

Chapter 2

CMOS Metamaterial Devices

2.1 Introduction

Metamaterial was first demonstrated by [54] with the use of split ring resonator (SRR) and metallic wire, among which SRR and metallic wire show the properties of negative permeability (μ) and negative permittivity (ε) at the resonance frequency, respectively. Metamaterial is not a traditionally defined material. It comprises many periodic or non-periodic unit cells. By giving different structure and property to these unit cells, the whole array of unit cells, which is the metamaterial, would show some properties that do not naturally exist. A more clear definition can be found in Figure 2.1 [55], where both x and y axes correspond to the material relative permittivity (ε_r) and permeability (μ_r), respectively. Most natural materials lie on the horizontal line in the 1st quadrant ($\varepsilon_r > 0, \mu_r > 0$) with a relative permittivity larger than 1 and a nearly unity relative permeability. But with metamaterial, by giving different design for unit cells, theoretically we can construct a material located in any of the regions of Figure 2.1 that enables many interesting applications. According to the transmission and reflection property, metamaterial can be categorized into two types: non-resonant-type and resonant-type.

Metamaterial in the 1st and 3rd quadrants are transmission-types, where EM wave is able to propagates inside. The EM wave that propagates in the 1st quadrant ($\varepsilon_r > 0, \mu_r > 0$) has a positive phase velocity, which is a linear function of frequency. But when metamaterial appears in the 3rd quadrant ($\varepsilon_r < 0, \mu_r < 0$), it is called left-handed material. Left-handed material has a non-linear negative phase velocity, which means when the energy propagates

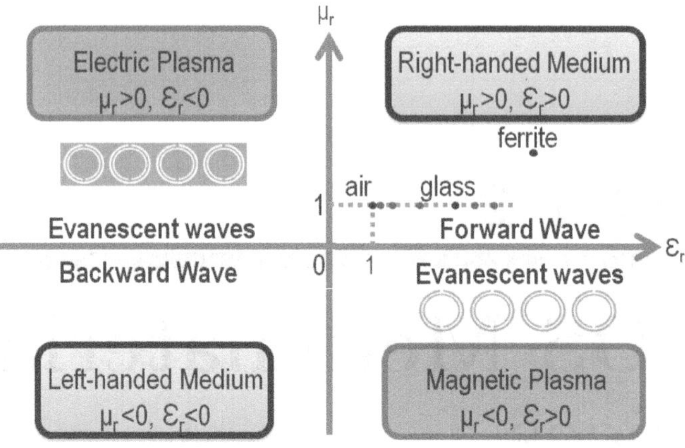

Figure 2.1: Definition of metamaterial.

forward in this material, the phase actually propagates backward. One application of left-handed material is to composite with right-handed material to provide zero phase propagation. Note that transmission-type metamaterial with zero phase propagation is located on the X or Y axes with $\varepsilon_r = 0$ or $\mu_r = 0$.

Metamaterial in the 2nd and 4th quadrants are resonant-types, where wave propagation is prohibited. When metamaterial appears in the 2nd quadrant ($\varepsilon_r < 0, \mu_r > 0$), it is called electric plasma. Evanescent wave will also be formed to strongly reflect the EM wave entering it. Such medium can be achieved by coupled right-handed material with a negative ε structure such as complementary split ring resonator (CSRR). When metamaterial appears in the 4th quadrant ($\varepsilon_r > 0, \mu_r < 0$), it is called magnetic plasma. An evanescent wave will be formed to strongly reflect the EM wave entering it. Such medium can be achieved by coupled right-handed material with a negative μ structure such as SRR.

2.2 Non-Resonant-Type Metamaterial

Non-resonant-type metamaterial such as magnetic plasmon waveguide (MPW) or composite right/left-handed (CRLH) T-line can be applied to achieve zero-phase-shifter with compact size. Magnetic coupled resonators have been extensively explored in the mm-wave filter designs since 1958 [56, 57]. But not until 2002, was MPW first proposed as a transmission medium by E. Shamonina and his colleagues [58]. In recent years, MPW is also applied in the middle distance wireless energy transmission systems [59, 60]. On the other hand, the applications of CRLH T-line have also been widely explored at PCB scale for the designs of various passive devices below 10GHz such as antennas, filters, hybrid couplers, baluns and power combiners [61, 62, 63, 64, 65, 66]. In addition, it can also be applied in the design of active devices such as distributed power amplifiers [67, 68]. Both MPW and CRLH T-line provide much more flexible phase control to the RF circuit with positive, negative or zero phase propagation modes, and their nonlinear phase-to-length relationships also enable much more compact designs compared to the ones with conversional T-line. When the operating frequency is further increased to THz region, potentially the application of the non-resonant-type metamaterial could largely reduce the size and increase the efficiency of on-chip devices. In this work, both MPW and CRLH T-line are explored for on-chip CMOS applications and used to overcome the fundamental limitations posed by conventional T-line for the CMOS designs from mm-wave to THz.

2.2.1 Composite Right-/Left-Handed T-Line

Metamaterial can be classified into two types: resonant type [69] and non-resonant type [70]. For applications that require wide bandwidth, non-resonant type metamaterial is preferred [71]. Typically, the left-handed property of T-line is realized with capacitors connected in series (C_s) and inductors connected in parallel (L_p). However, due to the unavoidable parasitics which are normally serial inductor (L_s) and parallel capacitor (C_p), the resulted T-line is actually a combination of left-handed T-line and normal right-handed (RH) T-line, and therefore called a composite right/left-handed (CRLH) transmission line [70]. Due to the distributive nature of T-line, one unit cell has the equivalent circuit as Figure 2.2(a).

The circuit can be viewed as two resonators connected together. L_s and C_e form the serial resonator, while L_p and C_p form the parallel resonator. Their impedance (admittance) can be represented as Z_s (Y_p). Here, all components (L_s, a_p, C_s, C_p) are normalized to unit cell length. According to transmission line theory, the propagation constant (γ) and characteristic impedance (Z_0) can be calculated as:

$$\gamma = \alpha + j\beta = \sqrt{\mathrm{Z_s} \times \mathrm{Y_p}} = \sqrt{-\frac{\left[\left(\frac{\omega}{\omega_\mathrm{s}}\right)^2 - 1\right] \times \left[\left(\frac{\omega}{\omega_\mathrm{p}}\right)^2 - 1\right]}{\omega^2 \times \mathrm{L_p} \times \mathrm{C_s}}} \tag{2.1}$$

$$Z_0 = \sqrt{Z_s \div Y_p} = \sqrt{\frac{(\frac{\omega}{\omega_s})^2 - 1}{(\frac{\omega}{\omega_p})^2 - 1} \times \frac{L_p}{C_s}} \tag{2.2}$$

where ω_s and ω_p are resonant frequencies for serial and parallel resonators, respectively. In addition, α and β are the attenuation constant and phase constant.

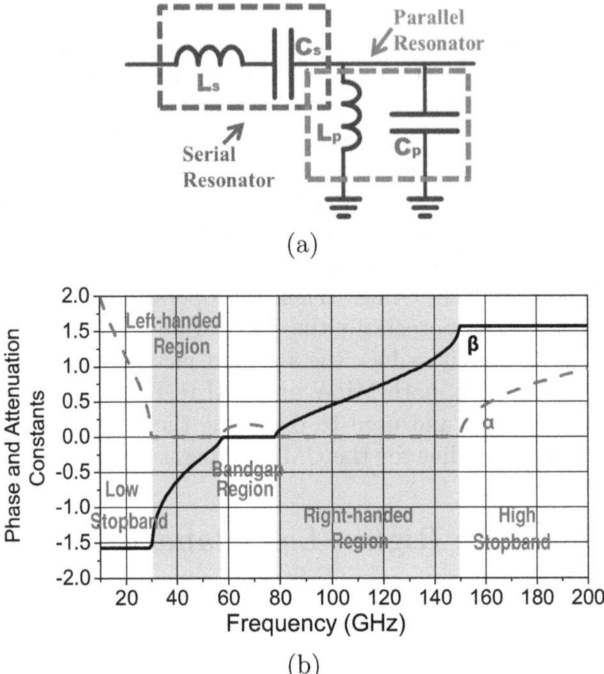

Figure 2.2: CRLH T-line: (a) equivalent circuit for T-line unit cell, (b) operating regions.

2.2.1.1 *Unbalanced CRLH T-Line*

From (2.1) we can see that if signal frequency is below the two resonant frequencies,

$$\alpha = 0, \beta = -\sqrt{\frac{\left[1-\left(\frac{\omega}{\omega_s}\right)^2\right]\times\left[1-\left(\frac{\omega}{\omega_p}\right)^2\right]}{\omega^2\times L_p\times C_s}} \tag{2.3}$$

the signal propagates backward. The transmission line operates in the left-handed (LH) region, where the phase contribution from LH components (L_p and C_s) dominate. In this region, a negative phase constant is achieved with low frequency, which can be used to replace traditional T-line to realize the same phase requirement with much more compact size and low loss. Based on this region, a tunable negative-phase CRLH T-line is implemented, with detailed discussion in Section 3.3.

If signal frequency is above the two resonant frequencies,

$$\alpha = 0, \beta = \sqrt{\frac{\left[\left(\frac{\omega}{\omega_s}\right)^2 - 1\right] \times \left[\left(\frac{\omega}{\omega_p}\right)^2 - 1\right]}{\omega^2 \times L_p \times C_s}} \tag{2.4}$$

the signal propagates forward. The transmission line operates in the right-handed (RH) region, where the phase contribution from RH components (L_s and C_p) dominates. The circuit behaves similarly to the traditional RH T-line.

If signal frequency is between the two resonant frequencies,

$$\alpha = \sqrt{-\frac{\left[\left(\frac{\omega}{\omega_s}\right)^2 - 1\right] \times \left[\left(\frac{\omega}{\omega_p}\right)^2 - 1\right]}{\omega^2 \times L_p \times C_s}} > 0, \beta = 0 \tag{2.5}$$

the signal doesn't propagate. The T-line operates in the band-gap region, where the phase contributions from LH and RH components cancel each other. A zero-phase can thus be realized to replace traditional RH $\lambda/2$ T-line with much more compact area and low loss. Based on this region, a Zero-Phase-Shifter (ZPS) is implemented, with detailed discussion in Section 3.2.

The relationship between β and frequency ω defines the dispersion diagram. Note here a lossless system is assumed. If lossy components are introduced, β cannot stay 0 in the band-gap region, and α can never became 0.

An example for ideal CRLH T-line unit cell is plotted in Figure 2.2(b) with L_s=100pHt^{-1}, L_p=100pHn^{-1}, C_s=50fFm^{-1}, and C_p=70fFm^{-1}. The dotted line displays attenuation constant α, and the solid line displays phase constant β. Negative (positive) phase constant is obtained in the left (right) hand region, where signal propagates backward (forward). Two additional stop-bands appear in the very low- and high-frequency regions due to CRLH T-line unit cell's nature as a band pass filter.

The CRLH T-line can he extended to a 2D system. The resulting left-handed region can be characterized by negative refractive index n.

$$n = \frac{c}{v} = \frac{c}{f\lambda} = \frac{c\beta}{\omega} \tag{2.6}$$

An example is shown in Figure 2.3. Note the refractive index below 60GHz should be negative and is mirrored to the positive side for easier observation.

2.2.1.2 Balanced CRLH T-Line

One special case occurs when the serial and parallel resonators have the same resonance frequency ($\omega_s = \omega_p$), and this is called the balanced case.

In this case, equations (2.1) and (2.2) reduce to:

$$\alpha = 0, \beta = \beta_R + \beta_L = \omega\sqrt{L_s C_p} - (\omega\sqrt{L_p C_s})^{-1} \tag{2.7}$$

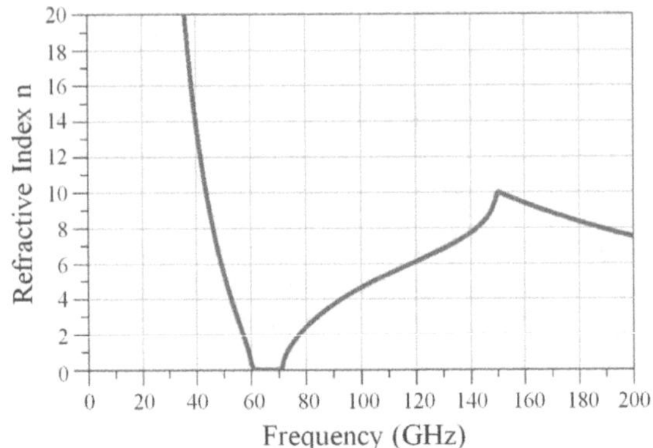

Figure 2.3: Refractive index for 2D CRLH metamaterial.

$$Z_0 = \sqrt{\frac{L_p}{C_s}} \tag{2.8}$$

where β_R and β_L are phase constants contributed from RH and LH T-line portions.

Notice the phase constant can now be split into RH and LH portions, and has a uniform equation for all frequencies. Furthermore, unlike the characteristic impedance for unbalanced case whose value varies with frequency, the characteristic impedance for the balanced case stays frequency independent.

With the dispersion relation between β and ω, the phase velocity (v_p) and group velocity (v_g) can be further obtained for the balanced case:

$$v_p = \frac{\omega}{\beta} = \frac{\omega_B^2\sqrt{L_pC_s}}{1-(\frac{\omega_B}{\omega})^2} \tag{2.9}$$

$$v_g = \frac{\partial\omega}{\partial\beta} = \frac{\omega_B^2\sqrt{L_pC_s}}{1+(\frac{\omega_B}{\omega})^2} \tag{2.10}$$

where ω_B is a constant. These two equations indicate opposite directions for v_p and v_g which suggest the LH region where a negative phase shift is obtained; and the same direction for v_p and v_g which suggest the RH region where a positive phase shift is obtained.

The dispersion diagram for ideal CRLH T-line unit cell in balanced condition is shown in Figure 2.4. The balanced resonance frequency ω_B is assigned at 60GHz. As the figure shows, the LH region and RH region locate side by side without a band gap between them.

Compared with the conventional RH T-line, which always has a positive phase-shift linearly proportional to the T-line length, CRLH T-line shows some

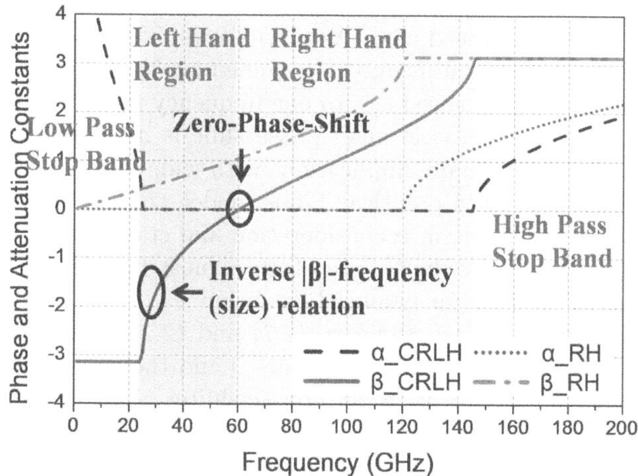

Figure 2.4: Dispersion diagram for CRLH T-line in the balanced case with comparison of RH T-line.

unique features such as zero-phase-shift at ω_B and high nonlinear negative-phase-shift in the LH region. These features are analyzed in detail in the following sections.

2.2.1.3 CRLH T-Line-based Zero-Phase-Shifter

ZPS by CRLH T-Line

For applications as mm-wave frequencies, the lumped capacitors and inductors to build CRLH T-line structure are more compact and less lossy and hence feasible for on-chip implementation in CMOS technology. More importantly, CRLH T-line can easily achieve the zero-phase-shift by combining the two phase-shifts in opposite directions for: 1) traditional right-handed T-line portion and 2) left-handed metamaterial portion (L_p and C_s).

An intuitive method to design a CRLH T-line-based ZPS is to bias the unit cell to operate in its band gap region, as shown in Figure 2.2(b). According to (2.5), when the operating frequency is in the band gap region ($\omega_s \leq$ d $\leq \omega_p$or $\omega_n \leq \omega \leq \omega_s$) the phase constant equals to 0 ($\beta = 0$). In this case, signals passing through CRLH T-line will not have any phase advance or delay. In other words, a zero phase shift is achieved. This condition, however, assumes the impedance matching from port to T-line is always maintained. As (2.2) shows, CRLH T-line's characteristic impedance (Z_0) is normally frequency dependent, which affects the matching for the whole SEDFDA (Single-ended dual-fed distributed amplifier), and therefore limits the actual bandwidth that can be achieved for zero-phase-shift region. A simple solution is to design the CRLH T-line in the balanced case. As (2.8) shows, in this case, Z_0 becomes frequency ω independent and is only determined by L_p and C_s. Although the band gap region in this case reduces to one frequency point, according to the following chapter, as long as a small phase shift is maintained, the CRLH T-line still works well in many applications with wide-band performance.

On the other hand, in a practical T-line model, the attenuation constant takes all loss from parasitic into consideration and stays positive ($\alpha > 0$) in all regions. Therefore, to reduce T-line loss, α must be reduced as much as possible, which is the case for balanced condition.

In the balanced case, according to (2.7) and (2.9), when the frequency equals to ω_B, the pease constant β becomes 0 and the phase velocity v_p becomes infinity. In other words, a zero-phase-shifter (ZPS) is obtained. The zero-phase CRLH T-line can replace $\lambda/2$ T-line in traditional RH design with the same phase requirement. Different from traditional RH T-line, the CRLH T-line phase-shift does not depend on its physical length. As a result, the T-line can be designed in a compact area with low loss. Furthermore, the large phase shift (π) in traditional $\lambda/2$ T-line means that a small percentage change can lead no a large phase error, which severely limits the bandwidth. The zero-phase CRLH T-line, on the other hand, centers at zero-phase and thus can achieve a smaller phase error. Therefore, the zero-phase CRLH T-line has appealing advantages to replace traditional $\lambda/2$ T-line with more compact size, lower loss and wider bandwidth.

In addition, for the sake of low loss and wide-band performance of CRLH T-line-based ZPS, both attenuation constant and phase constant need to be kept small. Eq. (2.1) gives the relation: $\alpha, \beta \propto \sqrt{\frac{1}{L_p \times C_s}}$. Although the formula is developed from a lossless system, the relation can be extended into lossy system. As a result, a large parallel inductor (L_p) and a large serial capacitor (C_s) reduce both T-line loss and phase error. To maintain the same serial and parallel resonant frequencies and thus the same operating frequency, a small parallel capacitor (C_p) and a small serial inductor (L_s) are required accordingly. In practice, C_p and L_s are realized by parasitic and wire connections to achieve maximized values for L_p and C_s.

Simulation and Measurement Results

To further characterize the performance of CRLH T-line-based ZPS and verify its benefits compared with a traditional $\lambda/2$ T-line, one ZPS unit cell is implemented in UMC 65nm logic and mixed-mode low-leakage low-K CMOS technology with 6-metal layers (1 thick metal layer). The circuit is designed and verified by EM simulation (ADS-Momentum) before fabrication.

As shown in Figure 2.5(a), a unit cell for CRLH T-line can be constructed by combining a serial capacitor (C_s) with a parallel inductor (L_p). The right-handed part of CRLH T-line comes from the Coplanar Waveguide (CPW) transmission line that connects unit calls, and parasitic capacitance between

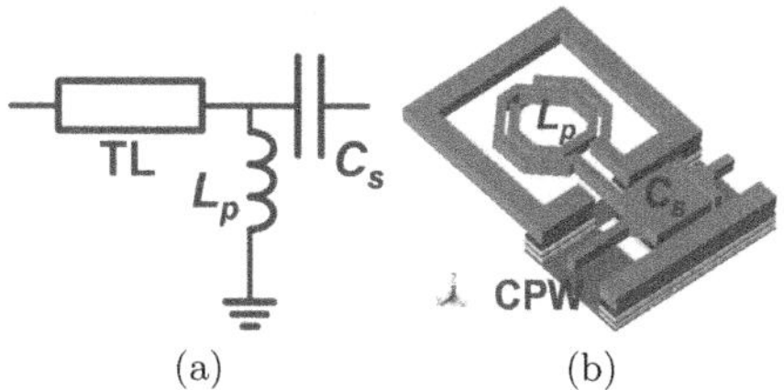

Figure 2.5: CRLH T-line-based ZPS unit cell: (a) schematic (b) layout.

unit cells and ground. Figure 2.6(b) shows the layout version of this unit cell, where L_p is a spiral inductor formed by top Metal layer (M6). The thick metal ring around L_p serves as ground to improve isolation between unit cells and to form a better distribution of ground, as described in [72]. C_s is a MOM capacitor constructed with multiple metal layers (M4-M6) in an inter-digit manner for better quality factor at 60GHz range. Notice the two ground traces of CPW are connected by metal 1 (M1) below, and the size of M1 can be adjusted to tune the total parallel capacitance to ground.

The ZPS unit cell is fabricated along with an open-short-through de-embedding structure. L_p is implemented with inductance of 220pH and Q factor of 13.4 at 70 GHz. C_s is implemented with capacitance of 150fF and Q factor of 19 at 70 GHz. The simulated and measured S parameters for CRLH T-line-based ZPS are shown in Figure 2.6, and are compared with the measured results of the conventional $\lambda/2$ T-line. According to Figure 2.6(a), the fabricated CRLH unit cell achieves a 30GHz bandwidth (57~87GHz) for a phase error less than 10°, which is 4 times wider than the 7GHz bandwidth (67~74GHz) for $\lambda/2$ T-line. The measured results agree well with EM simulation with a frequency shift-down of 4 GHz. According to Figure 2.6(b), the return loss is greater than 14dB for the entire near-zero-phase-shift region, indicating 50Ω characteristic impedance. The worst-case insertion loss is kept below 1.2dB, which is 3 times smaller than $\lambda/2$ T-line. There is a 0.8dB deviation from EM simulation for insertion loss, which is due to inaccurate substrate parameters.

Moreover, measurement demonstrates a low loss (<1.2dB) wide-band (30GHz) performance for the proposed CRLH T-line bused ZPS, which proves the feasibility for metamaterial application for CMOS designs in mm-wave region. Compared with the traditional $\lambda/2$ T-line, 4 times wider frequency band and 3 times less loss are achieved with 11 times reduction of physical length (86μm).

Note that to observe the left-handed property, its phase shift and effective phase constant can be obtained from s parameters [73]. Following is the formula used:

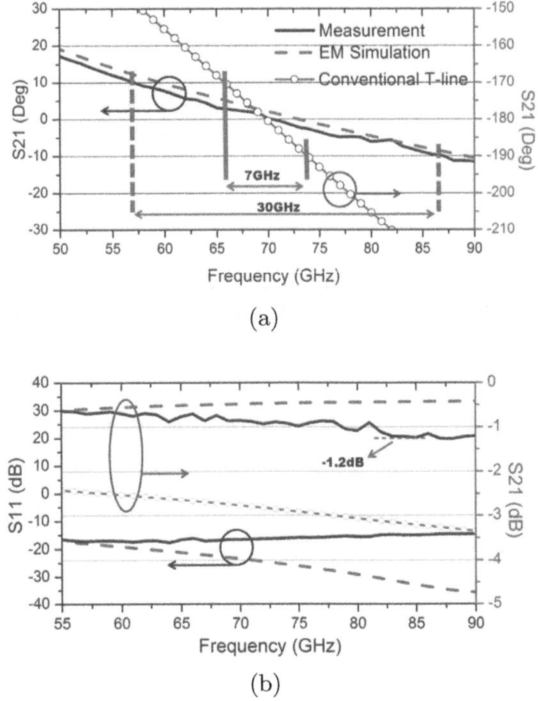

Figure 2.6: Simulated and measured S parameters for unit cell of CRLH T-line-based ZPS. Both (a) phase and (b) loss performances are compared with measured results for conventional $\lambda/2$ T-line.

$$\gamma \times p = cosh^{-1}\left(\frac{1 - S11 \times S22 + S12 \times S21}{2 \times S21}\right) \tag{2.11}$$

where p is the physical length of unit cell, and S is the propagation constant. For this design, p equals 86μm.

From Figure 2.7(a), we can see $\beta \times p$ and phase of S21 overlap with each other, which is justified by the fact that phase shift of unit cell approximately equals the product of phase velocity (β) and unit cell length (p) under impedance match. A small β within a wide frequency range therefore leads to wide-band performance.

The dispersion diagram is plotted in Figure 2.7(b), where the phase constant β ia obtained by dividing the phase shift ($\beta \times p$) to unit cell physical length (p). Notice absolute value of β is taken for easier observation. A fall-down curve for $|\beta|$ is observed below the zero-phase-shift region, indicating the left-handed region. Above the zero-phase-shift region is the right-handed

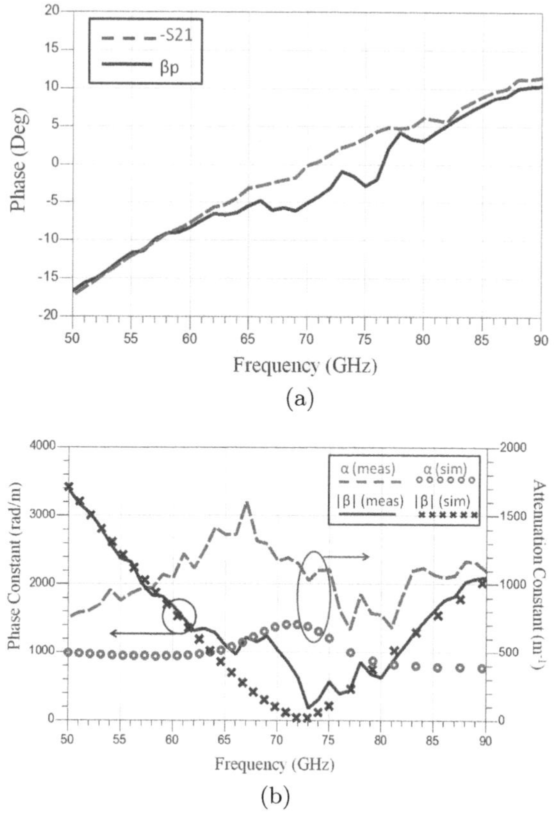

Figure 2.7: Characterization of CRLH T-line unit cell: (a) ZPS performance, (b) propagation constant.

region, where β becomes positive and keeps rising. The low-pass stop-band and high-pass stop-band are located around DC and very high frequency, respectively, and is not shown in the plot.

Differential ZPS

In many applications, differential topology is preferred for compact size, reduced loss and rejected noise. As it is unknown how to design an on-chip active differential zero-phase-shifter, in this section, differential CRLH T-lines are designed to obtain zero-phase-shift with circuit and layout diagrams shown in Figure 2.8. The serial capacitor C_s is realized with inter-digital capacitors for compact size. M1 shielding is used to improve the e_s quality factor. The parallel inductor L_p is implemented by a loop inductor. Thick top metal is used to minimize ohm and substrate loss. M1 shielding around the induc-

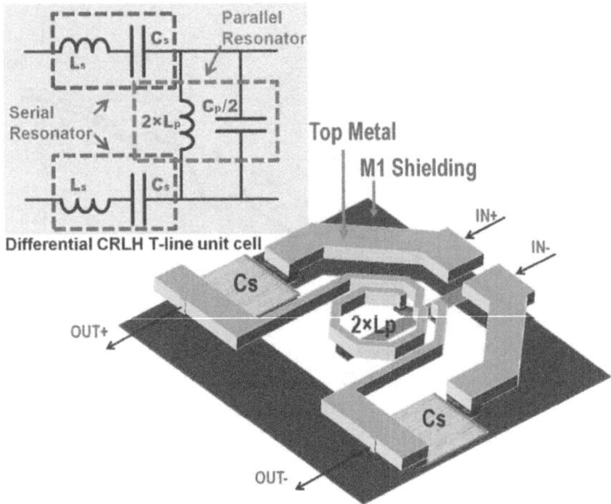

Figure 2.8: Equivalent circuit and layout diagrams for one unit cell of differential CRLH T-line-based zero-phase shifter.

tor reduces the loss in return ground and also improves isolation. Parasitic from transistors and connections form the RH T-line portion (L_s and C_p). Connection lines and M1 shielding are used to adjust L_s and C_p values for a zero-phase-shift at the targeted frequency ω.

Due to the differential design, the parallel inductor for the two differential branches can be merged together with reduced area and improved isolation. In addition, due to virtual ground on the central tap of the merged inductor, de-coupling capacitor is removed with further reduced area. As a result, zero-phase-shift can be achieved at designed frequency with compact area. For example, the differential ZPS unit cell in Figure 2.8 further reduces the size to only 61μm$\times$81μm while achieving the same ZPS frequency point (60GHz) as the single-ended design.

2.2.1.4 Tunable Negative-Phase CTLH T-Line

Another unique feature of CRLH T-line is the inverse relation between phase-shift and T-line size in its LH region. As (2.7) and Figure 2.4 show, the magnitude of phase constant in CRLH T-line is inversely dependent on its LH components (L_C and C_s) and frequency. In contrast, the phase change in RH T-line is linearly dependent on the LC values and frequency and stays positive. As such, the same phase shift in the RH T-line at a given frequency can be realized by CRLH T-line in the negative-phase region in Figure 2.4 with much smaller LC values and thus T-line size. For example, as shown in Figure 2.9, a $\lambda/4$ T-line can be realized by RH T-line at around 90GHz, but can be replaced with a CRLH T-line with -90° phase-shift at around 30GHz

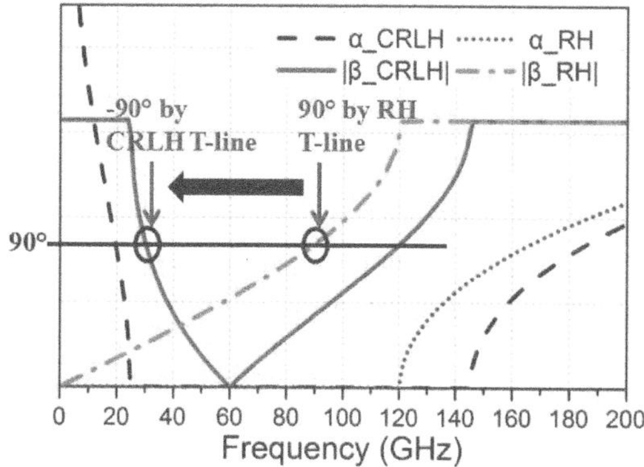

Figure 2.9: Compact size for negative-Chase CRLH T-line to achieve the same 90° phase-shift compared to traditional RH T-line.

with similar lumped component values and thus similar size. As a result, the required $\lambda/4$ T-line can be realized at the same frequency by -90° CRLH T-line biased in the LH region with much more compact size.

Though the negative-phase in the LH region shows a higher sensitivity to frequency and thus smaller bandwidth compared to ZPS, it does not impact the frequency tuning range (FTR). In fact, except for compact size, another benefit for the negative-phased CRLH T-line is the potential to achieve a wide FTR for VCO design. The tunability of CRLH T-line is analyzed here with balanced condition as shown in Figure 2.4 for simplicity, and similar analysis and conclusion can be extended to more general conditions.

As discussed, T-line is normally used in VCO design to realize traveling wave to generate multi-phase and low-noise clock outputs, by achieving certain phase-shift requirements (e.g., 360° phase-shift forms a loop). According to (2.7) in Section 2.2, the total phase shift of one CRLH T-line unit cell (θ) is contributed from two portions: the left-hand portion, and the right-hand portion:

$$\theta = \beta_R p + \beta_L p = \omega\sqrt{L_S C_p} - (\omega\sqrt{L_S C_p})^{-1} \tag{2.12}$$

where p is the T-line's physical length. Note that, different from (2.7), lumped components here are the normalized value to consider the phase shift instead of phase constant.

As shown above, CRLH T-line operating in the nonlinear LH region can replace the traditional RH T-line to achieve the same phase-shift requirement with much more compact size. When operating in nonlinear LH region, $\beta_L p$ dominates. The formula can thus be simplified to

$$\theta = \beta_L p = -(\omega\sqrt{L_p C_s})^{-1} = constant \tag{2.13}$$

$$\omega = (-\theta\sqrt{L_p C_s})^{-1}. \tag{2.14}$$

By taking the product of the LH components (L_p,C_s) as P_L, and the product of the RH components (L_s,C_p) as P_R, the tunability can then be analyzed as

$$\frac{\partial\omega}{\partial P_L} = \frac{1}{2\theta}(P_L)^{-\frac{3}{2}}. \tag{2.15}$$

The frequency tuning range (FTR) with CRLH T-line operating in non-linear LH region can then be estimated as

$$FTR_{LH} = \frac{\Delta\omega}{\omega} \approx \frac{1}{\omega} \times \frac{\partial\omega}{\partial P_L} \times \Delta P_L = \frac{\Delta P_L}{2P_L}. \tag{2.16}$$

Similarly, the FTR with traditional RH T-line can be estimated as

$$FTR_{RH} \approx \frac{\Delta P_R}{2P_R}. \tag{2.17}$$

Based on (2.16) and (2.17), the FTR depends on the tunability of the lumped component itself($\Delta P_e/P_R$ and $\Delta P_L/P_L$). Conventional RH T-line is mostly tuned by varactor and capacitor bank, where the tuning range is limited by the parasitic capacitance from transistors and constraint tuning ability of varactor and capacitor bank in millimeter-wave region. CRLH T-line, on the other hand, provides more choices of tunable elements such as inductive-loaded transformer [74] and avoids the effect of parasitic capacitance. As will be explained in Chapter 5, a much wider tuning range can be achieved.

In summary, by using tunable negative-phase CRLH T-line in nonlinear NH region to replace traditional RH T-line, the FTR can be largely improved with more compact size. Note that the high nonlinear dispersion curve in the LH region can be also used to generate dual-band or multi-band operation [75], which can further extend the tuning range.

2.2.1.5 Active CRLH T-Line

Most of the time, transistors need to be loaded in T-line to achieve desired functions. For example, in power combiner design for mm-wave PA, transistors need to be periodically loaded in the combining network where the output power of each transistor is combined in phase. While in mm-wave RTW-VCO design, transistors need to be distributed in the T-line loop to compensate the loss and facilitate oscillation. When considering transistors as a part of CRLH T-line, an active CRLH T-line or T-line network is obtained.

Traditional active CRLH T-line loads active devices as negative resistors to compensate the propagation loss. As shown in Figure 2.10(a), by loading a tunnel diode, negative resistance is introduced. Simultaneous negative α and negative β are demonstrated in [76], indicating the loss is compensated with maintained LH property. The same results can be obtained in a differential manner by replacing the tunneling diode with a cross-coupled transistor pair,

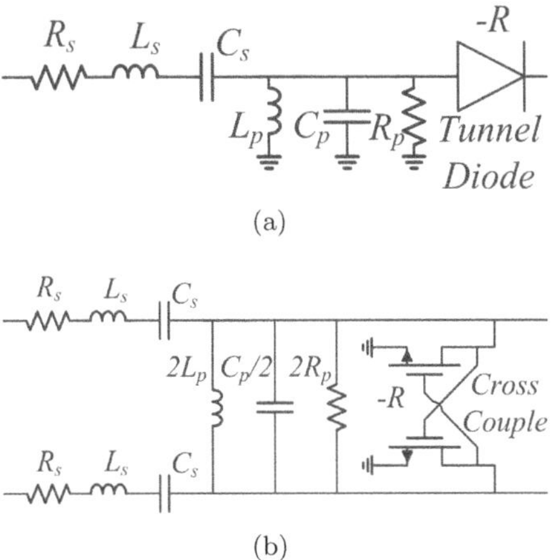

Figure 2.10: Traditional active CRLH T-line using tunnel diode or cross-coupled transistor to compensate for the propagation loss, (a) with tunneling diode, (b) with cross-coupled transistors.

as shown in Figure 2.10(b). The topology is used for CRLH T-line-based RTW-VCO design in Chapter 5.

However, these active CRLH T-line topologies are not feasible for PA design which requires signal amplification with maintained amplitude. Alternatively, transistor output power can be in-phase combined by directly connecting their outputs with zero-phase connections, which can be realized by the zero-phase CRLH T-line with transistor parasitic absorbed into the T-line design. Since zero-phase CRLH T-line can realize in-phase power combining both in parallel and in series, a 2D active CRLH T-line network is introduced in the following section, where a compact and high output power combining can be achieved.

2.2.2 Magnetic Plasmon Waveguide

MPW with zero phase propagation can be introduced in the coupling network design with $2k/N = 0$ to largely improve the output power within a compact area. It operates based on the inductive coupling between periodic resonators. The equivalent circuit of an ideal 1D MPW is shown in Figure 2.11(a). The plasmon resonators are coupled by the magnetic flux between adjacent resonators, which are represented by the LC networks with mutual inductances (M). Assuming the magnetic coupling only exists between adjacent resonators, each unit-cell consists of two magnetic coupled resonators. As

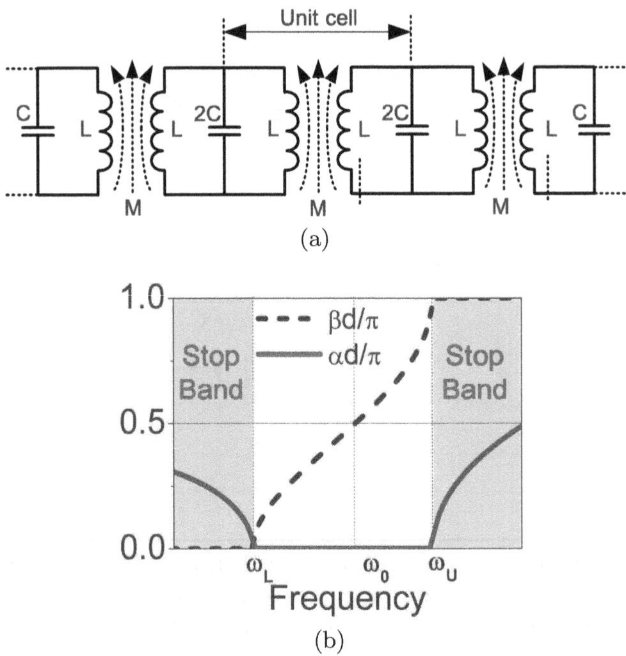

Figure 2.11: (a) Equivalent circuit of magnetic plasmon waveguide (MPW); (b) dispersion diagram of MPW.

such, the dispersion relationship can be written as:

$$\omega_0^2/\omega^2 - 1 = \frac{2M}{L}cos[(\alpha + j\beta)d] \tag{2.18}$$

where $j = \sqrt{-1}$, $\omega_0 = 1/\sqrt{LC}$ is the self-resonance frequency of the LC resonator, d is the distance between adjacent unit-cells, α and β are the attenuation coefficient and phase constant, respectively. Figure 2.2.1.5 shows the dispersion diagram. One can observe that both α and β are zero at the lower stop bands boundary ω_L with

$$\omega_L = \omega_0/\sqrt{1 + 2M/L} \tag{2.19}$$

where the zero phase propagation exists. When multiple MPW unit-cells are serially connected, the in-phase EM-energy can be stored in each unit-cell in zero phase propagation mode. A zero phase propagation mode operation is important for not only power combination but also phase noise reduction. The noise coupling network becomes reciprocal in the zero phase propagation mode, and the total phase noise will be reduced by N times when coupling N free running oscillators [77].

2.3 Resonant-Type Metamaterial

Metamaterial-based resonators have been explored recently for CMOS MMIC applications. The planar SRR structure can be considered as a magnetic dipole excited by the magnetic field (H-Field) along the ring axis as shown in Figure 2.12(a). Figure 2.12(c) shows the equivalent circuit of SRR unit cell, in which the equivalent inductance is coupled to the external applied magnetic flux. As the dual counterpart of SRR, CSRR shown in Figure 2.12(b) was proposed by [78] based on the well-known complementary theory. CSRR shows the metamaterial property of negative permittivity (ε) at resonance frequency, and can be considered as an electric dipole excited by the electric field (E-Field) along the ring axis. Figure 2.12(d) shows the equivalent circuit of CSRR unit cell, in which the equivalent LC resonator is driven by the external applied electric field.

In the recent years, there are several works proposed for the oscillator design with high-Q metamaterial resonators. SRR or CSRR-based oscillator design is explored in PCB scale at 5.5~5.8GHz [79, 80, 81]. TL-SRRs have also been studied on PCB substrate with operating frequencies below 10 GHz [82, 83]. A single-ended T-line loaded with SRRs (STL-SRRs) was designed with silicon substrate for 60 GHz MMIC applications [84]. This structure with multiple SRRs occupies a large silicon area and has weak EM coupling between T-line and SRR load, both of which will contribute to more energy loss. A 24 GHz CMOS oscillator based on open-loop multiple-SRR is presented as another kind of metamaterial resonator in [85].

In the regime from millimeter-wave to THz, the challenge is how to design

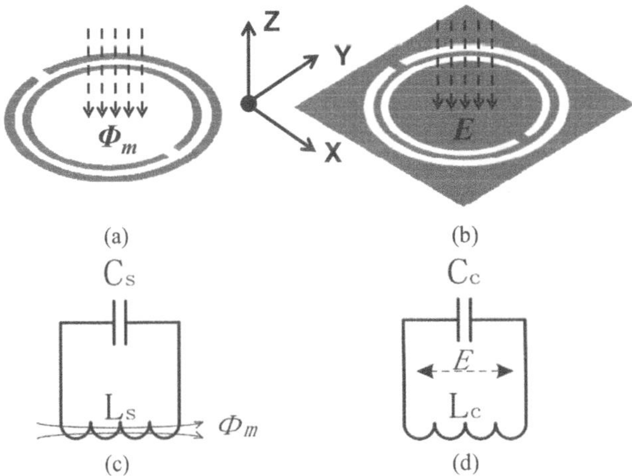

Figure 2.12: Layout topologies of SRR in (a), CSRR in (b), equivalent circuits of SRR in (c), CSRR in (d).

a low-energy-loss, strong EM coupling and high-area-efficiency metamaterial resonator for the MMIC applications. As explored in the mm-wave region, both SRR and CSRR can be applied as the load for a T-line to build compact on-chip metamaterial-based resonators with high-Q factor. When coupling either SRR or CSRR as load to a host T-line, a plasmonic medium with single negative ε or μ could be formed, called electric or magnetic plasmonic medium. A sharp band-gap or stop-band is formed in such a medium at the resonant frequency such that the EM-wave can be perfectly reflected back into the host T-line to form a stable standing-wave. Ideally, the EM-energy is stored in the compact SRR or CSRR structure, where the energy density can be significantly increased with a high-Q factor.

2.3.1 T-Line Loaded with Split Ring Resonator

As shown in Figure 2.13(a), T-line loaded with SRR (TL-SRR) can be implemented on chip by the topmost metal layer. By exciting SRR with the magnetic flux generated from the differential current in the host T-line, a magnetic plasmonic medium is formed by TL-SRR in the vicinity of SRR resonance frequency. SRRs are excited by the magnetic flux generated by the differential current flowing in the host T-line. The equivalent circuit of TL-SRR unit-cell is depicted in Figure 2.13(b). L and C are the intrinsic series inductance and shunt capacitance of T-line, while L_s and C_s are the equivalent inductance and capacitance of SRR. M is the mutual inductance between SRR and T-line.

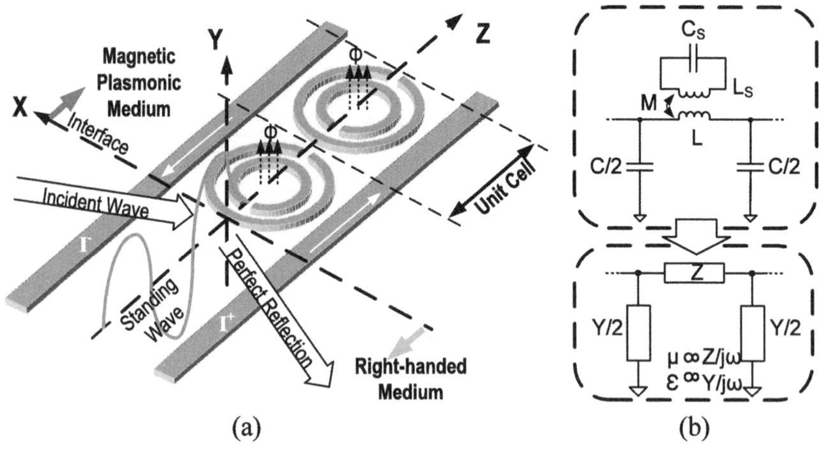

Figure 2.13: (a) Standing-wave formed by perfect reflection at DTL-SRR; (b) equivalent circuit of DTL-SRR with condition to form perfect reflection.

The metamaterial property for TL-SRR can be analyzed by T-line model [86]. Recall that T-line is usually modeled by distributed series impedance (Z) and shunt admittance (Y) with determined ε and μ, respectively. It can be shown that $\varepsilon > 0$ and $\mu < 0$ condition can be satisfied by TL-SRR in the frequency range

$$\sqrt{\frac{1}{L_s'C_s'}} < \omega < \sqrt{\frac{L + L_s'}{LL_s'C_s'}} \tag{2.20}$$

where $L_s' = C_sM^2\omega^2$ and $C_s' = L_s/(M^2\omega^2)$ are the equivalent series inductance and capacitance of SRR. Note that M needs to be sufficiently high for a negative μ. As such, differential host T-line is deployed in the design with SRRs placed in between as close as possible.

2.3.2 T-Line Loaded with Complementary Split Ring Resonator

What is more, as shown in Figure 2.14(a), T-line loaded with CSRR (TL-CSRR) can be implemented on chip by engraving CSRRs on the T-line with the use of the topmost metal layer. By exciting CSRR with the E-Field in the host T-line, an electric plasmonic medium is formed by TL-CSRR in the vicinity of CSRR resonance frequency. The equivalent circuit of TL-CSRR unit-cell is depicted in Figure 2.14 (b). L_C and C_C are the equivalent inductance and capacitance of the CSRR resonator. By comparing the equivalent circuit of TL-CSRR unit-cell with the T-line unit-cell, it can be observed that

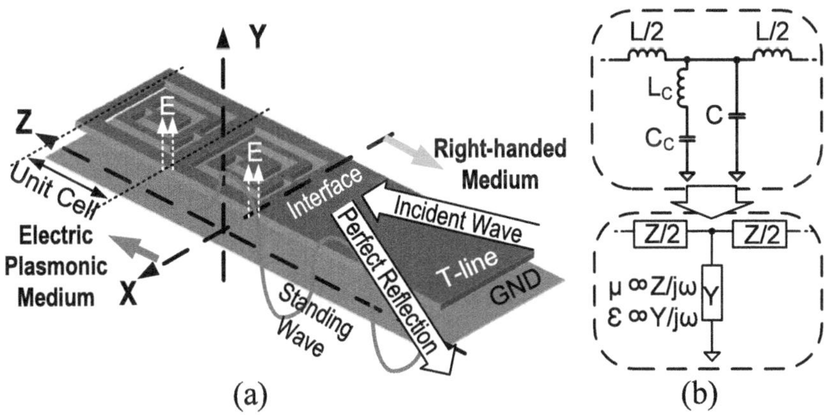

Figure 2.14: (a) Standing-wave formed by perfect reflection at DTL-CSRR; (b) equivalent circuit of DTL-CSRR with condition to form perfect reflection.

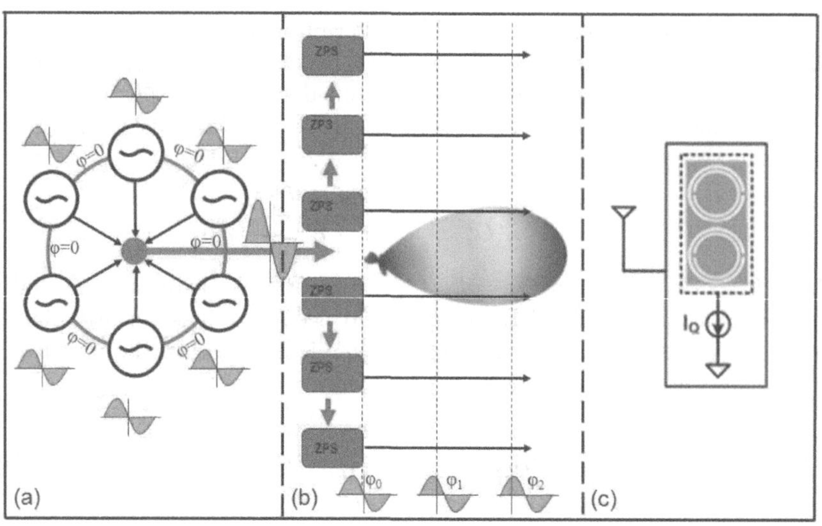

Figure 2.15: Metamaterial-based THz transceiver design including (a) high power THz signal source by MPW based zero-phase coupled oscillator network (CON), (b) high gain THz antenna by CRLH T-line, and (c) high sensitivity THz super-regenerative receiver by TL-SRR/TL-CSRR based quench-controlled oscillator.

the $\varepsilon < 0$ and $\mu > 0$ condition is satisfied in TL-CSRR in the frequency range

$$\sqrt{\frac{1}{C_c L_c}} < \omega < \sqrt{\frac{C + C_c}{C C_c L_c}} \tag{2.21}$$

where an evanescent wave is formed.

2.4 CMOS Coherent THz Electronics by Metamaterial

2.4.1 *Coherent Source*

Coupled oscillator network (CON) [87] is a well-known structure to synchronize output power and reduce phase noise. For a closed-loop CON with N oscillators, the phase shift ($\Delta\phi$) between adjacent oscillators need to satisfy the condition of $\Delta\phi = 2k\pi/N, (k = 0, \pm1, \pm2, ...)$ as illustrated in Figure 2.16.

The combined output admittance ($Y_{OUT}(\omega_0)$) and current ($I(t)$) of all

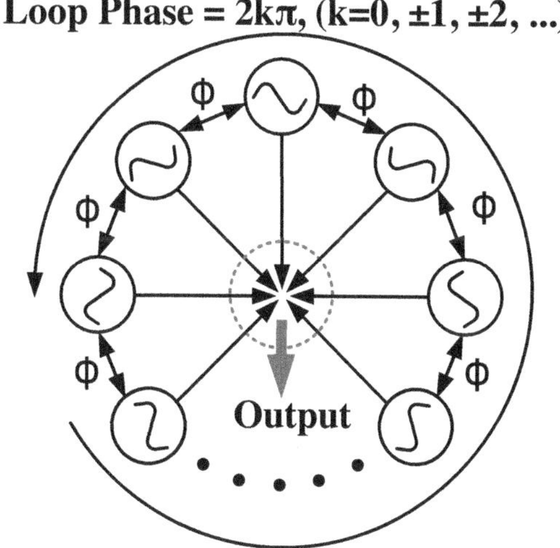

Figure 2.16: Closed-loop coupled oscillator network with center combined output.

oscillators can be calculated as:

$$\begin{cases} Y_{OUT}(\omega_0) = \sum_{i=1}^{n} Y_i(\omega_0) \\ I_{OUT}(t) = I_0 \cdot \sum_{i=1}^{n} \cos(\omega t + \phi_i) \end{cases} \tag{2.22}$$

where Y_i, I_0 and ϕ_i are the output impedance, the amplitude and phase of the output current from each oscillator unit-cell, respectively. Clearly, $I(t)$ is maximized as $N \cdot I_0$ when all oscillator outputs are in-phase ($2k/N = 0, \pm1, \pm2, \ldots$). Because Y_{OUT} is also N times larger by parallel connecting N oscillator outputs, the total available output power is N times increased by the CON due to $P_{OUT} = 0.5 \cdot |I_{OUT}|^2/Y_{OUT}$ when compared to that of a single free-running oscillator. However, if the coupling network is implemented by the conventional T-line, at least an equivalent length of $\lambda/2$ is required with $2k/N = 1$, which is not compact with large loss.

The resulting phase noise ($L(\Delta\omega)$) at frequency offset $\Delta\omega$ can also be improved under the zero-phase condition satisfied for the CON (in $1/f^2$ region) is [88]:

$$L(\Delta\omega) = 10log\left(\frac{8\pi Z_0 \omega_0^2 \overline{i_T^2}}{N P_{diss} Q_L^2 \Delta\omega^3}\right) \tag{2.23}$$

where $\overline{i_T^2}$ is the squared noise current density; P_{diss} is the power dissipated; and ω_0 is the oscillation frequency. Z_0 and Q_L are the impedance and the quality factor of the coupling T-line, respectively. Ideally, with N oscillator unit-cells coupled, the phase noise is N times smaller compared to the single free-running oscillator. Note that similar improvement cannot be achieved by spending the same amount power at one single oscillator. Firstly, increasing the supply voltage close to the breakdown voltage has serious reliability issues; secondly, phase noise cannot be reduced when increasing the supply voltage.

2.4.2 Coherent Transmission

A single-ended dual-fed distributed amplifier (SEDFDA) topology can be used to realize distributed amplification with extra bandwidth traded for better power performance. CRLH T-line-based ZPS is implemented in SEDFDA to optimize all transistors' power performance simultaneously with compact size and low loss.

A 2D active CRLH T-line network is further proposed as the power-combining topology with high power-combining efficiency. The ZPS connections in the proposed 2D active CRLH T-line network are adjusted such that each combining branch resembles a SEDFDA with ZPS connection. In this way, both high-efficient power combining and distributed amplification can be simultaneously achieved.

Figure 2.17 shows the singe-ended version of the proposed power-combining topology. By using CRLH T-line realized ZPS, a new 2D distributed power-combining network can be constructed. The CRLH unit-cell can replace the traditional $\lambda/2$ T-line foe in-phase distributed amplification along horizontal direction to achieve the serial power combining. The parallel power combining for all horizontal branches is then realized by zero-degree power combiner with short equal-length T-lines along the vertical direction. With the serial power combining in the 1st level and parallel power combining in the 2nd level, a 2D distributer power combining network is realized for simultaneous distributed amplification and power-combining. Such a topology can be further extended for phased-array applications by replacing ZPS with an array of tunable phase-shifters.

The proposed topology can simultaneously improve power and bandwidth performance of PA. For example, PA power performance can bo viewed from two aspects: output power per area (P_{out}/area) and output power per DC power consumption (PAE). The 2D power-combining network provides a high density of transistor, and therefore improves P_{out}/area. The distributed topology provides a wide bandwidth, while the SEDFDA implemented with CRLH T-line-based ZPS trades extra bandwidth with improved efficiency, thus improving PAE. As a result, the power performance can be improved together with bandwidth performance.

Note that for a fixed transistor size, the total output power depends on the number of distributed stages N and parallel combining branches M. Therefore, the power handling ability of the proposed PA partially depends on distributed stage number N, which is limited by the T-line loss and phase error.

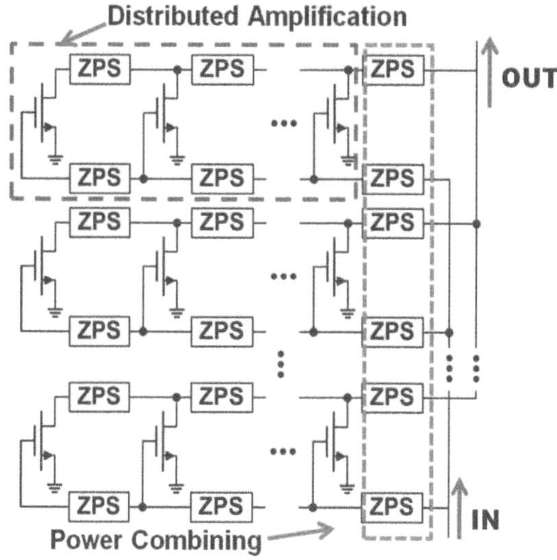

Figure 2.17: Single-ended version on proposed SEDFDA PA topology based on 2D distributed power-combining network with the use of CRLH ZPSs.

2.4.3 Coherent Detection

Millimeter-wave (mm-wave) imaging systems have been demonstrated to detect covered objects for security and pharmacy screenings [89, 90, 91, 92, 93]. Compared to other semiconductor implementations of mm-wave imaging circuits, CMOS is favored for system-on-chip integration of mm-wave circuits with digital baseband as well as large-arrayed imagers. However, due to the loss in propagation path as well as substrate and inefficient transmitting power of MOS transistors, a highly sensitive receiver is much more desirable.

The sensitivity is mainly relevant to bandwidth and noise figure. Super-regenerative receiver (SRX) is proven to have a superior sensitivity over direct-conversion one due to its higher oscillatory amplification [89, 90, 93, 94]. For example, in [93], the sensitivity was improved by a passive structure with a high-Q metamaterial resonator in terms of higher oscillatory amplification. But the passive approach has limitation to improve the sensitivity further because of its single oscillator. As an alternative, active structures, such as coupled oscillator network (CON) have been used to reduce the noise and improve the output power at the same time, and improve the sensitivity in further [95]. But in that structure, the coupling of two oscillators is not in-phase, which results in limited oscillatory amplification.

2.4.4 Transceiver Architecture

Figure 2.15 shows the block diagram of the proposed metamaterial-based THz transceiver design. Non-resonant-type metamaterial can be used in the designs of high power signal sources and high-gain on-chip antennas; resonant-type metamaterial can be used in the designs of high sensitivity signal detection. In the design of high-power signal sources by MPW-based zero-phase coupled oscillator network (CON), N oscillators can be coupled in-phase to generate a N times higher combined output power as well as N times lower phase noise. In the design of high-gain CRLH T-line-based on-chip LWA, the zero-phase propagation in the CRLH T-line can generate in-phase radiation to largely increase the antenna gain in a very small area. In the design of high-sensitivity super-regenerative receivers by TL-SRR/TL-CSRR-based quench-controlled oscillators, with the sharp stop-band introduced by the metamaterial resonators, high-Q oscillatory amplifications are generated to largely improve the receiver sensitivity.

Chapter 3

CMOS THz Modeling

3.1 Introduction

Accurate device models that can take into account the loss from strong frequency-dependent dispersion and non-quasi-static effects must be considered in CMOS-based THz design. As the most fundamental passive structure, the accurate modeling of transmission line (T-line) is very important in various designs [96, 97]. T-line is traditionally characterized by distributed integer-order RLGC model as shown in Fig. 3.1(a) [98]. Drude's classical relaxation-effect model is deployed for the skin effect with R_S [99, 100]. In addition, the loss due to dielectric polarization and dipole rotation can be modeled by a dielectric-loss of G_D. However, such an integer-order model is insufficient to describe the T-line performance at THz region because the loss term in T-line is difficult to model the dispersion loss and non-quasi-static effects [101], which can cause large deviation at THz frequency region. Such impact is further verified by the measurement results and circuit level simulations in this paper. Moreover, the traditional T-line model has a causality issue. Physically, the real and imaginary parts of both permittivity $\varepsilon(\omega)$ and permeability $\mu(\omega)$ in a propagation medium are not independent of each other, but follow the Kramers–Kronig relation [102]. As such, the extracted RLCG parameters in the traditional T-line model may result in a non-causal response in the model that can induce both accuracy and convergence problems in the time-domain simulation.

The concept of fractional-order model has been examined to model capacitor (C) and inductor (L) at high frequency region. The I-V relation of a capacitor is found to follow the fractional-order [103], and the eddy current and hysteresis effect in inductors are also observed with fractional-order relation [104]. It motivates us to re-examine the RLCG T-line model at THz

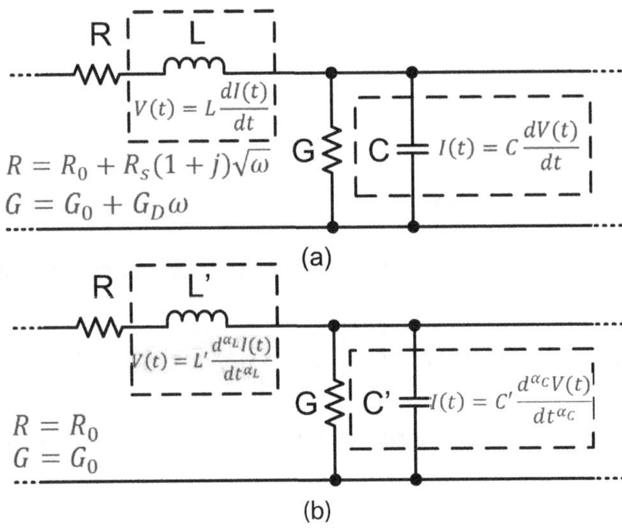

Figure 3.1: RLGC unit-cell equivalent circuits of T-line: (a) integer-order model; and (b) fractional-order model.

during device characterization [105]. Note that the fractional-order model has been deployed to model the surface impedance [106] and describe the abnormal diffusion of voltage and current wave [107]. The fractional-order-based impedance-matching network [108, 109] and resonator design [110] have also been studied. However, no studies investigating the model causality have been carried on with measurement verifications at THz.

In this chapter, two fractional-order T-line models have been developed for both CMOS on-chip conventional RLCG T-line modeling and metamaterial-based CRLH T-line modeling at THz with the following advantages. Firstly, the fractional-order T-line models can describe dispersion and non-quasi-static effect in THz. Secondly, by properly deciding the range of fractional-order, the fractional-order RLCG T-line model does not have the causality issue. Lastly, the fractional-order models are still in compact forms that can be extracted from measurement results. The proposed factional-order RLCG and CRLH T-line modes are verified by S-parameter measurement results in 10 MHz $\sim$ 110 GHz and 220 GHz $\sim$ 325 GHz, respectively. Compared to the conventional integer-order models, the proposed fractional-order T-line models demonstrate improved accuracy of characteristic impedance and propagation constant, which have significant impacts on THz circuit design.

3.2 Fractional-Order T-Line Model

3.2.1 Fractional Calculus

Generally, most of dynamic systems can be described with fractional dynamics, though the fractionality is rather low to be considered than the integer-order behavior. Recently, the fractional-order models are re-examined when considering loss terms in many fields [111] including electronics [103, 112, 113], electromagnetic [114], fluidic-dynamics [115], material technology [116], quantum mechanics [117], etc.

Fractional calculus was initiated by a question of half-order derivative by L' Hopital in 1695 and was generalized by Euler in [118]. In fractional calculus, the integration and differentiation can be generalized by the operator ${}_aD_t^\alpha$ [119],

$$ {}_aD_t^\alpha = \begin{cases} \frac{d^\alpha}{dt^\alpha}, & \alpha > 0 \\ \int_a^t (d\tau)^\alpha, & \alpha < 0 \end{cases} \tag{3.1}$$

where α is a real number, a and t are the lower and upper bounds. The differentiation and integration can be treated as the special cases when α equals 1 or -1, respectively. By Riemann–Liouville definition, the fractional operation can be expressed by the following equation ($n-1 < \alpha < n$),

$$ {}_aD_t^\alpha f(t) = \frac{1}{\Gamma(n-\alpha)} \frac{d^n}{dt^n} \int_a^t \frac{f(\tau)}{(t-\tau)^{\alpha-n+1}} d\tau, \tag{3.2}$$

where $\Gamma(\cdot)$ is the Euler's gamma function.

Assuming the lower bound $a = -\infty$, one can take the Fourier transform of 3.2 to obtain the generalized expression of fractional integral in frequency domain for $0 < \alpha < 1$,

$$ \mathfrak{F}\{{}_{-\infty}D_t^{-\alpha} f(t)\} = (j\omega)^{-\alpha} G(\omega). \tag{3.3}$$

Similarly, the generalized expression of fractional derivative in the frequency domain is

$$ \mathfrak{F}\{D^\alpha f(t)\} = (-j\omega)^\alpha G(\omega). \tag{3.4}$$

As shown in 3.3 and 3.4, the fractional-operator in the frequency domain can be treated as the product of a magnitude scaling factor ω^α and a phase rotation factor $j^{-\alpha}$. Theoretically, the physical behavior of any electronic device can be described by these two fractional factors. More importantly, both scaling factor and rotation factor are linked by a fractional-order α, which ensures the reality of one dynamic system with dissipation. Therefore, in order to examine the loss terms for electronic devices at THz, the aforementioned fractional calculus can be applied with many interesting observations as explored in the following sections.

3.2.2 Fractional-Order Capacitance and Inductance

Fractional-order model for T-line can be built by introducing fractional-order terms in the conventional RLGC model as shown in Fig. 3.1 (b). A fractional-order capacitor model [103] with the I-V relation can be given by

$$I(t) = C' \frac{d^{\alpha_C} V(t)}{dt^{\alpha_C}} = C'{}_0 D_t{}^{\alpha C} V(t) \tag{3.5}$$

where C′ is the fractional capacitance with order α_C, and $\alpha_C \in (0, 1]$ is the fractional-order relating to the loss of capacitor.

Similarly, the I-V relation of fractional-order inductor [112] is

$$V(t) = L' \frac{d^{\alpha_L} I(t)}{dt^{\alpha_L}} = L'{}_0 D_t{}^{\alpha L} I(t) \tag{3.6}$$

where L′ is the fractional inductance with order α_L, and $\alpha_L \in (0, 1]$ is the fractional-order relating to the loss of inductor. The admittance and impedance of fractional-order capacitor and inductor can be obtained from (3.5) and (3.6) by

$$Y'(\omega) = \omega^{\alpha_C} C' e^{0.5\pi j \alpha_C} \tag{3.7}$$

$$Z'(\omega) = \omega^{\alpha_L} L' e^{0.5\pi j \alpha_L}. \tag{3.8}$$

When α_L or $\alpha_C \neq 1$, we can expect the existence of real-parts at the right-hand sides of (3.7) and (3.8), which represent the frequency-dependent loss. Physically in a particular device, the fractional-order operator indicates the transfer of the energy storage to energy loss. As such, the distributed frequency-dependent terms are considered by L′ and C′ elements in fractional-order terms.

3.2.3 Fractional-Order T-Line Model

Note that the fractional-order T-line can be analyzed in a similar fashion as the traditional T-line. The characteristic impedance (Z_0) of T-line can be found by $\sqrt{Z/Y}$, where Z and Y are the series impedance and shunt admittance, respectively. Based on (3.7) and (3.8) with consideration of resistance R_0 and conductance G_0, one can have

$$Z_0 = \sqrt{\frac{R_0 + \omega^{\alpha_L} L' e^{0.5\pi j \alpha_L}}{G_0 + \omega^{\alpha_C} C' e^{0.5\pi j \alpha_C}}}. \tag{3.9}$$

In THz frequency region, ω is in the order of $10^{11} \sim 10^{13}$. At such a high frequency, we have $R_0 << \omega^{\alpha_L} L' e^{0.5\pi j \alpha_L}$ and $G_0 << \omega^{\alpha_C} C' e^{0.5\pi j \alpha_C}$, so (3.9) can be approximated as

$$Z_0 = \sqrt{\frac{L'}{C'}} \cdot \omega^{\frac{\alpha_L - \alpha_C}{2}} \cdot \left[\cos \frac{(\alpha_L - \alpha_C)\pi}{4} + j \sin \frac{(\alpha_L - \alpha_C)\pi}{4} \right]. \tag{3.10}$$

Comparing characteristic impedance by the fractional-order and the conventional integer-order RLGC models, one can observe that the fractional-order Z_0 has nonlinear frequency dependency in THz. If $\alpha_L < \alpha_C$, magnitude of Z_0 has an inverse-square-root-like decreasing function of frequency. This reveals the existence of an imaginary part in Z_0, which accounts for the dispersion and non-quasi-static effects. Both effects are confirmed in the THz T-line measurements.

Moreover, the propagation constant (γ) is

$$\gamma = \alpha + j\beta \tag{3.11}$$

where α is the attenuation constant and β is the phase constant.

As $\gamma = \sqrt{ZY}$, with (3.7) and (3.8), one can have

$$\gamma = \sqrt{(R_0 + \omega^{\alpha_L} L' e^{0.5\pi j \alpha_L})(G_0 + \omega^{\alpha_C} C' e^{0.5\pi j \alpha_C})}. \tag{3.12}$$

In the THz frequency region, since $R_0 << |\omega^{\alpha_L} L' e^{0.5\pi j \alpha_L}|$ and $G_0 << |\omega^{\alpha_C} C' e^{0.5\pi j \alpha_C}|$, (3.12) can be approximated as

$$\gamma = \sqrt{L'C'} \cdot \omega^{\frac{\alpha_L+\alpha_C}{2}} \cdot \left[\cos\frac{(\alpha_L+\alpha_C)\pi}{4} + j\sin\frac{(\alpha_L+\alpha_C)\pi}{4}\right]. \tag{3.13}$$

Comparing propagation constant by the fractional-order and the conventional integer-order RLGC models, one can observe that the fractional-order γ also has nonlinear frequency dependency in THz. The attenuation constant α will become non-zero when $\alpha_L + \alpha_C < 2$ in (3.13), and the energy loss is introduced accordingly. What is more, note that the S-parameters of T-line are determined by Z_0 and γ [120].

$$\begin{bmatrix} S11 & S12 \\ S21 & S22 \end{bmatrix} = \begin{bmatrix} \frac{A+B/Z_0-CZ_0-D}{A+B/Z_0+CZ_0+D} & \frac{2(AD-BC)}{A+B/Z_0+CZ_0+D} \\ \frac{2}{A+B/Z_0+CZ_0+D} & \frac{-A+B/Z_0-CZ_0+D}{A+B/Z_0+CZ_0+D} \end{bmatrix}, \tag{3.14}$$

where A, B, C and D are the transfer matrix of uniform T-line:

$$\begin{bmatrix} A & B \\ C & D \end{bmatrix} = \begin{bmatrix} \cosh\gamma l & Z_0\sinh\gamma l \\ \frac{\sinh\gamma l}{Z_0} & \cosh\gamma l \end{bmatrix}. \tag{3.15}$$

By substituting (3.9) and (3.12) into (3.14), one can obtain the S-parameters of the fractional-order T-line model. As such, the models can be verified by the S-parameter measurement results. In addition, it is well known that the propagation velocity of the EM wave front (V_p) equals to ω/β. In the fractional-order T-line model, one can have

$$V_p = \frac{\omega^{2-\frac{\alpha_L+\alpha_C}{2}}}{\sqrt{L'C'}\sin\frac{(\alpha_L+\alpha_C)\pi}{4}}. \tag{3.16}$$

In the fractional-order T-line model, when $\alpha_L + \alpha_C < 2$ in (3.16), V_p becomes non-linearly frequency dependent in a high-frequency region like THz.

This reveals the dispersion effect when propagating through lossy media. On the other hand, in the integer-order T-line model, when $\alpha_L + \alpha_C = 2$ in (3.16), V_p equals $1/\sqrt{L'C'}$, which is not frequency dependent, to model the dispersion effect in high frequency region like THz.

3.2.4 Fractional-Order CRLH T-Line Model

Note that the fractional-order CRLH T-line can be analyzed in a similar fashion as fractional-order T-line. Based on the integer-order CRLH T-line model with general series and shunt loss terms (R and G) in Fig. 3.2(a), fractional-order terms are introduced in the fractional-order CRLH T-line model as shown in Fig. 3.2(b). Note that R_0 and G_0 only represent the series resistance and the shunt conductance at DC condition, respectively. Based on 3.7 and 3.8 with consideration of R_0 and G_0, one can have the characteristic impedance of CRLH T-Line as

$$Z_0 = \sqrt{\frac{R_0 + \omega^{\alpha_{L_S}} L'_S e^{0.5\pi j \alpha_{L_S}} + \frac{1}{\omega^{\alpha_{C_S}} C'_S e^{0.5\pi j \alpha_{C_S}}}}{G_0 + \omega^{\alpha_{C_P}} C'_P e^{0.5\pi j \alpha_{C_P}} + \frac{1}{\omega^{\alpha_{L_P}} L'_P e^{0.5\pi j \alpha_{L_P}}}}}. \tag{3.17}$$

From the equivalent circuit of CRLH T-line, we find that each cell consists of parallel and series LC resonators, and there is a gap between parallel resonate frequency (ω_P) and series resonate frequency (ω_S). When $\omega = \omega_P$,

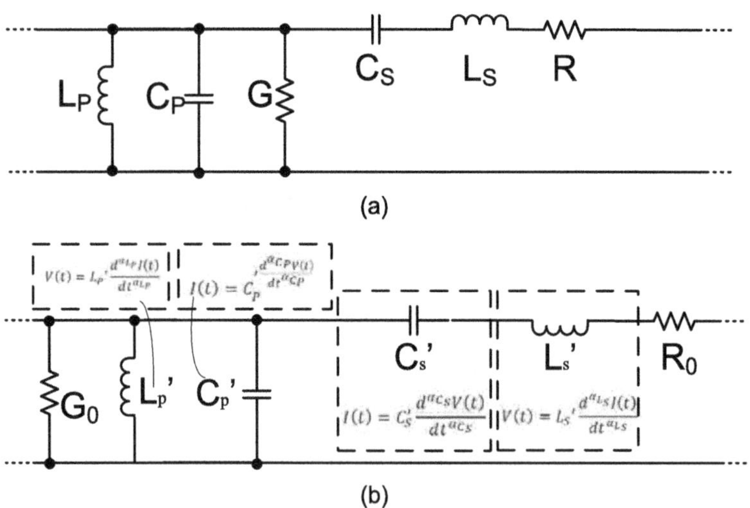

Figure 3.2: Equivalent circuits of CRLH unit-cell: (a) integer-order model; and (b) fractional-order model.

Z_0 reaches maximum value, when $\omega = \omega_S$, Z_0 reaches its minimum value, thus Z_0 shows a peek-valley or valley-peek curve as frequency grows within the whole range. This will be verified by simulation and measurement results shown in Fig. 3.14. According to (3.17), real terms of series resonator and parallel conductance are expressed as

$$\begin{cases} \Re(Z) = R_0 + \omega^{\alpha_{L_S}} L'_S \cos(0.5\pi j\alpha_{L_S}) + \dfrac{\cos(0.5\pi j\alpha_{C_S})}{\omega^{\alpha_{C_S}} C'_S} \\ \Re(Y) = G_0 + \omega^{\alpha_{C_P}} C'_P \cos(0.5\pi j\alpha_{C_P}) + \dfrac{\cos(0.5\pi j\alpha_{L_P})}{\omega^{\alpha_{L_P}} L'_P} \end{cases}. \tag{3.18}$$

One can observe from (3.18) that, different from conventional integer order model, fractional model introduces frequency-depended terms to loss and conductance equations that greatly affect the peak and valley magnitudes of Z_0.

In THz frequency region, ω is in the order of 10^{11} 10^{13}, such that $R_0 << \omega^{\alpha_{L_S}} L'_S e^{\frac{j\alpha_{L_S}\pi}{2}}$, and $G_0 << \omega^{\alpha_{C_P}} C'_P e^{\frac{j\alpha_{C_P}\pi}{2}}$. At a frequency that is much lower than zero-phase-shift frequency, the left-handed terms ($\frac{1}{\omega^{\alpha_{C_S}} C'_S e^{0.5\pi j\alpha_{C_S}}}$ and $\frac{1}{\omega^{\alpha_{L_P}} L'_P e^{0.5\pi j\alpha_{L_P}}}$) becomes dominant in (3.17). Thus Z_0 can be approximated as

$$Z_0 = \sqrt{\frac{L'_P}{C'_S}} \cdot \omega^{\frac{\alpha_{L_P}-\alpha_{C_S}}{2}} \cdot \left[\cos\frac{(\alpha_{L_P}-\alpha_{C_S})\pi}{4} + j\sin\frac{(\alpha_{L_P}-\alpha_{C_S})\pi}{4}\right]. \tag{3.19}$$

On the other hand, at a frequency that is much lower than zero-phase-shift frequency, the right-handed terms ($\omega^{\alpha_{L_S}} L'_S e^{0.5\pi j\alpha_{L_S}}$ and $\omega^{\alpha_{C_P}} C'_P e^{0.5\pi j\alpha_{C_P}}$) becomes dominant in (3.17). As such, Z_0 can be approximated as

$$Z_0 = \sqrt{\frac{L'_S}{C'_P}} \cdot \omega^{\frac{\alpha_{L_S}-\alpha_{C_P}}{2}} \cdot \left[\cos\frac{(\alpha_{L_S}-\alpha_{C_P})\pi}{4} + j\sin\frac{(\alpha_{L_S}-\alpha_{C_P})\pi}{4}\right]. \tag{3.20}$$

From (3.20) and (3.20), one can observe that Z_0 is a frequency-dependent parameter, which is determined by $\omega^{\frac{\alpha_{L_P}-\alpha_{C_S}}{2}}$ and $\omega^{\frac{\alpha_{L_S}-\alpha_{C_P}}{2}}$ at low and high frequencies outside the band-gap, respectively. For an on-chip CRLH T-line design, the fractional orders for inductive elements (α_{L_S} and α_{L_P}) is usually smaller than that of capacitive elements (α_{C_S} and α_{C_P}) due to a lower Q factor of inductors. Therefore, both $\omega^{\frac{\alpha_{L_P}-\alpha_{C_S}}{2}}$ and $\omega^{\frac{\alpha_{L_S}-\alpha_{C_P}}{2}}$ are negative values. As a result, Eq. (3.17) becomes a negative function of frequency outside the band-gap.

Moreover, since R_0 and G_0 are negligible at THz, the propagation constant of CRLH T-Line can be written as

$$\gamma = \sqrt{\left(\omega^{\alpha_{L_S}} L'_S e^{0.5\pi j\alpha_{L_S}} + \frac{1}{\omega^{\alpha_{C_S}} C'_S e^{0.5\pi j\alpha_{C_S}}}\right) \cdot \left(\omega^{\alpha_{C_P}} C'_P e^{0.5\pi j\alpha_{C_P}} + \frac{1}{\omega^{\alpha_{L_P}} L'_P e^{0.5\pi j\alpha_{L_P}}}\right)} \tag{3.21}$$

Assuming the fractionality for both inductance and capacitance are all constants that $\alpha_{L_S} = \alpha_{L_P}$ and $\alpha_{C_S} = \alpha_{C_P}$, (3.11) can be simplified as

$$\gamma = \sqrt{\omega^{\alpha_{L_S}+\alpha_{C_P}} L'_S C'_P e^{0.5\pi j(\alpha_{L_S}+\alpha_{C_P})} + \frac{1}{\omega^{\alpha_{C_S}+\alpha_{L_P}} C'_S L'_P} e^{-0.5\pi j(\alpha_{C_S}+\alpha_{L_P})}}. \tag{3.22}$$

The zero-phase-shift frequency (ω_0) can be obtained from (3.22) with $\beta = 0$:

$$\omega_0 = (L'_S C'_P C'_S L'_P)^{\frac{1}{\alpha_{L_S}+\alpha_{C_P}+\alpha_{C_S}+\alpha_{L_P}}}. \tag{3.23}$$

Eq. (3.23) reveals an exponential relationship between the prefactors and fractional-order terms, which can be used as a guideline in the fractional-order modeling of CRLH T-line network.

3.3 Model Extraction and Causality Analysis

T-line is a passive, linear and time-invariant (LTI) network. The extracted T-line model is thereby needed to be causal. The extraction flow of fractional-order T-line model is introduced with the additional causality checking and enforcement followed by comparison with the traditional integer-order counterpart.

3.3.1 Fractional-Order Model Extraction

A fractional-order model parameters extraction flow for T-line at THz is illustrated in Fig. 3.3. The extraction begins with the measurement data obtained from a Vector Network Analyzer. Firstly, the measurement data is converted into transfer matrix (T matrix) for an easy operation, and the error terms contributed by the testing pads are removed by de-embedding process. Secondly, characteristic impedance Z_0 and propagation constant γ are calculated from de-embedded T-matrix according to [121]. Afterward, one can define the modeling frequency interval $[\omega_1, \omega_2]$ in the THz region based on his interests.

From (3.10), one can have

$$\alpha_L - \alpha_C = 2log_{\frac{\omega_1}{\omega_2}} \left|\frac{Z_0(\omega_1)}{Z_0(\omega_2)}\right| \tag{3.24}$$

where $Z_0(\omega_1)$ and $Z_0(\omega_2)$ are the characteristic impedances at frequencies ω_1 and ω_2 in THz region, respectively.

From (3.13), one can have

$$\alpha_L + \alpha_C = 2log_{\frac{\omega_1}{\omega_2}} \left|\frac{\gamma(\omega_1)}{\gamma(\omega_2)}\right| \tag{3.25}$$

where $\gamma(\omega_1)$ and $\gamma(\omega_2)$ are the propagation constants at frequencies ω_1 and ω_2

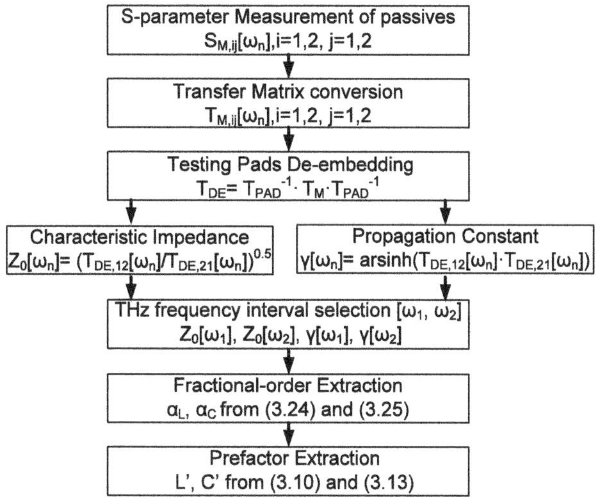

Figure 3.3: Fractional-order T-line modeling parameters extraction flow.

in THz region, respectively. By combining (3.24) and (3.25), α_L and α_C can be obtained in the fractional-order model; and by substituting α_L and α_C into (3.24) and (3.25), fractional-order L' and C' can be obtained as well. Note that L' and C' are the p.u.l. (per-unit-length) prefactors with corresponding units of $Vs^{-\alpha_L}A^{-1}/m$ and $As^{-\alpha_C}V^{-1}/m$, respectively, but not p.u.l. inductance and capacitance anymore.

Moreover, in order to apply the fractional-order T-line model in the time-domain simulator to Cadence Spectre, the model needs to be converted from frequency domain into time-domain by rational functional approximation

$$f(s) \approx \sum_{j=1}^{N} \frac{c_j}{s - a_j} + d + sh. \tag{3.26}$$

Here, N is the rational order, a_j and c_j are the poles and residues in complex conjugate pairs, d and h are real. The coefficients in (3.26) can be obtained by vector fitting algorithm as introduced in [122]. Note that the error introduced by the frequency-to-time conversion is well controlled by increasing the rational-fitting order.

3.3.2 Causal LTI System and Causality Enforcement

To understand the causality for the extracted fractional-order T-line model, the fundamentals of the causal LTI system are first reviewed here. In a LTI system, the impulse response $h(t)$ to an input $x(t)$ can be expressed as [123]:

$$y(t) = x(t) * h(t) = \int_{-\infty}^{+\infty} h(t - \tau)x(\tau)d\tau \tag{3.27}$$

where $x(t)$ and $y(t)$ represent the input and output voltages, currents or powers of T-line network, and $h(t)$ is the corresponding admittance or impedance state matrix.

The principle of causality states that no effect happened before its cause. As such, a causal LTI system $h(t)$ can be mathematically defined as:

$$h(t) = 0, \forall t < 0. \tag{3.28}$$

The causality of T-line model can be verified by this definition in the time-domain. (3.28) can be equivalently represented as

$$h(t) = sign(t)h(t), \tag{3.29}$$

where sign function $sign(t)$ equals -1 when $t < 0$ and equals 1 when $t > 0$.

By taking the Fourier transform of (3.29), we can obtain the impulse response of $h(t)$ in frequency domain with a complex function

$$H(\omega) = \mathfrak{F}\{h(t)\} = \Re[H(\omega)] + j\Im[H(\omega)]. \tag{3.30}$$

with

$$\Re[H(\omega)] = \frac{2}{\pi}\int_{0}^{\infty} \frac{\omega'\Im[H(\omega')]}{\omega'^2 - \omega^2} d\omega'. \tag{3.31}$$

and

$$\Im[H(\omega)] = -\frac{2\omega}{\pi}\int_{0}^{\infty} \frac{\Re[H(\omega')]}{\omega'^2 - \omega^2} d\omega'. \tag{3.32}$$

Here $\Re[H(\omega)]$ and $\Im[H(\omega)]$ are the coefficients of real and imaginary parts of $H(\omega)$, respectively, which are both real numbers. Equation (3.28) is also addressed as Kramers–Kronig relation or Hilbert transform [102]. Note that (3.31) and (3.32) are bidirectional equations, which reveal the dependency of real and imaginary parts of impulse response, and also provide a necessary and sufficient condition for a causal LTI system. Note that the causality of a LTI system can be enforced by correcting the real or imaginary part in (3.31) and (3.32) with truncation. However, a truncation error could be also introduced with largely reduced accuracy for simulation.

One criteria to verify causality by tabulated S-parameters is to measure the error difference (e_ij) between the imaginary part and its Hilbert transform of the real part

$$e_{ij}(\omega_n) = |Hilbert\{\Re[S_{ij}(\omega_n)]\} - \Im[S_{ij}(\omega_n)]|. \tag{3.33}$$

Whether a system is causal or non-causal is determined by the error threshold that can be tolerated in the numerical analysis [124]. A smaller e_{ij} is usually desired to ensure the accuracy and the convergence in simulation. A flow

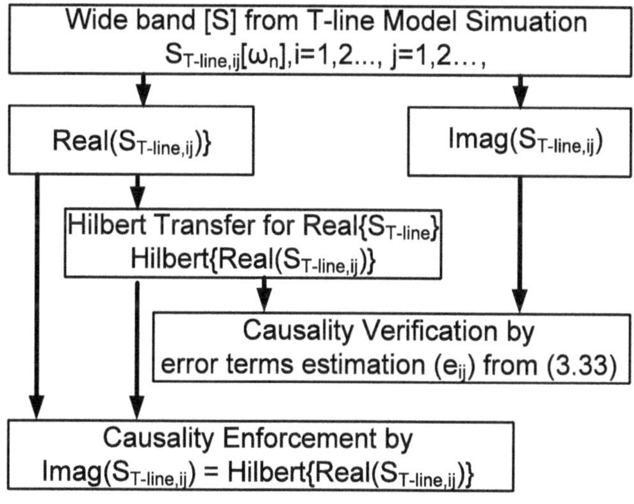

Figure 3.4: Causality verification and enforcement flow.

of causality verification and enforcement is illustrated in Fig. 3.4. Firstly, a very wide-band initial tabulated S-parameter needs to be generated by numerical calculation from the model under investigation. Secondly, both the real and imaginary parts are extracted, and a Hilbert transform is applied to the real parts according to (3.32). Finally, the causality is verified by calculating e_ij from (3.33); and enforced by replacing the imaginary part of the original tabulated data with the Hilbert transform of the real part in the frequency band of interest. Note that the bandwidth of initial data must be much larger than the final frequency band after causality enforcement to minimize reconstruction and discretization errors [125].

3.3.3 Causality of T-Line Model

The relationship between real and imaginary parts in (3.31) and (3.32) also relates the amplitude and phase. Provided the magnitude, one can calculate the phase and vice versa. According to the theory of linear system, any causal and stable impulse response $H(\omega)$ can be decomposed into the production of the minimum phase function and all-pass function [126] by

$$H(\omega) = H_{min}(\omega) \cdot H_{all}(\omega), \tag{3.34}$$

where $H_{min}(\omega)$ and $H_{all}(\omega)$ are the minimum phase function and all-pass function, respectively. Since $H_{all}(\omega)$ does not contain any magnitude information, the system causality can also be ensured if it satisfies the minimum phase function defined by the following condition [127, 128]:

$$\lim_{\omega\to\infty}\left[\frac{\gamma(\omega)}{j\omega}\right] \Rightarrow 0. \tag{3.35}$$

For T-line, the minimum phase function can be calculated by substituting (3.13) into (3.35) as

$$\lim_{\omega\to\infty}\left(\frac{\gamma(\omega)}{j\omega}\right)=\lim_{\omega\to\infty}\left[\omega^{\frac{\alpha_L+\alpha_C}{2}}\cdot\sqrt{L'C'}\cdot\left(\sin\frac{(\alpha_L+\alpha_C)\pi}{4}-j\cos\frac{(\alpha_L+\alpha_C)\pi}{4}\right)\right]. \tag{3.36}$$

We can observe that (3.36) shows very different responses for fractional-order and integer-order T-line models. For the fractional-order model, (3.36) equals zero when $\alpha_L + \alpha_C < 2$. So the causality is always ensured as the minimum phase function condition when (3.35) is satisfied. On the other hand, α_L and α_C are both equal to one for the integer-order T-line model, and (3.36) results in a constant value of $\sqrt{L'C'}$, where L' and C' become the normal inductance and capacitance, respectively. Thus the minimum phase function condition in (3.35) is violated and the model becomes non-causal.

Note that the major reason for the non-causal issue in the traditional integer T-line model is due to the linear frequency dependence of the propagation constant $\gamma(\omega)$ when $\alpha_L + \alpha_C = 2$ in (3.13). This cannot model the dispersion loss and non-quasi-static effects in the high-frequency application like THz. The reality of the integer-order T-line model is lost in the THz region, and so is the causality. In contrast, the non-ideal effects are considered in the proposed fractional-order T-line model by fractional-order dispersion terms, which can largely improve the model reality. As such, both the model accuracy and causality are improved. The causality of the fractional-order model can also be verified in numerical calculation by computing the error terms in (3.33), which will be discussed in the following section.

3.4 Prototyping and Measurement

3.4.1 T-Line Fractional-Order Model Verification

As shown in Fig. 3.5(a), a coplanar waveguide transmission line (CPW-TL) testing structure with RF-PADs is fabricated with Global Foundry 1P8M 65nm CMOS process, of which the dimensions are given in Fig. 3.5(b). The CPW-TL is implemented on the top metal layer with thickness of 3.3 μm. It is measured on a CASCADE Microtech Elite-300 probe station by Agilent PNA-X (N5247A) with frequency sweep up to 110 GHz. The measurement setup of S-parameters up to 110 GHz is illustrated in Fig. 3.6. The reference plane of PNA is calibrated to the ends of GSG probes by SOLT method. Note that both the probes and the impedance standard substrate are provided by Cascade Microtech. RF-PADs on both sides are de-embedded from the

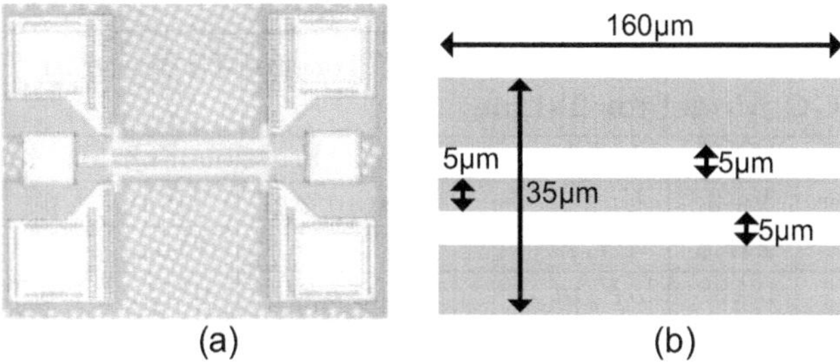

Figure 3.5: T-line testing structure: (a) die photo, and (b) detailed dimensions.

measurement results with the "open-short" method. Table 3.1 summarizes extracted model parameters of both integer-order and fractional-order models based on measurement results. The parameters of the traditional integer-order model are extracted according to the procedure by [121]. The parameters of fractional-order model are extracted according to Section 3.3.1.

The resulting S-parameters and characteristic impedance (Z_0) of integer-order and fractional-order RLGC models are compared in Fig. 3.8. We can observe that both the traditional integer-order model and the proposed fractional-order model can fit the measurement results in magnitude in Fig. 3.7. Here a relatively large deviation is observed in magnitude of S11 between the simulation and measurement results. This deviation comes from the equipment noise and calibration error, which is unavoidable as the absolute magnitude of S11 is small ($-15 \sim -50$ dB). Moreover, the phase delay of both the

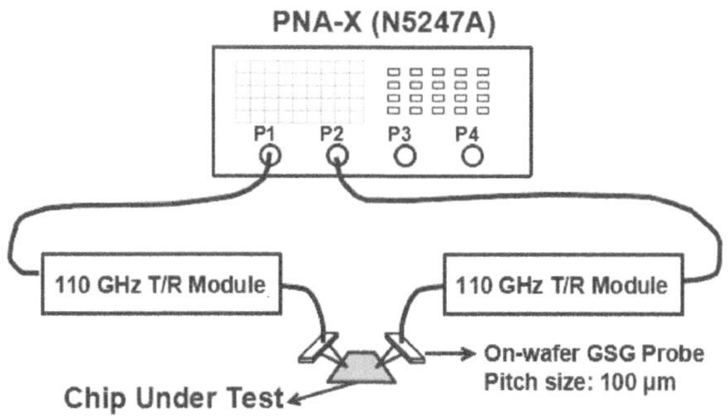

Figure 3.6: Measurement setup of on-wafer S-parameter testing up to 110 GHz.

Table 3.1: Modeling Parameters of Integer-Order and Fractional-Order RLGC Model for T-Line

Integer-Order Model			Fractional-Order Model		
Parameter	Value	Unit	Parameter	Value	Unit
L	247.5	nH/m	α_L	0.862	—
C	0.188	nF/m	L'	10022	$Vs^{-\alpha_L}A^{-1}/m$
R	1200	Ω/m	α_C	0.988	—
R_S	12.56	$m\Omega/m \cdot rad$	C'	0.278	$As^{-\alpha_C}V^{-1}/m$
G	0.079	S/m	R	1200	Ω/m
G_D	19.33	$pS/m \cdot rad$	G	0.079	S/m

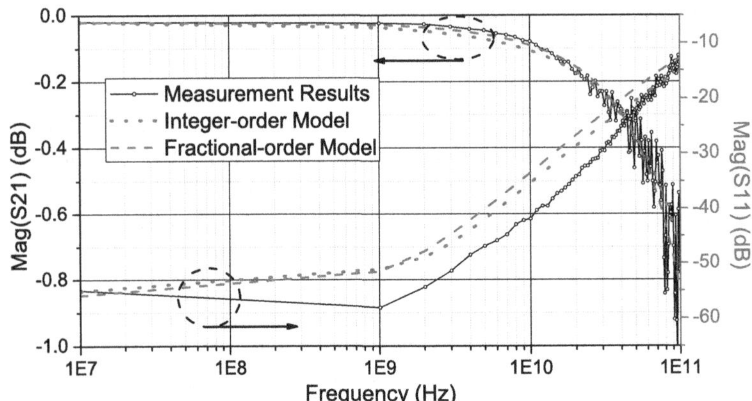

Figure 3.7: Verification of fractional-order T-line model with measurement results for magnitude of S11 and S21 in dB.

traditional integer-order model and the proposed fractional-order model agree well with the measurement results as shown in Fig. 3.8. However, it is observed that characteristic impedance Z_0 in the traditional integer-order RLGC model has deviated from measurement results above 10 GHz, and almost approaches a constant above 40GHz. On the other hand, the fractional-order RLGC model closely fits the measured Z_0 up to 110 GHz, because it can accurately consider frequency-dependence loss yet in a compact RLGC form. At 100 GHz, the Z_0 from fractional-order and measurement results are 34.3 Ω, which is 3.1 Ω lower than the one from integer-order model. Note that such difference will keep increasing with frequency and largely affects the model accuracy in traditional integer-order T-line model at THz. Physically, the values of fractional-order terms (α_L and α_C) model the frequency-dependent dispersion loss of the device at THz. For the T-line fabricated by on-chip CMOS process, larger loss is

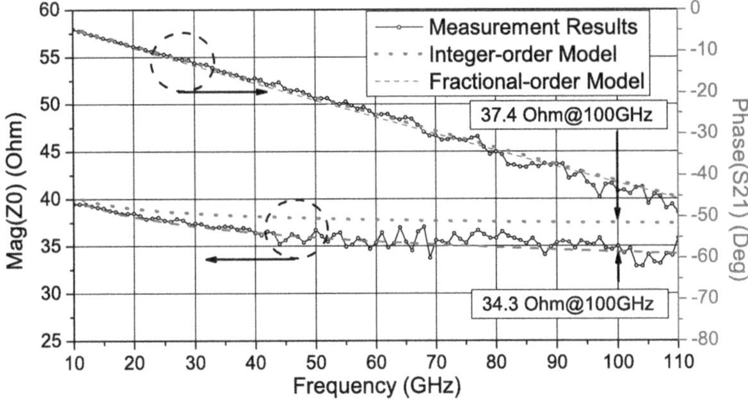

Figure 3.8: Verification of fractional-order T-line model with measurement results for phase delay of S21 and characteristic impedance.

observed in metal layer than in dielectric layer. As a result, α_L has a relatively large deviation from 1, while α_C is close to 1. But note that a slight change in the order-terms (α_L and α_C) could bring huge changes in the prefactors (L' and C') in the THz region as observed in (3.7) and (3.8).

3.4.2 CRLH T-Line Fractional-Order Model Verification

In order to minimize the characterization error of each CRLH T-line unit-cell, one 13-cell CRLH T-line is fabricated with Global Foundry 1P8M 65nm CMOS process. As shown in Fig. 3.9, it has a chip size of $145\mu m \times 660\mu m$ excluding the RF Pads. The layout and dimension of each unit cell is shown in Fig. 3.10. The topmost aluminum layer (LB) is exclusively employed as signal layer for the maximum distance to the bottom ground layer (M1) to improve the radiation efficiency. Various components in the CRLH T-line cell in Fig. 3.2(a) are synthesized by on-chip structures. The L_P of the CRLH T-line is synthesized by a microstrip line connected to the ground and C_S is implemented with inter-digital capacitor. Both right-handed elements L_S and C_P are contributed by the intrinsic parasitic. Note that a mesh structure is applied in the ground layer to satisfy the metal density rule.

The 13-cell CRLH T-line design is verified by circuit simulation in ADS from 220 to 325 GHz. From this we get the integer-order and fractional-order simulation results. The fabricated 13-cell CRLH T-line structure is measured on probe station (CASCADE Microtech Elite-300) with VNA extender (VDI WR3.4-VNAX). Two waveguide GSG probes with 50 μm pitch are used for the S-parameter measurement from 220 to 325 GHz, as shown in Fig. 3.11. Note

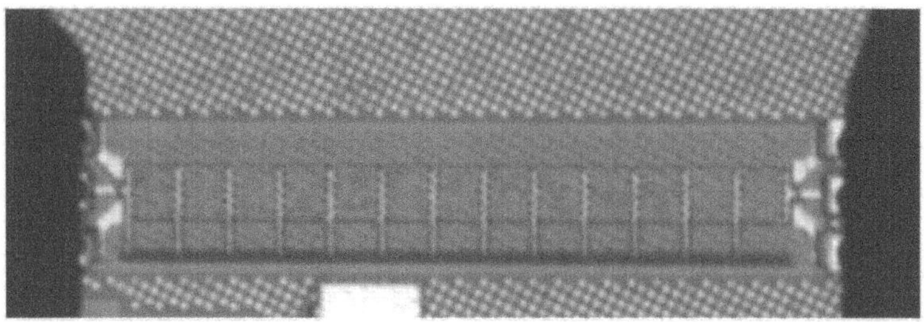

Figure 3.9: Chip micrograph of fabricated CRLH T-line in 65 nm CMOS process.

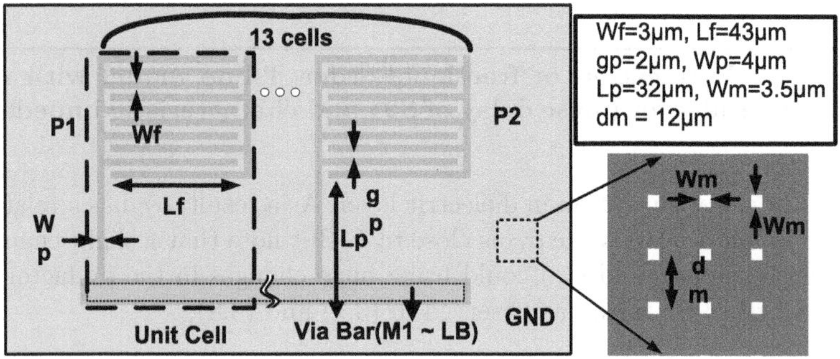

Figure 3.10: Dimension of each unit-cell and layer configurations of LWA.

that the testing pads and traces are de-embedded (open, short) from both sides with recursive modeling technique [129]. We also compare the measurement results of fabricated CRLH T-line with integer-order and fractional-order circuit simulation as well as EM-simulation by HFSS. The circuit simulations are conducted with the equivalent circuits of unit-cell shown in Fig. 3.2, and the values of circuit elements are summarized in Table 3.2, obtained by curve fitting technique.

As shown in Fig. 3.12 and 3.13, the phase and magnitude of S21 are almost identical for both fractional-order and integer-order models in the measured frequency range of 220–325GHz. But the extracted phase constant (β) of fractional-order model is closer to measurement than that of integer-order one while considering the dispersion effects. More importantly, the fractional-order model accurately fits the measurement results at the frequency with $\beta = 0$, which is the boundary between left-handed and right-handed regions, while that from integer-order model is 13 GHz less. Moreover, Fig. 3.14 shows

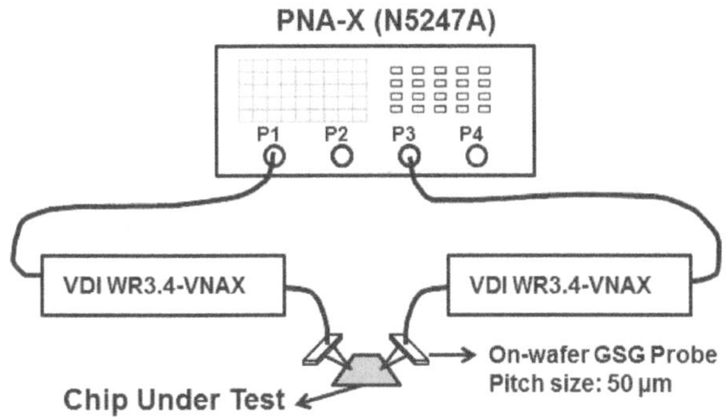

Figure 3.11: Measurement setup of on-wafer S-parameter testing from 220 GHz to 325 GHz.

Table 3.2: Modeling Parameters of Integer-Order and Fractional-Order Models of CRLH T-Line Unit Cell

Integer-Order Model			Fractional-Order Model		
Parameter	Value	Unit	Parameter	Value	Unit
L_S	15.6	pH	$\alpha_{L_S}/\alpha_{L_P}$	0.9847/0.9766	—
C_S	14.7	fF	$\alpha_{C_S}/\alpha_{C_P}$	0.9939/0.9973	—
G	1.3	mS	L'_S	14	$Vs^{-\alpha_{L_S}}A^{-1}$
R	2.8	Ω	C'_P	1732.1	$As^{-\alpha_{C_P}}V^{-1}$
C_P	13.8	S/m	L'_P	39.41	$Vs^{-\alpha_{L_P}}A^{-1}$
L_P	28.3	pH	C'_S	1408	$As^{-\alpha_{C_S}}V^{-1}$
—	—	—	R_0/G_0	0.3396/902	Ω/mS

a remarkable difference between integer-order and fractional-order results in terms of characteristic impedance Z_0. The measurement Z_0 fit very well to fractional-order model at zero-phase-shift region from 260 GHz, also a smaller error of Z_0 at low-frequency region compared to integer-order fitting result. The average accuracy improvement of 78.8% is obtained by fractional-order model compared to the integer-order counterpart with correlated measurement and simulation results of Z_0. Moreover, the measurement results of CRLH T-line agree well with the EM simulation results for the frequency range of 220 $\sim$ 325 GHz.

3.4.3 Causality Verification and Comparison

The causality of the proposed fractional-order T-line model can be verified by comparing imaginary parts of S-parameters with the Hilbert transform of

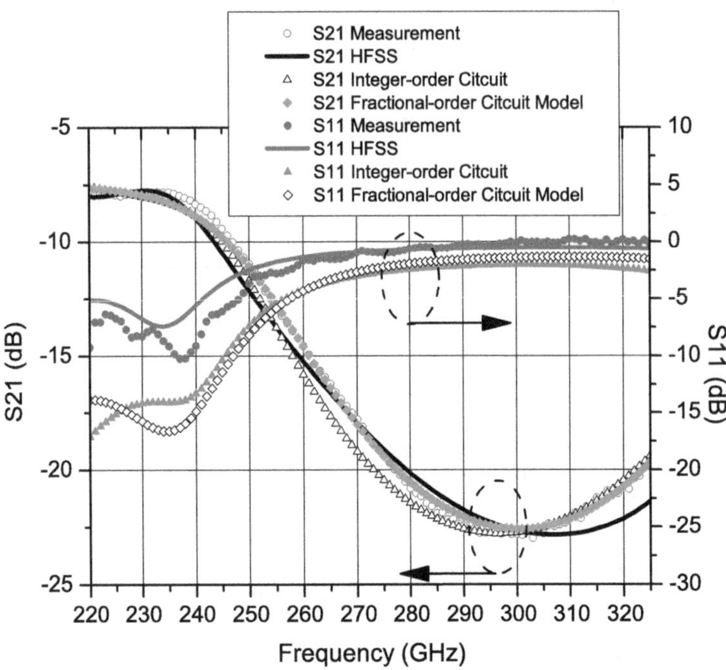

Figure 3.12: Measurement, EM, integer-order and fractional-order circuits simulation results: magnitude of S21 and S11 in dB.

real parts. Then, the error term $e_{ij}\ (\omega_n)$ is calculated by (3.33) as discussed in Section 3.3. For the purpose of comparison, the causality of traditional integer-order T-line model is also verified in the same way. The tabulated results for both models are obtained by two-port S-parameter simulation in Agilent Advanced Design System (ADS) based on the extracted model parameters shown in Table 3.1. For a two-port network, four sets of complex S-parameter results can be obtained including S11, S22, S12 and S21. However, according to the reciprocal property of the T-line structure (S11 = S22 and S12 = S21), only S11 and S21 are considered in the causality analysis. In order to minimize reconstruction and discretization errors [125] introduced by finite spectrum, the S-parameter simulation is conducted from 0Hz to 20THz with a step size of 1GHz.

Firstly, the causality of return loss (S11) is verified for both integer and fractional order T-line models. Figs. 3.15 and 3.16 show the comparison between $\Im(S11)$ and the value obtained by Hilbert transformation from the real part HilbertReal(S11) for both integer-order and the proposed fractional-order T-line models in the frequency range of 0.001 $\sim$ 1 THz, respectively. For the traditional integer-order RLCG T-line model, the $\Im(S11)$ starts to deviate

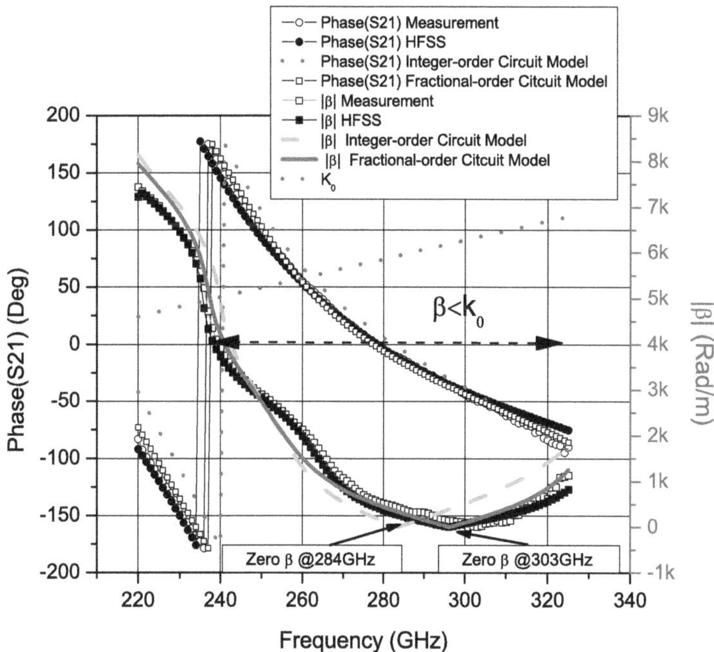

Figure 3.13: Measurement, EM, integer-order and fractional-order circuits simulation results: phase of S21 in degree and the absolute value of extracted phase constant β.

from the causal response at 10 GHz and shows large deviation in 0.1 $\sim$ 1 THz as depicted in Fig. 3.15. But for the proposed fractional-order T-line model as shown in Fig. 3.16, we can observe that the $\Im(S11)$ closely fits the causal response obtained from the Hilbert transformation $Hilbert\{\Re(S11)\}$. The error magnitude of $\Im(S11)$ from both models are compared in Fig. 3.17, where a dramatic error reduction is observed by the application of fraction order T-line model. Note that the error magnitude is calculated by

$$e_{11} = |Hilbert\{\Re(S11)\} - \Im(S11)|. \tag{3.37}$$

Secondly, the causality of return loss (S21) is verified for both integer and fractional-order T-line model. The comparison between Imag(S21) and causal response for both models are illustrated in Figs. 3.18 and 3.19. For the traditional integer-order RLCG T-line model, the $\Im(S21)$ obtained from the integer-order RLCG T-line model deviates from the causal response (1$\sim$10 GHz) as depicted in Fig. 3.18. But for the proposed fractional-order T-line model as shown in Fig. 3.19, we can observe that the $\Im(S21)$ of the fractional-order T-line model closely fits the causal response. A clear comparison by

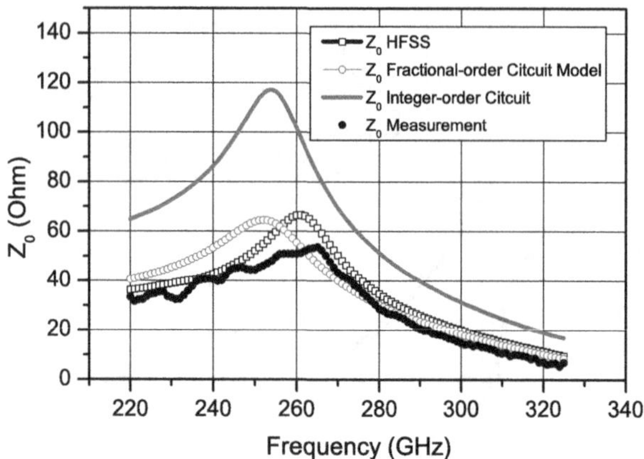

Figure 3.14: Measurement, EM, integer-order and fractional-order circuits simulation results: characteristic impedance of CRLH T-line (Z_0).

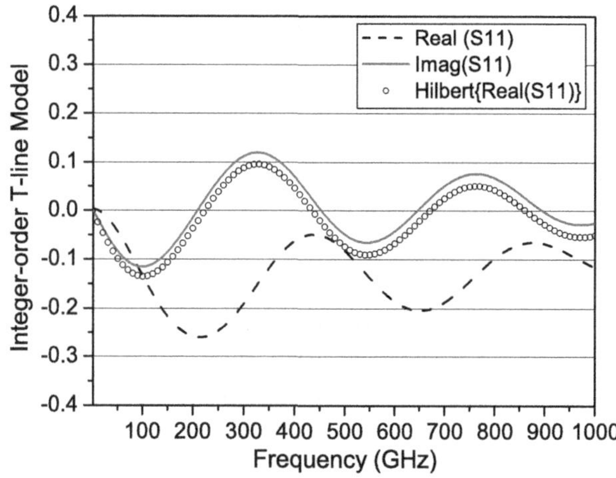

Figure 3.15: Causality verification by Hilbert transformation: integer-order T-line model S11.

error magnitude of $\Im(S21)$ from both models is illustrated in Fig. 3.20, where a dramatic error reduction is also observed by the proposed fractional-order T-line model. Note that the error magnitude is calculated by

$$e_{21} = |Hilbert\{\Re(S21)\} - \Im(S21)|. \tag{3.38}$$

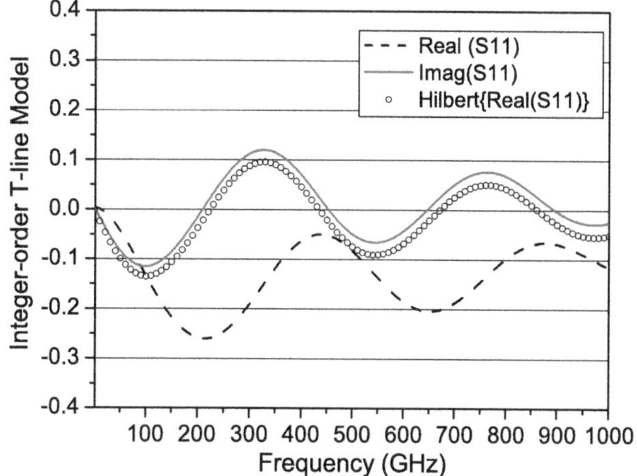

Figure 3.16: Causality verification by Hilbert transformation: fractional-order T-line model S11.

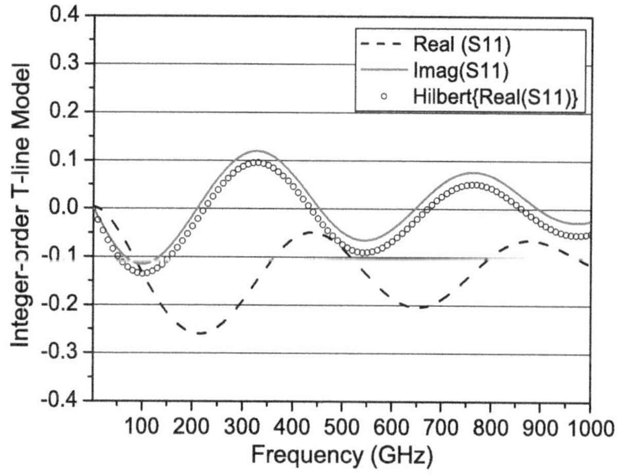

Figure 3.17: Causality verification by Hilbert transformation: error magnitude comparison of S11.

Note that since both e_{11} and e_{21} for the fractional-order T-line model are rather small, the causality enforcement by (3.31) and (3.32) is not required. The resulting frequency model can be directly used to estimate the time-domain model by the rational fitting. As such, the best accuracy could be ensured in the time-domain simulation such as Transient Analysis or Periodic

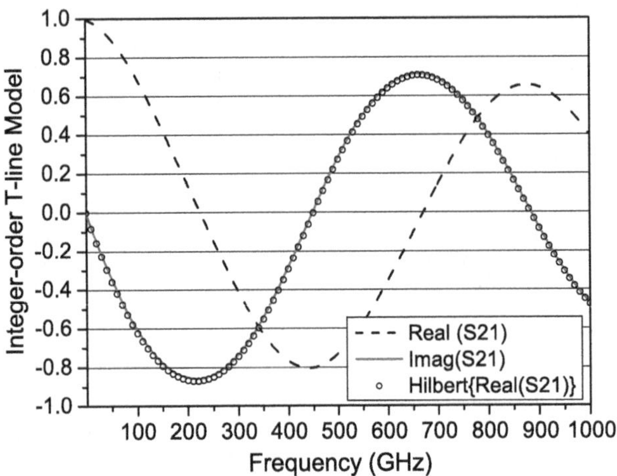

Figure 3.18: Causality verification by Hilbert transformation: integer-order T-line model S21.

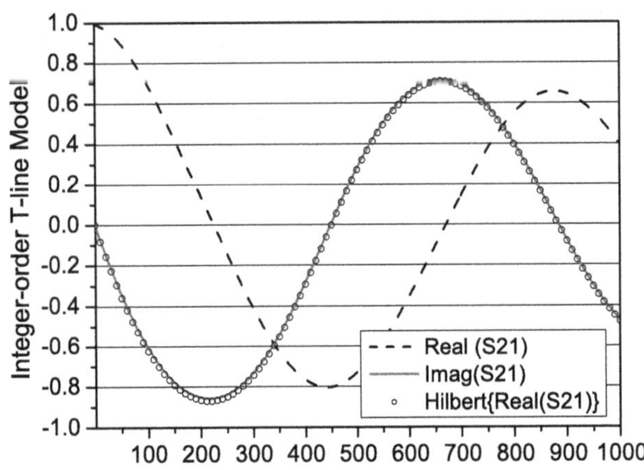

Figure 3.19: Causality verification by Hilbert transformation: fractional-order T-line model S21.

Steady State (PSS) analysis. But for the traditional integer-order RLCG T-line model, the non-causal effect could have convergence issues. One way to alleviate the causality issue of the integer-order RLCG T-line model is by truncating the model data with the causality enforcement, but the accuracy is lost in this way as discussed in Section 3.3.

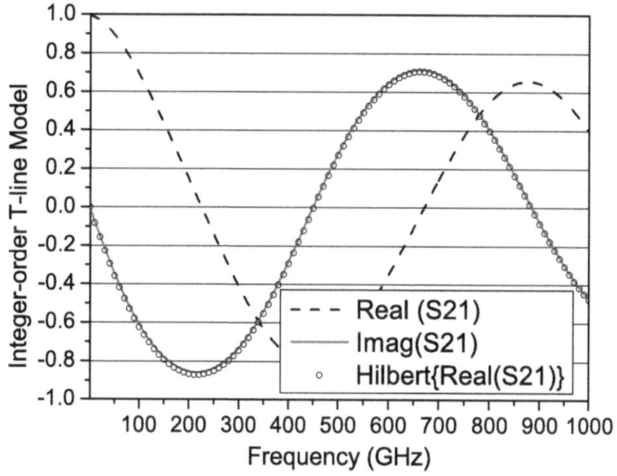

Figure 3.20: Causality verification by Hilbert transformation: error magnitude comparison of S21.

3.5 Conclusion

An accurate device model is critical for CMOS-based THz circuit design. Since transmission line (T-line) is one of the most fundamental passive device commonly used in the THz circuit design; an in-depth study of T-line model at THz is thereby important. Note that dispersion and non-quasi-static effects are difficult to be modeled by traditional methods such as the integer-order RLCG model with causality. By the proposed compact and causal fractional-order T-line model, the causality concern is resolved for T-line by considering the frequency-dependent dispersion loss and non-quasi-static effect at THz. The measured results have confirmed that the proposed fractional-order RLGC T-line model and CRLH T-line model have improved accuracy over the traditional integer-order models from mm-wave to THz region. Accordingly, the proposed fractional-order T-line models will be applied in the design for CMOS-based THz circuits in the following sections.

CMOS THZ SIGNAL GENERATION

Chapter 4

Oscillator

4.1 Introduction

Voltage controlled oscillator (VCO) is another critical block required in the 60 GHz transceiver to provide sufficient tuning range to cover the wide spectrum and large PVT variations with maintained phase noise and compact area, which is becoming a challenge with conventional tuning methods in CMOS technology. In this chapter, one inductive tuning method is first proposed based on configuration of current return paths in the secondary coil of a transformer, which demonstrates a wide frequency tuning range for CMOS VCO at mm-wave frequencies and shows great potential for integration in 60-GHz transceiver design. The inductive tuning method is further applied to realize a tunable CRLH T-line for Mobius-ring RTW-VCO design in mm-wave region. By utilizing the unique features of CRLH T-line to achieve a negative phase shift with compact area and wide tuning capability, state-of-the-art performance is demonstrated.

Phase noise and tuning range are the two primary design targets for VCO designs. During the last decade, substantial knowledge about the wide frequency bands at 60 GHz and beyond has been accumulated to develop the next generation big-data-rate wireless terminals [39, 130, 74, 131, 132]. The recent IEEE 802.15.3c standard for wireless local personal network (WPAN) has defined radio-frequency (RF) allocation composed of 4 RF sub-bands at 60 GHz, each with bandwidth of 2.16GHz. Considering the large frequency range and large process variation in nano-scale CMOS, the utilization of one single varactor cannot cover such a wide range with good phase noise performance, which has introduced a grand challenge for 60-GHz VCO designed in CMOS technology.

At mm-wave frequencies, the most widely used VCO topology is LC VCO [131, 133, 134, 135, 136]. It consists of an LC tank as resonator, and a cross-coupled transistor pair to generate negative resistance. LC VCO is widely used at 60 GHz and beyond due to its high oscillation frequency, low phase noise, simple structure and differential output. The challenge, however, is its limited tuning range due to the large parasitic capacitance from cross-coupled transistor pair.

Except for phase noise and tuning range, multi-phase or quadrature output is often required for many big-data communication and imaging applications at millimeter-wave frequencies [137, 138, 132, 134, 139, 140]. Multi-phase and quadrature oscillators are normally realized by traveling wave to generate multi-phase clock outputs with good phase noise performance [137, 138, 141, 142]. Mobius-ring rotary-traveling-wave (RTW) VCO topology is commonly adopted due to its advantages such as easy placement of cross-coupled transistors, good matching of differential blocks and compact area [142].

Traditionally, RTW-VCO is implemented with conventional right-handed (RH) transmission line (T-line), with a phase delay directly proportional to the T-line physical length [141, 142, 143]. Since a total phase delay of 360-degrees is required for oscillation, a large area is induced. Recently, left-handed (LH) T-line has shown to provide a superior performance at high frequency [144], and also unique features such as the nonlinear dispersion curve [75]. Due to large parasitic capacitors from cross-coupled transistors that are RH in nature, the actual implemented T-line is a composite right/left-hand (CRLH) T-line. By merging the phase shifts from LH and RH components together, CRLH T-line provides a phase delay independent of its physical size, and thus can be designed to be much more compact than conventional RH T-line for VCO. On the other hand, as big-data communication or imaging applications require a wide-band to ensure high data rate and also to cover process variation by CMOS MMIC at advanced technology, tuning ability of RTW-VCO has not been thoroughly studied and achieved as far.

Multi-sub-band operation is normally adopted to enhance the total frequency tuning range (FTR) with reduced VCO gain (K_{VCO}) [131]. Conventionally, multi-sub-band operation is implemented with capacitive tuning by switched capacitor banks. When operation frequency scales up to 60 GHz, the parasitic capacitance from the capacitor bank becomes too large and the quality factor of capacitor becomes too low [131, 145], which would severely limit the achievable FTR. Recently, inductive tuning has become a promising substitute to replace the capacitive tuning [131, 132, 145, 146], and is normally implemented by a loaded transformer topology [131, 145, 147]. By tuning inductance instead of capacitance, the limit of parasitic capacitance on FTR is relaxed. As a result, very wide FTR or multi-band operation can be achieved [131, 132, 145, 146]. The inductive tuning can also be combined with conventional capacitive tuning to realize more sub-bands to reduce K_{VCO} [132, 147].

Besides a wide FTR, inductive tuning can also provide the benefit of isolated DC noise from the tuning element.

The loads on transformer for inductive tuning can be categorized into three types: resistor [131], capacitor [147], and inductor [145]. Wide FTR is then achieved by controlling the value of the load. However, traditional loaded transformer topologies suffer from various limitations. For example, resistor-loaded transformer has a nonlinear tuning-curve with large effective K_{VCO}, which can make PLL difficult to lock [131]. Capacitor-loaded transformer suffers from a narrow FTR due to the limited tuning range and poor quality factor of the varactor at high frequency region [147]. Inductor-loaded transformer requires the use of multiple number of transformers, which constrain the effective number of sub-bands due to layout size and design complexity [145].

4.2 Frequency Tuning by Loaded Transformer

4.2.1 Inductive Tuning Analysis

The mechanism of loaded transformers applied for inductive tuning can be explained by Figure 4.1. The loaded transformer is utilized to tune the effective inductance (c_{eff}) in a LC-tank, while C_t consists of the total capacitance in the LC-tank. Note the 3 types of loaded transformers can all be approximately equalized to a RC tank and analyzed with the same equivalent circuit as shown in Figure 4.1.

The transformer is assumed to be ideal with coupling factor k, and with L_1 and L_2 as the primary inductance and secondary inductance, respectively. The equivalent circuit with l_{eq} and R_{eq} can then be calculated as

$$\begin{cases} L_{eq} = L_1 \times \dfrac{R^2[1-\omega^2 CL_2(1-k^2)]^2 + \omega^2 L_2^2(1-k^2)^2}{R^2\left(1-\omega^2 CL_2\right)\left[1-\omega^2 CL_2\left(1-k^2\right)\right] + \omega^2 L_2^2(1-k^2)} \\ R_{eq} = \dfrac{R^2 L_1[1-\omega^2 CL_2(1-k^2)]^2 + \omega^2 L_1 L_2^2(1-k^2)^2}{Rk^2 L_2}. \end{cases} \tag{4.1}$$

Thus the oscillation frequency becomes

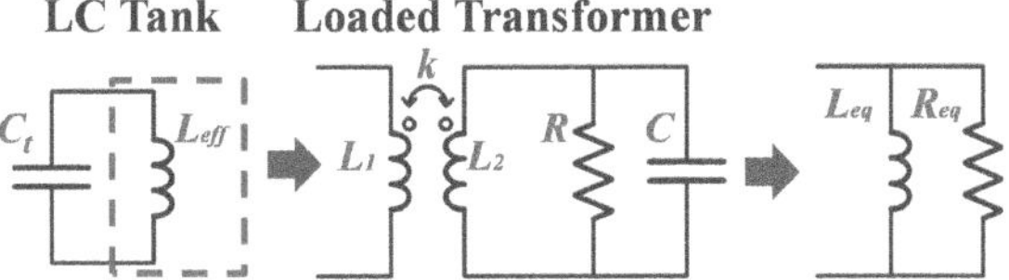

Figure 4.1: Equivalent circuit model for inductive tuning of loaded transformer.

$$\omega = \frac{1}{\sqrt{L_{eq}C_t}}. \tag{4.2}$$

For a resistor or inductor-loaded transformer, the FTR of the equivalent circuit can be estimated by considering the two extreme conditions of R in Figure 4.1:

$$\begin{cases} \mathrm{L_{eq\_max}} = \mathrm{L_{eq}}\left(\mathrm{R} \to \infty\right) = \mathrm{L_1} \times \frac{1-\omega^2\mathrm{CL_2}(1-\mathrm{k}^2)}{1-\omega^2\mathrm{CL_2}} \\ \mathrm{L_{eq\_min}} = \mathrm{L_{eq}}\left(\mathrm{R} \to 0\right) = \mathrm{L_1}\left(1-\mathrm{k}^2\right). \end{cases} \tag{4.3}$$

By substituting (4.3) into (4.2), the FTR for LC-tank oscillation frequency can be obtained:

$$\begin{cases} \omega_{\min} = \omega\left(\mathrm{R} \to \infty\right) = \sqrt{\frac{\omega_1^2+\omega_2^2-\sqrt{(\omega_1^2+\omega_2^2)^2-4\omega_1^2\omega_2^2(1-\mathrm{k}^2)}}{2(1-\mathrm{k}^2)}} \\ \omega_{\max} = \omega\left(\mathrm{R} \to 0\right) = \frac{\omega_1}{\sqrt{1-\mathrm{k}^2}} \end{cases}, \tag{4.4}$$

where $\omega_1 = \frac{1}{\sqrt{\mathrm{L_1C_t}}}$ and $\omega_2 = \frac{1}{\sqrt{\mathrm{L_2C}}}$. As shown in Figure 4.1, ω_1 and ω_2 represent the resonant frequencies at the primary side and the secondary side of the transformer, respectively.

Note that ω_1 is pre-determined by parameters of the transformer and the LC-tank, while ω_2 would be affected by the load. By defining $\omega_2 = \alpha\omega_1$, where $\alpha{>}0$ is the ratio between two resonant frequencies, we can further analyze the value based on different α values. Since $\frac{\partial\omega(\mathrm{R}\to\infty)}{\partial\alpha}$ stays positive for all α values, by taking the extreme conditions for α, the range for can be estimated as

$$\omega\left(\mathrm{R} \to \infty\right) \approx \begin{cases} \omega_2, 0 < \alpha \ll 1 \\ \omega_1, \alpha \gg 1. \end{cases} \tag{4.5}$$

According to (4.5), when ω_2 is much higher than ω_1 or equals ω_1, indicating negligible dependence between value of $\omega\left(\mathrm{R} \to \infty\right)$ and the load. However, as ω_2 drops below ω_1, $\omega\left(\mathrm{R} \to \infty\right)$ is decreased, approaching the value of ω_2 instead. This is actually tie mechanism for frequency-tuning of capacitor-loaded transformer.

The effect of ω_2 value on the quality factor for the effective LC-tank must be considered, which can be easily derived from (4.1) as

$$Q_{eq} = \frac{R_{eq}}{\omega L_{eq}} = \frac{R}{\omega L_2} \times \frac{\left(1 - {\omega^2}/{\omega_2^2}\right)\left[1 - \left(1-k^2\right){\omega^2}/{\omega_2^2}\right]}{k^2} + \frac{\omega L_2}{R} \times \frac{1-k^2}{k^2}. \tag{4.6}$$

Note that here the loss from the transformer and the LC-tank is not included in the calculation and Q_{eq} quantifies the additional loss coupled from transformer load into the LC-tank. As (4.6) shows, this coupled loss is contributed by two portions. When $R >> \omega L_2$, the first item on the right-side of the equation dominates. When $R << \omega L_2$, the second item dominates. Clearly, in the case of $\omega\,(\mathrm{R} \to \infty)$, the first item should be considered. Unfortunately, as ω_2 drops, it approaches the value of ω_2, forcing Q_{eq} degrade toward 0, which indicates a high degradation on the phase noise performance. As a result, the approach of lowering ω_2 value for larger FTR, suffers significant phase noise degradation. In fact, this is also one limitation for the capacitor-loaded transformer.

Therefore, for a resistor or inductor-loaded transformer, the condition $\omega_1 \ll \omega_2$ is required in design optimization. The FTR can then be estimated by

$$\mathrm{FTR} = \frac{\frac{\omega_1}{\sqrt{1-k^2}} - \omega_1}{\frac{\omega_1}{\sqrt{1-k^2}} + \omega_1} \times 2 = \frac{1 - \sqrt{1-k^2}}{1 + \sqrt{1-k^2}} \times 2. \tag{4.7}$$

According to (4.7), to achieve a large FTR, a large k is required. Moreover, according to (4.6), Q_{eq} approaches infinity when R approaches 0 or infinity, but drops when R moves from the two boundaries. This explains the performance degradation for resistor-loaded transformer since its major tuning region locates away from these two boundaries.

4.2.1.1 Model of Inductor-Loaded Transformer with Switches

The three types of loaded transformer (resistor, capacitor and inductor) are shown in Figure 4.2. In Section 4.2.2.1, they are analyzed by the same equivalent circuit shown in Figure 4.1. Since both resistor and capacitor-loaded transformers have the loading at one fixed location on the secondary coil of the transformer, their circuit behavior can be fully emulated by the same equivalent circuit shown in Figure 4.1. The inductor-loaded transformer, on the other hand, has switches located on several different locations on the secondary coil. When one part of the secondary coil is turned on and plays the major role in determining the effective inductance on the primary coil, the remaining part of the secondary coil can still affect the performance due to parasitic effect, which is ignored by the semilar equivalent circuit in Figure 4.1. As a result, one more comprehensive circuit model is developed in Figure 4.3 that can provide a more comprehensive model for an inductor-loaded transformer.

Figure 4.3 shows the circuit models for an traditional inductor-loaded transformer. Three inductors (L_1, L_2, and L_3) are used to form the simplest topology, and are coupled with each other by the mutual inductances M_{12}, M_{13}, and M_{23}. The terminal voltage and loop current for each inductor are represented by (V_1, I_1), (V_2, I_2), and (d_3, I_3), respectively. The loaded inductance is varied by switching on different combinations of L_2 and L_3, with their switches represented by (R_2, C_2, $\overline{i_{n2}^2}$) and (R_3, C_3, $\overline{i_{n3}^2}$), respectively. The resulting L_{eq} and R_{eq} can then be calculated by solving the following

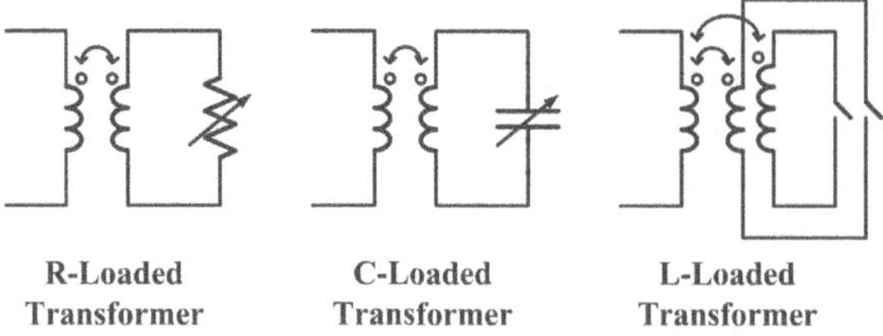

Figure 4.2: Traditional resistor-, capacitor-, and inductor-loaded transformers.

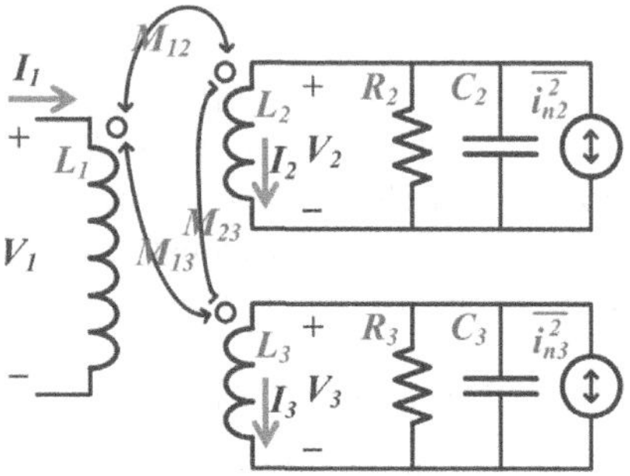

Figure 4.3: Equivalent circuit model for conventional inductor-loaded transformer.

equations:

$$\begin{cases} I_1 = V_1 \times \left(\frac{1}{R_{eq}} + \frac{1}{sL_{eq}}\right) + \overline{i_{neq}} \\ V_1 = sL_1I_1 + sM_{12}I_2 + sM_{13}I_3 \\ V_2 = sM_{12}I_1 + sL_2I_2 + sM_{23}I_3 \\ V_3 = sM_{13}I_1 + sM_{23}I_2 + sL_3I_3 \\ V_2 + \frac{R_2I_2}{1+sR_2C_2} = \frac{R_2\overline{i_{n2}}}{1+sR_2C_2} \\ V_3 + \frac{R_3I_3}{1+sR_3C_3} = \frac{R_3\overline{i_{n3}}}{1+sR_3C_3} \end{cases} \tag{4.8}$$

where an equivalent noise current (i_{eq}^2) parallel to the LC tank can be transferred from the noise components of the switches.

4.2.1.2 Switch Design Parameters

To have the performance analysis in (4.8), we need to extract and optimize switch parameters for performance.

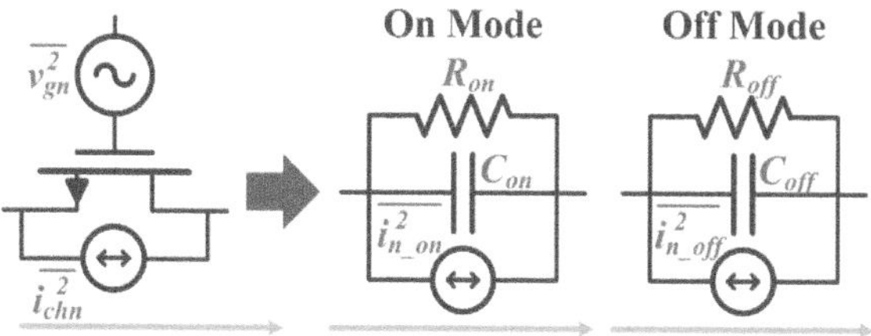

Figure 4.4: Equivalent circuit model for switches. R$_{on}$, C$_{on}$ and $\overline{i^2_{n\_on}}$ form the equivalent circuit of switch when it is turned on. R$_{off}$, C$_{off}$ and $\overline{i^2_{n\_off}}$ form the equivalent circuit of switch when it is turned off.

Table 4.1: Switch Parameters Extracted from CMOS 65 nm Technology

W_s (μm)	10	20	50	100	200	400
R_{on} (Ω)	41.4	20.5	8.16	4.07	2.04	1.02
R_{off} (Ω)	2.72K	1.36K	543	272	136	67.9
C_{on} (fF)	7.78	15.6	38.9	77.8	156	311
C_{off} (fF)	6.10	12.2	30.5	61.0	122	244

As shown in Figure 4.4, the switch state parameter in (4.8) is approximated by a RC-tank, where R_{on} and R_{off} are used to represent its effective resistance for the on and off states. Furthermore, the effective capacitances are represented by C_{on} and C_{off}. One can build an FC-library model for switches by extracting RC-values based on the 65-nm CMOS technology by sweeping as listed in Table 4.1. Note that since the minimum length of the switch is used to minimize parasitic capacitance, the size of the switch is determined by its width W_s.

For the switch noise parameter in (4.8), the gate noise ($\overline{v^2_{gn}}$) and channel noise ($\overline{i^2_{chn}}$) of the switch are transformed to equivalent current noise sources ($\overline{i^2_{n\_on}}$ and $\overline{i^2_{n\_off}}$) that are added to the RC tank in parallel. Since the transformer filters out the low-frequency noise, flicker noise is not considered in the model for simplicity. As a result, the noise sources ($\overline{i^2_{n\_on}}$ and $\overline{i^2_{n\_off}}$) of the switch are estimated at thermal noise in equivalent model.

4.2.2 *Inductor-Loaded Transformer by Switching Return-Path*

According to Figures 4.1 and (4.1), there are 4 variables: R, C, L_2, and k on the secondary coil of the transformer, which control the oscillation frequency. Resistor-loaded transformer tunes R, capacitor-loaded transformer tunes C, while inductor-loaded transformer tunes both L_2 and k. Conventionally, L_2 and k are tuned by switching on different combinations of transformers [145].

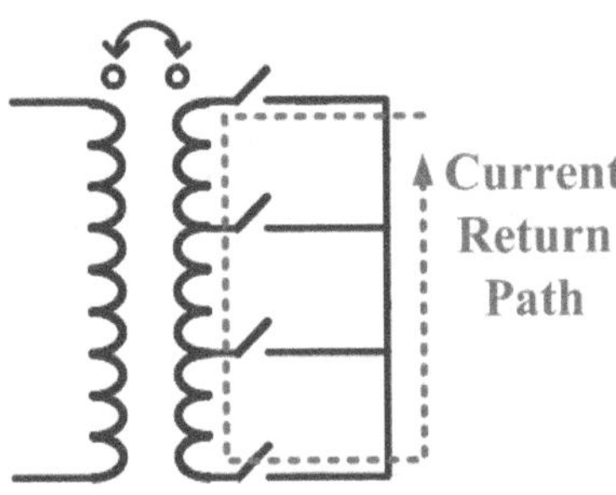

Figure 4.5: Proposed new inductor-loaded transformer by switching current return-paths with only one transformer.

However, the large layout size of the loop inductor and strong magnetic coupling with adjacent devices limit the number of transformers. Moreover, as more transformers are used, magnetic coupling from different transformers tend to cancel each other, and hence make the tuning less effective. As a result, the number of sub-bands achieved by the conventional inductor-loaded transformer topology often limits to 4 (with 2 transformers used) and below.

In this section, a new inductor-loaded transformer topology is proposed, which breaks through the limit of the conventional inductive tuning. The concept of the proposed topology can be explained in Figure 4.5. Only one transformer is used for the new inductor-loaded transformer, with switches placed at various locations of the secondary coil. When some combination of switches are turned on such that a closed-loop is constructed in the secondary coil, a current return-path forms. Different-sized current return-paths generate different magnetic fluxes, which are fed back to the primary coil and hence result in multiple sub-bands.

4.2.2.1 Comparison with Traditional Loaded Transformers

Since the proposed topology can increase the number of sub-bands by simply adding more switches, the sub-band number can be easily designed to be larger than 4 with compact layout area when compared to the conventional inductor-loaded transformer.

Moreover, different from the resistor-loaded transformer that has a highly nonlinear tuning-curve and large K_{VCO}, the new inductor-loaded transformer achieves a much smaller K_{VCO} through multi-sub-band operation within linear tuning-curve. As a result, the phase noise performance can be improved with no PLL locking difficulty. The small K_{VCO} may also be used to trade for a wider tuning range, which can be easily realized by implementing with a large coupling factor k, as explained in (4.7).

In addition, as mentioned in Section 4.2.2, frequency-tuning for capacitor-loaded transformer is realized by varying the value of C and thus ω_2. However,

Table 4.2: Trade-Offs between Different Loaded Transformer Topologies

Topology	Benefits	Limitations
R-loaded transformer	• wide tuning range large sub-band number • large sub-band number	large effective K_{VCO}
C-loaded transformer	• large sub-bend number	limited tuning range
Traditional L-loader transformer	• wide tuning range	limited sub-band number
Proposed L-loaded transformer	• wide tuning range	asymmetric current return path

according to (4.6), as C increases or ω_2 drops, Q_{eq} is severely degraded. As a result, the FTR that can be achieved is limited. Furthermore, the FTR for the varactor or capacitor-bank is further limited by parasitic capacitance from switches and transformers.

Trade-offs between different loaded-transformer topologies are summarized in Table 4.2. However, one design challenge is how to deal with asymmetric current return-paths in certain sub-bands, which will be discussed in detail in Section 4.4.3.

4.2.2.2 Model of Proposed New Inductor-Loaded Transformer with Switches

Similar to the modeling or conventional inductor-loaded transformer, a more comprehensive circuit model is developed in Figure 4.6 for the proposed new inductor-loaded transformer which can take the parasitic effects from the off part of the secondary coil into consideration.

Figure 4.6 shows the circuit models for the proposed inductor-loaded transformer. Its secondary coil is split into two portions: L_2 and L_3. The L_3 portion is switched on to form a current return-path to generate feedback to L_1, while the remaining portion of the secondary coil (L_2) is left floating by keeping the switch terminating L_2 off. The change of loaded inductance is then emulated by varying the ratio between L_2 and L_3. The resulted L_{eq} and R_{eq} can then be calculated by solving the following equations:

$$\begin{cases} I_1 = V_1 \times \left(\frac{1}{R_{eq}} + \frac{1}{sL_{eq}}\right) + \overline{i_{neq}} \\ V_1 = sL_1I_1 + sM_{12}I_2 + sM_{13}I_3 \\ V_2 = sM_{12}I_1 + sL_2I_2 + sM_{23}I_3 \\ V_3 = sM_{13}I_1 + sM_{23}I_2 + sL_3I_3 \\ V_2 + V_3 + \frac{R_2I_2}{1+sR_2C_2} = \frac{R_2\overline{i_{n2}}}{1+sR_2C_2} \\ V_3 + \frac{R_3(I_3-I_2)}{1+sR_3C_3} = \frac{R_3\overline{i_{n3}}}{1+sR_3C_3}. \end{cases} \tag{4.9}$$

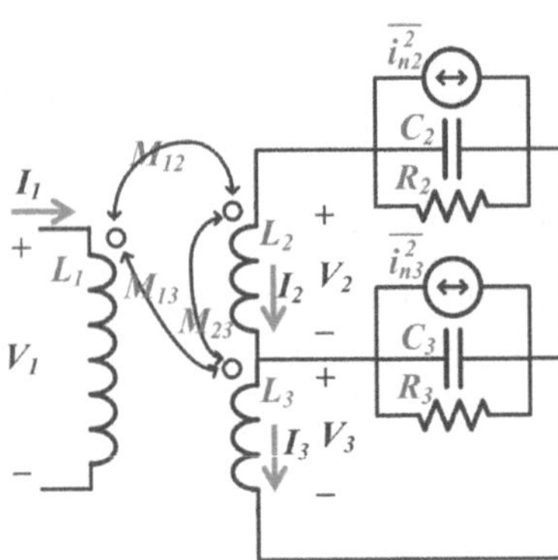

Figure 4.6: Equivalent circuit model for the proposed loaded transformer.

4.2.2.3 Performance Study

Based on the previously developed switch and transformer models, performance for the proposed inductor-loaded transformer topology can be further analyzed to obtain the optimized design with respect to switch sizing W_s. With extracted switch parameters such as in Table 4.1, switch performance under various sizes W_s can be studied. Based on the design parameters summarized in Table 4.3, we have the following detailed performance study.

Firstly, the impact of switches on the FTR performance is studied in Figure 4.7(a). Confirmed with our conclusion in (4.7), a larger coupling factor k leads to a wider FTR. When switch size is small, the FTR is also observed to increase with switch size. This can be explained by the analysis in Section 4.2.2, where a larger C_{on} would raise the FTR when R_{off} is sufficiently large. However, as switch size further increases, R_{off} becomes too small to fully switch off the current return path, and FTR starts to decrease.

Secondly, the impact of switches to phase noise performance can be also analyzed. Switches on a loaded transformer degrade the phase noise performance from two aspects. It can decrease output signal power by reducing the effective Q factor in LC-tank; and also increase phase noise by transferring noise power to output nodes. These two aspects are analyzed in Figure 4.7(b)

Table 4.3: Parameters for 60-GHz VCO Design Based on Proposed Loaded Transformer Topology

Switch	Transformer			Other
$W_s(\mu m)$	L_{prim} (pH)	L_{sec} (pH)	k	C_t (fF)
10~400	80	80	0.1~0.7	100

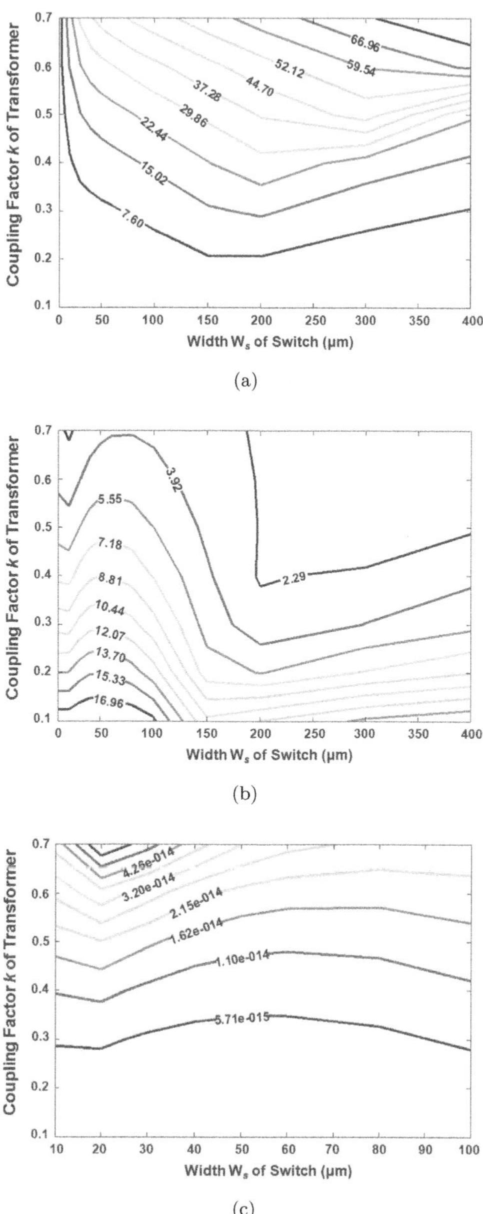

Figure 4.7: Design optimization for (a) frequency tuning range (%), (b) the minimum quality factor in the tuning range, and (c) the maximum output noise spectral density at 10 MHz offset in tuning range.

and (c), by examining the minimum Q factor of the LC-tank and the maximum output noise spectral density at the offset frequency. One can observe that there is an optimal switch size for the minimum phase noise degradation.

4.2.2.4 Design Optimization Flow

As such, we present a design flow in Figure 4.8 to optimize the specific performances of the proposed inductor-loaded transformer topology. The targeted frequency (*freq.*) and tuning range (*FTR*) define the minimum frequency (f_{min}) and maximum frequency (f_{max}) to be designed. With the proposed tuning topology, f_{min} is mainly determined by the inductance of the primary coil (L_{prim}) and the total capacitance in LC-tank (C_t). Due to the single-loop topology adopted for the proposed transformer, the inductance on its secondary coil (L_{sec}) can be accordingly determined.

Firstly, with the given *FTR* and targeted K_{VCO}, we can calculate the number of sub-bands (N_{band}) needed, thus determining how many switches are required as well as their locations on the secondary coil. Each sub-band is then to be fully covered by a varactor pair as fine tuning. Therefore the tuning capacitance (C_{tune}) is determined for varactor design. Besides C_{tune}, the rest part of C_t is mainly contributed from the parasitic capacitance in the cross-coupled transistors, which can help determine the transistor sizes.

Next, given L_{prim}, L_{sec}, and C_t, f_{max} is mainly determined by the coupling factor k of the transformer. For a specific k value, an optimized switch size can be found to minimize the phase noise (*PN*) as Figure 4.7 (b) and (c) shows. Note that since both phase noise and power consumption are related

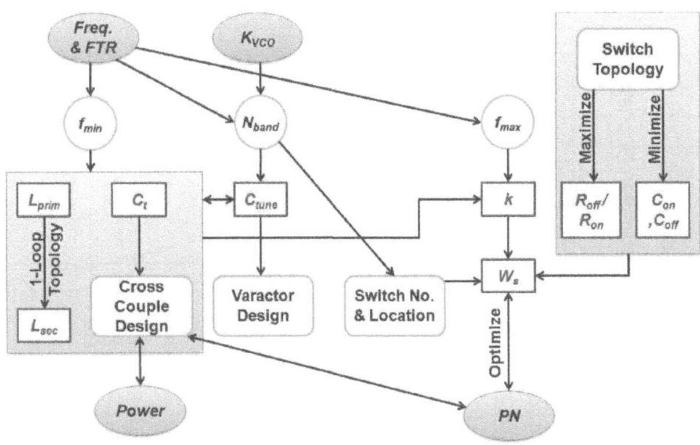

Figure 4.8: Design optimization flow for wide-tuning VCO based on the proposed inductor-loaded transformer, where performance metrics are frequency, FTR, K_{VCO}, power, and phase noise.

Table 4.4: EM Extracted Parameters at 60 GHn for the Proposed Loaded-Transformer Implementation

L_1 (pH)	L_2 (pH)	M_{12} (pH)	k
154.2	175.5	77.3	0.470

to the sizing and biasing of cross-coupled transistors, a few design iterations are required to meet the targeted performance for all specifications.

4.2.2.5 Loaded-Transformer Simulation Results

4.2.2.6 Model Validation

The proposed model in Section 4.3.2 is used to analyze one asymmetrical implementation for the proposed loaded transformer, whose topology will be shown in Figure 4.14 in Section 4.4.2. Transformer parameters are extracted from EM simulation, as summarized it Table 4.4. C_t from Figure 4.1 is adjusted to be 92fF. Calculated VCO oscillation frequency and noise density contributed by switches are plotted in Figure 4.9 both of which can roughly fit the simulation results from Cadence. This validates the proposed model. Note a larger deviation occurs at lower frequency bands, which is due to neglect of flicker noise in the switch model, as will be addressed in Section 4.4.1.2 and 4.4.2.2.

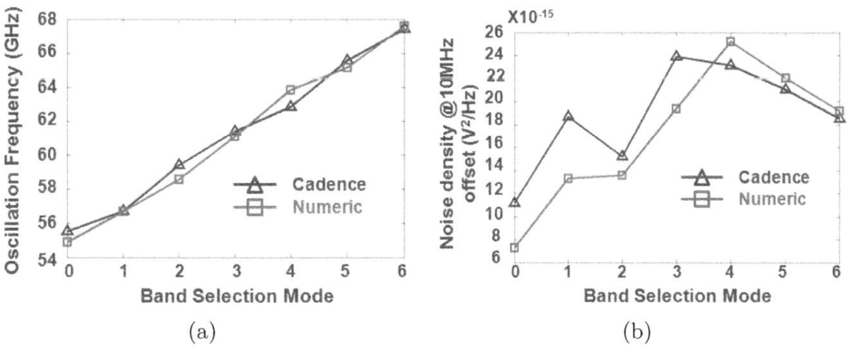

Figure 4.9: Model validation: (a) oscillation frequency, (b) output noise density contributed by switches.

4.2.2.7 Comparison between Loaded Transformer Topologies

The four topologies in Figures 4.2 and 4.5 are simulated numerically in MATLAB for performance comparison. To achieve a fair comparison, while both resistor and capacitor-loaded transformers are simulated by the equivalent circuit shown in Figure 4.1, the inductor-loaded transformers are simulated based on more comprehensive models shown in Figures 4.3 and Figure 4.6 to consider parasitic effects on the secondary coil. Parameters derived in Section 4.2.2.3 are used to assist numeric analysis for the proposed inductor-loaded transformer topology. The same parameters are utilized to simulate resistor-loaded transformer (Table 4.5), with its resistance linearly varies between the on and off resistances (R_{on} and R_{off}) of the 50μm switch in Table 4.1. The linear change can be achieved by splitting the switch into a parallel array of smaller switches [131]. Similarly, for the capacitor-loaded transformer, a switched capacitor bank can be used to obtain linear and large tuning range than single varactor. The penalty is the parasitic from the switches in the capacitor bank, which is also the major limitation for its tuning range. With the extracted switch parameters in Table 4.1, the effective capacitance ratio when the switch is on and off for each bank (p_{datio}=C_{off}/C_{on}) is analyzed. A value of 3.206 is obtained for C_{ratio} and is used for this analysis.

All loaded transformers are designed to provide the same oscillation frequency in 60-GHz band. The adjusted parameters are summarized in Table 4.5, and the simulated tuning range and quality factor are shown in Figure 4.10. To have a direct view of the extra loss coupled from the tuning elements into the LC-tank, a similar definition of quality factor as (4.6) is used. With this definition, the quality factor represents how much degradation on the whole LC-tank quality factor (or phase noise performance) will be caused by the tuning elements loaded on the transformer.

Firstly, as Figure 4.10(a) shows, the resister-loaded transformer has a highly nonlinear tuning-curve with respect to tuning resistance. Most of the frequency tuning is realized in a narrow region of the tuning resistance, where the lowest quality factor is also located. Next, the capacitor-loaded trans-

Table 4.5: Parameters for Different Loaded Transformers Biased for 60-GHz Band Oscillation

Loaded Transformer	R-loaded	C-loaded	L-loaded	Proposed
L_{prim} (pH)	80	60	80	80
L_{sec} (pH)	80	60	N.A.	80
Coupling factor	k=0.5	k=0.5	k_{12}=k_{13}=0.5 k_{23}=0.4	k=0.5
L_{ratio}	N.A.	N.A.	0.3	0$\rightarrow$ 1
C_{ratio}	N.A.	3.206	N.A.	N.A.

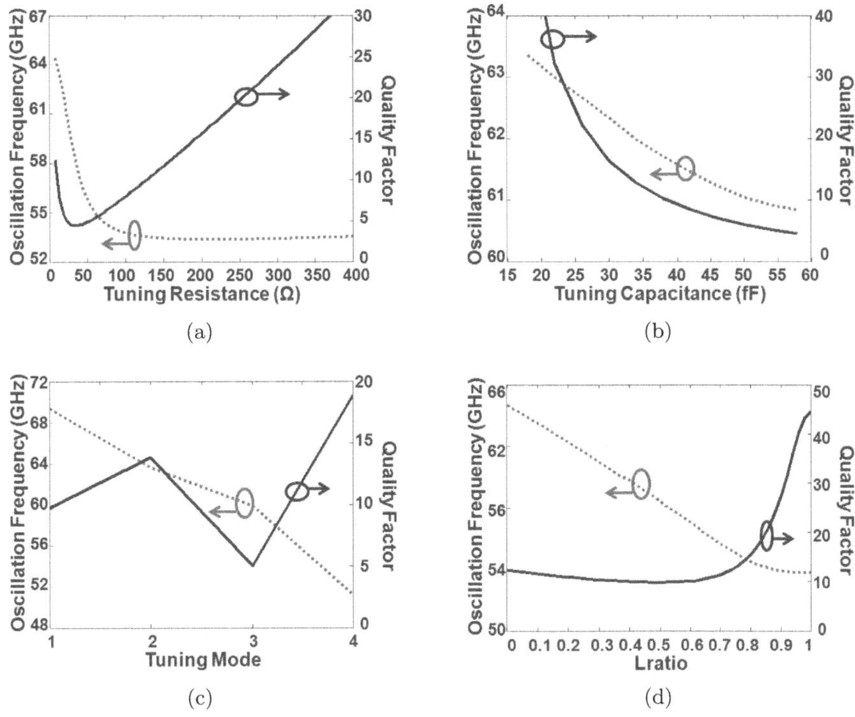

Figure 4.10: Numeric simulation for tuning range and quality factor of different loaded transformers: (a) R-loaned transformer, (b) C-loaded transformer, (c) traditional L-loaded transformer, (d) proposed new loaded transformer.

former, as Figure 4.10(b) shows, has a very linear tuning-curve. Besides its quality factor degradation in the lower frequency region, its major limitation is the narrow tuning range which comes from the limited tuning ability of varactor or capacitor bank. Lastly, for the traditional inductor-loaded transformer shown in Figure 4.10(c), there are only 4 sub-bands within the tuning range. Besides its limitation on the number of sub-bands that can be achieved, the inductor-loaded transformer also differs from high degradation on quality factor in the middle region (mode 3) of its tuning range. Different from the resistor-loaded transformer, this degradation comes from magnetic coupling from L_3 to L_2 when L_2 is switched on and L_3 is off. Recall that multiple transformers needed by the traditional inductor-loaded transformer would cause large area overhead as well.

In contrast, the proposed inductor-loaded transformer does not have this degradation. Due to the single-loop topology adopted for the transformer, the

Table 4.6: Performance Summary for Different Loaded Transformer Topologies Based on Numeric Analysis

Loaded Transformer	R-loaded	C-loaded	L-loaded	Proposed
Tuning Range	Large	Small	Large	Large
Linearity	Low	High	Medium	High
Quality Factor Degradation	High	Medium	Medium	Low
Band Number	Large	Large	Small	Medium

coupling between different portions on the secondary coil is much weaker. As Figure 4.10(d) shows, a linear tuning curve is obtained with a large FTR, and with low degradation on the quality factor in the whole tuning range at 60 GHz by the proposed inductor-loaded transformer.

The performances of different loaded transformers are summarized in Table 4.6. The numeric simulations confirm our observations in Section 4.3.1 that the proposed new inductor-loaded transformer can realize a wide FTR with high linearity and low K_{VCO} and also can achieve multiple sub-bands with compact size. Furthermore, low degradation on LC-tank quality factor and hence better VCO phase noise performance can also be maintained in the whole tuning range by the proposed inductor-loaded transformer. As shown in Figure 4.10(e), a 20% FTR with linear tuning curve is achieved with a Q factor above 10 for all sub-bands.

4.3 Frequency Tuning by CRLH T-Line

As mentioned in Section 4.1, Mobius-ring RTW-VCO is often utilized to generate multi-phase or quadrature output for many millimeter-wave applications such as big-data communication and imaging. Conventional RTW-VCO is mostly tuned by varactor and capacitor bank due to the RH topology [141, 142, 143]. Due to constrained tuning ability of varactor and capacitor bank in the millimeter-wave region, the achieved FTR in quite limited [141, 142, 143]. CRLH T-line, on the other hand, provides more choices of tunable elements to achieve a wide FTR in RTW-VCO design, but is not well explored at the millimeter-wave region [144]. In this section, a tunable CRLH T-line biased in the LH region is studied for RTW-VCO to achieve compact size and wide FTR. Assisted with the inductive tuning techniques presented in the above sections, a much wider FTR can be obtained.

4.3.1 CRLH T-Line-Based RTW-VCO

The topology for Mobius-rang RTW-VCO is shown in Figure 4.11. A Mobius-ring is evenly divided into N stages, with each stage loaded with a cross-

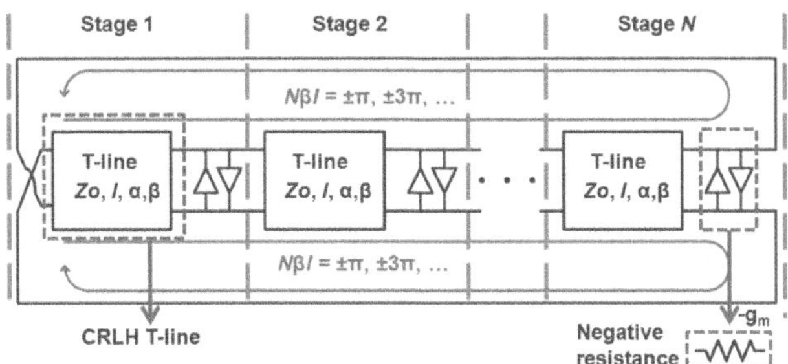

Figure 4.11: CRLH T-line-based Mobius-ring RTW-VCO.

coupled transistor pair. As a wave travels along the Mobius-ring, certain phase delay must be fulfilled to create a positive feedback for VCO oscillation. At the same time, cross-coupled transistors should generate enough power to compensate the loss from the T-line. In summary, the start-up condition of Mobius-ring RTW-VCO is

$$g_m > \frac{2\exp(\alpha l)}{Z_o}; \beta l = \frac{M\pi}{N} \tag{4.10}$$

where g_m is the transconductance of the cross-coupled pair, z_o, l, α, β are T-line characteristic impedance, physical length, attenuation constant, and phase constant, respectively. N is the stage number, and M=±1, ±3,... is an odd integer number.

In this section, a negative-phase CRLH T-line is deployed in the Mobius-ring RTW-VCO for both compact size and wide FTR. Assuming a balanced condition for simplicity, with (4.7) and (4.10), the oscillation frequency for an N-stage Mobius-ring RTW-VCO by CRLH T-line can be obtained

$$\omega_{CRLH} = \frac{\pi}{2Nl\sqrt{L_sC_p}} \times (\sqrt{1 + \frac{4N^2l^2}{\pi^2}\sqrt{\frac{L_sC_p}{L_pC_s}}} \pm 1). \tag{4.11}$$

Here, only the fundamental resonant condition M=±1 is considered for simplicity of illustration. The plus and minus signs in (4.11) correspond to CRLH T-line working in the RH region and LH region, respectively.

Furthermore, phase noise is an important specification for VCO design. Generally, for N-stage RTW-VCO, the phase variation $< \Phi^2(\mathrm{t}) >$ is proportional to *1/N* [141, 148, 149, 150], which is reduced by *1/N* when compared to single stage.

In this work, the LH operation is selected for compact size and superior performance when implemented in multiple stages [144]. However, there is no study of how to tune the CRLH T-line-based RTW-VCO, which will be addressed in the next part.

4.3.2 Wide-Band Tuning for CRLH T-Line-Based RTW-VCO

Note that in (4.11), there are 4 components that may be used for tuning: L_s, L_p, C_s, C_p. For easy analysis, we represent the product of the LH components $(L_p, C_s,)$ as P_L; and represent the product of the RH components $(L_s, C_p,)$ as P_R. Then, the oscillation frequency in the LH region becomes

$$\omega_{CRLH\_LH} = \frac{\pi}{2Nl\sqrt{P_R}} \times (\sqrt{1 + \frac{4N^2l^2}{\pi^2}\sqrt{\frac{P_R}{P_L}}} - 1). \tag{4.12}$$

Conventionally, P_R is used to realize FTR by varactor as part of C_p [144]. Unfortunately, with the omitted L_s component and thus small P_R value in [144], the tuning ability by P_R is very limited, not to mention the already constrained tuning ability as well as the limited quality factor of varactor at high frequency. In fact, for a small P_R / P_L value, approaches the operation frequency of a pure LH T-line-based RTW-VCO

$$\omega_{CRLH\_LH}|\frac{P_R}{P_L} \rightarrow 0 = \omega_{LH} = \frac{Nl}{\pi\sqrt{P_L}} \tag{4.13}$$

which is independent of P_R with poor tuning ability. Furthermore, a large portion of C_p is contributed by transistor parasitic with a fixed value, which severely limits tuning range of the whole C_p value, not to mention the already constrained tuning ability as well as the limited quality factor of varactor in the high-frequency region.

Intuitively, a wider FTR should be obtained by tuning P_L since the LH-components dominate in the LH region. Since $\frac{\delta\omega_{CRLH}}{\delta P_L}$ stays positive for all P_L values, the FTR can be calculated:

$$\Delta\omega_{CRLH_{LH}} = \frac{\pi}{2Nl\sqrt{P_R}} \times (\sqrt{1 + \frac{4N^2l^2}{\pi^2}\sqrt{\frac{P_R}{P_{L\_min}}}} - \sqrt{1 + \frac{4N^2l^2}{\pi^2}\sqrt{\frac{P_R}{P_{L\_max}}}}) \tag{4.14}$$

The extreme condition forms for a pure LH T-line with

$$FTR_{LH} = \frac{\frac{1}{\sqrt{P_{L\_min}}} - \frac{1}{\sqrt{P_{L\_max}}}}{\frac{1}{\sqrt{P_{L\_min}}} + \frac{1}{\sqrt{P_{L\_max}}}} \times 2 \approx \frac{\alpha_{P_L}}{2} \tag{4.15}$$

where $\alpha_{P_L} = \frac{\Delta P_L}{P_L}$ measures the tunability of components in P_L. As (4.15) shows, FTR_{LH} is directly proportional to α_{P_L}.

However, since the loss in C_s adds directly into the signal path, it is not feasible to tune C_s. On the other hand, one can realize a wide FTR by tuning L_p with a loaded transformer structure presented in the above sections. More specifically, the inductive-loaded transformer can achieve a large α_{P_L}, which is adopted in this work.

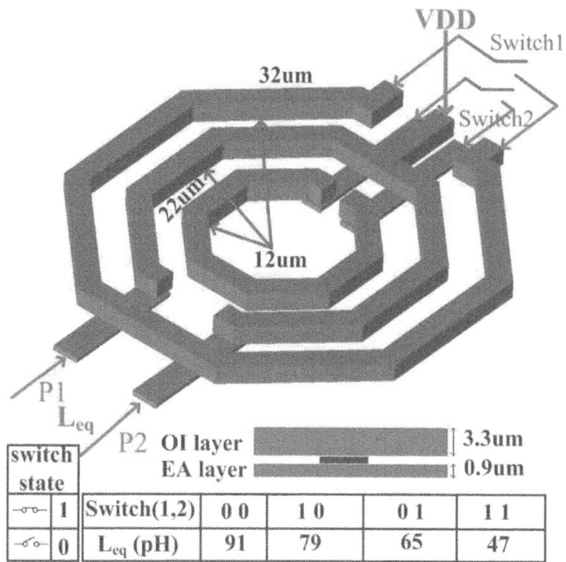

Switch(1,2)	0 0	1 0	0 1	1 1
L_{eq} (pH)	91	79	65	47

Figure 4.12: Layout implementation for inductor-loaded transformer where tuned inductance is determined by states of two switches.

The mechanism for the inductive-loaded transformer has been explained in Section 4.2.2. As (4.3) indicates, a large α_{P_L} can be easily obtained by implementing a large coupling factor k for the transformer. Furthermore, multiple inductors can be switched on and off to further increase α_{P_L} with a wide FTR achieved by creating multiple sub-bands.

The designed switched coupled-inductor for inductive tuning is shown in Figure 4.12. Inductors are realized by the top Cu layer to guarantee a high quality factor. Two transformers loaded with two switches are used to realize 4 sub-bands. As summarized in the tables shown in Figure 4.12, the resulted L_{eq} can be varied over a large range from 47 pH to 91 pH. As such, wide FTR can be realized with 4 sub-bands: (75.67–83.11 GHz), (79.65–87.78 GHz), (86.18–94GHz) and (93.89–102.01 GHz). To realize a continuous tuning, fine-tuning by varactor is used in each sub-band. To increase the tuning ability of varactor as (4.13) indicates to fully cover each sub-band, a relatively large L_s value is adopted in this design.

The resulting tuning mechanism for the proposed CRLH T-line-based RTW-VCO can be explained in Figure 4.13. Inductive-loaded transformer creates multiple sub-bands by shifting the dispersion curve to different resonant frequency points. Each sub-band is then covered with fine-tuning by a varactor.

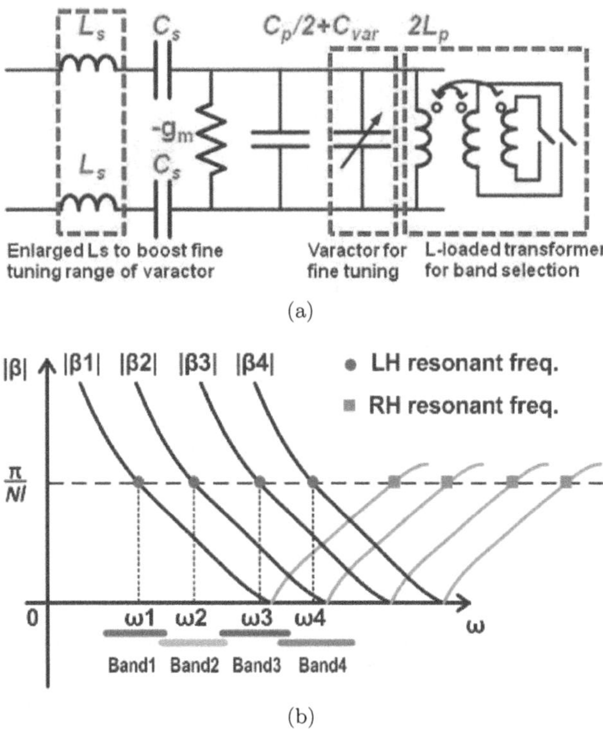

Figure 4.13: Tuning mechanism for the proposed tunable CRLH T-line-based Mobius-ring RTW-VCO: (a) Equivalent circuit, (b) Dispersion diagram.

Compared with conventional RTW-VCO, the proposed CRLH T-line-based RTW-VCO provides alternative choices of tunable elements. Assisted with the inductive tuning techniques presented in above sections, a much wider FTR can be obtained.

4.4 Circuit Prototyping and Measurement

4.4.1 60-GHz VCO Prototype with Asymmetric Implementation of Inductive Tuning

To further verify the proposed inductive tuning mechanism by switching return-path in Section 4.3, two 60-GHz VCO prototypes are demonstrated in CMOS 65nm technology in this section [74] and the following section [151].

As shown in Section 4.3, to realize multiple sub-bands for the proposed inductor-loaned transformer, switches are loaded at various locations on the secondary coil of one transformer. As the number of switches increases, the total capacitance and resistance loaded on the transformer increases and decreases, respectively. According to the analysis in Section 4.2.2, for the conditions when switches are turned off, both a larger C and a smaller R would weaken the domination of the terms $R^2[1-\omega^2 CL_2(1-k^2)]^2$ and $R^2\left(1-\omega^2 CL_2\right)\left[1-\omega^2 CL_2\left(1-k^2\right)\right]$ in (1), resulting in a smaller FTR. As a result, the number of switches loaded on the transformer should be minimized while providing enough sub-bands.

As a result, one layout topology is designed in this section, which can realize the maximum number of sub-bands with the least number of switches, thus can achieve the maximized FTR. The penalty is an asymmetric layout implementation, which may cause certain degradation in the phase noise performance. This problem can be solved with another symmetric topology to be presented in Section 4.4.3.

4.4.1.1 60-GHz VCO Design

Loaded Transformer Design

The proposed topology targets the maximum FTR, with layout implementation shown in Figure 4.14. A transformer is loaded with 4 switches (S1˜S4) at different locations. The inner loop is the primary coil, which serves as the inductor of the LC-tank. The outer loop is the secondary coil, which is loaded with 4 switches to control the current return-paths. Lengths of the 4 sections in the secondary coil are marked with unit length l. Different combinations of the switches and corresponding effective lengths of the current return-paths are summarized in Table 4.7. There are in total 7 modes or sub-bands established. For example, by turning on switches S1 and S2, the mode 3 is invoked with a current return-path formed with length $3l$. Moreover, as shown in Table 4.7, the effective length of return-path in secondary coil varies from 0 to $6l$ linearly, resulting in 7 evenly distributed sub-bands. Evenly distributed sub-binds can facilitate PLL design and also improve its performance.

Note that more sub-bands can be realized by implementing more switches but may also degrade the phase noise performance. As derived in Section 4.2.2 and 4.3, a small switch R value is desired to minimize phase noise degradation. As such, the number of switches should be minimized when connected in serial in the activated current return-path. The proposed band selection method in Figure 4.14 and Table 4.7 can minimize the number of switches in the current return-path to be 2 or below for all selection modes.

With an asymmetric allocation of switches, this layout implementation realizes 7 sub-bands with only 4 switches. As a result, a maximized FTR can be achieved. The trade-off is that the asymmetric twitch locations and current return-paths would have a large phase noise variation due to different current return-paths in each sub-band.

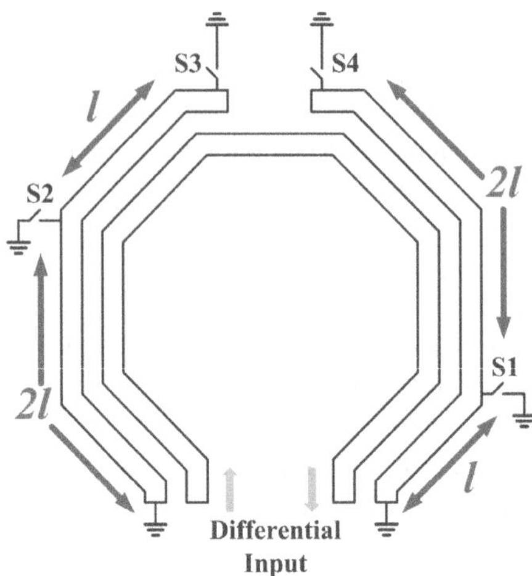

Figure 4.14: Asymmetric layout implementation for the proposed new inductor-loaded transformer.

Table 4.7: Effective Return Path Lengths in Secondary Coil for Different Sub-Band Selection Modes in Asymmetric Layout Implementation

Sub-band Selection Mode	0	1	2	3	4	5	6
On Switches	Nil	S1	S2	S1+S2	S1+S3	S2+S4	S3+S4
Effective Length of Return Path	0	l	$2l$	$3l$	$4l$	$5l$	$6l$

VCO Design

To verify the proposed inductive tuning, one VCO prototype is designed at 60 GHz. The VCO can provide multiple frequency sub-bands to cover the wide frequency band at 60 GHz. As shown in Figure 4.15, power supply is fed on the central tap. A varactor-pair is used for fine tuning within each sub-band. The LC-tank loss is compensated by a cross-coupled NMOS pair. Two output buffers are utilized for the power gain and isolation. The transformer is implemented with the top metal layer for high Q. To implement a proper k value, a gap size of 3.5μm is designed between transformer primary and secondary coils. Once the coupling factor of transformer is determined, an optimized switch size can be found. A size of 50μm/60nm is adopted for switch transistors.

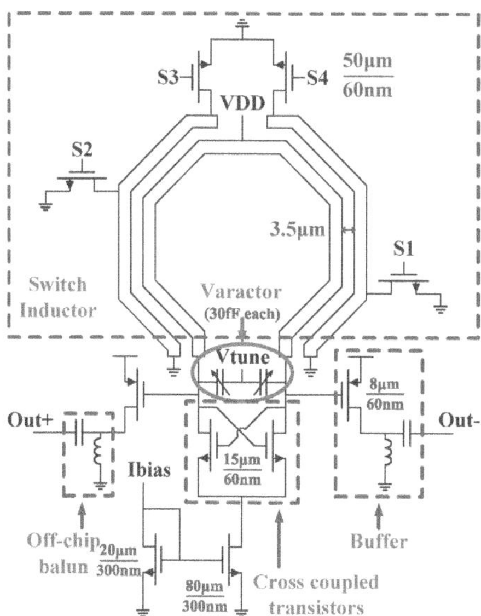

Figure 4.15: Schematic of the 60-GHz inductive-tuning VCO with asymmetric implementation of the proposed new inductor-loaded transformer.

With the tuning scheme proposed in Table 4.7, there are 7 sub-bands generated by the VCO. Compared with the symmetric implementation as will be shown in Section 4.4.3, the asymmetric VCO provides a wider FTR due to more sub-bands and fewer loaded switches, and thus smaller parasitic capacitance.

4.4.1.2 Simulation and Measurement Results

The designed 60-GHz VCO is implemented in STM 65nm 1P7M CMOS technology. EM simulation (ADS-Momentum) is used for circuit design and verification before the fabrication. The extracted parameters for the designed transformer are summarized in Table 4.4, and the equivalent circuit parameters under various band selection modes are plotted in Figure 4.16.

Phase Noise Analysis

To further analyze the proposed loaded-transformer influence on VCO phase noise (*PN*) performance, percentage of noise contribution from switches on loaded transformer to output is simulated and plotted in Figure 4.17. The analysis is carried out at both offset frequencies of 1MHz and 10MHz. Around 10–15% phase noise is contributed from the proposed loaded transformer.

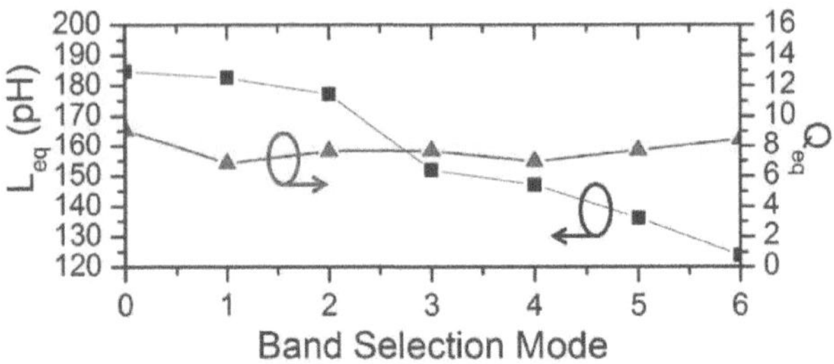

Figure 4.16: Parameter extraction for the asymmetric loaded transformer design under various band selection modes.

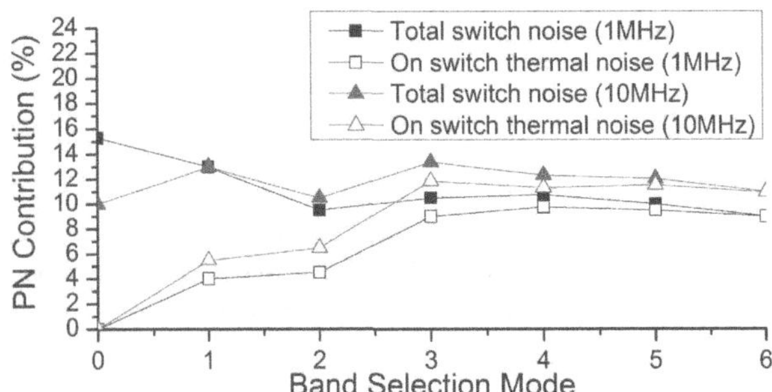

Figure 4.17: Percentage of noise contribution from switches on asymmetric loaded transformer implementation at 1 MH offset and 10 MHz offset. Both total noise from all switches and drain-to-source thermal noise from "on" switches are plotted.

The drain-to-source thermal noise from the ON switches in the current return path is also analyzed in Figure 4.17. In high-frequency bands, where a large current return path is formed, thermal noise from the ON switches dominate the total noise contribution. However, at lower-frequency bands, where a large portion of secondary coil is left floating, noise contribution from OFF switches not in the current return path comes in.

The deviation of total switch noise between 1 MHz offset and 10 MHz offset shows the role of flicker noise from switches. In our numeric analysis in Section 4.3, flicker noise was ignored due to DC blocking and low up-conversion ratio of switches biased in triode region. However, a large AC signal on the secondary coil of transformer could drive the switch toward saturation region with negative voltage swing, leading to higher up-conversion ratio. In lower-frequency bands, where a large portion of secondary coil is left floating, a standing wave would be formed on the floating coil, introducing a large voltage swing at the floating end, which drives switches into the saturation region. As a result, more flicker noise is up-converted and coupled to output. In higher-frequency bands, the floating coil becomes shorter and the contribution of flicker noise from switches becomes negligible, as indicated in Figure 4.17.

Furthermore, a comparison is done with switches removed from loaded transformer and replaced with ideal open and short connections. This analysis aims to check the effect of a switch alone on VCO performance, and is carried out with pre-layout simulation and with EM simulation for loaded transformer. The results are compared an Figure 4.18 with the case where actual switches are used.

From low to high frequencies in Figure 4.18, the loaded transformer is switched from Mode 0 to Mode 6 according to Table 4.7. In Mode 0, all switches are turned off and has minimum degradation on phase noise performance. In this case, the parasitic capacitance from switches lowers the oscillation frequency from around 65 GHz to 60 GHz. However, as switches are turned on to form a current return path, according to analysis in Section 4.2.2, parasitic capacitance from switches increases the FTR, while both parasitic capacitance and resistance from switches degrades the phase noise performance. Note that as capacitance from switches further increases, the FTR would degrade again as shown in Figure 4.7(a), and is the case for symmetric implementation.

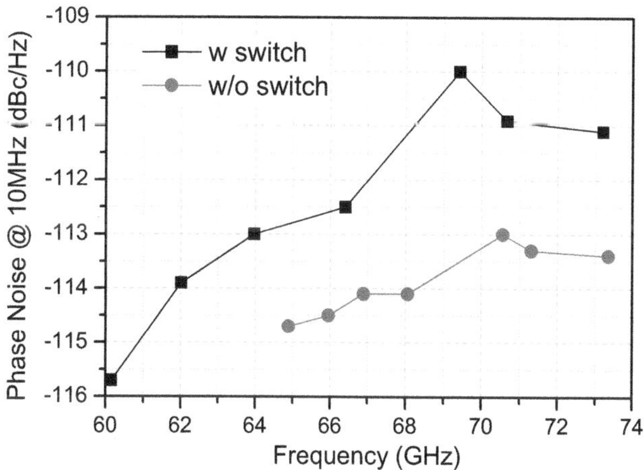

Figure 4.18: Simulation comparison for VCO performance (phase noise and oscillation frequency) with and without switches.

Measurement Results

The measurements are then done on the CASCADE Microtech Elite-300 probe station, with Agilent PNA-X spectrum analyzer, E5052 source signal analyzer, and 11970V harmonic mixer. A 67GHz bias-T is used to provide load to the buffer.

As mentioned in Section 4.4.2.1, there tends to be a large variation for VCO phase noise performance at different sub-bands due to the wide FTR and different switching conditions. Since a large phase noise variation across sub-bands would significantly degrade the PLL performance, we introduce a new phase noise (PN) performance in this work with the following equation

$$\mathrm{FTR} = \frac{\frac{\omega_1}{\sqrt{1-k^2}} - \omega_1}{\frac{\omega_1}{\sqrt{1-k^2}} + \omega_1} \times 2 = \frac{1-\sqrt{1-k^2}}{1+\sqrt{1-k^2}} \times 2 \tag{4.16}$$

where $\overline{PN}$ and σ_{PN} are the mean and variation of phase noise across all sub-bands. The phase noise variation (σ_{PN}) can then be used as a new figure-of-merit for wide FTR VCO design at 60 GHz.

The die photo for the designed asymmetric 60-GHz VCO is shown in Figure 4.19. Decoupling capacitors are implemented by MIM capacitors and used to stabilize DC signals. The total area is $852\times451\mu\mathrm{m}^2$, which Fs mainly constrained by PADs. The core area takes only $163\times190\ \mu\mathrm{m}^2$.

With 1V VDD and Vtune varied from 0.5 to 1.5 V, the obtained tuning curves under different sub-band selection modes are plotted in Figure 4.20. The entire tuning range is divided into 7 sub-bands. Within each sub-band, a tuning range of 2.5 $\sim$ 4.5 GHz is achieved by a smell varactor. Evenly distributed sub-bands are preferred for easy PLL implementation, which can be

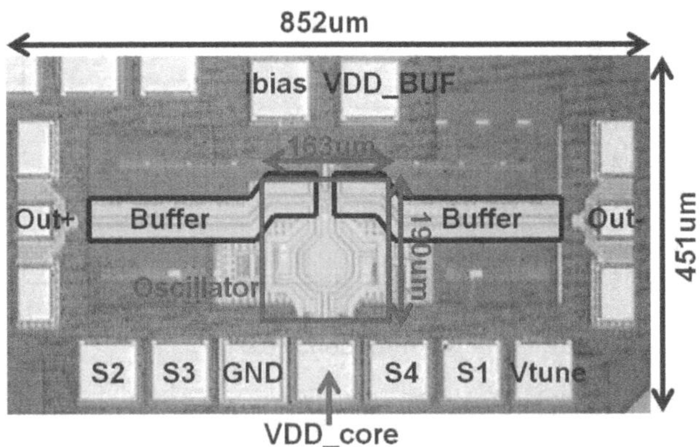

Figure 4.19: Die photo for the 60-GHz asymmetric VCO with fabricated in STM 65 nm CMOS technology.

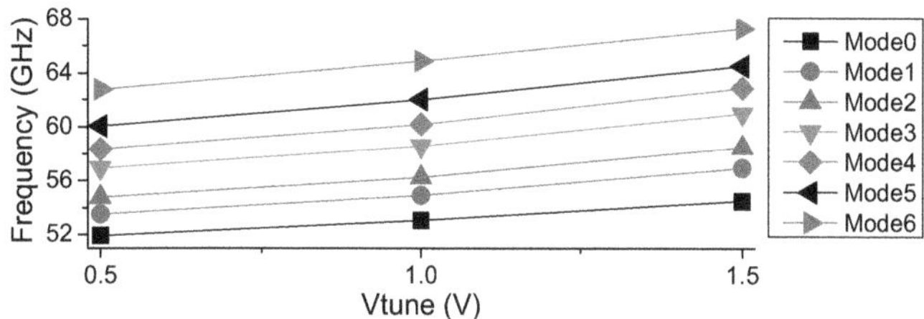

Figure 4.20: Measured tuning curves under different band selection modes for the 60-GHz asymmetric VCO.

achieved by adjusting locations of switches. The obtained oscillation frequency varies from 51.9 to 67.3 GHz, which covers tho whole 60-GHz band in IEEE 802.15.3c standard and provides a FTR of 25.8%. The effective K_{VCO} in each band varies from 2.1 to 3.8 GHz/V. Note the tuning voltage (0.5 $\sim$ 1.5V) is selected to provide maximum tuning range for varactor, and can be easily changed to 0 $\sim$ 1 V by adding a serial capacitor between varactor and power supply.

A sample phase noise plot is shown in Figure 4.21(a). At 60 GHz, the phase noise is -106.7 dBc/Hz at 10MHz offset. The measured phase noise performance for all modes is shown in Figure 4.21(b). Due to the low output power, there is around 10dB deviation in phase noise from simulation, which may be due to the low output power, inaccurate noise model and non-ideal ground around VCO. Moreover, as expected in Section 4.4.2.1, degradation in phase noise variation is observed in Figure 4.21(b), which mainly comes from asymmetric sub-band selection topology. As a result, a large phase noise variation (σ_{PN}) of 8.2 dB is observed.

4.4.2 60-GHz VCO Prototype with Symmetric Implementation of Inductive Tuning

Though the topology presented in Section 4.4.2 can achieve a maximized FTR, the asymmetric layout would degrade the phase noise performance. To solve this problem, in this section, another topology is designed with a symmetric layout implementation and optimized tuning mechanism for the switches [151]. Both phase noise and phase noise variation are thus improved. The penalty is the use of more switches than in the first topology, leading so a relatively narrower FTR. These two topologies can be utilized for different applications with different design targets. A comparison is also made between the two topologies.

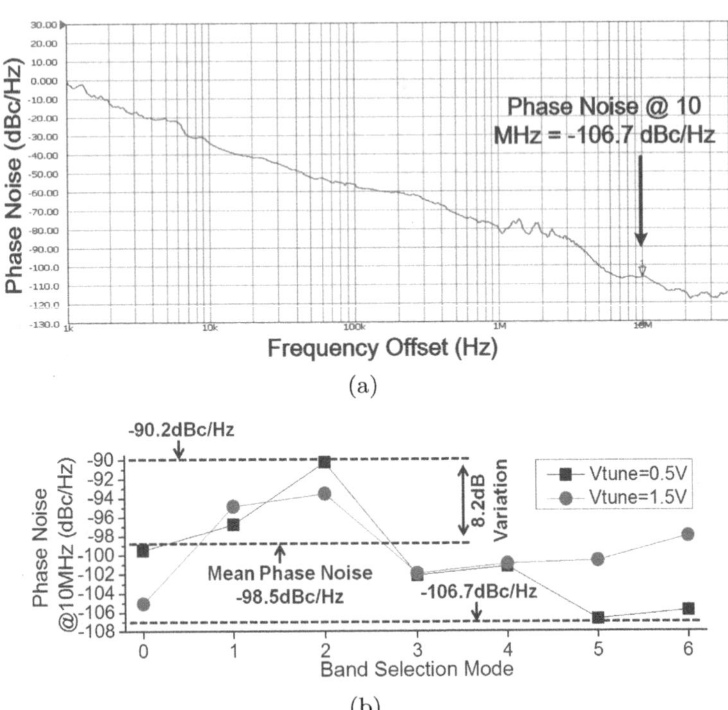

Figure 4.21: Measured phase noise performance for the 60-GHz asymmetric VCO. (a) Phase noise at 60 GHz. (b) Phase noise variation for all selection modes.

4.4.2.1 60-GHz VCO Design

Loaded Transformer Design

The proposed topology in this section targets a balanced performance of both FTR and phase noise variation in each sub-band, with symmetric layout implementation shown in Figure 4.22. Since a symmetric topology with differential operation lowers undesired common-mode effects such as substrate aid supply noise amplification and up-conversion [152], the phase noise performance is improved. In Figure 4.22, the symmetric topology is realized by placing 3 pairs of switches (S1P/N˜S3P/N) on the secondary coil of transformer with vertical symmetry.

Note that with symmetric switch locations, if the current return-path is also configured symmetrically, the number of sub-bands is highly limited. For N pairs of switches, only $N+1$ sub-bands can be created. To realize a targeted FTR and K_{VCO}, more pairs of switches would then be required to generate enough sub-bands, which would add loss to the loaded transformer and de-

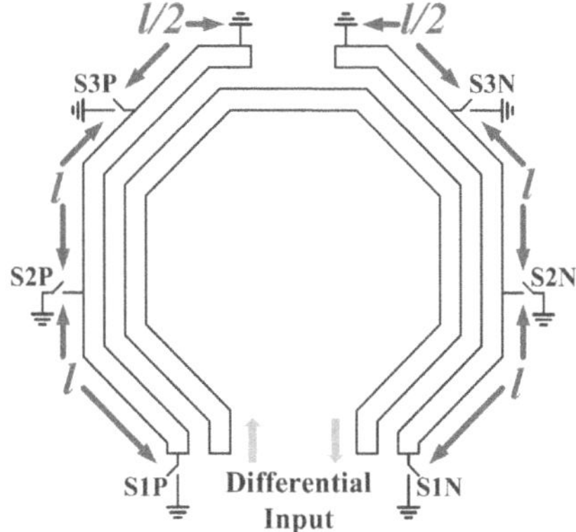

Figure 4.22: Symmetric layout implementation for the proposed new inductor-loaded transformer.

Table 4.8: Effective Return Path Lengths in Secondary Coil for Different Sub-Band Selection Modes in Symmetric Layout Implementation

Sub-band Selection Mode	0	1	2	3	4	5
On Switches	Nil	S3N+S3P	S2N+S3P	S2N+S2P	S2N+S1P	S1N+S1P
Effective Length of Return Path	0	l	$2l$	$3l$	$4l$	$5l$

grade phase noise performance. Furthermore, because switches with large size contribute large parasitic capacitance to the loaded transformer, if a large number of switches are used, the FTR would be limited by indicated by Figure 4.7(a).

In this section, the following tuning scheme is designed to overcome the aforementioned challenge. As shown in Figure 4.22, one switch on each side of virtual ground is turned on in all sub-band selection modes except the default node 0 where all switches are off. Different sub-bands are then changed by shifting the ON-switch locations on each side alternately. In this fashion, the number of sub-bands created is nearly doubled while maintaining a small difference in the selected current return-path lengths on both sides. For N pair of switches, $2N$ sub-bands can be created.

One example is shown in Table 4.8, 6 sub-bands are generated using 3 pairs of switches. The effective length of return-path in secondary coil varies from 0 to $5l$ linearly when the mode is switched from 0 to 5. In addition, the

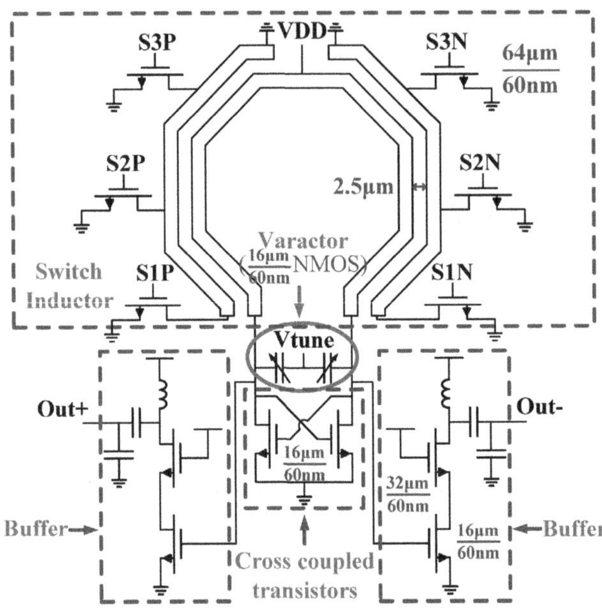

Figure 4.23: Schematic of the 60 GHz inductive tuning VCO with symmetric implementation of the proposed new inductor-loaded transformer.

maximum difference in the effective length on both sides is maintained within l. Compared with asymmetric implementation, the proposed symmetric implementation only introduces limited extra number of switches with small FTR reduction, but can significantly improve phase noise with constraint phase noise variation. As verified by measurement, this symmetrical configuration results in low phase noise with small variation across all sub-bands, while still maintaining a high FTR.

VCO Design

To verify the proposed symmetric implementation of inductive tuning, another VCO prototype is designed at 60 GHz which can also provide multiple frequency sub-bands to cover the wide frequency band at 60 GHz.

As shown in Figure 4.23, power supply is fed on the central tap. A varactor-pair is used for fine tuning within each sub-band. The LC-tank loss is compensated by a cross-coupled NMOS pair. Two output buffers are utilized for the power gain and isolation. The transformer is implemented with the top metal layer for high Q. Different from the asymmetric implementation, a gap size of 2.5 μm instead of 3.5 μm is designed between transformer primary and secondary coins. Once the coupling factor of transformer is determined, an

Table 4.9: EM Extracted Parameters at 60 GHz for Symmetric Loaded Transformer Implementation

L_1 (pH)	L_2 (pH)	M_{12} (pH)	k
153.1	136.9	44.6	0.308

optimized switch size can be found. Again, a different size of 64 μm/60 nm is adopted for switch transistors in the symmetric implementation compared with the size of 50 μm/60 nm in the asymmetric implementation. The size differences between two designs come from technology and topology differences, as we will discuss in Section 4.4.3.2.

With the tuning scheme proposed in Table 4.8, there are 6 sub-bands generated by the symmetric VCO. Compared to the asymmetric VCO introduced in Section 4.4.2 which can provide a wider FTR due to more sub-bands and fewer loaded switches thus smaller parasitic capacitance, the symmetric VCO significantly improves the phase noise performance with highly suppressed phase noise variation and can still achieve a wide FTR.

4.4.2.2 Simulation and Measurement Results

The designed symmetric 60-GHz VCO is implemented in Global Foundries 65-nm CMOS 1P8M technology. EM simulation (ADS-Momentum) is used for circuit design and verification before the fabrication.

For a fair comparison to the asymmetric 60-GHz VCO presented it Section 4.4.2, different transformer and switch sizes are designed for the two fabrications to achieve the same primary inductance L_1 as well as equivalent Q-factors Q_{eq}. In this way, similar oscillation frequency as well as similar loss introduced by loaded transformer can be ensured. The extracted parameters for the transformer used for the symmetric VCO are summarized in Table 4.9, and the equivalent circuit parameters under various band selection modes are plotted in Figure 4.24. Also note that a square shape is adopted for the transformer for ease of switch allocation. Though an octagonal shape is theoretically less lossy, the effect is minimal for single-loop transformer at 60 GHz according to simulation.

Phase Noise Analysis

Similar to the asymmetric leaded transformer, percentage of noise contribution from switches on loaded transformer to output is simulated and plotted in Figure 4.29 for symmetric loaded transformers at offset frequencies of 1 MHz and 10 MHz. Compared with asymmetric implementation, less noise contribution is observed for symmetric implementation. Although similar Q_{eq} values in Figure 4.16 and Figure 4.24 indicate similar loss introduced by loaded transformers, a smaller k value means less noise coupling from switches, which gives better PN performance at the penalty of smaller FTR. As such, one can

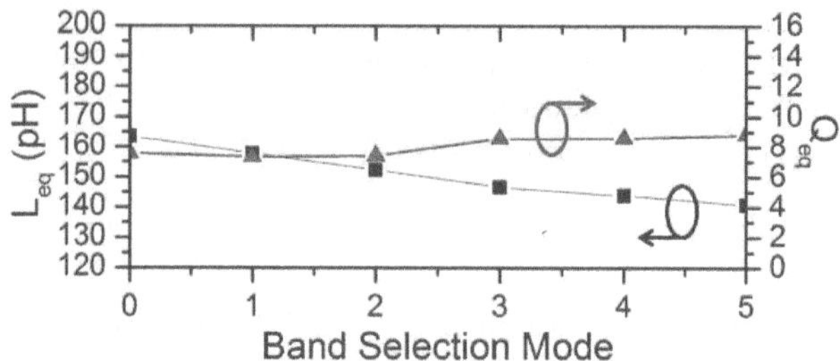

Figure 4.24: Parameter extraction for the symmetric loaded transformer design under various band selection modes.

observe 4-dB improvement of average *PN* performance for symmetric loaded-transformer design.

Similar to the asymmetric loaded transformer, the drain-to-source thermal noise from "ON" switches dominate the total noise contribution in high frequency bands, while noise contribution from OFF switches not in the current return path becomes larger at lower frequency bands where a large portion of secondary coil is left floating.

Again, the deviation of total switch noise between 1-MHz offset and 10-MHz offset shows the role of flicker noise from switches. In lower frequency bands, where a large portion of secondary coil is left floating, a standing wave would be formed on the floating coil, introducing a large voltage swing at the floating end, which drives switches into saturation region. As a result, more flicker noise is up-converted and coupled to output. In higher frequency bands, the floating coil becomes shorter and the contribution of flicker noise from switches become negligible.

Measurement Results

The measurements are then done on CASCADE Microtech Elite-300 probe station, with Agilent PNA-X spectrum analyzer, E5052 source signal analyzer, and 11970V harmonic mixer. Different from asymmetric VCO which requires a bias-T to provide load to buffer, in this design, the whole buffer is realized on-chip.

The die photo for the designed symmetric 60-GHz VCO is shown in Figure 4.26. The VCO core occupies an area of 140 × 220 μm^2. The overall chip size is 840 × 750 μm^2, including the test buffer and all the pads.

The DC power dissipation of the VCO is 6 mW at supply voltage of 1.0 V. The lower power consumption compared to asymmetric 60-GHz VCO is due to the designed high-quality factor of the symmetrical transformer. Figure 4.27 shows the measured tuning curves with dependence on the control voltages. One can observe that the VCO can exhibit 6 sub-bands with oscillation in

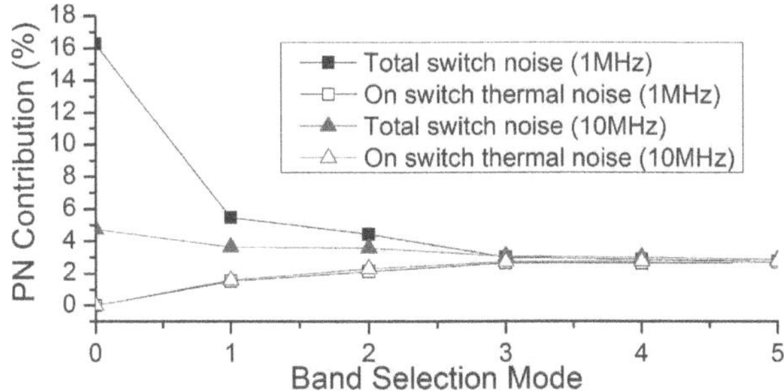

Figure 4.25: Percentage of noise contribution from switches on symmetric loaded transformer implementation at 1 MHz offset and 10 MHz offset. Both total noise from all switches and drain-to-source thermal noise from "on" switches are plotted.

a wide FTR from 57.0 GHz to 65.5 GHz, which covers the whole 60 bands in IEEE 802.15.3c standard. The tuning range is 8.5 GHz with 14.2% of the center frequency. The effective K_{VCO} in each band varies from 1.8 to 2.4 GHz/V.

Moreover, Figure 4.28 shows the measured phase noise at 10-MHz offset frequency of the VCO. In the required frequency range (58.32–64.80 GHz), the phase noise at 10MHz frequency offset is lower than -105 dBc/Hz. Both the mean phase noise ($\overline{PN}$) and phase noise variation (σ_{PN}) has been significantly improved over the first asymmetric design due to symmetric tuning adopted, with σ_{PN} improved to -108.3 dBc/Hz and σ_{PN} reduced to 2.5 dB. Though the trade-off is reduced FTR, a large tuning range of 14.2% is still achieved.

In addition, the measured spectra of the output signals under different modes are shown in Figure 4.29. The starting frequency under different modes distribute evenly as expected, with a small variation from 1 GHz to around 1.6 GHz. Note that this variation could be further suppressed by adjusting switch locations.

The performance of the symmetric VCO prototype is summarized in Table 4.10 and compared with the asymmetric VCO prototype as well as previously published 60-GHz VCOs. The asymmetric VCO is able to achieve a very wide FTR of 25.8% with the moderate figure-of-merits (FOM and FOM_t) defined in ITRS. A large phase noise variation of 8.2 dB is observed because of asymmetric design. The symmetric VCO shows improved phase noise with noise variation (σ_{PN}) of 2.5 dB achieved in the table with a phase noise mean (σ_{PN}) of -108.3dBc/Hz while a high FTR of 14.2% is still maintained, leading to a state-of-the-art FOM_t of -179.4 dBc/Hz.

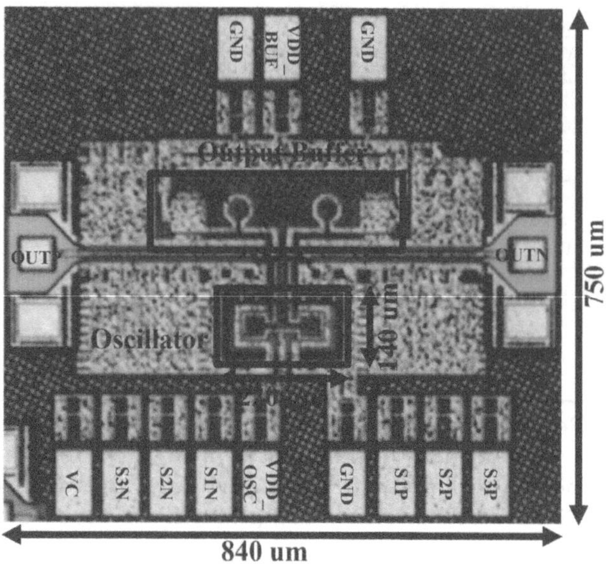

Figure 4.26: Die photo for the 60-GHz symmetric VCO fabricated in Global Foundries 65 nm CMOS technology.

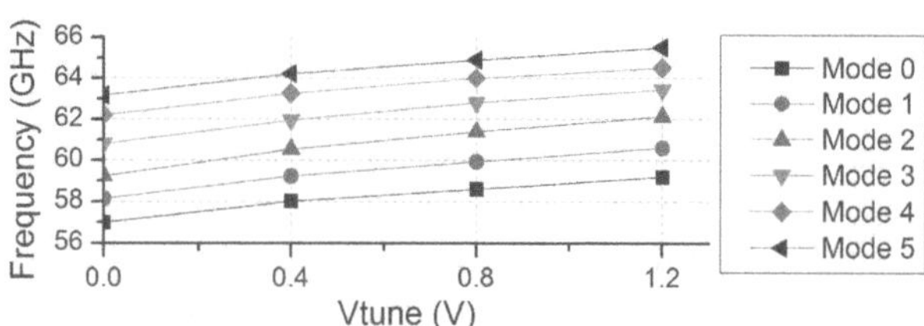

Figure 4.27: Measured tuning curves under different band selection modes for the 60-GHz symmetric VCO.

4.4.3 90-GHz VCO Prototype with CRLH T-Line-Based RTW

The above two VCO prototypes verify the proposed inductive tuning method, which is applied in tunable CRLH T-line in Section 4.4.1 for RTW VCO design. To verify the proposed CRLH T-line-based RTW VCO, one 90-GHz VCO prototype is demonstrated on CMOS 65-nm technology in this section

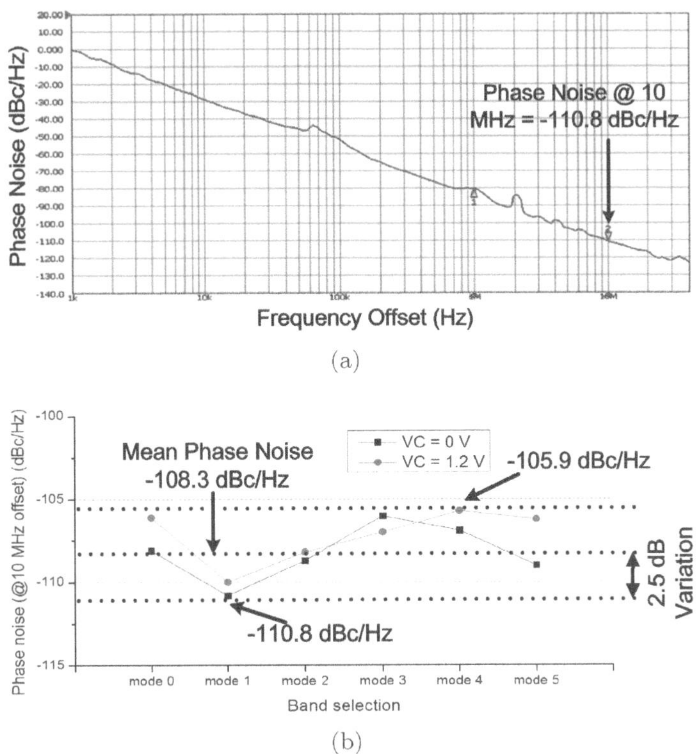

Figure 4.28: Measured phase noise performance for the 60-GHz symmetric VCO. (a) Phase noise at 60.8 GHz. (b) Phase noise variation for all selection modes.

[63]. Note a higher frequency is adopted to further demonstrate the advantages of CRLH T-line at higher frequencies.

4.4.3.1 90GHz VCO Design

The proposed tunable CRLH T-line-based Mobius-ring RTW-VCO shown in Figure 4.13(a) is fabricated in 65-nm CMOS Global Foundries 1P8M RF CMOS technology as shown in Figure 4.30(a). To push the cut-off frequencies away from operation frequency region, each stage is implemented with 2 distributed CRLH T-lone unit-cells. As a result, 180-degree phase shift is required due to the Mobius-ring connection, which leads to a 90-degree phase shift in each unit-cell. The EM simulation results for the designed unit-cell are shown in Figure 4.30(b). At the frequency of interest 100 GHz, one unit-cell can provide 90-degree phase-shift with loss at -1.86 dB, which is compensated by the negative resistors realized by a cross-coupled pair. Note the unit-cell

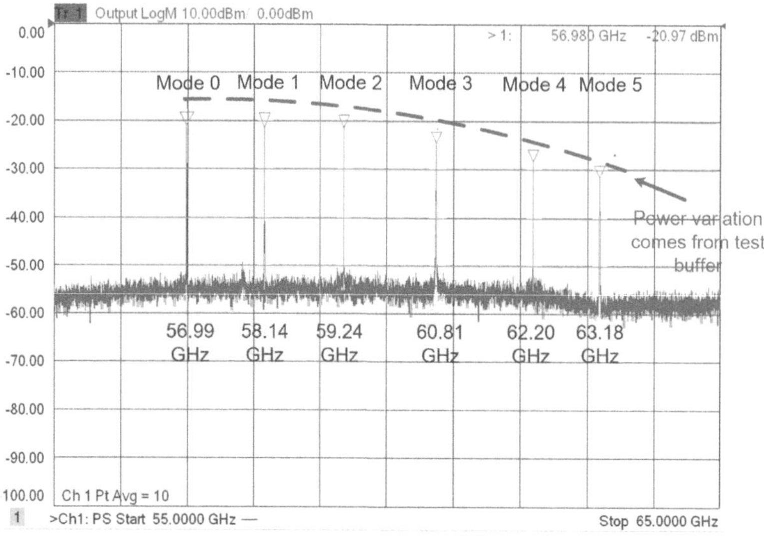

Figure 4.29: Measured output spectrum of equally spaced starting frequencies under 6 different modes for the 60-GHz symmetric VCO.

Table 4.10: Performance Summary and Comparison of Wide-Tuning 60-GHz VCOs

		[135]	[134]	[136]	**Asym. VCO Prototype**	**Sym. VCO Prototype**
Technology (CMOS)		90 nm	65nm	65 nm	65 nm	65 nm
Freq. (GHz)	f_{OSC}	76.5	70.2	77	59.6	61
Freq. Tuning Range (%)	FTR	7.0	9.6	14.5	**25.8**	**14.2**
Phase Noise (dBc/Hz)	PN	-110.6	-106.0	-112	-106.7	-110.8
Phase Noise Mean (dBc/Hz)	$\overline{PN}$	-107.1	-99.5	-108.5	-98.5	-108.3
Phase Noise Variation (dB)	σ_{PN}	3.5	6.5	3.5	8.2	**2.5**
Power (mW)	P_{DC}	19.4	5.4	190	**5.4**	**6.0**
Area (mm^2)	A	0.01	0.003	0.15	0.031	0.031
Figure of Merit (dBc/Hz)	$FOM^{(1)}$	-171.9	-169.1	-163.4	**-166.7**	**-176.2**
Figure of Merit (dBc/Hz)	$FOM_t{}^{(2)}$	-168.8	-168.8	-166.7	**-174.9**	**-179.3**

$^{(1)}FOM = \overline{PN} - 20\log\left(\frac{f_{OSC}}{\Delta f}\right) + 10log(P_{DC}/1mW)$

$^{(2)}FOM_t = \overline{PN} - 20\log\left(\frac{f_{OSC}}{\Delta f} \times \frac{FTR}{10}\right) + 10log(P_{DC}/1mW)$

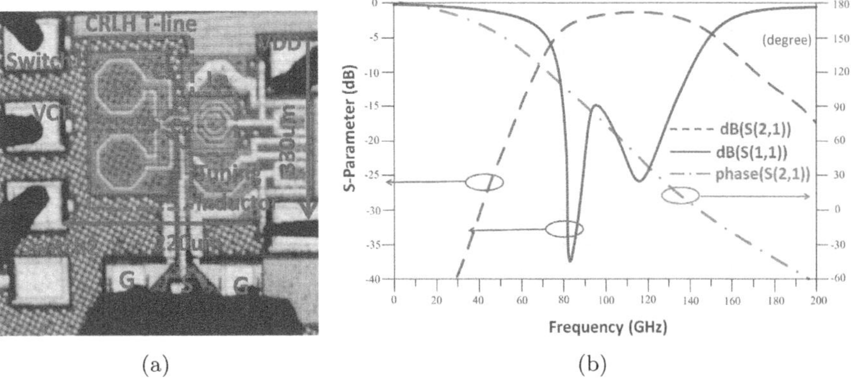

Figure 4.30: (a) Die micrograph of the proposed VCO. (b) The EM simulation for one CRLH T-line unit-cell. Note that Lp is shared by two unit-cells and its value is purposely designed doubled.

is biased to operating in the LH region, with the resonant mode in the RH region (-90-degree phase shift) highly suppressed.

4.4.3.2 Simulation and Measurement Results

The proposed VCO is fabricated 65-nm CMOS Global Foundries 1P8M RF CMOS technology. The VCO core area is about 0.0812mm^2. The output spectrum is measured by E4408B spectrum analyzer through one 11970W harmonic mixer. The supply voltage for buffer is 1.2 V and for VCO is 1 V. The measured current for the core VCO is 14 mA.

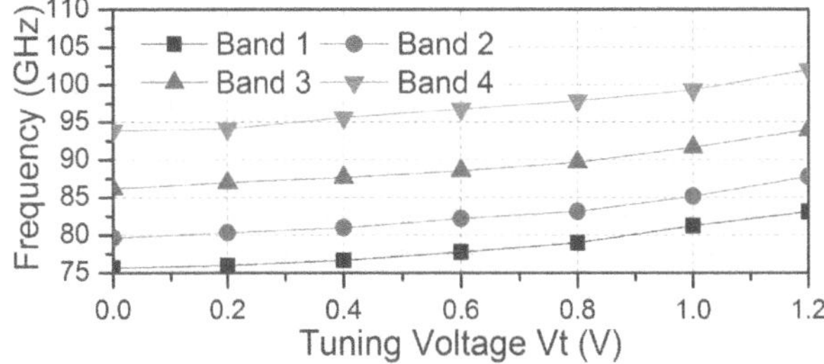

Figure 4.31: Measured frequency tuning range by 4 sub-bands.

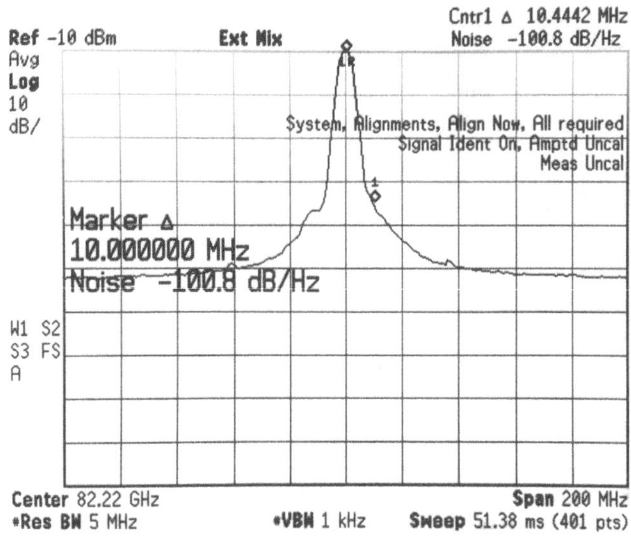

Figure 4.32: Measured phase noise at 82.22 GHz with 10 MHz offset frequency.

As shown in Figure 4.31, by using the proposed tunable CRLH T-line, a wide FTR of 29.6% is achieved from 76.59GHz to 102.01GHz, with a center frequency at 89.33 GHz. The full FTR is formed from the four sub-bands controlled by two switches: (75.67–83.11GHz), (79.65–87.78GHz), (86.18–94 GHz) and (93.89–102.01 GHz). With a tuning voltage for varactor from 0 V to 1.2 V, each sub-band is fully covered. The measured phase noise varies from −100.1 dBc/Hz to −98.7 dBc/Hz with a sample plot shown in Figure 4.32, where 6–9 dB deviation is observed compared with simulation, which may be due to inaccurate device and noise models at such high frequency and imperfect ground provided during measurement. The measured output power is from -23 dBm to -15 dBm as shown in Figure 4.33. The output power variation is about 8 dBm.

As summarized in Table 4.11, the performance of the proposed VCO is further compared with other published millimeter-wave VCOs in 65nm CMOS technology. According to the Table 4.11, the phase noise is comparable with others, and the widest FTR and the best FOM_T are achieved by the proposed VCO.

$$FOM = PN - 20\log\left(\frac{f_{OSC}}{\Delta f}\right) + 10log(P_{DC}/1mW)$$

$$FOM_T = PN - 20\log\left(\frac{f_{OSC}}{\Delta f} \times \frac{FTR}{10}\right) + 10log(P_{DC}/1mW).$$

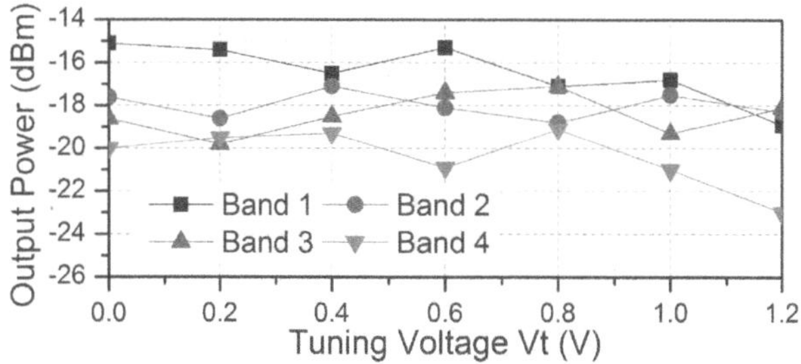

Figure 4.33: Measured output power across the entire frequency tuning range.

Table 4.11: Performance Summary and Comparison

Parameters	[139]	[140]	[134]	**This Work**	Unit
f_{osc}	95.7	101	70.4	89.3	GHz
VDD$_{core}$	1.5	0.8	1.2	1	V
P_{DC}	9	11.9	5.4	14	mW
Phase Noise (*PN*) @10MHz	-106	-104.5	-106.1	-100.8	dBc/Hz
FTR (%)	3.6	11.2	9	**29.6**	%
FOM	-176.1	-173.8	-175.7	-168.4	dBc/Hz
FOM$_{T}$	-167.2	-174.8	-174.8	**-177.8**	dBc/Hz
Tech.	CMOS 65	CMOS 65	SOI CMOS 65	CMOS 65	nm

4.5 Conclusion

This chapter studies techniques to achieve a wide frequency tuning range for CMOS VCO at mm-wave frequencies. More specifically, a new inductive tuning by inductor-loaded transformer is proposed in this chapter to design a wide frequency tuning range (FTR) VCO for all sub-bands at 60 GHz. Different from previously published inductive tuning methods, by configuring different current return-paths in the secondary coil of one transformer, wide multi-sub-band tuning can be achieved within a compact area with only one transformer. With the use of the proposed new inductive tuning method, two VCO topologies are realized in 65-nm CMOS with design targets for the maximum FTR and the balanced performance (FTR and phase noise), respectively. Measurement results show that the first VCO achieves a FTR of 25.8% from 51.9 to 67.3 GHz, and a 10-MHz-offset phase noise varied from -90.2 to -106.7 dBc/Hz across all sub-bands; and the second VCO achieves a FTR of 14.2% from 57.0 GHz to 65.5 GHz, and a 10-MHz-offset phase noise varied from -105.9 to -110.8 dBc/Hz across all sub-bands. The demonstrated VCOs have shown great potential for integration in 60-GHz transceiver design with wide-tuning ability.

The inductive tuning method is further applied to realize a tunable CRLH T-line for Mobius-ring RTW-VCO design in mm-wave region. Inductor-loaded transformer is implemented in CRLH T-line to realize 4 sub-bands. Each sub-band is covered by a varactor with fine-tuning. The proposed tunable CRLH T-line-based RTW-VCO is fabricated in 65nm GF RF-CMOS technology with a wide FTR of 75.7–102 GHz and area of 0.0821 mm^2. The measured results show a current consumption of 14mA under supply voltage of 1 V, a FTR of 29.5% with center frequency at 89.3GHz, and a phase noise of -100.8 dBc/Hz with 10-MHz offset at 82.2 GHz frequency. The state-of-the-art figure-of-merit FOM_T is demonstrated at -177.8 dBc/Hz.

Chapter 5

Coupled Oscillator Network

5.1 Introduction

CMOS-based THz signal sources have been recently demonstrated for compact system-on-chip implementation [153, 154, 155, 156, 157, 158, 159, 160, 161] with applications in high-data-rate communication and non-invasive imaging. As THz signal suffers from large propagation loss, the generated signal strength must be strong enough to have sufficient signal-to-noise ratio (SNR) for detection, which imposes grand challenges for high-power signal source designs in CMOS.

It is challenging to design a high-output power THz signal source by single CMOS oscillator source with high efficiency as well as a wide frequency tuning range (FTR). In the CMOS process, one single oscillator usually has small output power that is limited by single CMOS transistor with commonly observed low output power level [162, 154, 77], which is incapable of delivering a strong THz signal for transmission and processing. Similar to the approach utilized in a power amplifier [163, 164], output power combining of multiple CMOS oscillators can be considered to achieve a large output power at THz frequency. Several coupled-oscillator-network (CON) structures have been proposed for high-output power [161, 87]. A phase/delay tuning design is utilized in [161] but cannot ensure the in-phase coupling condition. In-phase synchronization by half λ transmission line (T-line) is reported in [87], which is bulky and lossy when deployed for a large-scale phase-arrayed design. There is great interest to explore a high-output power signal source by combining the outputs of an array of CMOS oscillators such as CON [165].

The combined output power of CON is maximized when all the oscillator unit-cells are in-phase coupled with a phase difference of $2n\pi$ ($n = 0, 1, 2, \ldots$). In the conventional CON design [165], adjacent oscillators are coupled by a T-line or an equivalent delay network with at least an electrical length of half λ ($n = l$), which is bulky and lossy and hence largely reduces the output power and efficiency. The recent work in [163] has shown that the CMOS metamaterial devices can be utilized for phase-arrayed design such as zero-phase-shifters ($n = 0$) for power combing in CMOS mm-wave PAs with very high-output power. Compared to the coupling by half λ T-line, the zero-phase-shifter can result in zero-phase coupling with low loss and compact area.

Recently, plasmon polariton-based waveguide structures have been explored for low loss energy transfer [166, 167, 168, 59, 60, 169]. As one type of plasmon polariton-based waveguide structures, magnetic plasmon waveguide (MPW) has been already applied to the middle distance wireless energy transmission systems [59, 60] as well as one-dimensional sub-wavelength power transfer in the mm-wave range [166, 167, 168]. Similar to CRLH T-line, MPW has a zero-phase propagation mode. But it also has several advantages over CRLH T-line in the CON design. Firstly, MPW has lower propagation loss in the practical CMOS layout. As introduced in Sec. 2.2.1, there will be a band-gap in CRLH T-line if the series and parallel resonance frequencies of unit-cell are not same, which will contribute the propagation loss. On the other hand, MPW only has one zero-phase mode at the boundary of the stop-band, where its attenuation factor is zero. Secondly, the plasmon resonators inside MPW can be easily transferred into oscillator unit-cells by replacing their equivalent capacitance with transistor-based negative resistance. As such, a distributed zero-phase CON is proposed with magnetic-plasmon-waveguide (MPW)-based oscillator unit-cells. When a number of zero-phase oscillator unit-cells are serially connected in a ring with a centralized placement of active devices, in-phase coupling can be achieved with low loss. The resulting CON output can be significantly improved with a reduced phase noise because outputs of all zero-phase coupled (ZPC) oscillator unit-cells are synchronized for an in-phase combination. With the further use of inductive tuning [170], a wide FTR can be achieved for each ZPC oscillator unit-cell.

In this chapter, firstly, a zero-phase CON with 4 unit-cells is implemented at 60 GHz in 65nm CMOS process. The measured results show a peak output power of 2 mW with 2.2% power efficiency, phase noise of -116.7 dBc/Hz at 10-MHz offset and FTR of 16% from 58 to 69.1 GHz. Secondly, an injection-locked THz signal source with zero-phase coupled oscillator network is proposed to provide high output power and low phase noise within compact chip area. A zero-phase oscillator unit-cell is developed by inter-digital coupler with 0.4-dB loss at 70 GHz. With four in-phase coupled unit-cells and push-push frequency doublers, high output power signal is generated at the center of the proposed CON at 140 GHz. The measured results show a peak output power of 3.5 mW with 2.4% power efficiency, power density (or output power/area) of 26.9 mW/mm^2 and 9.7% FTR centered at 133.5GHz.

5.2 In-Phase Signal Generation by MPW

In this work, a magnetic plasmon waveguide (MPW) with zero phase propagation is introduced in the coupling network design with $2k/N = 0$ to largely improve the output power within compact area. A zero phase propagation is not only important for power combination but also the phase noise reduction. The noise coupling network becomes reciprocal in zero-phase mode, and the phase noise at CON output becomes $1/N$ of a single free-running oscillator [77].

The MPW unit-cell can be implemented on-chip by coupled T-line-based resonator with C contributed by the parasitic capacitances of transistors as shown in Figure 5.1(a). The two-port Y-parameters for a conventional coupled T-lines structure can be expressed as [171]:

$$\begin{bmatrix} Y11 & Y12 \\ Y21 & Y22 \end{bmatrix} = \begin{bmatrix} \frac{-j(Y_{0o}+Y_{0e})\cot\theta}{2} & \frac{-j(Y_{0o}-Y_{0e})\cot\theta}{2} \\ \frac{-j(Y_{0o}-Y_{0e})\cot\theta}{2} & \frac{-j(Y_{0o}+Y_{0e})\cot\theta}{2} \end{bmatrix} \tag{5.1}$$

where Y_{0o}, Y_{0e} denotes the odd-mode and even-mode admittance, respectively; $\theta = \beta l$ is the electrical length of the coupler.

When two identical capacitors (C) are introduced on both sides of the coupler, the two-port Y-parameters becomes:

$$\begin{bmatrix} Y11' & Y12' \\ Y21' & Y22' \end{bmatrix} = \begin{bmatrix} \frac{-j(Y_{0o}+Y_{0e})\cot\theta}{2} + j\omega C & \frac{-j(Y_{0o}-Y_{0e})\cot\theta}{2} \\ \frac{-j(Y_{0o}-Y_{0e})\cot\theta}{2} & \frac{-j(Y_{0o}+Y_{0e})\cot\theta}{2} + j\omega C \end{bmatrix}. \tag{5.2}$$

Equation (5.2) can be converted into S-parameters according to the

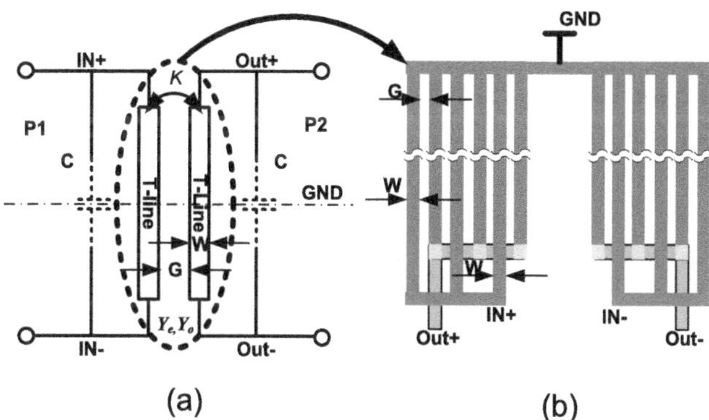

Figure 5.1: (a) Equivalent circuit of differential ZPC loaded with parasitic capacitance; (b) on-chip realization of inter-digital coupled T-lines.

method introduced in [172];

$$\begin{bmatrix} S11 & S12 \\ S21 & S22 \end{bmatrix} = \begin{bmatrix} \frac{1+Z_0^2(Y_{0o}\cot\theta-\omega C)(Y_{0e}\cot\theta-\omega C)}{\Delta Y} & \frac{jZ_0(Y_{0o}-Y_{0e})\cot\theta}{\Delta Y} \\ \frac{jZ_0(Y_{0o}-Y_{0e})\cot\theta}{\Delta Y} & \frac{1+Z_0^2(Y_{0o}\cot\theta-\omega C)(Y_{0e}\cot\theta-\omega C)}{\Delta Y} \end{bmatrix} \tag{5.3}$$

with

$$\begin{aligned} \Delta Y &= Z_0^2[\omega C(Y_{0o}+Y_{0e})\cot\theta-\omega^2C^2-Y_{0o}Y_{0e}\cot^2\theta] \\ &\quad + jZ_0[2\omega C-(Y_{0o}+Y_{0e})\cot\theta]+1. \end{aligned} \tag{5.4}$$

As such, the coupling phase (ϕ) can be expressed as:

$$\phi = \frac{\pi}{2} - \tan^{-1}\left\{\frac{2\omega Z_0 C - Z_0(Y_{0o}+Y_{0e})cot\theta}{1+Z_0^2[\omega C(Y_{0o}+Y_{0e})\cot\theta-\omega^2C^2-Y_{0o}Y_{0e}\cot^2\theta]}\right\}. \tag{5.5}$$

When the impedance of both ends are perfectly matched ($Z_0^2 Y_{0o}Y_{0e}=1$), a zero coupling phase condition ($\phi=0$) is satisfied in (5.5) with

$$\left[\cot(\beta l)-\frac{\omega C}{Y_{0e}}\right]\left[\cot(\beta l)-\frac{\omega C}{Y_{0o}}\right]=1. \tag{5.6}$$

The required physical length l can be derived as

$$l=\frac{1}{\omega\sqrt{\mu\varepsilon}}\cot^{-1}\left\{\frac{\omega C(Y_{0o}+Y_{0e})}{2Y_{0o}Y_{0e}}+\sqrt{1+\left[\frac{\omega C(Y_{0o}-Y_{0e})}{2Y_{0o}Y_{0e}}\right]^2}\right\}. \tag{5.7}$$

Note that (5.7) is obtained as the minimum positive solution of (5.6), which provides the smallest feature size of zero-phase-coupler in the practical IC layout.

With an inter-digital configuration layout, as shown in Figure 5.1(b), lower coupling loss can be achieved [173]. The coupling coefficient in zero-phase mode $|S21_{ZP}|$ can be derived from (5.3) and (5.6):

$$|S21_{ZP}|=\left|\frac{(Y_{0e}\cot\theta-\omega C)-(Y_{0o}\cot\theta-\omega C)}{(Y_{0e}\cot\theta-\omega C)+(Y_{0o}\cot\theta-\omega C)}\right|, \tag{5.8}$$

which can be optimized for the start-up condition by a higher odd-mode admittance (Y_{0o}) or a lower even-mode admittance (Y_{0o}).

Clearly, a low loss can be obtained by a much smaller physical length l and a lower Y_e for multiple ZPC-based oscillator unit-cells under the zero-phase condition. Compared to the conventional coupler design with T-line by single strip on each side, the proposed ZPC structure can simultaneously increase Y_{0o} and reduce Y_{0e}, which can be further optimized based on the relation of coupler length l vs. loaded capacitances and even-mode admittance as shown in Figure 5.2. The coupling loss needs to be compensated to start oscillation, which means $|S21_{G_m}|\cdot|S21_{ZP}|>1$, where $S21_{G_m}$ is the equivalent gain of shunt negative conductance from active devices.

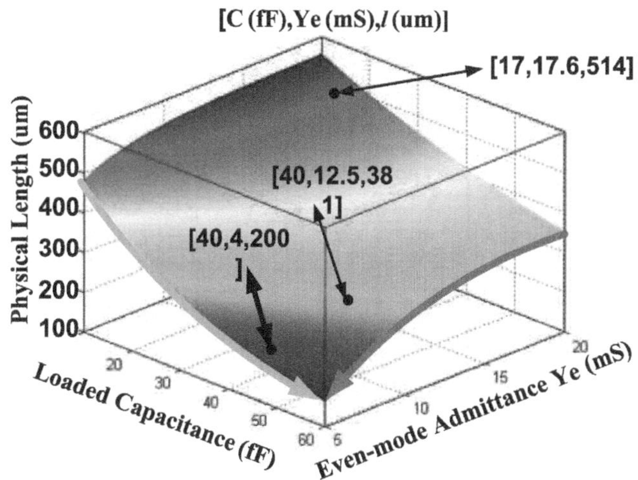

Figure 5.2: The calculated l for zero coupling phase vs. loaded capacitance and even-mode characteristic admittance at 60 GHz.

5.3 Circuit Prototyping and Measurement

5.3.1 60 GHz CON Signal Source

5.3.1.1 Differential ZPC Unit-Cell

Figure 5.3 shows the schematic and layout to implement a differential ZPC by the topmost copper layers (M5, M6) and aluminum layer (AL) with interdigital coupling topology in 65-nm CMOS process. The average length of the coupler is 182μm. The sizes of transistors are pre-determined by the required output power and the frequency range. Their parasitic capacitances are extracted from post-layout simulation as the load of one ZPC. These capacitances are then incorporated into the EM simulation to satisfy (5.6). The design satisfies the zero-phase condition at 60GHz as illustrated in Figure 5.4. In addition, the S11 is smaller than -20 dB and the differential S21 is greater than -0.5 dB at the vicinity of 60 GHz, which confirm a low coupling loss. As a comparison, a conventional coupler using two coupled T-lines with the minimum allowed gap (1.5 μm) is also simulated. With the same capacitance load (40 fF), the proposed ZPC obtains 2-dB better S21, leading to a lower coupling loss. The propagation constant of the proposed ZPC as illustrated in Figure 5.5. β is negative before 60 GHz, which presents the left-handed property. A zero β is achieved at 60 GHz leading to the zero-phase coupling condition. At the same time, the attenuation constant α is also minimized at around 60 GHz, resulting in the minimum coupling loss. As shown in Figure

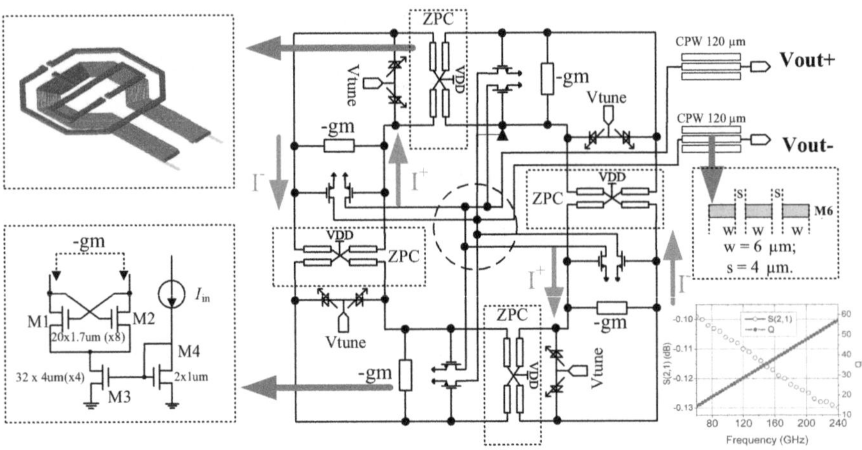

Figure 5.3: Layout of inter-digital differential ZPC with effective electrical length controlled by MOS switches.

5.5, the negative relative permittivity (ε_r) realized by the CMOS on-chip ZPC confirms the metamaterial characteristic.

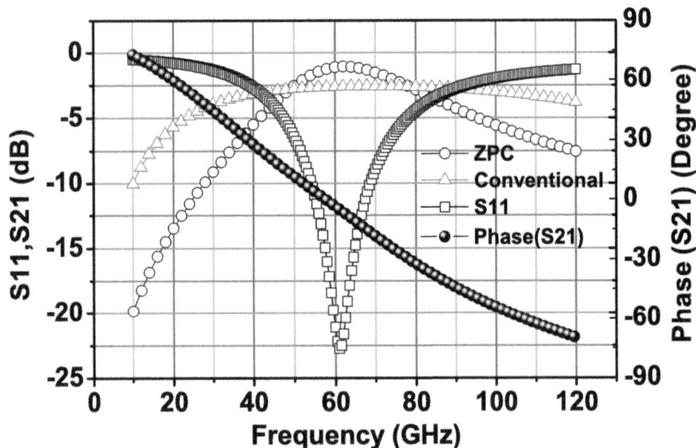

Figure 5.4: Simulated magnitude of S11 and S21 in dB and phase of S21 of the proposed coupler structure with comparison of S21 magnitude to the conventional one by coupled T-line.

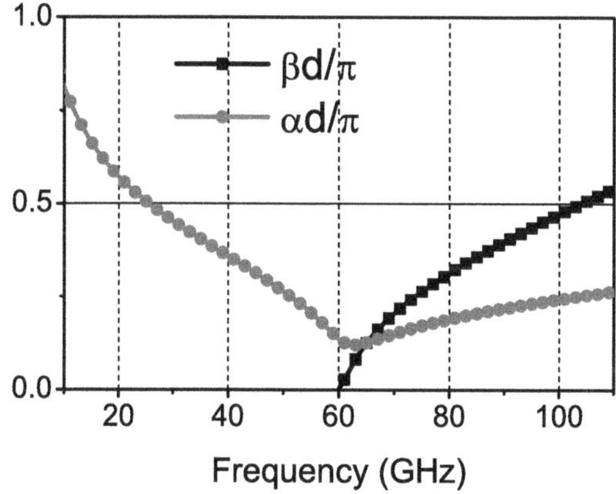

Figure 5.5: The extracted dispersion diagram and relative permittivity (ε_r).

5.3.1.2 ZPC-Based Oscillator with Tuning

Since a broadband zero coupling phase is desired, based on (5.6) and (5.7) the frequency tuning can also be achieved by changing the effective length of the coupler. The inductive loading method [170] is applied to achieve the wide tuning range. Two metal loops are formed above the coupler in the aluminum PAD layer (LB). By configuring the on-off status of MOS switches $M_{a1,2}$ and $M_{b1,2}$ shown in Figure 5.3, the effective electrical length of the coupler is changed, which in turn changes ZPC oscillator frequency as shown below

$$\omega_{0,mn} = \frac{1}{\sqrt{C_{eq}(L_{eq} + mM_A + nM_B)}} \tag{5.9}$$

where $C_{eq}L_{eq}$ defines the maximum operation frequency; $m = 0, 1$, $n = 0, 1$ denotes the modes of configurations; M_A and M_B are the loaded mutual inductances. As such, the minimum FTR without considering varactor tuning can be calculated by

$$FTR = 2\left[\frac{\omega_{0,00} - \omega_{0,11}}{\omega_{0,00} + \omega_{0,11}}\right]. \tag{5.10}$$

In order to achieve higher FTR, larger M_A and M_B are required.

The loading capacitance is contributed by the parasitic of the cross-coupled NMOS pair (M_1 and M_2), output buffers (M_3 and M_4) and varactors (D_1 and D_2). M_1 and M_2 provide a negative resistance to compensate the energy loss. The sizes of M_1 and M_2 are optimized with the maximum tuning range. The drain-source current of cross-coupled pair is controlled by a tail current connected NMOS M_5, of which the biasing can be adjusted. To facilitate output

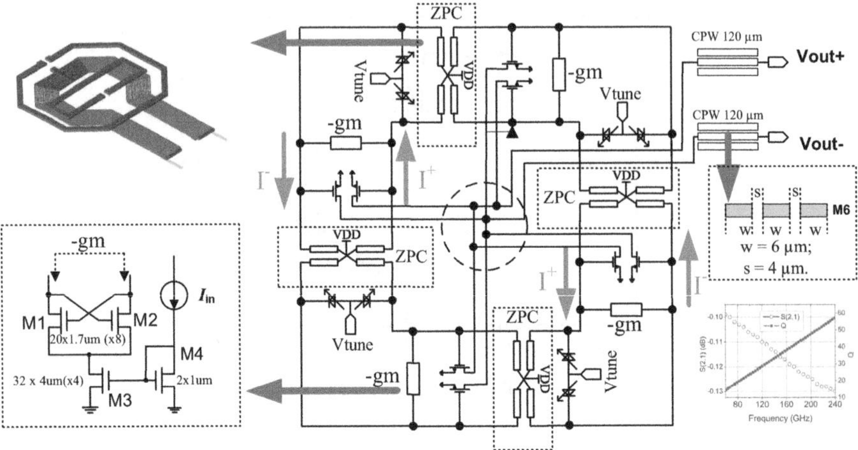

Figure 5.6: Schematic of proposed VCO with differential outputs combined at the center.

impedance matching and isolate the VCO core from peripherals, common source NMOS M_3, M_4 are employed as output buffers. The width of M_3, M_4 are optimized for high output power.

5.3.1.3 60-GHz Zero-Phase-Coupled Oscillator Network

The schematic of the distributed zero-phase-coupled VCO network is shown in Figure 5.6. Four differential ZPC unit-cells are connected in serial with a closed-loop. Their power outputs are combined at the geometry center of the layout. A CPW T-line with 120 μm length and 50 Ω characteristic impedance is used to connect the center output to the RF PADs. The cross-section of CPW T-line is also shown in in Figure 5.6. According to the EM-Simulation at 60 GHz, the CPW T-line has an insertion loss and Q-factor (Q) of 0.1 dB and 15, respectively. Note that all the tail currents of all oscillator unit-cells are controlled by the same current mirror with diode-connected NMOS.

5.3.1.4 Measurements

As shown in Figure 5.7, the distributed 4-way ZPC-based CON was fabricated in the UMC 65-nm CMOS process with f_T/f_{MAX} of 170/190 GHz. The core chip area is 330μm×320μm excluding Pads. It was measured on CASCADE Microtech Elite-300 probe station and Agilent PNA-X (N5247A), E5052 source signal analyzer with spectrum swept up to 70 GHz. Bias-T, probe and cable loss are calibrated before the measurements. The proposed VCO consumes 91-mW DC power under 1.2-V power supply. Note that the

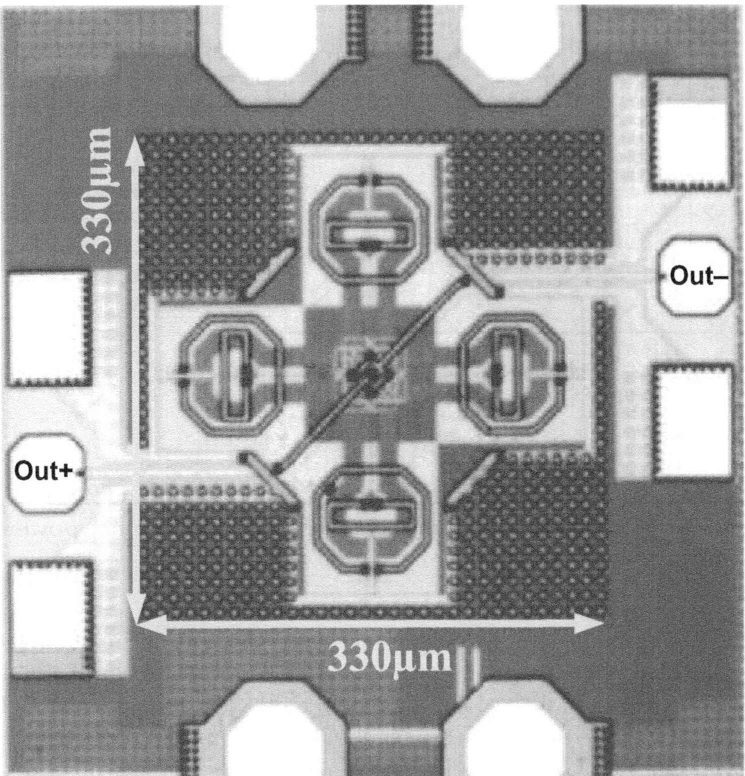

Figure 5.7: Die micrograph of the fabricated 60 GHz VCO chip in 65 nm CMOS.

differential outputs are on different sides of the chip. Since the measurement is performed at single-ended RF output with GSG Pads, +3 dB is added to the output power level. In addition, the simulation results are obtained from Cadence Spectre post-layout simulation.

Figure 5.8 shows the simulated and measured output power of VCO in each mode. Similar to the simulation results, the measured output power of VCO is highest when Sa = 1.2 V and Sb = 1.2 V. This is mainly due to a higher transconductance of NMOS transistors at a lower frequency. The proposed VCO achieves the highest output power of 2 mW (3 dBm) at V_{Tune} = 0 condition, where the oscillation frequency is 58.1 GHz. The corresponding maximum DC-RF efficiency is 2.2%, which is defined by P_{OUT}/P_{DC}, where P_{OUT} and P_{DC} are the output power and DC power consumption of VCO, respectively. Figure 5.9 shows four modes of VCO with different frequency bands obtained from both simulation and measurement, which are generated

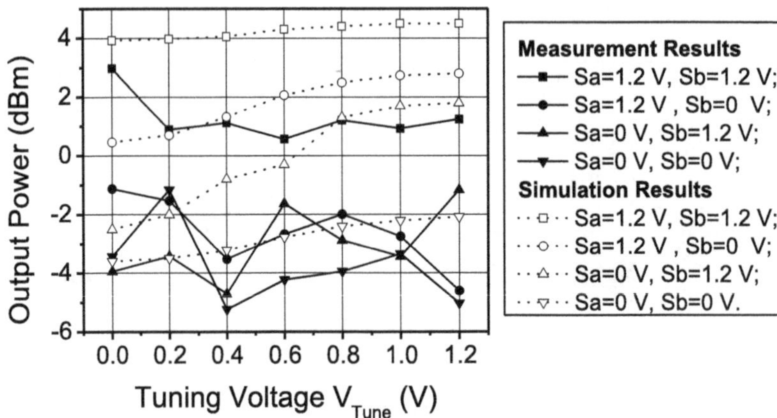

Figure 5.8: Measured and simulated output power and power efficiency of proposed VCO over entire 60 GHz band.

by switching the inductive loadings from Sa and Sb. The entire 60-GHz band under the IEEE 802.15.3c standard is completely covered in both simulation and measurement. Note that the measured FTR of proposed VCO is 15.8% from 58.1 to 68.1 GHz, which is slightly lower than the simulation result of 16.8% from 58.4 GHz to 69.1 GHz. Figure 5.10 shows the measured and simulated phase noise at 60 GHz output frequency. The measured phase noise correlates very well with the simulation results. A -116.7-dBc/Hz phase noise is observed at 10-MHz offset, which is about 2.5-dB lower than the simulation result at the same frequency offset.

The performance of the proposed VCO is summarized in Table 5.1 with comparison of other similar designs at 60 GHz. It can be observed that the proposed design has the highest output power of +3 dBm, the highest power efficiency of 2.2% and the widest FTR of 15.8%. Note that the phase noise of the proposed VCO is very close to the best reported result of -118.8 dBc/Hz at 10-MHz offset in [174]. However, the output power of the proposed VCO is almost 10 times (9.6-dB) higher. This leads to the state-of-the-art figure of merit (FOM) and figure of merit with tuning range (FOMt) as well, which are defined by the following equations:

$$\begin{cases} FOM = PN(\Delta f) - 20log(\frac{f_{osc}}{\Delta f}) + 10log(\frac{P_{diss}}{1mW}) \\ FOMt = PN(\Delta f) - 20log(\frac{f_{osc}}{\Delta f} \times \frac{FTR}{10}) + 10log(\frac{P_{diss}}{1mW}) \end{cases} \tag{5.11}$$

where PN(Δf) is the phase noise at the offset frequency Δf, f_{osc} is the oscillation frequency and P_{diss} is the DC power consumption in mW. The highest output power and lowest phase noise both confirm the feasibility of applying the proposed ZPC in mm-wave IC designs. The maximum power density of

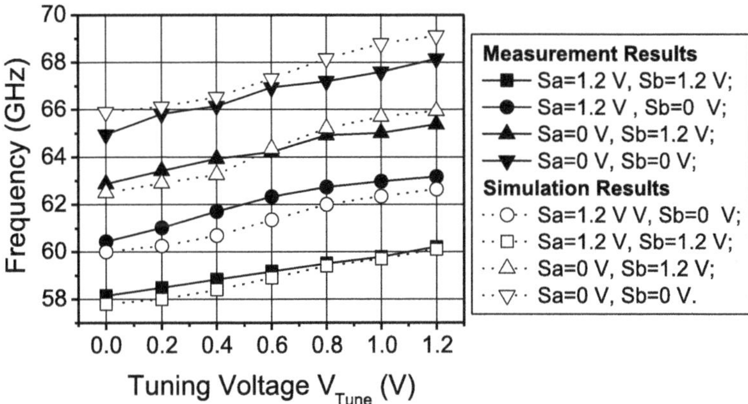

Figure 5.9: Measured and simulated VCO FTR under various switch configurations to cover 58.3–64.8 GHz continuously.

the proposed VCO is 18.4 mW/mm^2, which is more than 8 times higher than the previous VCO design in [174]. Note that power density is defined as the output power generated in unit chip area (P_{OUT}/A_{CORE}).

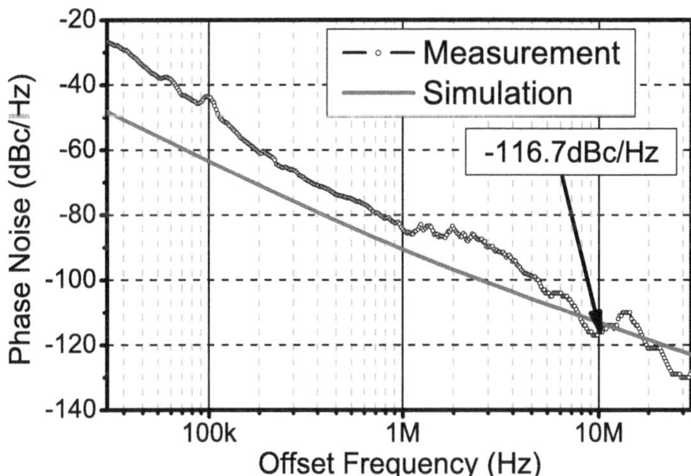

Figure 5.10: Measured and simulated VCO phase noise at 60 GHz.

Table 5.1: Performance Comparison of State-of-the-Art VCO Designs around 60 GHz

Parameters	[162]	[154]	[77]	[174]	This Work
Technology	0.13-μm CMOS	32-nm CMOS SOI	65-nm CMOS	90-nm CMOS	65-nm CMOS
f_{osc} (GHz)	56.5	102.2	40	57	63.1
FTR (%)	10.3	4.1	10.5	14.3	15.8
Phase Noise @10MHz (dBc/Hz)	−108 @10M	−100.8 @10M	−85 @10M	−118.8 @10M	−116.7 @10M
Output Power (dBm)	−18	−30.7	−13	−6.6	+3
Power Efficiency (%)	<0.16	0.013	<0.1	1.5	2.2
FOM (dBc/Hz)	−173.1	−172.45	−162	−184.3	−172.9
FOM_t (dBc/Hz)	−173.4	−164.75	−162.4	−187.4	−177.3
A_{CORE} (mm^2)	0.06	0.0014	—	0.1	0.11
P_{OUT}/A_{CORE} (mw/mm^2)	0.26	0.6	—	2.2	18.4

5.3.2 140 GHz CON Signal Source

Figure 5.11 shows the block diagram of the proposed 140-GHz signal source, of which the core is a 70-GHz CON with four zero-phase-coupled oscillator unit-cells. Since the output signals after frequency doublers are still in-phase, they are directly combined at the center of CON to generate a four times higher output power. The oscillation frequency of CON is controlled by the injection locking method. Compared to the direct frequency control by a 70-GHz phase lock loop (PLL) with the bulky and power hungry frequency dividers, the injection locking method has higher power and area efficiency. In this work, the 70-GHz injection signal is obtained by doubling the frequency of a 35-GHz reference input, which can be easily generated by an on-chip or off-chip signal generator. The design of each circuit block is shown in the following section.

5.3.2.1 Zero-Phase Oscillator Unit-Cell at 70GHz

Figure 5.12 shows the schematic and layout of an on-chip MPW-based oscillator unit-cell with coupled T-line implemented in the topmost copper layer (M8) and parasitic capacitances from transistors in the 65-nm CMOS process. Here an inter-digital coupling topology is deployed to largely increase the magnetic coupling inside each unit-cell. Both input and output of the unit-cell are on the same side due to the dumbbell-shaped routing with an effective length of 40 μm. Switch-controlled inductive loadings by Sa and Sb are applied to increase the number of the available zero-phase modes of unit-cell as well as the tuning range of CON. The unit-cell EM-simulation results and

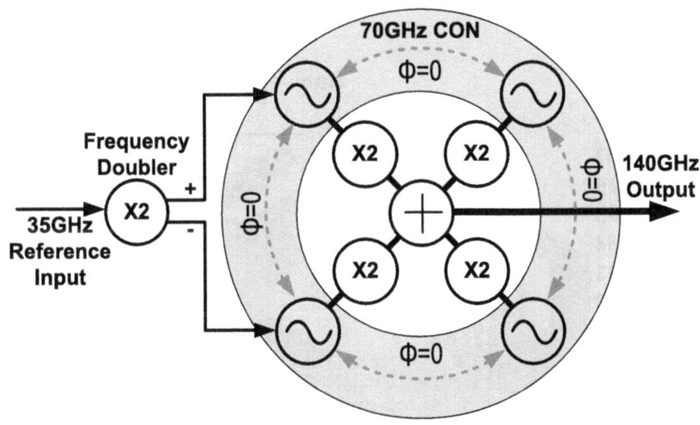

Figure 5.11: Block diagram of proposed 140 GHz signal source with center combined output from four 70 GHz zero-phase-coupled oscillator unit-cells.

the dispersion diagram extracted by the method introduced in [175] without any inductive loadings are shown in Figure 5.13 and 5.14, respectively, where a very small insertion loss of 0.4dB is observed in zero-phase mode at 70 GHz. Note that a parasitic capacitance of 40fF from active devices is also considered in the simulation. Moreover, the metamaterial properties of proposed on-chip unit-cell design are verified by a similar dispersion diagram to Figure 2.2.1.5 except the loss-induced non-zero α at zero-phase mode.

5.3.2.2 70GHz Zero-Phase Coupled Oscillator Network

The schematic of the 70-GHz CON is shown in Figure 5.15. Four MPW-based oscillator unit-cells are serially connected in a closed-loop form. Due to the strong in-phase inductive coupling inside each zero-phase oscillator unit-cell, the differential output signals at locations A, B, C and D have the same phase, magnitude and frequency, which are locked to the injected 70-GHz reference signal with largely amplified strength. The oscillation signal is generated by compensating the energy loss in each unit-cell with a negative resistance formed by cross-coupled NMOS pair (M1 and M2). Usually larger M1 and M2 are preferred to ensure the oscillation condition, but the available output power will be correspondingly reduced. Additionally, in order to reduce the impacts of the process variation, a central symmetrical layout is deployed and all active devices are placed as close as possible to the geometrical center of CON.

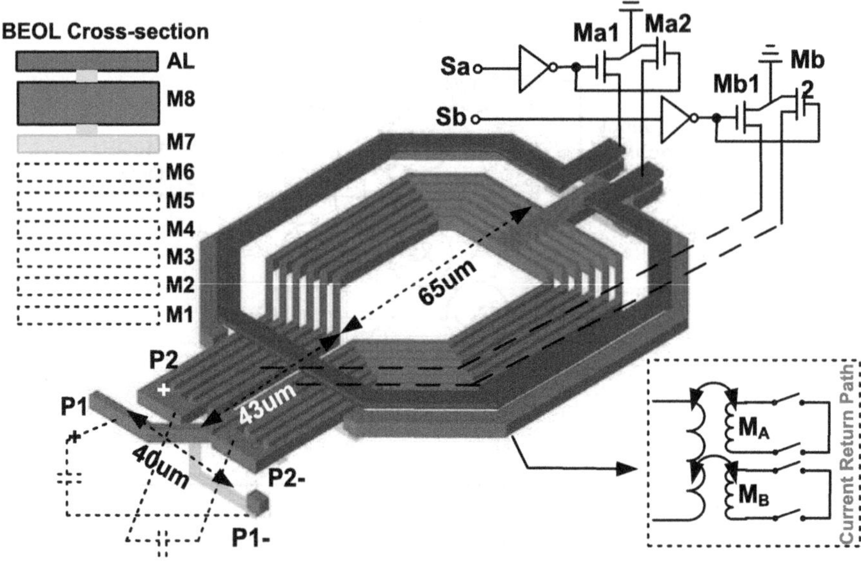

Figure 5.12: Schematic of on-chip ZPC-based oscillator unit-cell at 70-GHz band with inter-digital coupled T-line and switch-controlled inductive loadings.

5.3.2.3 70GHz to 140GHz Output Frequency Doublers

Figure 5.16 shows the schematic of four 70-GHz to 140-GHz push-push frequency doublers with center combined output. The 70-GHz differential output signals at A, B, C and D are coupled to the push-push frequency doubler by 28fF DC-block capacitors. Therefore, all the frequency doublers can be externally biased to the threshold level (VG1) to maximize the frequency conversion efficiency. The resulting four in-phase 140-GHz output signals are directly tied together to generate a high power output signal at the center with a combined output impedance of 50 Ω. Moreover, a LC resonator-based AC-GND is applied to reduce the output leakage of the 70-GHz fundamental signal. A CPW T-line with 210-μm length and 50-Ω characteristic impedance is used to connect the center output to the RF PADs. The cross-section of CPW T-line is also shown in in Figure 5.16. According to the EM-Simulation at 140 GHz, the CPW T-line has an insertion loss and Q-factor (Q) of 0.45 dB and 13.5, respectively.

5.3.2.4 35-GHz to 70-GHz Input Reference Frequency Doubler

Figure 5.17 shows the schematic of the 35-GHz to 70-GHz Reference Frequency Doubler. One transformer-based balun is deployed to generate a differential

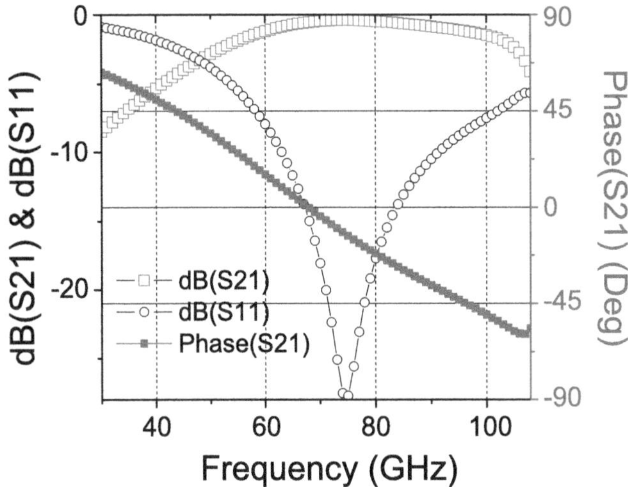

Figure 5.13: EM simulation results of 70-GHz ZPC with inter-digital coupled T-line.

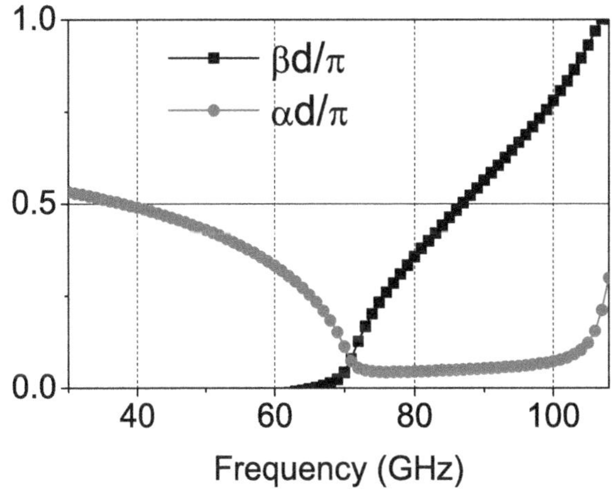

Figure 5.14: Extracted dispersion diagram of 70 GHz ZPC with inter-digital coupled T-line.

35-GHz reference signal to drive M3 and M4, which also have threshold-level biasing. However, the transformer-based balun suffers from the output mismatch above 60 GHz. As such, another Marchant balun with inter-digital

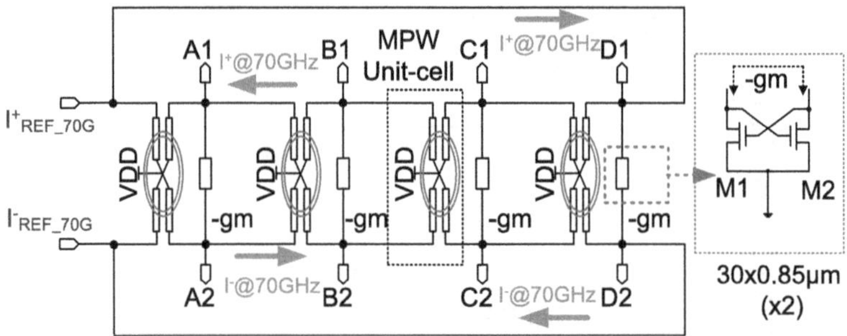

Figure 5.15: Schematic of injection-locked 70-GHz CON with 4 oscillator unit-cells.

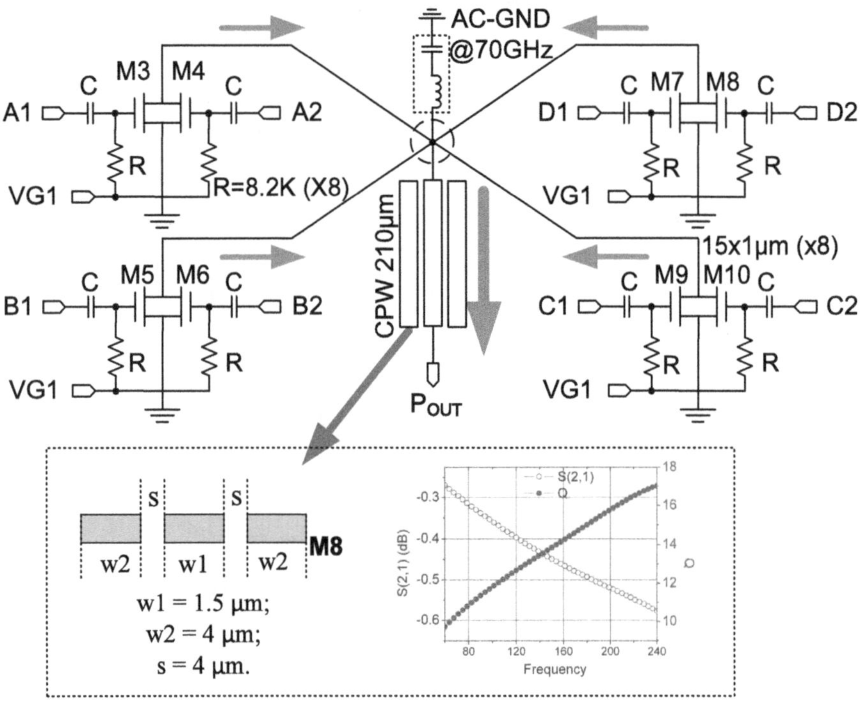

Figure 5.16: Schematic of four 70-GHz to 140-GHz push-push frequency doublers with center combined output.

coupling is deployed at 70 GHz to have balanced differential outputs as well as low insertion loss. As verified by EM simulation in Figure 5.18, the pro-

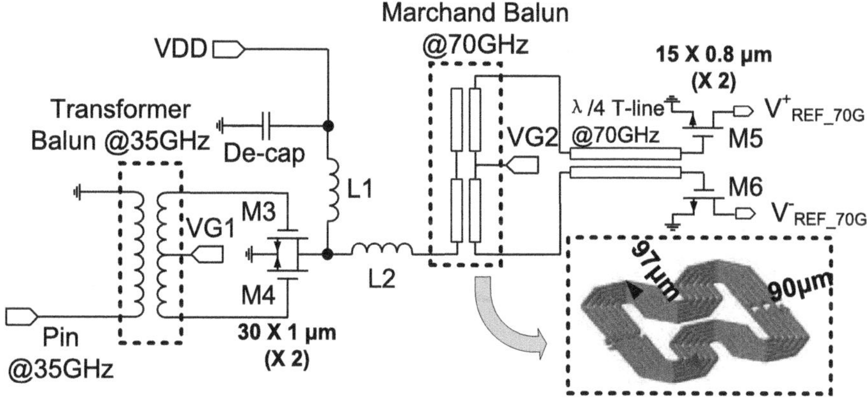

Figure 5.17: Schematic of 35 GHz to 70 GHz frequency doubler with inter-digital Marchand balun at 70 GHz.

posed Marchand balun has an average intrinsic loss of 1.1 dB at 70 GHz. The magnitude and phase mismatches at 70 GHz are only 0.4 dB and 4 degrees, respectively. The 70-GHz differential signal is then injected into the CON by a common source buffer stage (M5 and M6). Figure 5.19 shows the post-layout simulation results of the entire frequency doubler with 5-dBm reference power. The conversion gain is above -15 dB in 33–39 GHz. Moreover, a good input matching is observed with S11 smaller than -6 dB in 33–37.5 GHz.

5.3.2.5 Measurements

As shown in Figure 5.20, the proposed injection-locked 140GHz signal source is implemented in Global Foundries 65-nm CMOS RF process with f_T/f_{MAX} of 180/530 GHz. The die area including DC and RF pads is 750 × 550 μ^2m, and the CON core area is 0.13 mm^2. It was measured on a probe station with a 6-pin DC probe for biasing, a normal GSG probe for reference signal input and a D-band GSG to waveguide probe for output, which is connected to the R&S FSUP signal source analyzer with a D-band waveguide harmonic mixer. Operating from a 1.2-V power supply, the CON core of signal source consumes 145 mW, while the input frequency doubler consumes another 3.8 mW. Note that the simulation results are obtained from Cadence Spectre post-layout simulation.

Figure 5.21 shows the output power obtained from both measurement and simulation. By controlling the inductive loading modes of MPW unit-cells, the entire tuning range of signal source from 127 to 140 GHz is covered by three available bands. Compared to the simulation results, the measured output power is 0.5 $\sim$ 2.5-dB higher in 128 $\sim$ 132 GHz and 1.5 $\sim$ 3-dB lower in 134 $\sim$ 140 GHz. This is probably due to the process variation. The maximum

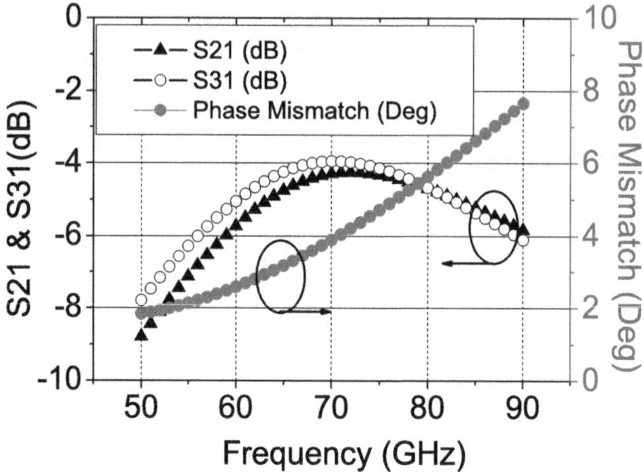

Figure 5.18: EM simulation results of the proposed Marchand balun at 70 GHz.

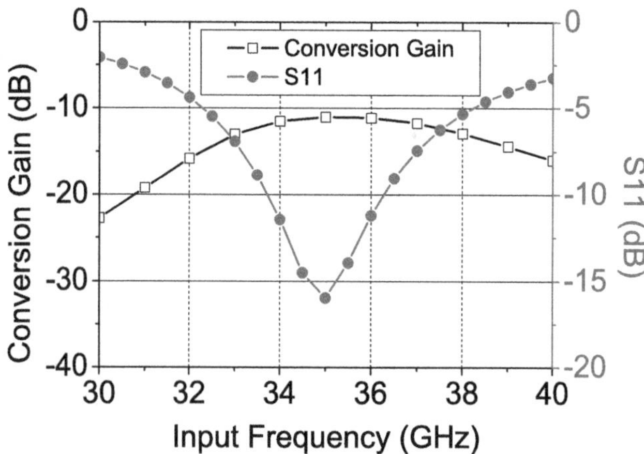

Figure 5.19: Post-layout simulation results of the 35-GHz to 70-GHz frequency doubler.

output power of 5.4 dBm is observed at 132 GHz in mode 2 with a DC-RF efficiency of 2.4%. Figure 5.22 shows the measured and simulated spectrum of 132-GHz output signal when locked to a 5-dBm reference signal at 33 GHz. Note that the simulated spectrum is offset to the same output signal power level at 132 GHz. Compared to the simulation results, a raised noise floor is

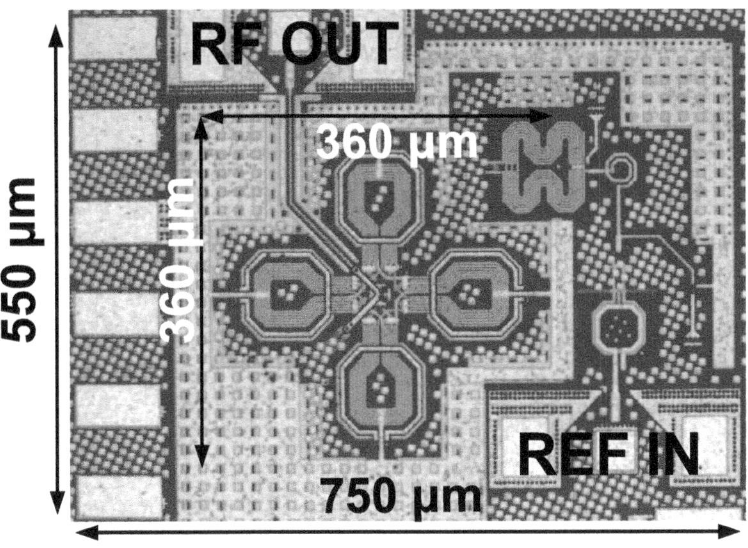

Figure 5.20: Die micrograph of the fabricated THz source in CMOS.

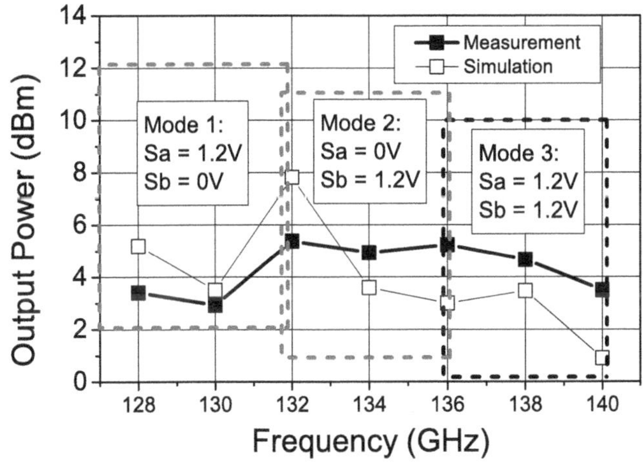

Figure 5.21: Measured and simulated output power of signal source with three different inductive loading modes.

observed in the measurement within ±25 MHz of 132 GHz. This is probably contributed by the noise coupled from DC power supplies, because there are not any de-coupling capacitors in the DC probe. In such case, a phase noise of

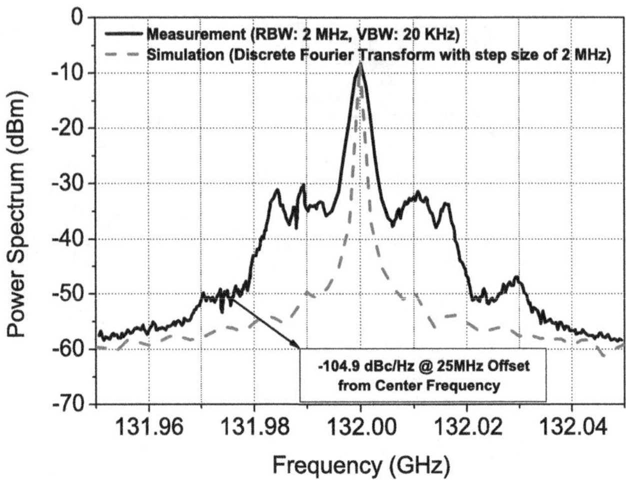

Figure 5.22: Measured and simulated output spectrum of the proposed signal source at 132 GHz.

Table 5.2: Performance Comparison with Recently Published THz Signal Source

Parameters	[153]	[161]	[156]	[160]	This Work
Technology	65-nm CMOS	65-nm CMOS	SiGe	65-nm CMOS	65-nm CMOS
f_{osc} range (GHz)	113.6–118.8	100–110	125–138	159–169	127–140
P_{OUT} (dBm)	−3.5	4.5	3	1	5.4
Power Efficiency (%)	2.2	5.2	4	1.38	2.4
FTR (%)	4.4	9.5	9.8	6.1	9.7
A_{CORE} (mm^2)	0.21	0.18	0.21	0.1	0.13
P_{OUT}/A_{CORE} (mw/mm^2)	2.1	15.6	9.5	4.16	26.9

-104.9 dBc/Hz is measured at 25-MHz offset. Moreover, the maximum power density of the proposed signal source is 26.9 mW/mm^2, which is defined as the output power generated in unit chip area (P_{OUT}/A_{CORE}). The performance of the proposed signal source is summarized in Table 5.2 with comparison to the recent state-of-the-art THz source designs in both CMOS and SiGe processes. It can be observed that the proposed design has the highest output power and power density.

5.3.3 280 GHz CON Signal Source

Figure 5.23 shows the block diagram of the proposed 280-GHz signal source. The input of the proposed 280GHz signal source is a 17.5-GHz reference signal, of which the signal frequency is four times increased by a frequency quadrupler. Based on the 35 GHz to 70 GHz input reference frequency doubler in Sec. 5.3.2.4, the proposed frequency quadrupler is designed with another push-push frequency doubler with differential signal input at 17.5 GHz. The resulting differential 70-GHz reference signal is amplified by the injection-locking of a 70-GHz zero-phase CON with two oscillator unit-cells, each of which has already been introduced in Sec. 5.3.2.1. Similar to the 140-GHz signal source in Sec. 5.3.2, the output signals of two 70-GHz zero-phase oscillator unit-cells are first frequency-doubled. Then the resulting two in-phase 140GHz signals are combined at the center of 70-GHz CON to generate a two times higher 140-GHz output power. The combined single-ended 140-GHz reference signal is further split and converted into two in-phase differential 140-GHz reference signal by transformer-based baluns. Each differential 140GHz reference signal is further amplified by injection-lock of a 140-GHz zero-phase CON with four oscillator unit-cells. The output signals of four 140GHz zero-phase oscillator unit-cells in each 140GHz CON are also frequency-doubled. Then the resulting four in-phase 280-GHz signals are combined at the center of each 140-GHz CON to generate a four times higher output power at 280 GHz. Two resulting in-phase 280-GHz output signals are finally combined to have a total eight times higher output power at 280 GHz. The design of each circuit block is shown in the following section.

5.3.3.1 Zero-Phase Oscillator Unit-Cell at 140 GHz

Figure 5.24 shows the schematic and layout of an on-chip 140-GHz MPW-based oscillator unit-cell with inter-digital coupled T-line implemented in the top most copper layer (M8) and parasitic capacitances from transistors in 65-nm CMOS process. Compared to the 70-GHz oscillator unit-cell in Sec. 5.3.2.1, the size of 140-GHz oscillator unit-cell is about 50% smaller due to a shorter wavelength at 280 GHz. The unit-cell EM-simulation results are shown in Figure 5.25, where a very small insertion loss of 1 dB is observed in zero-phase mode at 140 GHz. Note that a parasitic capacitance of 32 fF from active devices is also considered in the simulation.

5.3.3.2 140-GHz Zero-Phase Coupled Oscillator Network with Output Frequency Doublers

The schematic of the 140-GHz CON is shown in Figure 5.26(a). Similar to the design of 70-GHz zero-phase CON, four 140GHz MPW-based oscillator unit-cells are serially connected in a closed-loop form to generate four in-phase differential output signals at locations A, B, C and D with the same magnitude and frequency, which is injection-locked to the 140-GHz reference

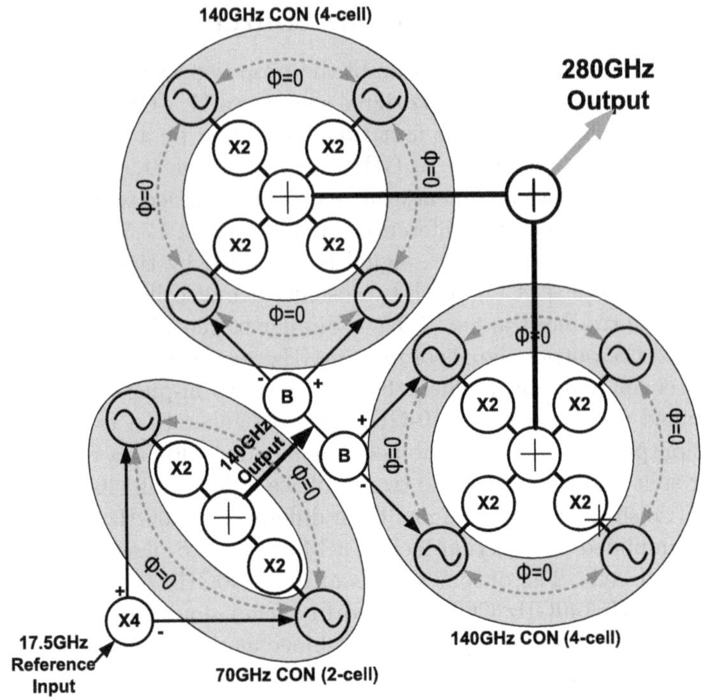

Figure 5.23: Block diagram of proposed 280 GHz signal source.

signal. The oscillation signal is generated by compensating the energy loss in each unit-cell with a negative resistance formed by cross-coupled NMOS pair (e.g., M1 and M2). Different from the 70-GHz CON with external push-push frequency doubler, the 2nd harmonics of differential signal in 140-GHz CON are directly extracted from the tail of the cross-coupled NMOS pair shown in Figure 5.3.3.2. This method eliminates the parasitic capacitance contributed by the push-push frequency doubler, and enables the CON to operate at a higher frequency such as 140GHz. However, there are several considerations when applying this method. First, the biasing network such as a one-side shorted $\lambda/4$ T-line is required at the tail of each cross-coupled NMOS pair with small resistance at DC and high impedance at the output frequency. As such, two $\lambda/4$ T-lines at 280 GHz are connected in parallel to increase the power efficiency of the 140-GHz CON. Secondly, the output impedance of each cross-coupled NMOS pair cannot be flexibly adjusted, because the size of NMOS transistors are usually maximized to have a large output current. As such, an additional T-line-based impedance transformer at 280 GHz is required to convert the output impedance to the targeted value.

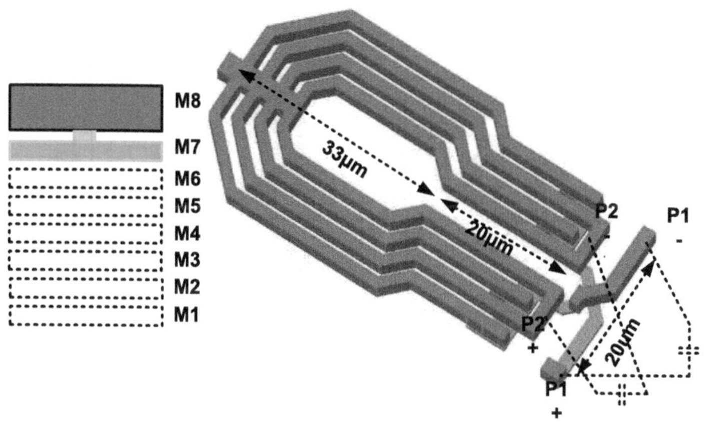

Figure 5.24: Schematic of on-chip MPW base oscillator unit-cell at 140-GHz band with inter-digital coupled T-line.

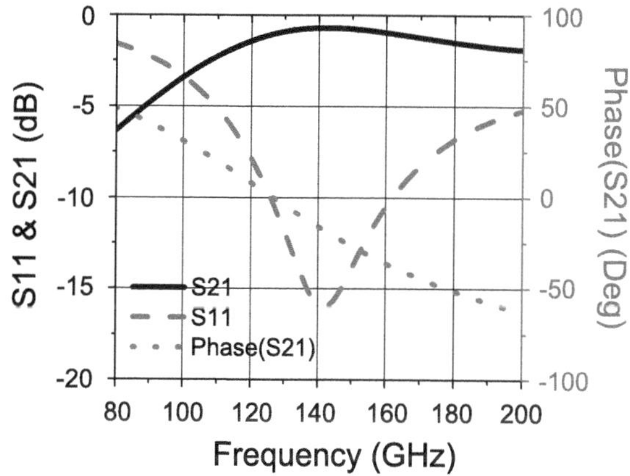

Figure 5.25: EM simulation results of 140-GHz on-chip MPW unit-cell with inter-digital coupled T-line.

The optimum output impedance at point "a" is found to be 18Ω by the load-pull analysis in the post-layout simulation. It is further matched to the single size output impedance of 152 Ω at point "b" by a $\lambda/4$ T-line with characteristic impedance of 52.3 Ω. Note that the resulting output impedance for the entire 280-GHz signal source is 76 Ω, which is half of the impedance of the single branch due to the parallel in-phase power combination. Compared

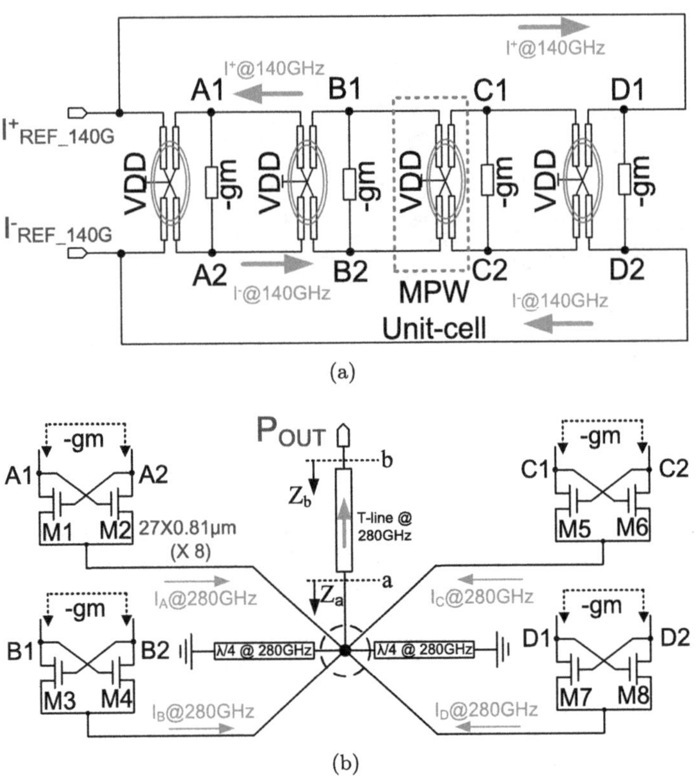

Figure 5.26: (a) Schematic of injection-locked 140 GHz CON with 4 MPW unit-cells; (b) 2nd harmonic outputs power combining network.

to the conventional 50 Ω system, a 76 Ω system has a larger voltage to drive the gate of a CMOS transistor as well as a smaller current to reduce the propagation loss.

5.3.3.3 70-GHz Zero-Phase Coupled Oscillator Network with Inter-stage Frequency Doublers

The schematic of the closed-loop 70-GHz CON is shown in Figure 5.27. Since this 70GHz CON functions as an inter-stage buffer with less stringent output power requirement, a minimum number of two MPW-based oscillator unit-cells is deployed to form a loop with a central symmetrical layout. Compared to the 70-GHz CON design with four oscillator unit-cells in Sec. 5.3.2.1, the output power is reduced by half as well as the power consumption. As such, a output power of around 0 dBm can be ensured at 140 GHz.

A 140-GHz power splitter is designed to convert the single-ended 140GHz reference signal output into two identical differential signals. The layout of the

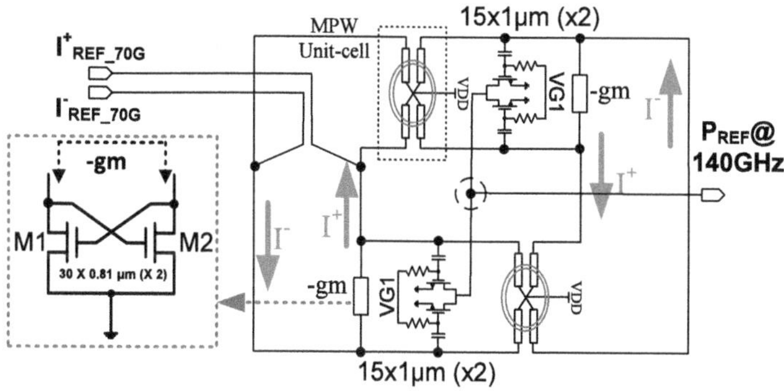

Figure 5.27: Schematic of injection-locked 70 GHz CON with 2 MPW unit-cells.

proposed power splitter is shown in Figure 5.28(a). The inlet single-ended 140-GHz signal (P1) is first split into two path "a" at point; each of the resulting single-ended 140GHz signals is further converted into differential signal by a compact transformer-based balun ($25\times25\mu m^2$) due to the limited inter-stage chip area. The primary and secondary loops of the transformer-based baluns are designed in the topmost (M8) and second topmost (M7) copper layers, respectively. The grounding layer (M1) is removed under the balun to enhance the inductive coupling between the primary and secondary loops. The phase and magnitude mismatch between P2 and P3 (P4 and P5) can be improved by adjusting the trace length and AC-GND locations of the secondary coils, respectively. A symmetric layout of the whole splitter ensure the magnitude and phase balance among differential port (P2-P3 and P4-P5) with $S21 = S41$ and $S41 = S51$. As verified by EM simulation in Figure 5.3.3.3, the proposed the proposed power splitter has an average intrinsic loss of 9 dB at 140 GHz. The magnitude and phase mismatches at 140 GHz are only 0.7 dB and 5.8 degrees, respectively.

5.3.3.4 17.5-GHz to 70-GHz Input Reference Frequency Quadrupler

Figure 5.29 shows the schematic of the 17.5 GHz to 70 GHz input reference frequency quadrupler. Based on the frequency doubler discussed in Sec. 5.3.2.1, the proposed quadrupler is designed with additional push-push frequency doubler from 17.5 GHz to 35 GHz. One transformer-based balun is deployed to generate a differential 17.5 GHz reference signal to drive M1 and M2. Figure 5.30 shows the post-layout simulation results of the entire frequency quadrupler with 0-dBm reference power. The conversion gain is above -20 dB in 16 $\sim$ 19 GHz. Due to the low coupling factor between the primary and the secondary coil in on-chip transformer-based balun at 17.5 GHz, the input S11

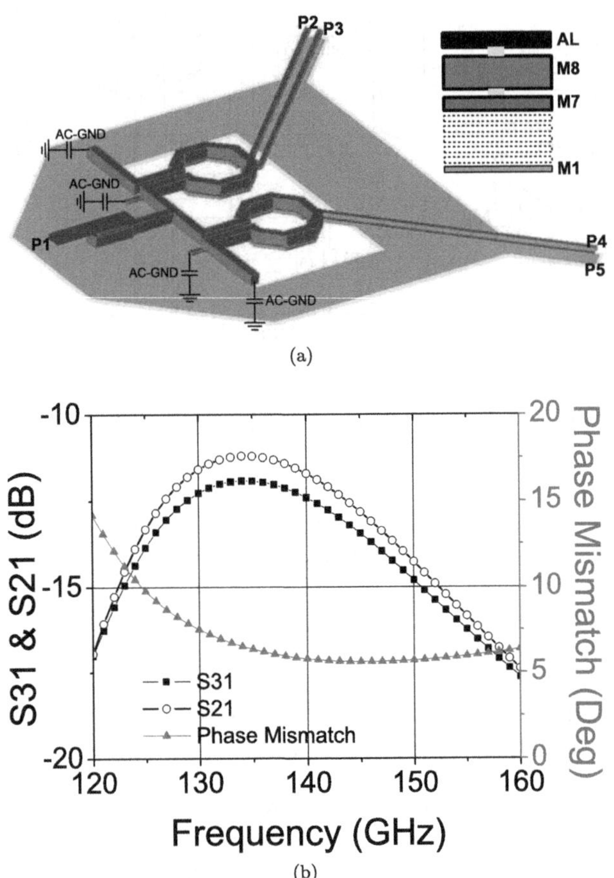

Figure 5.28: 140 GHz power splitter from one single-ended input to two differential outputs. (a) On-chip layout, (b) EM-simulation results.

is only smaller than -6 dB in 16 $\sim$ 17.3 GHz. This can be resolved by the additional matching network in PCB.

5.3.3.5 Simulation Results and Discussion

The proposed injection-locked THz signal source is implemented in the 65nm CMOS RF process with the Cadence layout shown in Figure 5.31. It has a total area of 750 $\times$ 550 μm^2, and a core area of 0.12 mm^2 including CONs at 70 GHz and 140 GHz. A post layout simulation is conducted to evaluate the performance of the proposed 280-GHz signal source. Operating from a 1.2-V power supply, the core of signal source consumes 288 mW, while the input frequency quadrupler consumes another 7.6 mW.

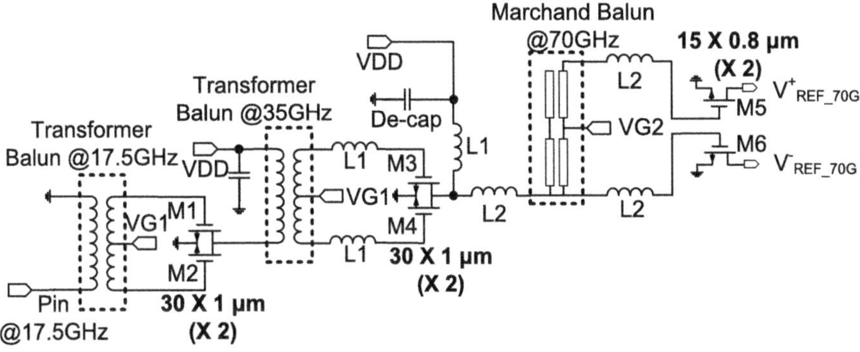

Figure 5.29: Input reference frequency quadrupler from 17.5 GHz to 70 GHz.

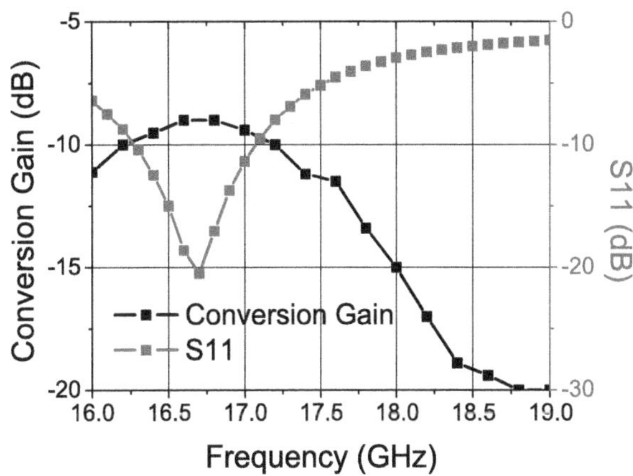

Figure 5.30: Post-layout simulation results of 17.5 GHz to 70 GHz quadrupler.

Figure 5.32 shows the simulation results of output power. By adjusting the reference signal around 17.5 GHz with 0-dBm power level, a 10.5% tuning range centered at 286 GHz is obtained. The maximum output power of 1.9 mW is observed at 276 GHz with a DC-RF efficiency of 0.66%. Moreover, the maximum power density of the proposed signal source is 31.1 mW/mm^2. The performance of the proposed 280 GHz signal source is summarized in Table 5.3 with comparison to the recent state-of-the-art THz signal source designs in CMOS process. It can be observed that the proposed 280 GHz signal source has the highest power density as well as the outstanding output power and

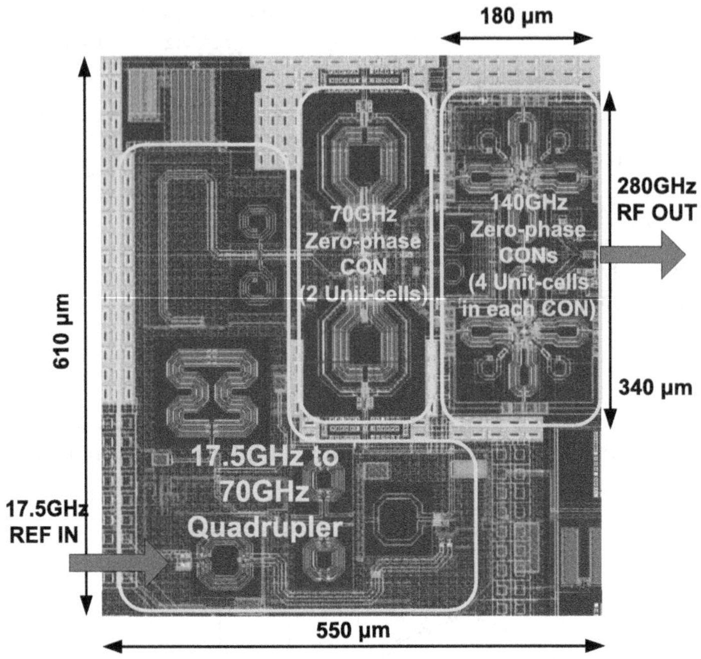

Figure 5.31: Cadence layout of the proposed 280 GHz source in CMOS.

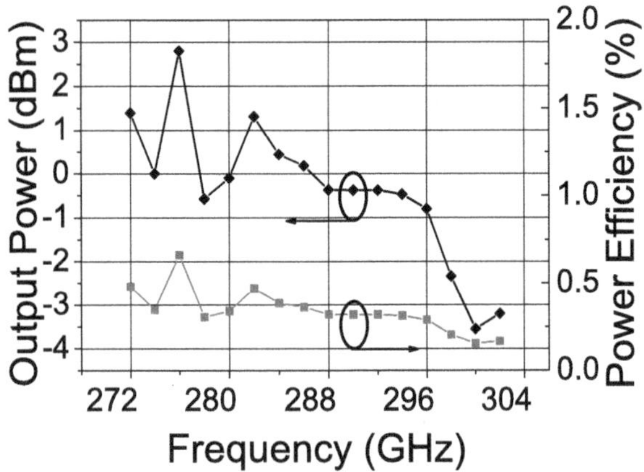

Figure 5.32: Simulated output power of the proposed 280 GHz source in CMOS.

Table 5.3: Performance Comparison with Recently Published THz Signal Sources

Parameters	[176]	[177]	[178]	[179]	This Work (Simulated)
Technology	65-nm CMOS	65-nm CMOS	65-nm CMOS	65-nm CMOS	65-nm CMOS
Center Frequency (GHz)	290	294	288	256	286
FTR (%)	4.5	1.1	1.7	6.5	10.5
P_{OUT} (dBm)	−1.2	−3.3	−1.5	4.1	2.8
Integrated DC Bias Network	NO	YES	NO	NO	YES
DC Power (mW)	325	258	275	227	288
Power Efficiency (%)	0.23	0.19	0.25	1.14	0.66
A_{CORE} (μm^2)	600×600	630×330	240×150*	640×470	180×340
P_{OUT}/A_{CORE} (mw/mm^2)	2.1	2.3	19.7	8.2	31.1

*The area of the power combining network is included in the core area calculation.

power efficiency performance. The output power of the proposed design is slightly lower than [179] due to integration of DC bias network, which will at least contribute 1.5-dB loss to the output signal. Note that a signal source with DC Bias Network can be directly used for on-chip integration with function blocks such as a mixer or antenna.

5.4 Conclusion

The CMOS high-output power signal sources are demonstrated from mm-wave to THz by coupled oscillator network with ZPC-based oscillator unit-cells, which helps greatly increase the output power and efficiency by the in-phase power combination. The fabricated 60-GHz VCO in 65-nm CMOS has a compact core chip area of 0.11 mm^2, and it is measured with 2-mW output power, -116.7-dBc/Hz phase noise at 10MHz offset, and 15.8% frequency tuning range (FTR) centered at 63.1 GHz. The fabricated 140GHz signal source with injection locking in 65-nm CMOS has a compact core chip area of 0.13 mm^2, and it is measured with 3.5-mW peak output power, 2.4% power efficiency, 26.9-mW/mm^2 power density and 9.7% FTR centered at 133.5 GHz. A 280-GHz high-power signal source is designed by connecting the 2nd harmonic outputs of two 140GHz CONs in parallel, which are both injection locked with the same phase and magnitude. It is simulated with an output power of +2.8 dBm, a power efficiency of 0.66%, and a frequency tuning range of 10.5% from 272 GHz to 302 GHz. In the following section, CMOS-based THz signal detection will be discussed.

Chapter 6

Phase-Locked Loop

6.1 Introduction

Recently, with the increasing demand for high-data-rate communication system such as 60GHz band applications, the requirements for integrating PLLs with an on-chip transceiver becomes more challenging. The conventional methodology to achieve fully coverage of the IEEE 802.15.3c 60GHz band (58.3–64.8GHz) by using multiple capacitor bands seems to be a good candidate. However, the quality factor of the tuning capacitor implemented by MOSFET varactors is low at such high frequency, leading to lower drivability of the VCO which in turn may make the VCO fail to lock the prescaler. In stead of using capacitive tuning in the VCO, in this chapter, a novel 60GHz VCO using inductive tuning by switching return path is employed to cover the whole band with high output power almost unaffected. The PLL provides the four source frequencies defined by the IEEE 802.15.3c 60GHz communication standard with the attained phase noise suitable for various short-range applications.

Figure 6.1 shows the schematic of the designed 60-GHz PLL. It mainly consists of a 60-GHz VCO, a divider chain, a phase frequency detector (PFD), a charge pump, a law pass filter (LPF) and a reference clock. The 60-GHz VCO adopts the proposed symmetric inductive tuning method in Chapter 4 to achieve a wide FTR. The divider chain includes a 60-GHz divide-by-2 divider, a 30-GHz divide-by-2 divider, a dynamic current-mode logic (DCML) divide-by-4 divider, and a programmable divider. The LPF is realized off-chip, and the reference clock is generated through a 54-MHz crystal oscillator.

Figure 6.2 shows the implemented layout of the 60-GHz PLL in GF CMOS 65-nm technology, with an active area of 0.68 × 0.64 mm^2 excluding pads.

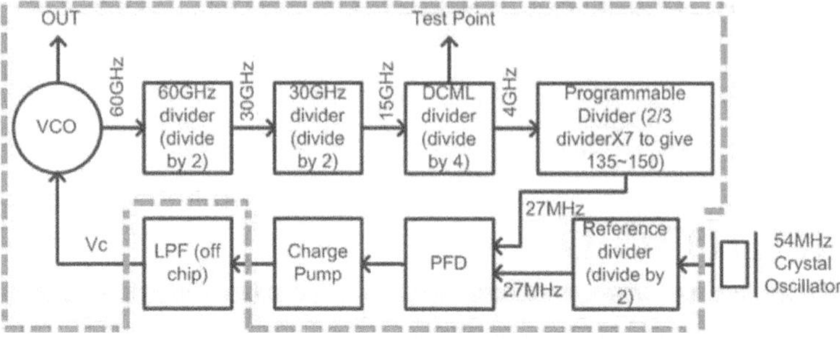

Figure 6.1: Schematic of designed CMOS 60-GHz PLL.

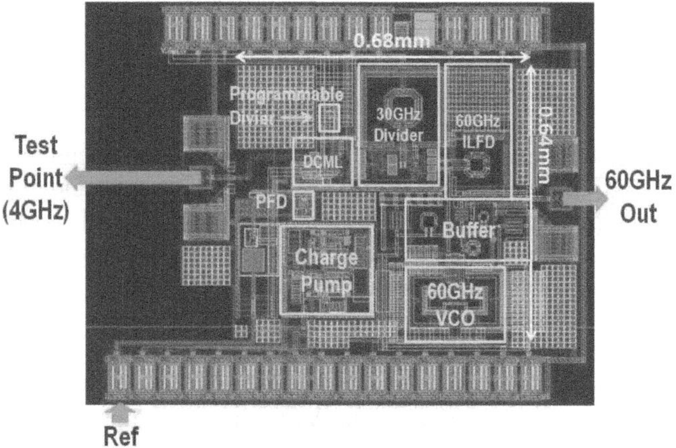

Figure 6.2: Layout of designed CMOS 60-GHz PLL.

One testing point is inserted after the DCML divider for tuning of bias and debugging.

Voltage-controlled oscillator (VCO) and high-frequency dividers are two major designing blocks in PLL at 60 GHz. Considering the required wide-band at 60 GHz and process variation in nano-scale CMOS, a wide frequency locking range is typically required for 60-GHz PLL design, which demands the wide frequency-tuning-range (FTR) of VCO and wide locking range of a divider. In the following sub-sections, the design details for the VCO and a high-frequency portion of divider chain are provided.

6.2 60-GHz PLL Design

The proposed new inductive tuning in Chapter 4 is utilized for VCO design in the 60-GHz PLL. To achieve a wide FTR with maintained phase noise performance, the VCO prototype presented in Section 4.4.3 with symmetric inductive tuning is selected.

Various frequency dividers have been explored for different applications. Generally, frequency dividers can be classified into digital and analog classes. The digital class of dividers can be sub-divided into current-mode logic (CML) dividers [180] and dynamic divider [181]; and the analog class of dividers can be sub-divided into Miller dividers [182] and injection-locked frequency dividers (ILFD) [183, 184, 185]. Dynamic dividers are easy to design that operate at low frequency with wide range and variable division-ratio. CML and Miller dividers can operate at higher operating frequency with wide locking range, but usually suffer from high power consumption. Compared with Miller frequency dividers and CML dividers, ILFD can achieve higher operating frequency with lower power consumption. Its major limitation, however, is the limited locking range.

In the design of the divider chain in 60-GHz PLL, according to different operating frequencies, the choice of the divider structure in each dividing stage will be different. The first stage divider operates at the highest frequency in the divider chain, and thus the ILFD is usually employed. The last stage divider operates at the lowest frequency in the chain, and thus a dynamic divider is usually employed due to the simple structure and variable division-ratio. The remaining stages can be designed with CML and Miller dividers for their wide locking range. The major challenge is to design the first stage divider with a wide locking range to cover the wide frequency range at 60 GHz. To increase the locking range of the ILFD, varactors are usually deployed to tune the self-oscillation frequency of ILFD. However, a large varactor will severely degrade the phase noise of ILFD and PLL. Capacitor banks can be used to realize multi-band operation [183]. However, as frequency scales up to 60-GHz, the large parasitic capacitance from the capacitor bank becomes too large and the quality factor of capacitor decreases significantly [145, 186].

As introduced in Chapter 4, inductive tuning has recently become a promising substitute to replace the capacitive tuning, and is used in 60-GHz VCO design to realize a wide FTR. Besides a wide FTR, inductive tuning can also provide the benefit of isolated DC noise from the tuning element. The same mechanism could be used in high-frequency divider design to realize a large locking range. In this section, an inductor-loaded transformer is introduced into the conventional ILFD structure to improve its locking range by creating multiple frequency bands.

The locking range (LR) for an injection locked oscillator is given by [184]

$$LR = \frac{1}{2Q} \cdot \frac{I_{inj}}{I_{osc}} \cdot \frac{1}{\sqrt{1 - \frac{I_{inj}^2}{I_{osc}^2}}} \tag{6.1}$$

where I_{osc}, I_{inj} and t are the oscillator and injection current and quality factor of the LC-tank, respectively. Thus, for larger LR, the quality factor of the LC-tank should be balanced. The second important consideration of LR is on the effective injection current (I_{inj}) reaching the oscillator core. To enhance the LR, the internal injection power while using the same external injection should be maximized. The input signal can be injected at the tail-node or direct across the LC-tank [187]. Due to the loss of injection power in the parasitic capacitance of the tail-node injection, direct injection is employed to improve the injection efficiency in this work.

The introduced switching inductor loaded transformer in Chapter 4 is utilized here for the 60-GHz divider design, where one new type of ILFD is proposed in this section. As shown in Figure 6.3, the input injection transistor is placed across the LC-tank. The cross-coupled transistors generate negative Solid-State Circuits and resistance to compensate the energy loss in the LC-tank. The injection locking will occur when the self-oscillation frequency of the ILFD is close to the half of the input signal. The switching inductor loaded transformer can change the inductance of the LC-tank, and then finally change the self-oscillation frequency, which leads to multi-band operation for a wide locking range.

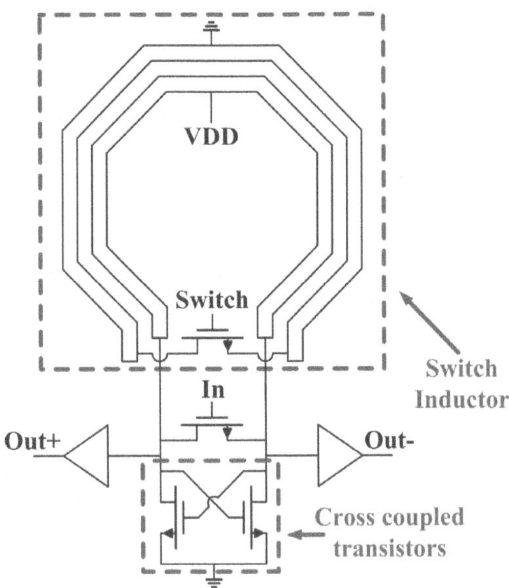

Figure 6.3: Schematic of switch-inductor loaded transformer-based ILFD.

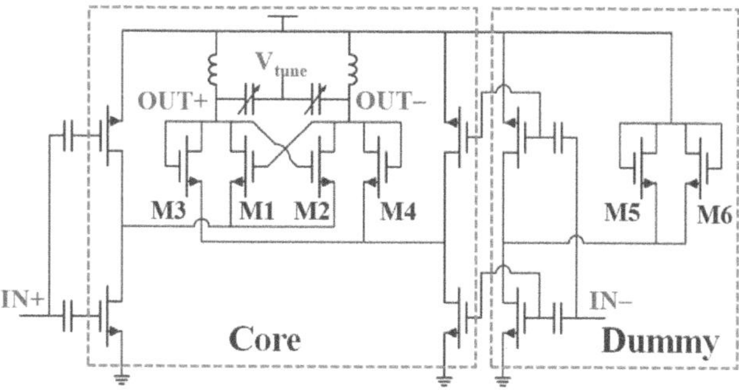

Figure 6.4: Schematic of the 30-GHz ILFD.

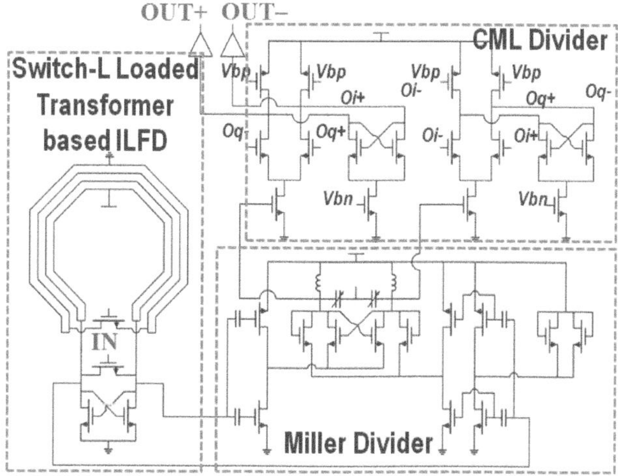

Figure 6.5: Schematic of the 60-GHz divider chain.

In addition to the divide-by-2 operation, another two divide-by-2 dividers are implemented at a lower frequency region to realize a divide-by-8 divider chain. The second stage divider is implemented with Miller divider topology [182] as shown in Figure 6.4. Transistors M3 and M4 are designed with smaller size than M1 and M2 to lower the Q-factor in LC tank, thus increasing the locking range. M5 and M6 are dummy transistors to provide a balanced matching condition for differential inputs. The third stage divider is implemented with a common CML topology. Figure 6.5 shows the schematic for the whole 60-GHz divider chain.

6.3 Circuit Prototyping and Simulation

The designed 60-GHz PLO prototype is implemented in Global Foundries 65nm CMOS 1P8M technology as shown in Fig. 6.6 with a die size of 700μm $\times$ 680μm excluding pads. Both the 60-GHz VCO and 60-GHz divider chain have been fabricated separately with measurement results. The VCO measurement was shown in Section 4.4.3.

6.3.1 Divider Measurement Results

Figure 6.7 shows the chip micro-photo of the fabricated divider, which occupies a core area of 0.058 mm^2. The DC power of the ILFD is 6.3 mW under 0.75-V power supply. The whole divider circuit is designed and verified with EM simulation (ADS-Momentum) before fabrication. The measurements are then done on a CASCADE Microtech Elite-300 probe station with Agilent PNA-X spectrum analyzer.

Figure 6.8 shows the measured input sensitivity curve. Two sub-bands are clearly observed by switching inductor loaded transformer. The first sub-band has a free-running frequency around 63 GHz, and the second sub-band has a free-running frequency around 66 GHz. The input power is 0 dBm, and the locking range for the first band is from 60.8 to 65.1 GHz, while the locking

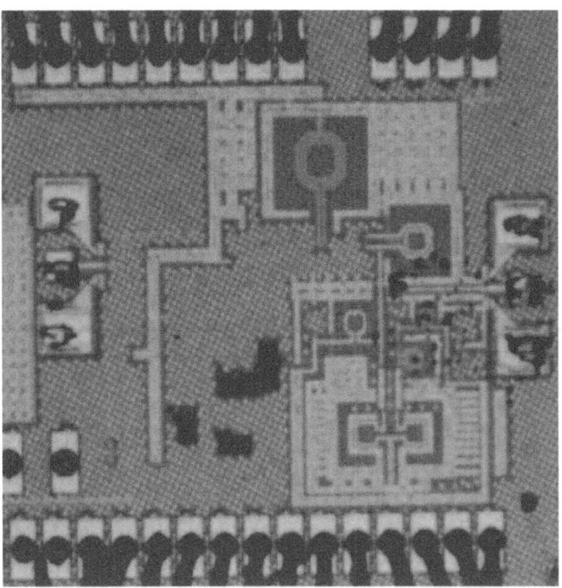

Figure 6.6: Chip micrography of 60-GHz PLL in Global Foundries 65 nm technology.

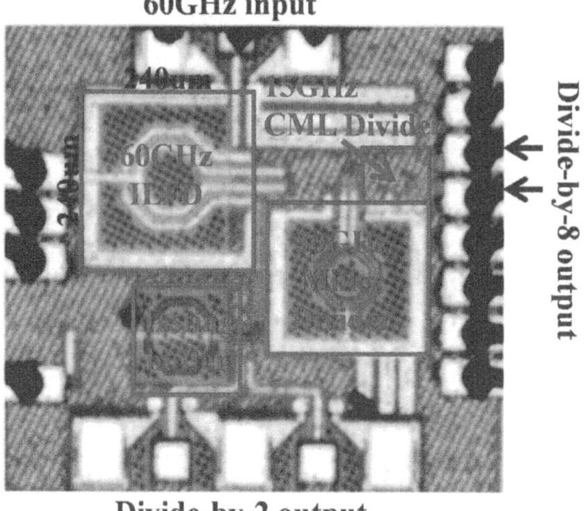

Figure 6.7: 60-GHz divider chain die photo.

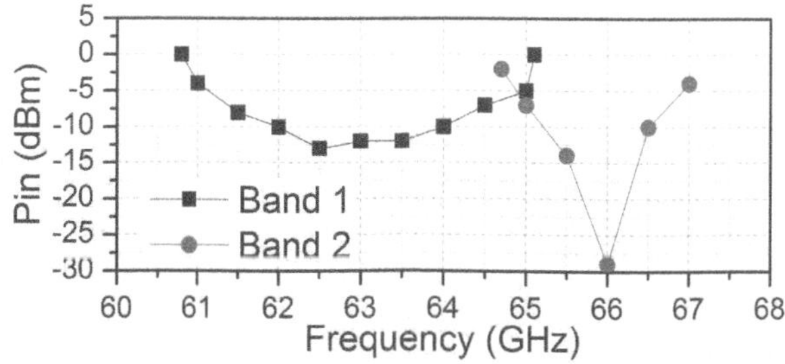

Figure 6.8: Measured sensitivity curve of the 60-GHz ILFD.

range for the second band is from 64.7 to 67GHz. The obtained total locking range is thus 9.7% from 60.8 to 67 GHz, with a center frequency of 63.9 GHz. Figure 6.9(a) shows the ILFD output spectrum at 63 GHz after the first division, where a 31.5-GHz signal is obtained. The functionality of the full divider chain is also examined. Figure 6.9(b) shows the divide-by-8 divider chain output spectrum at 63 GHz, where a 7.875-GHz output is obtained.

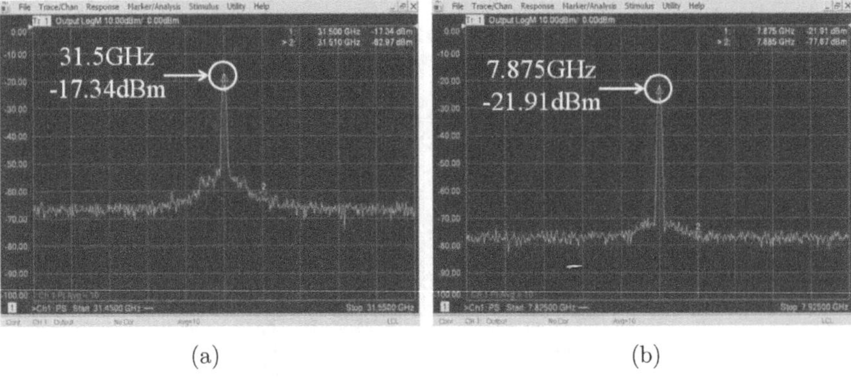

(a) (b)

Figure 6.9: Measured divide-by-2 and divide-by-8 output spectrums at 63-GHz input signal.

6.3.2 PLL Simulation Results

The designed PLL is simulated in Cadence. Figure 6.10 shows the transient simulation of the locking process at the 3rd band (62.64 GHz). The control voltage is settled to 783 mV at around 7 μs.

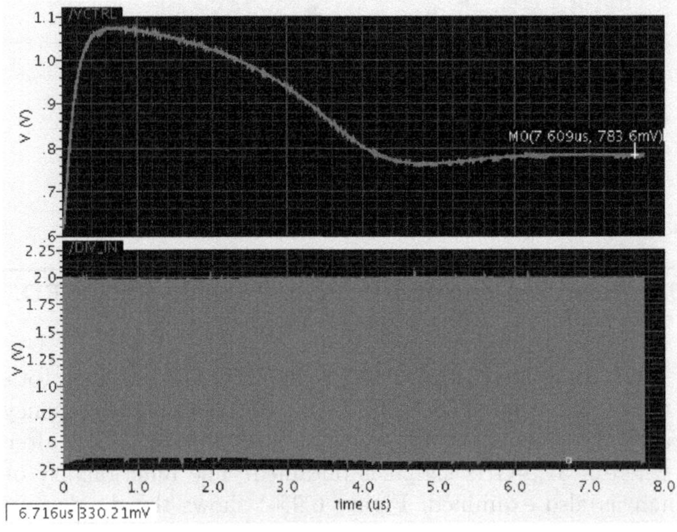

Figure 6.10: Simulated locking process of designed 60-GHz PLL at 62.64 GHz.

Table 6.1: Simulated DC Power Comparison

Building blocks	Current (mA)	Supply (V)	Power (mW)
Charge Pump	2	1.2	2.4
PFD			
Programmable Divider	1.85	1.2	2.22
Shaping Buffer			
DCML /4 divider	3	1.2	3.6
30 GHz divider	5.5	1.2	6.6
60 GHz divider	9	0.8	7.2
LO buffer	15	1.2	18
Oscillator	22	1.2	26.4
Total			66.4

Table 6.2: Performance Summary and Comparison with State-of-the-Art CMOS 60-GHz PLLs

	[188]	[189]	[190]	[191]	This work (sim.)
Technology (CMOS)	90nm	90nm	90nm	65nm	65nm
VCO tuning range (GHz)	61.1-63.1	58-60.4	78.1-78.8	75.6-76.3	57-65.5
Phase noise (dBc/Hz @1MHz)	-80	-85.1	-85	-85.3	-95 -89
Supply (V)	1.2	1.2	1.2	1.2	1.2
Reference freq. (MHz)	60	234.1	75	700	27
Power (mW)	78	80	101	73	66.4
Core area (mm^2)	0.36	0.95	0.62	N.A.	0.41 (w/o LPF)

Table 6.1 summarizes the DC power consumption in each block of the PLL. The total power consumption is 66.4 mW including buffers.

The PLL performance is summarized in Table 6.2 with comparison to state-of-the-art CMOS 60-GHz PLLs. Our work can provide a wide tuning range (57–65.5 GHz) with good phase noise performance (-95 dBc/Hz @1 MHz).

III

CMOS THZ SIGNAL AMPLIFICATION AND TRANSMISSION

Chapter 7

Power Combiner

7.1 Introduction

Power combining can improve output power and PAE at 60GHz [192, 193]. Numerous power combining techniques have been published for 60GHz CMOS applications [194, 192, 193, 195, 196, 197]. The most straightforward method is to use a Wilkinson power divider/combiner as implemented in [194]. It has the advantage of easy implementation, low loss, and good isolation between ports. However, the required $\lambda/4$ transmission like (T-line) occupies a large area. Two modified techniques are implemented in [193] and [192]. The first one merges the power combining/dividing function into the existing matching network, which is still bulky in area. The latter one, on the other hand, uses a zero-degree power divider instead, which eliminates the resistor and only requires equal-length short T-line and is thus much more compact. However, to achieve high output power, it still requires many branches to be combined with a large power combiner area due to its 1D power combining nature. Another widely explored device for power combining is Transformer. The distributed active transformer (DAT) has been proven as an efficient method for power combining [195, 196, 198]. However, the DAT topology limits the number of combined transistors, which in turn limits the achievable output power. As a result, to achieve high output power, either a larger DAT size needs to be adopted or multiple branches need to be used, both of which degrade the output power density due to its 1D power combining nature. One 2D power combining is introduced in [199], where an electrical "funnel" is constructed by 2D T-line network, which still suffers from bulky size for impedance transformation, low PAE and difficulty of matching.

T-line is commonly utilized in power combining topologies to provide power transmission for the required impedance and phase transformation.

As such, all combined transistors can be periodically loaded in the combining network where their output powers are merged in phase. Unfortunately, in many power combiner topologies, a long T-line proportional to wavelength (λ) is often required to achieve the in-phase power combining of transistors. Since advanced technology only scales active devices while the passive devices remain relatively the same size, the power combiner size is normally dominated by the passive elements. As a result, due to the usage of a long RH T-line, high output power normally leads to bulky combiner size which is not appealing for mm-wave system integration. On the other hand, CRLH T-line with its unique phase-change property could be used to replace the RH T-line with the same chase requirement but much more compact size and lower loss. In the following section, an active in-phase distributed CRLH T-line network is proposed to improve the power combining efficiency and with high output power and high output power density achieved simultaneously at mm-wave frequency region.

7.2 In-Phase Signal Transmission by CRLH Zero-Phase-Shifter

In order to achieve high output power/output power density performance with improved power combining efficiency and wide bandwidth, multiple transistors need to be periodically loaded in the combining network in compact size with distributed topology where the output power of each transistor is combined in phase. With a compact CRLH T-line to replace the traditional RH T-line, the challenge is how to load transistors in T-line network and have their output power combined in phase. The loading method for traditional active CRLH T-line is not feasible for PA design as a negative resistor would pause oscillation. Alternatively, transistor output power can be in-phase combined by directly connecting their outputs with zero-phase connections, which can be realized by the CRLH T-line-based zero-phase-shifter (ZPS) with transistor parasitic absorbed into the T-line design. Since zero-phase CRLH T-line can realize in-phase power combining both in parallel and in series, a 2D active CRLH T-line network is introduced in Figure 7.1.

As shown in Figure 7.1, the power combining is achieved in 2 levels: serial power combining (1st level) realized in each branch; and parallel power combining (2nd level) further implemented at the output. Active CRLH T-line unit cells are realized by absorbing the parasitic capacitance of the loaded transistors into design. In the 1st level combining, by designing the active CRLH T-line with zero-phase-shift in the target frequency, all transistor outputs in each branch can be serially combined in phase. The load-pull optimization process is also simplified as load-line impedance of all transistors can be viewed directly fed to output. As a result, the optimized power performance can be achieved by simply feeding a load impedance $R_g = R_{opt}/N$ to the output of the

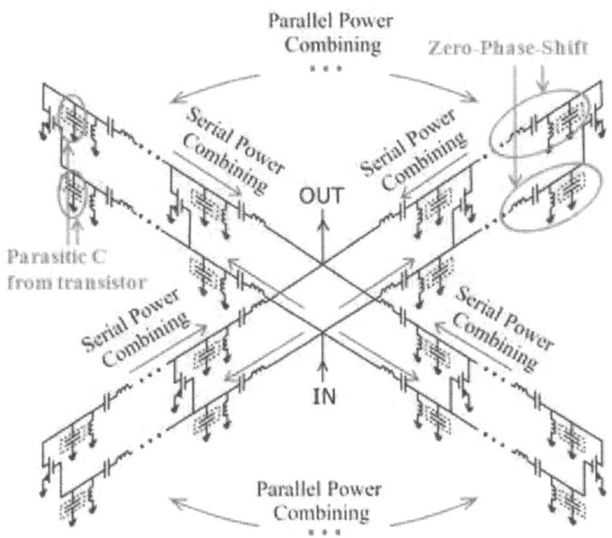

Figure 7.1: Proposed 2D active CRLH T-line network. By absorbing parasitic C from transistors into zero-phase CRLH T-line design, in-phase power combining is realized both in series and in parallel, resulting 2D distributes power combining.

branch, where R_{opt} is the optimized load-line impedance which can be easily calculated. For example, for class-A amplifier design, the optimized efficiency can be achieved by implementing: $R_{opt} = (V_{max} - V_{min})/I_{max}$, where V_{max} and V_{min} are the maximum and minimum output voltage of transistors for class A operation and I_{max} is the maximum output current [200].

Due to the power pre-combining in the 1st level, the size of the parallel power combiner in the 2nd level can be largely reduced with use of compact transformers, which perform output matching at the same time. Moreover, a differential structure could be implemented in both CRLH T-line and PA with benefits of compact size and reduced loss. As a result, more (>10) power transistors can be combined for high output power with high power combining efficiency and wide bandwidth.

Note there may be various connection methods to achieve in-phase power combining using CRLH T-line-based ZPS. However, the exact zero-phase-shift is only realized at one frequency point. To achieve wide-band performance, the ZPS connections for the serial power combining is adjusted to resemble one distributed amplification topology named single-ended dual-fed distributed amplifier (SEDFDA) topology [9], but with the bulky $\lambda/2$ T-line replaced with compact zero-phase CRLH T-line, thus achieving wide bandwidth with much reduced size and loss. In the following section, the feature of SEDFDA would be reviewed first followed by detailed analysis for on-chip implementation toward PA design.

7.3 PA Design with Power Combining Network

7.3.1 SEDFDA-Based PA Design

7.3.1.1 Review of SEDFDA

Wide bandwidth is usually achieved by distributed amplification in the mm-wave region. One major limitation for traditional distributed PA is its low PAE. As shown in Figure 7.2(a), each transistor outputs different power; therefore the transistors cannot be optimized simultaneously [7]. The power wasted in the resistive terminations further degrades the efficiency. Both transmission-line and transistor sizes are tapered in [7] to realize the maximized output voltage swing at all distributed stages (Figure 7.2(b)). Although each transistor still outputs different power, the same voltage swings are maintained due to scaled transistor sizes. However, the large scaling ratio between transistor stages limits the achievable number of distributed stages and thus output power. Furthermore, resistive terminations still consume power and degrade efficiency. A new distributed amplifier called the dual-fed distributed amplifier (DFDA) was proposed in [8], which can significantly improve the PAE limitation for distributed PAs. As shown in Figure 7.2(c), the input signal is split into 2 paths and fed into both ends of the gate line. The two outputs from the drain line are then combined again as the output signal. It has been proven that when a phase-shift of $\pm n\pi$ (n=0,1,2...) is maintained between transistors in both gate and drain lines, all transistors can see the same load, and output the same power [200]. As a result, they can be optimized simultaneously. Moreover, the resistive terminations are eliminated in DFDA, and there is no additional power wasted. As a result, the PAE limitation of distributed PAs can be resolved fundamentally. DFDA is further developed in [9] as single-ended to eliminate the need of hybrid. The resulted topology is shown in Figure 7.2(d), which is called the single-ended dual-fed distributed amplifier (SEDFDA). Both input and output signals propagate to the open-circuit ends and are reflected back. Since both forward and reflected signals add up to each other under certain phase-shift of the T-line, the power gain is further improved.

Note that both DFDA and SEDFDA require a phase-shift of $\pm n\pi$ (n=0,1,2...) to be maintained between transistors in both gate and drain lines. Since zero-phase-shift (n=0) is impossible to be realized by the traditional T-line (which introduces phase-shift proportional to the T-line length), $\lambda/2$ T-line is used at PCB level to fulfill the phase-shift requirement, which is however too bulky and lossy for on-chip implementation. One type of meta-material called composite right/left-handed (CRLH) T-line can be used to

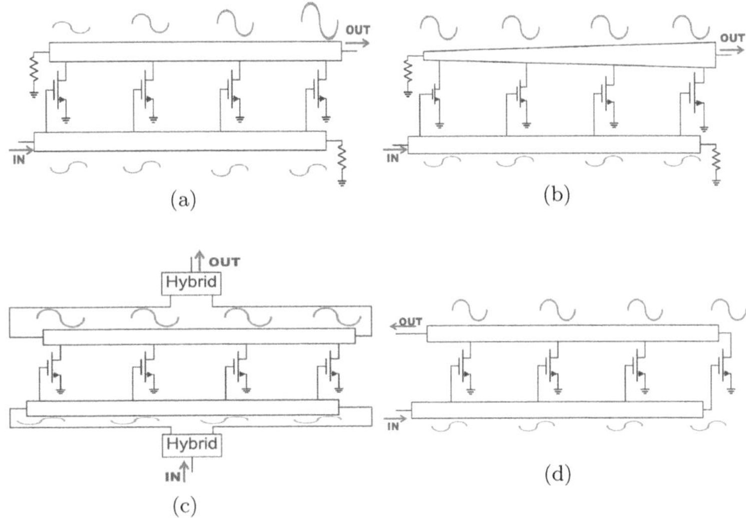

Figure 7.2: Distributed amplifier (DA) topologies: (a) conventional DA, (b) tapered DA [7], (c) DFDA [8], (d) SEDFDA [9].

realize a real zero-phase-shift, and is implemented for distributed amplifier design in [200] and [201] at the PCB level for GHz region applications. However, at this frequency region, CRLH T-line is too bulky and lossy for on-chip implementation in CMOS technology.

With frequency pushed into the mm-wave frequency region, such as 60GHz, the lumped capacitor and inductor to build CRLH T-line structures are more compact and less lossy and hence feasible for on-chip implementation in CMOS technology. In this chapter, CRLH T-line-based ZPS is studied for the first time in on-chip power amplifier design at 60GHz [202]. Detailed design considerations are studied for ZPS to achieve low loss and wide-band performance for 60GHz PA applications.

Both DFDA and SEDFDA have been analyzed in [200] and [203] but targeted for PCB design at the GHz level, where T-lines are normally assumed ideal. For on-chip power amplifier design at 60GHz and beyond, T-lines are no longer ideal and the amplifier performance can be greatly affected. In the following, we present the design analysis background of SEDFDA, and then show the design implications when considering the non-ideal T-line targeted for on-chip 60GHz applications.

7.3.1.2 SEDFDA Performance Analysis under Ideal T-Line Model

Figure 7.3 shows the equivalent circuit for one N-stage SEDFDA. The upper half is the gate line and the lower half the drain line. All parasitic components

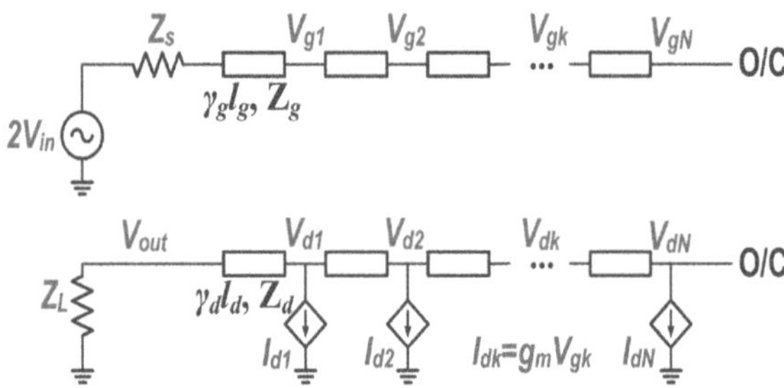

Figure 7.3: Equivalent circuit for single-ended dual-fed distributed amplifier (SEDFDA).

from transistors can be absorbed into the T-line model. Resulted T-lines for each section in both gate and drain paths are then characterized with characteristic impedance Z_g/Z_d, propagation constant γ_g/γ_d, and physical length l_g/l_d. The input impedance and load impedance are termed as Z_S and Z_L. Perfect open circuits are assumed for terminations on both gate and drain lines. The input signal travels along the gate line, meets open-circuit termination, and is reflected back again. Forward and backward signals add together to form transistor gate voltage V_{gk} (for the k-th distributed stage), which controls the corresponding drain current I_{dk}. Assume n_S=Z_g, gate voltages for all transistors can be calculated by directly adding the forward and backward voltages:

$$V_{gk} = V_{in}\left[e^{-k\gamma_g l_g} + e^{-(2N-k)\gamma_g l_g}\right]. \tag{7.1}$$

One special property for a distributed amplifier is that transistor drain voltage (V_{dk}) is affected by all transistor drain currents. Assume Z_L=Z_d, with a similar method as [200], all drain voltages for SEDFDA can be calculated:

$$V_{dk} = \frac{g_m V_{in} Z_d \left(A1+A2+B1+B2\right)}{1+coth\left[\left(N-k\right)\gamma l_d\right]} \tag{7.2}$$

where $A1$, $A2$, $B1$, $B2$ are:

$$\begin{aligned}
A1 &= \mathrm{e}^{-\mathrm{k}\gamma_\mathrm{g}\mathrm{l}_\mathrm{g}} \times \mathrm{e}^{-\mathrm{k}(\gamma_\mathrm{d}\mathrm{l}_\mathrm{d}-\gamma_\mathrm{g}\mathrm{l}_\mathrm{g})/2} \times \frac{\sinh[(\mathrm{k}-1)(\gamma_\mathrm{d}\mathrm{l}_\mathrm{d}-\gamma_\mathrm{g}\mathrm{l}_\mathrm{g})/2]}{\sinh[(\gamma_\mathrm{d}\mathrm{l}_\mathrm{d}-\gamma_\mathrm{g}\mathrm{l}_\mathrm{g})/2]},\\
A2 &= \mathrm{e}^{-(2\mathrm{N}-\mathrm{k})\gamma_\mathrm{g}\mathrm{l}_\mathrm{g}} \times \mathrm{e}^{-\mathrm{k}(\gamma_\mathrm{d}\mathrm{l}_\mathrm{d}+\gamma_\mathrm{g}\mathrm{l}_\mathrm{g})/2} \times \frac{\sinh[(\mathrm{k}-1)(\gamma_\mathrm{d}\mathrm{l}_\mathrm{d}+\gamma_\mathrm{g}\mathrm{l}_\mathrm{g})/2]}{\sinh[(\gamma_\mathrm{d}\mathrm{l}_\mathrm{d}+\gamma_\mathrm{g}\mathrm{l}_\mathrm{g})/2]},\\
B1 &= \mathrm{e}^{-\mathrm{k}\gamma_\mathrm{g}\mathrm{l}_\mathrm{g}} \times \mathrm{e}^{-(\mathrm{N}-\mathrm{k})(\gamma_\mathrm{d}\mathrm{l}_\mathrm{d}+\gamma_\mathrm{g}\mathrm{l}_\mathrm{g})/2} \times \frac{\sinh[(\mathrm{N}-\mathrm{k}+1)(\gamma_\mathrm{d}\mathrm{l}_\mathrm{d}+\gamma_\mathrm{g}\mathrm{l}_\mathrm{g})/2]}{\sinh[(\gamma_\mathrm{d}\mathrm{l}_\mathrm{d}+\gamma_\mathrm{g}\mathrm{l}_\mathrm{g})/2]},\\
B2 &= \mathrm{e}^{-(2\mathrm{N}-\mathrm{k})\gamma_\mathrm{g}\mathrm{l}_\mathrm{g}} \times \mathrm{e}^{-(\mathrm{N}-\mathrm{k})(\gamma_\mathrm{d}\mathrm{l}_\mathrm{d}-\gamma_\mathrm{g}\mathrm{l}_\mathrm{g})/2} \times \frac{\sinh[(\mathrm{N}-\mathrm{k}+1)(\gamma_\mathrm{d}\mathrm{l}_\mathrm{d}-\gamma_\mathrm{g}\mathrm{l}_\mathrm{g})/2]}{\sinh[(\gamma_\mathrm{d}\mathrm{l}_\mathrm{d}-\gamma_\mathrm{g}\mathrm{l}_\mathrm{g})/2]}.
\end{aligned} \tag{7.3}$$

The load line impedance for all transistors can then be obtained:

$$Z_{dk} = \frac{V_{dk}}{I_{dk}} = \frac{V_{dk}}{g_m V_{gk}}. \tag{7.4}$$

If the same load line impedance can be maintained for all transistors, their power performance can be optimized simultaneously. For lossless T-line as in the case for GHz region applications at PCB level, it can be achieved by maintaining a same phase shift ±nπ (n=0,1,2...) of both gate and drain lines:

$$Z_{dk} = NZ_d \quad when\ \beta_d l_d = \beta_g l_g = \pm n\pi\ (n = 0, 1, 2\ldots) \tag{7.5}$$

where β_g and β_d are the phase constants for T-lines on gate and drain paths, respectively. In this case, all transistors can be fully utilized, and efficiency of the whole amplifier depends on that of each transistor. For example, for class-A amplifier design, the optimized efficiency can be achieved by implementing: $Z_{dk} = (V_{max} - V_{min})/I_{max}$, where V_{max} and V_{min} are the maximum and minimum output voltage for class A operation and I_{eax} is the maximum output current.

The improvement in efficiency can also be observed through the improvement in power gain. With (7.5) satisfied, the power gain can be calculated as:

$$Gain = \frac{P_{out}}{P_{in}} = 4N^2 g_m^2 Z_g Z_d \tag{7.6}$$

which is 16 times larger than the conventional distributed amplifier with the same number (N) of transistors.

However, for on-chip distributed amplifier design at 60GHz and beyond, T-lines can no longer be assumed as ideal. Large parasitic components of transistors which are absorbed into the T-line design further degrade its performance. Both loss and phase error on the T-line can severely degrade amplifier performance, and therefore should be taken into consideration with detailed analysis as shown below.

7.3.1.3 Effect of T-Line Loss on SEDFDA

As frequency pushes up into the mm-wave region and transistor size shrinks down to below 100nm, the lossy substrate, thin metal layer, and strong coupling between them severely degrades the quality factor of passive components. What is worse, the large and low-Q parasitics of the transistor, which are absorbed into the T-line design, can severely degrade the effective Q-factor of T-line. For a practical on-chip amplifier such as the PA design at 60GHz, loss on T-line must be taken into consideration.

Recall that (7.5) and (7.6) assumed ideal T-lines in both gate and drain paths, i.e., where α_g and α_d are the attenuation constants for T-lines on gate and drain paths, respectively. For the practical on-chip design, α_A and α_d can no longer be assumed zero and are used to represent the loss on T-line. As a result, the conclusion in (7.6) can be affected.

The impact of T-line loss to the SEDFDA design is further illustrated by one simulation example. Figure 7.4 shows the impact of T-line loss on SEDFDA power gain. Here g_m is assumed to be 20mS and characteristic impedance on both gate and drain lines are set as 50ω. Loss per distributed

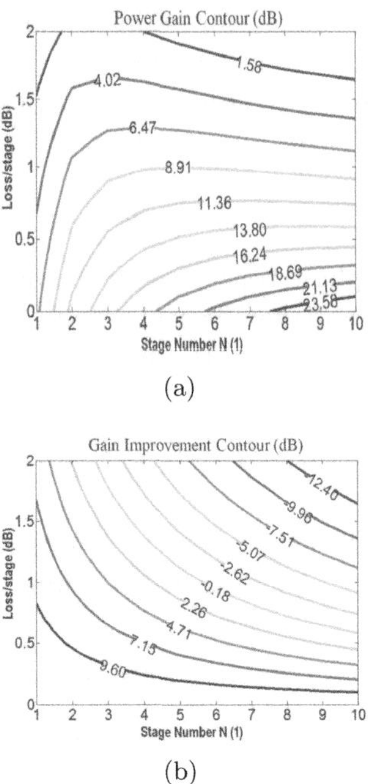

Figure 7.4: Effect of T-line loss on SEDFDA performance.

stage on T-lines are defined as $\alpha_g l_g$ $(\alpha_d l_d)$ and assumed identical on both gate and drain paths. As Figure 7.4(e) shows, loss on the T-line severely degrades the power gain in an exponential manner. For example, for a 10-stage SEDFDA, the power gain reduces from above 25dB to below 0dB as loss on the T-line increases from 0dB/stage to 2dB/stage. It can also be observed that the impact of loss on power gain becomes more severe as the number of stages (N) increases. This can be understood because as N increases the signal needs to propagate through more lossy stages to the output and therefore it experiences more degradation. As a result, there exists an optimum N for a specific value of loss in order to achieve the highest power gain. This optimum N decreases as loss per stage increases. In other words, loss on the T-line limits the maximum number of stages that can be implemented in the SEDFDA.

The advantage of SEDFDA over the conventional distributed amplifier is its improvement on power gain and efficiency. As (7.6) shows, an ideal SEDFDA can improve power gain by 12dB, and improves the efficiency proportionally. However, as loss in T-line increases, this advantage gradually diminishes. Figure 7.4(b) shows the impact of T-line loss on the power gain improvement, which is calculated by dividing the obtained power gain by the power gain of a conventional distributed amplifier with the same number of stages and with ideal T-line. As shown in Figure 7.4(b), in a high-loss region the gain ratio decreases below 0dB. This effect again becomes more severe as N increases. In other words, loss on the T-line again limits the maximum number of stages (N) that can be implemented in the distributed amplifier. For example, with loss of 2dB per stage, SEDFDA with stage number above 2 can have no advantage over conventional topology (with ideal T-line) on power and efficiency performance. Note that although identical loss is assumed on both gate and drain lines for easy simulation, a similar conclusion can be drawn if divergent losses are used.

7.3.1.4 Effect of T-Line Phase Error on SEDFDA

As mentioned above, the performance of SEDFDA is optimized when phase shift in both gate and drain lines are identical and equals to ±mπ (n=0,1,2...). It is relatively easy to keep identical phase shift in gate and drain line, but very difficult to maintain the phase shift to a fixed value. The major reason is that phase shift in T-line is often frequency dependent. At 60GHz and beyond it is very expensive to implement phase compensation with extra circuits, and the large process variation further degrades the problem. Here we denote the difference between actual phase shift and target value as the "phase error" and analyze its impact on SEDFDA power performance.

Recall that to obtain the conclusions in (7.5) and (7.6) the phase shift condition $\beta_d l_d = \beta_g l_g = \pm n\pi (n = 0, 1, 2\ldots)$ must be satisfied, where β_g and β_d are the phase constants for T-lines. The identical phase shift ($\beta_d l_d = \beta_g l_g$) is relatively easier to achieve and is assumed βl. Since we target a phase shift of ±nπ, the phase error can then be represented as $mod(\beta l, \pi)$.

Figure 7.5 shows the simulation result, with the same parameters used as an Figure 7.4. The phase error per stage is swept from -20° to +20°. As Figure 7.5 shows, the power gain degrades as phase error increases. Since phase error is normally proportional to frequency shift, this gain drop determines the bandwidth of SEDFDA. It also explains the trade-off of SEDFDA bandwidth over the conventional distributed amplifier, since the conventional topology only requires identical phase shift in gate and drain lines, and therefore has no such bandwidth limitation.

It can be observed again that as number of stages (N) increases, the power gain degradation by phase error becomes more severe. As a result, phase error on T-line also limits the maximum number of stages that can be implemented in SEDFDA.

7.3.1.5 CRLH T-Line-Based SEDFDA

As discussed above, both loss and phase error of T-line can degrade SEDFDA performance and also limit the number of stages (N) to be implemented. As will be shown in the following session, the value of N affects the power handling capability of the proposed Po topology when using SEDFDA. A T-line that can achieve a phase shift of ±nπ (n=0,1,2...) with low loss and small phase

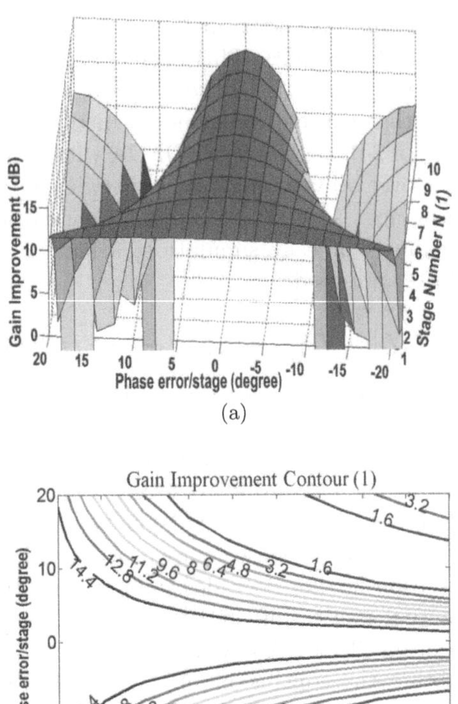

Figure 7.5: Effect of T-line phase error on SEDFDA performance: (a) 3D diagram, (b) contour diagram.

error is thereby required. Unfortunately, a 0° phase shift cannot be obtained in nature when using the traditional T-line since its phase-shift is proportional to a non-zero length. As a result, $\lambda/2$ T-line is used instead at PCB level for SEDFDA design, which achieves a phase shift of 180°. When implemented on chip, this T-line is very bulky and lossy. Furthermore, its large phase shift (π) means a small percentage change can lead to a large phase error, which severely limits the bandwidth. As a result, a traditional T-line approach is impractical for on-chip implementation of SEDFDA.

Alternatively, one non-resonant type metamaterial T-line called CRLH T-line is shown to be able to achieve a real zero-phase-shift, and can be utilized to replace $\lambda/2$ RH T-line for SEDFDA-based on-chip PA design at 60GHz with compact size, low loss and wide bandwidth.

Except for compact T-tine size itself, zero-phase CRLH T-line also allows more compact design of the whole distributed amplifier topology. In distributed amplifier design, as parasitic capacitance in transistor is to be absorbed into the T-line design, the effective T-line is realized with the lumped model. Figure 7.6 shows the lumped model of a traditional RH T-line. By equalizing Z_n and Z_{n+1}, following impedance is obtained:

$$Z_n = Z_{n+1} = \sqrt{\frac{L}{C} - \left(\frac{\omega L}{2}\right)^2} + j\frac{\omega L}{2}, \tag{7.7}$$

where n is the distributed stage number, which is the cut-off frequency of traditional RH T-line. At low frequency, the term approaches 0, and Z_n is roughly equal to the T-line characteristic impedance $Z_o = \sqrt{\frac{L}{C}}$. However, as $\frac{\omega L}{2}$ becomes more significant at higher frequency, Z_n deviates from Z_o, causing an impedance mismatch which degrades distributed amplifier's gain. Furthermore, as the Smith Chart in Figure 7.2 shows, due to the additional term, the obtained Z_n moves in a circle near Z_o as n changed. The radius of this circle increases as $\frac{\omega L}{2}$ increases, leading to large impedance variation in different distributed stages. As a result, the power performance is degraded as transistors cannot be optimized simultaneously. In order to achieve proper operation in high frequency such as the mm-wave region, the inductance L needs to be reduced to keep $\frac{\omega L}{2}$ small. For a given Z_o, the capacitance C needs to be reduced proportionally. As large portion of C cores from parasitic capacitance in transistor, the transistor size in each distribution stage has to be reduced as well. As a result, in order to maintain the total transistor size and thus output power, more distributed stages need to be designed, which leads to larger layout size and lower output power density.

Zero-phase CRLH T-line, on the other hand, does not have this problem. As illustrated by Figure 7.3, the impedance at each distributed stage can be matched exactly to the designed impedance and is irrelevant to the transistor parasitic or designed frequency. As a result, large transistor size can be adopted with reduced distributed stages, leading to a compact distributed amplification.

7.3.2 ZPS-Based 2D Distributed Power Combining for PA

Since low output power/output power density and narrow bandwidth are two primary design challenges for CMOS PA it 60GHz, a new power combining topology is introduced to simultaneously improve PA's output power and bandwidth performance. One straightforward approach is to merge one power combining topology with high power combining efficiency and distributed amplification with wide bandwidth.

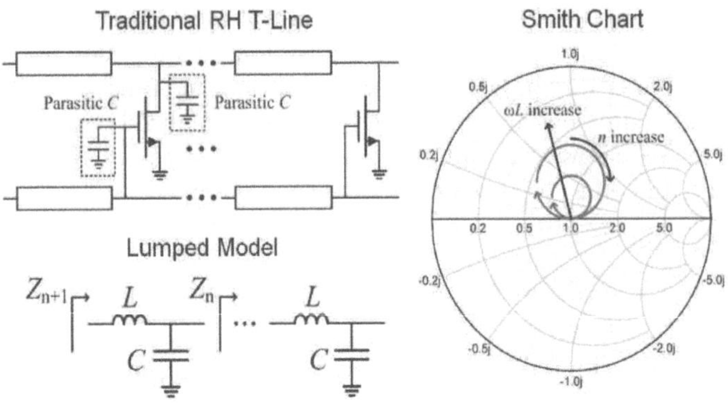

Figure 7.6: Traditional right-handed T-line analysis: lumped model and Smith Chart. Impedance on Smith Chart is obtained by loading the theoretical characteristic impedance Z_o and varying both parameter ωL and stage number n.

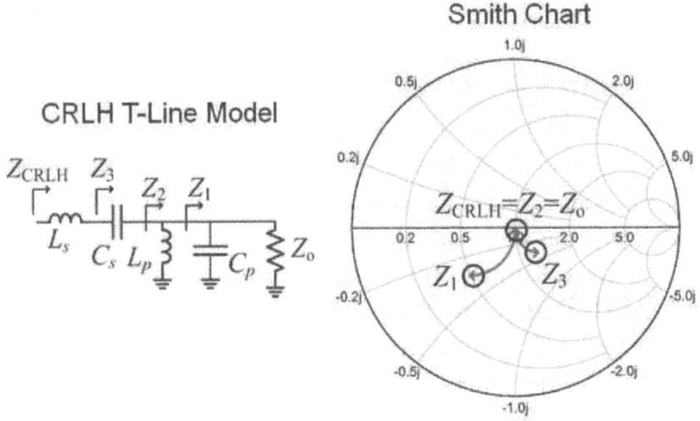

Figure 7.7: Zero-phase CRLH T-line analysis: lumped model and Smith chart. Impedance at various nodes of CRLH T-line model is plotted on Smith Chart.

7.3.2.1 Design Optimization of ZPS-Based Power Combining

A detailed design consideration can be viewed in Figure 7.8. With bandwidth performance fulfilled with distributed nature of the proposed topology, PAE and output power density (P_{out}/area) become two major targets during PA design. By knowing the application for the PA, the proper PA class can then

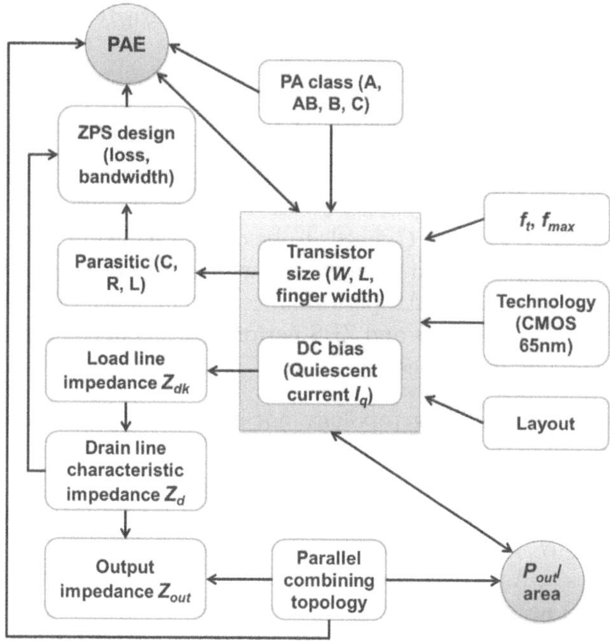

Figure 7.8: Design consideration for the proposed 2D distributed power combining network.

be selected. Together with the selected technology, f_t/f_{max} optimization, PAE and P_{out}/area requirement, and layout skills, the sizing and biasing of the transistors can be initially determined.

However, the inter-dependency between parameters calls for certain design iterations. There are mainly three considerations shown in the diagram that may require design iterations.

1. To improve the power density performance (P_{out}/area), large size is preferred for transistors. However, large transistor size brings large parasitic components, which are the major contributions for L_s and C_p in ZPS design, which leads to small L_p and C_s to maintain the same operating frequency, which in turn causes high loss and narrow bandwidth for the designed ZPS. As a result, PAE is degraded. A compromise therefore needs to be made between P_{out}/area and PAE.

2. DC bias of transistors determines PA operating class. Both P_{ont} and PAE performances for a single transistor is also determined by the bias. However, DC bias of transistors affects ZPS design through its optimized load line impedance. As shown in the diagram, given DC bias, for optimized performance of all transistors, the load line impedance (Z_{dk}) is

determined, which in turn determines the characteristic impedance of the drain line (s_d).

A balanced condition ($\omega_s = \omega_p$) is preferred for optimized ZPS performance, which leads to a characteristic impedance of $Z_o = \sqrt{\frac{L_p}{C_s}} = \sqrt{\frac{L_s}{C_p}}$ according to (). However, the actual parasitic reactance from transistors (L_s ' and C_p ') is unlikely to follow the above relation for L_s and C_p. As a result, the size of L_t or C_p needs to be over-designed to generate wanted i_d. Again, high loss and narrow bandwidth are caused for the designed ZPS, which degrades PAE performance. In summary, PAE is affected by both transistor DC bias and ZPS performance, and a compromise needs to be made between these two parts.

3. The parallel combining topology not only affects P_{out}/area and PAE performances directly through its efficiency, but also affects them indirectly through the output matching. As stated in (7.5), with a fixed load line impedance Z_{dk}, the characteristic impedance for the drain line is $Z_d = Z_{dk}/N$, where N is the distributed stages. Assuming M distributed amplifiers (DAs) are combined in parallel, the output impedance can be calculated as $Z_{out} = Z_{dk}/(MN)$ if the Z_d for all DAs are combined in parallel, which is the case for zero-degree power combiner.

   Though the combiner has the benefit of merging part of the DA design into itself with reduced loss, a large combining network (large MN) may lead to very small output impedance and degrade the whole PA performance. In this case, other combining topologies which can combine the Z_d for all DAs in serial may be used, which generates output impedance of $Z_{out} = MZ_{dk}/N$ instead, thus relaxing the stress on output matching. This is the case for transformer combiners.

In summary, selections and design iterations may be made to choose the most suitable power combining topology. Note that a zero-degree tower combiner is selected for parallel combining in one single-ended PA prototype with a small 2×2 combining network; while transformers are further implemented in differential PA prototypes with larger combining networks.

7.3.2.2 Differential Design

The aforementioned 2D distributed power combining topology in Figure 7.8 is implemented in single-ended manner. However, due to the single-ended topology with a large matching network deployed, the benefit to achieve wide-band high-density power combining is not fully demonstrated.

In this section, we introduce a differential 2D power combining network for 60GHz PA design in 65nm CMOS with further improved output power density. Transformer matching and neutralization capacitor are also deployed to enable a larger power combining network with further improved PA performance.

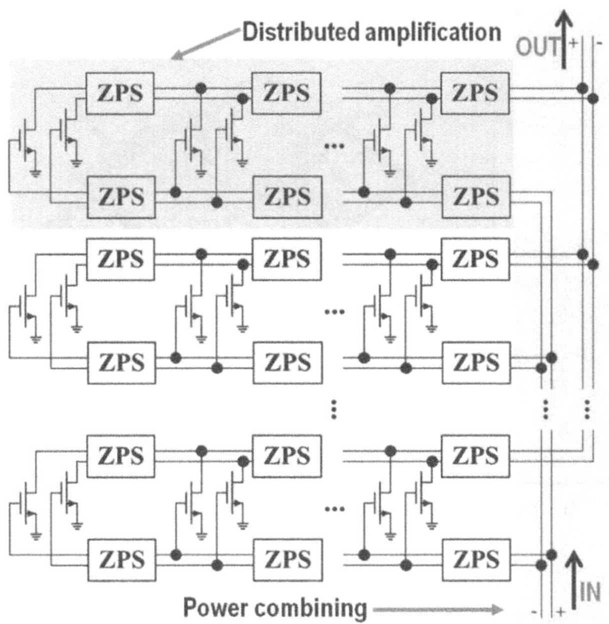

Figure 7.9: Differential version of proposed SEDFDA PA topology based on 2D distributed power combining network with the use of CRLH ZPSs.

With the use of differential CRLH T-line-based ZPS designed, one differential 2D power combining network can be realized as shown in Figure 7.9, with benefits of reduced area due to merged parallel inductors and the elimination of de-coupling capacitors. Moreover, loss is also reduced due to confined EM field and nullified parasitic at virtual ground in the differential topology. In addition, the differential topology also allows easy implementation of techniques such as transformer matching and neutralization capacitor. Transformer matching provides DC isolation with easy biasing and compact area. Neutralization capacitor improves stabilization, simplifies matching, and also boosts gain with minimized external loss.

There are, however, two design challenges for the proposed differential topology. First, for a differential implementation, it is desired to design the circuit as symmetric as possible. An asymmetric implementation would cause mismatch in the differential signals and degrade the pre-mentioned benefits. However, since transistor pairs, differential ZPS, and differential input and output terminals are all connected together, it is almost impossible to have a fully symmetric implementation. Second, the input and output terminals in Figure 7.9 are on the same side of the power combining network. This would

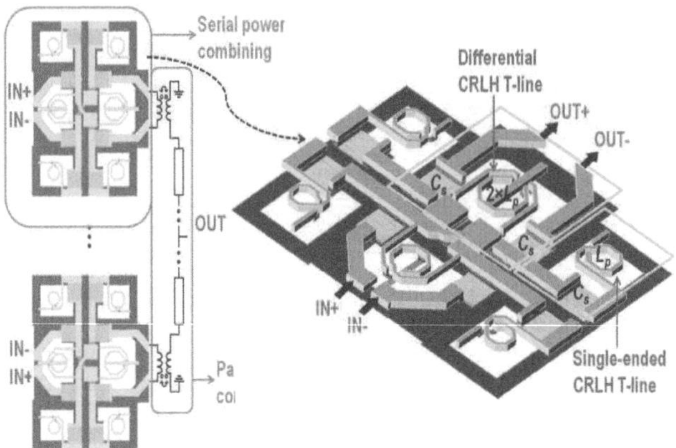

Figure 7.10: The proposed layout for differential 2D power combining network.

lead to long overlapped interconnection, which severely increases parasitics and degrades performance.

To solve the above-mentioned problems, one novel differential 2D power combining network is proposed in Figure 7.10. For each differential gate-line and drain-line, the differential ZPS is implemented in the first distributed stage only. The differential signals then flow into separate directions to 2 single-ended ZPSs on both sides. In this way, the differential topology can be maintained highly symmetrical, while input and output terminals are placed on opposite sides of the power combining network. Though some of the ZPSs are realized single-ended, the whole topology is still differential, allowing techniques such as transformer matching and neutralization capacitor toward compact matching and stabilization.

7.3.3 Stabilization Techniques

Stability is an important concern for all amplifier designs. Normally, additional circuit components or special amplifier topologies are required which either degrade PA's performance or have more stringent system requirements. In this section detailed analysis is provided for PA stabilization methods at mm-wave frequencies and possible solutions to minimize the risk of instability while maintaining PA performance from degradation.

7.3.3.1 Common PA Stabilization Techniques

Neutralization

In the mm-wave region, parasitic capacitance between gate and drain terminals of the transistor forms a feedback loop in common source amplifiers, which degrades both power gain and stabilization. For differential topology, a neutralization technique has been widely used recently [72, 204, 205, 206] to neutralize the feedback signal by introducing a negative path from the drain of one differential transistor to the gate of the other transistor. As shown in Figure 7.11, by introducing neutralization capacitors C_{neu} with similar capacitive coupling as the parasitic gate-drain capacitance C_{gd}, the feedback from the differential outputs cancel each other, and the PA can therefore be stabilized.

Neutralization technique is widely used recently for differential PA due to several advantages. Firstly, the topology is very simple. Only two very small capacitors are required with almost no layout overhead. Secondly, by neutralization of the feedback from C_{gd}, S12 of PA approaches 0. The amplifier becomes near unilateral, thus making input and output matching independent of each other, which greatly simplifies the matching process. Thirdly, C_{neu} actually introduces a positive feedback loop. By properly choosing C_{neu} value, in addition to achieving stabilization, the gain of PA can be slightly boosted.

However, the neutralization technique does have some limitations. Firstly, this technique is sensitive to process variation because the PA is only stable within a small region of C_{neu} values. In fact, with a large C_{neu} value the topology shown in Figure 7.11 becomes a cross-coupled transistor pair commonly

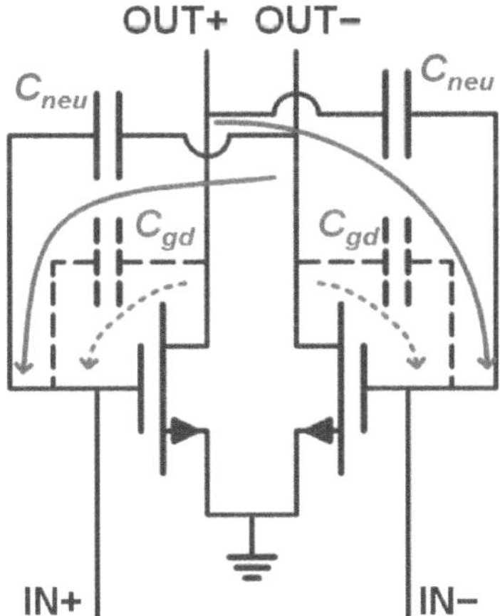

Figure 7.11: Neutralization technique for PA stabilization.

used in VCO to generate a negative resistor. As a result, the PA becomes a VCO. Secondly, due to additional capacitance loaded on the transistors, the parasitic of transistors almost doubled. This effect is more significant for input matching and for more advanced technology, as the gate impedance locates near the edge of Smith Chart, making the impedance matching narrow band.

Cascode

Cascode topology is commonly used at lower frequency regions for stabilization. It also helps to reduce the Miller effect from C_{gd} and improve power gain. In addition, cascade topology also shows on advantage for advanced technology with low break-down voltages. Due to serial connection of transistor junctions, a higher supply voltage can be used, thus increasing the achievable output power. However, as frequency pushes higher, the large capacitance at the source of cascode transistor ($C_{gs}+C_{gd}$) would cause performance degradation. A matching network such as a serial inductor L_s can be added between the cascode transistor and the common-source transistor [197, 207]. As shown in Figure 7.12, the added inductor (L_s) resonates out the two parasitic capacitors (C_{gt} and C_{gd}) by forming a low-pass filter. The penalty is additional area and loss introduced by the serial inductor. A hybrid design is commonly used where the previous stages are realized by cascode for stability and higher gain, while the power combining stage is realized by common source topology for better efficiency [197], which however requires multiple supply voltage levels. Nevertheless, at 60GHz, normal cascode topology can still function properly without inserted matching network, and is used to achieve a higher

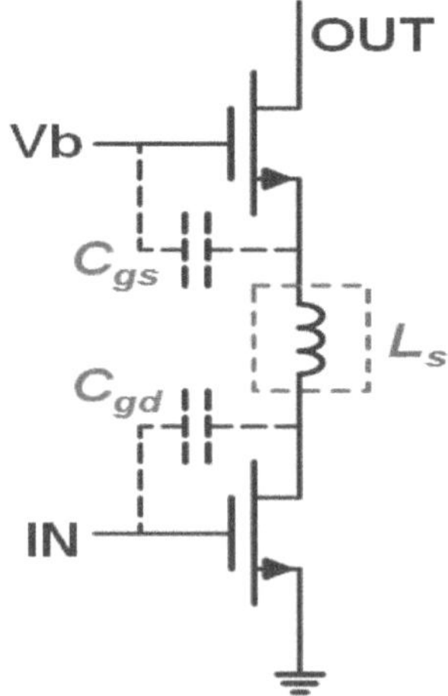

Figure 7.12: Cascode topology for PA stabilization.

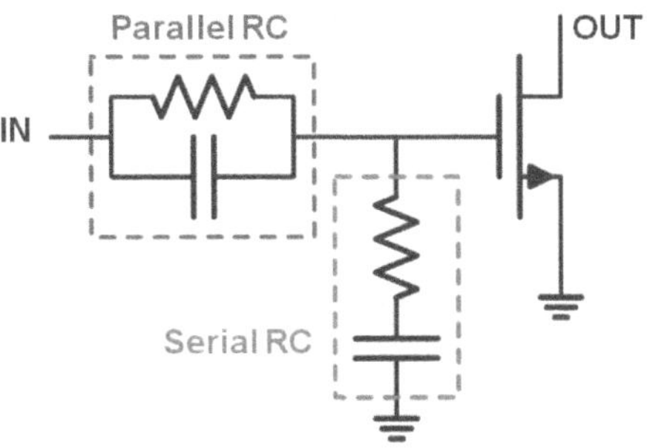

Figure 7.13: RC networks for PA stabilization.

output power with the requirement of a higher supply voltage such as 2V [192, 196, 208, 209, 210].

RC Network

The most conventional technique for PA stabilization is to use an RC network [211, 195]. As shown in Figure 7.13, with serial or parallel RC networks, high- and low-frequency regions can be stabilized, respectively. More specifically, a parallel RC network put in serial connection forms a high pass topology, with larger serial resistance introduced at lower frequency region, thus stabilizing the new frequency. Similarly, a serial RC network put in parallel connection forms a low pass topology, with smaller parallel resistance introduced at higher frequency region, thus stabilizing the high frequency. These stabilization techniques can be used by itself or work together with other techniques. Its penalty is obvious. To achieve a targeted stabilization level, additional losses are often introduced in the operating region, degrading PA's power gain and efficiency.

Technique Selection

Three stabilization techniques are summarized above. There are other stabilization techniques. For example, by properly designing the matching network, the PA can be stabilization without using additional devices [194, 212]. However, as the matching needs to take stabilization into design consideration, the performance of PA may not be fully optimized.

Based on the above analysis, the neutralization technique shows the best performance without additional requirements and is selected in this work. Although other techniques such as cascode topology and RC network may be less sensitive to process variation, additional performance penalties or system requirements can be caused.

In addition to the above introduced stabilization techniques, automatic digital control could also be used to mitigate PVT-variations [10, 213]. In the following section, a power detector is implemented to quantify the output power level with a DC signal. This DC signal could then be used for possible self-healing or automatic digital control of PA.

7.3.4 Digital Control

As mentioned above, automatic digital control could also be used to mitigate PVT-variations [10, 213]. High frequency in the mm-wave region and scaled CMOS transistor size below 100nm make transistor performance susceptible go process variation and make accurate modeling of both active and passive elements very challenging. Furthermore, power amplifier consumes large DC power and normally generates a high temperature variation. All these variations would cause the power transistor to deviate from its optimal operating point, which degrades performances much as output power, efficiency, linearity, gain and stability. Furthermore, the operating environment is also likely to vary, such as the variation of antenna load impedance. Aging is another concern, where transistor performance would gradually change with time. Automatic digital control provides solutions to all the above issues. With a feedback loop designed for self-healing, the PA biasing and matching can be automatically tuned for optimal performance.

Except to maintain optimum PA performance, another important function which can be provided by automatic digital control is to prevent circuit destruction [88]. The low breakdown voltage provided by scaled CMOS technologies makes transistors vulnerable to environment change. For example, a mismatch in antenna load impedance may cause a peak voltage higher than the breakdown voltage. With automatic digital control, biasing point of transistor can be monitored and controlled in the safe region, and emergency shutdown can also be provided. Furthermore, external testing contributes a large portion of expense for circuit production. With the help of on-chip feedback and digital control, a built-in self-test (BIST) mechanism can be provided which is much cheaper [10]. In addition, digital control is explored and implemented for the power back-off.

7.3.4.1 Power Back-Off in PA

Power back-off is often required for PA to conserve battery power, avoid interference with adjacent channels, and fulfill linearity requirement for adopted modulation scheme [214, 215, 216]. The power back-off is usually realized from baseband side by reducing input power to PA. Note that the high output power efficiency region for PA normally locates near P_{1dB} and P_{sat} points. When input power is reduced, the PA operating point is pulled away from the high-efficiency region, leading to a large power waste, which is even worse for CMOS PA design at 60GHz. To maintain high output power efficiency, digital control can be introduced in PA design with back-off realized by self-tuning, which reduces the PA output power along with DC power to maintain a high efficiency.

There are many techniques to enhance PA output power efficiency for back-off. A few were successfully implemented at 60GHz and beyond [204, 214, 215, 216]. Architectures such as the Doherty amplifier, out-phasing, and envelope elimination and restoration (BER) show boosted back-off efficiency at low-frequency regions, but have high design complexity or large power consumption from digital data pre-processing [216]. Multi-mode operation by turning on and off a different number of PA units is another popular technique at low frequency [217, 218, 219, 220, 221, 222, 223], but with two critical design issues at high frequency: power leakage to the PA units that are switched off, and mismatching due to the impedance variation of PA units at different modes [214]. There are two recent works [204, 214] with successful implementations of multi-mode operation at 60GHz. The work in [204] tunes the matching by shorting part of the power combiner, but the obtained PAE for low-power mode has a large degradation compared with high-power mode. The work in [214] isolates the PA units in power-off made by implementing a bulky quasi-quarter-wavelength transmission line to prevent current leakage.

In this work, power back-off is realized by controlling the current biasing of transistors without PA switched off during power tack-off. It thus avoids the power leakage and impedance mismatch issues in [204, 205, 206, 207, 208, 209, 210, 10, 213, 11, 214]. As DC power consumption is reduced along with output power, high output power efficiency can be maintained.

7.3.4.2 Power Detection

On chip power detection is widely used in mm-wave regions [10, 213, 11, 12, 13]. In addition to providing dynamic bias control to mitigate the effect of process, voltage and temperature variations (PVT-variations) [10, 213], it can also be used to cope with antenna impedance mismatch [10, 11], realize low-cost on-chip built-in self-test (BIST) [10, 12], and provide VSWR protection with consideration for transistor breakdown and system overload by offering protection mechanisms such as emergency shutdown [10].

As shown in Figure 7.14, a power detection unit is normally formed by two parts: a power coupler which senses the output power level, and a power detector which transfers the sensed signal's power level to a DC signal. Different topologies are analyzed and designed in this section for power coupler and power detector, respectively.

Power Coupler

Power coupler senses the output power by coupling a fraction of the output signal. In mm-wave regions, two types of power couplers are found in literature. The first type (Figure 7.15(a)), which is also the more common one, is to use a capacitive coupling from the transmission line feeding to the output port [10, 11, 12]. The capacitive coupling level is usually designed low so that the

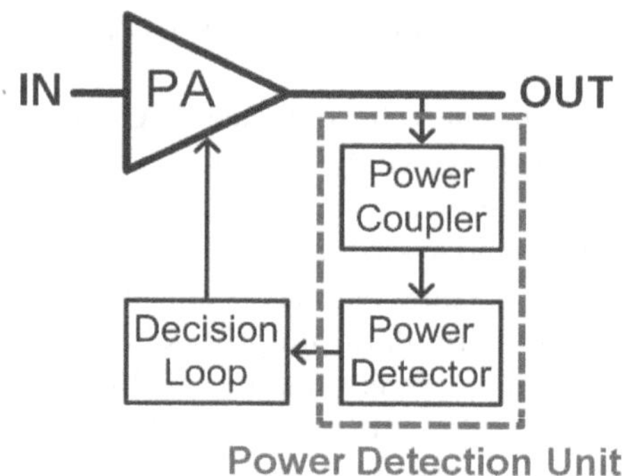

Figure 7.14: Power detection unit.

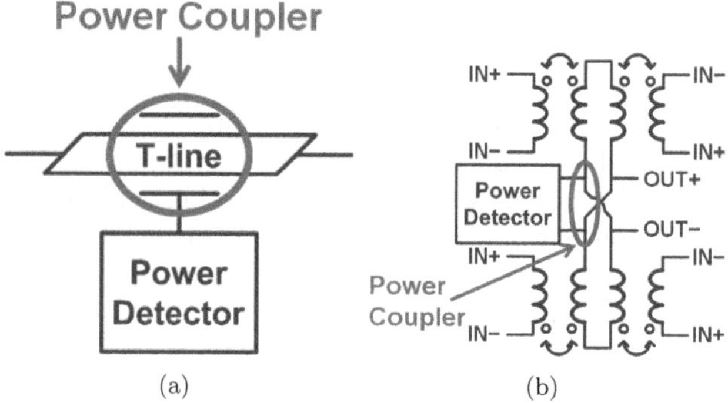

Figure 7.15: Power coupler topologies: (a) capacitive coupling from output [10, 11, 12]; (b) direct connection from output [13].

output level is merely affected. The coupled signal often goes underneath the T-line (and its ground if it's CPW topology) and suffers more loss from the substrate. Considering the low coupling level, the sensitivity of power detection is low. The second type of power coupler (Figure 7.15(b)) is proposed in [13], with the power coupler merged into the DAT power combiner. The power coupling is achieved through direct line connection. As a result, the output power level would be affected, and the input impedance for power detector must be considered as part of the output matching network. The benefit is the easy connection to power detector and high sensitivity of the power detection unit.

In this work, power detection is designed with the objective to control the DC power along with output power and improve PA efficiency during power

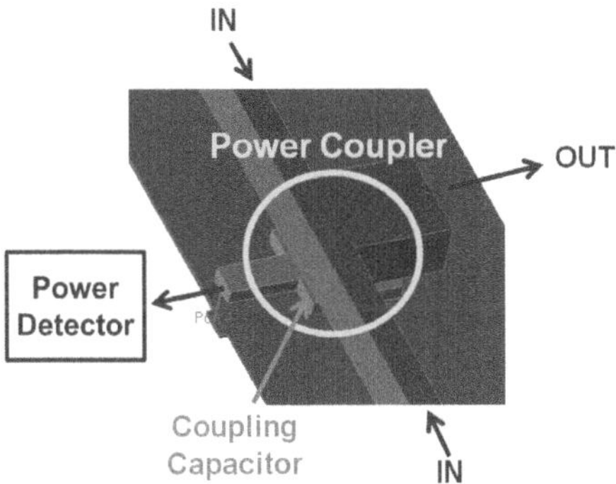

Figure 7.16: Designed capacitive power coupler.

back-off. Therefore, the degradation on output power level caused by power detection needs to be minimized, while the sensitivity requirement on power detection is not critical and can be relaxed. As a result, the first type of power coupler is selected. The designed layout is shown in Figure 7.16. A metal-plate capacitor is implemented at the conjunction of a two-branch combiner. The combiner is implemented at top metal level, and the coupled signal is fed to the power detector through the second top metal level. Since micro-strip topology is adopted for transmission line design, the resulting power coupler is very compact.

Power Detector

In the mm-wave region, square-law power detector is commonly used for on-chip applications [10, 11], with the simplified schematic shown in Figure 7.17. Coupled signals are fed into differential transistor pair Mn1 and Mn2, with their output terminals connected together. With an input signal of $V_{IN} \pm V_{ac}cos\omega t$, the combined current flowing through the two transistors (I_d1+I_d2) can be approximated with a simple square-law equation for CMOS transistors:

$$\begin{aligned} I_d1 + I_d2 &= K_n\left(2\overline{V_{eff}}^2 + 2V_{ac}^2cos^2\omega t\right) \\ &= K_n\left(2\overline{V_{eff}}^2 + V_{ac}^2cos2\omega t + V_{ac}^2\right) \end{aligned} \tag{7.8}$$

where $\overline{V_{eff}} = V_{IN} - V_{th}$ is an offset which can be canceled through current mirror. K_n is the coefficient in square-law equation for NMOS transistors Mn1 and Mn2. The amplitude of the AC signal is represented by V_{ac}.

When this current is mirrored through the low-pass filter, the high frequency term $V_{ac}^2cos2\omega t$ is filtered out. As a result, the output current I_{out} becomes proportional to V_{ac}^2, which represents the power level of the AC sig-

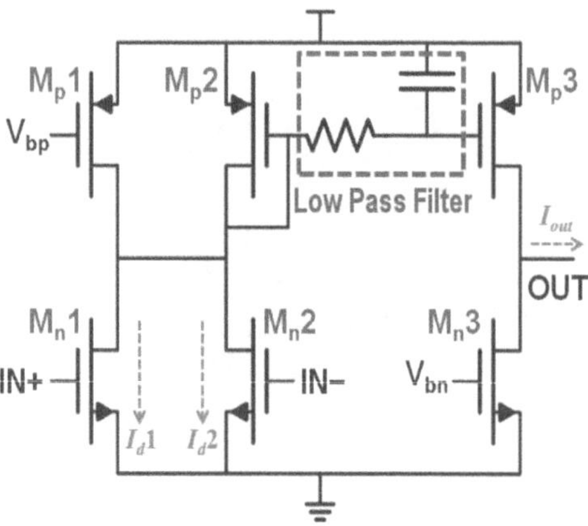

Figure 7.17: Square-law power detector.

nal (P_{ac}):

$$I_{out} \propto V_{ac}^2 \propto P_{ac}. \tag{7.9}$$

As a result, the power level of input signal is detected and represented by the DC level at output terminal. In this work, however, the output signal is single-ended, and so is the sensed signal from power coupler, as shown in Figure 7.16. Therefore, the design in Figure 7.17 is modified to single-ended, as shown in Figure 7.18. Although the fundamental and odd harmonics of the AC signal can no longer cancel each other as the differential power detector does, they can still be filtered out by the low-pass filter as the 60GHz operating frequency is far away from DC.

7.3.4.3 Digital Control System

The implemented digital control system is shown in Figure 7.19. The power level of PA output is detected by an on-chip power detector, and is converted to a digital signal through an ADC that returns a digital input to configure the PA biasing current, which in turn controls the gain and power consumption of PA. The power detention unit, 3-bit ADC/DAC are realized on-chip, while digital signal processing is implemented off-chip. Detailed block designs are shown in the following section.

7.3.4.4 Circuit Design

Detailed circuit designs for digital control blocks such as power detection unit, 3-bis ADC/DAC, as well at the power amplifier design are presented in this section.

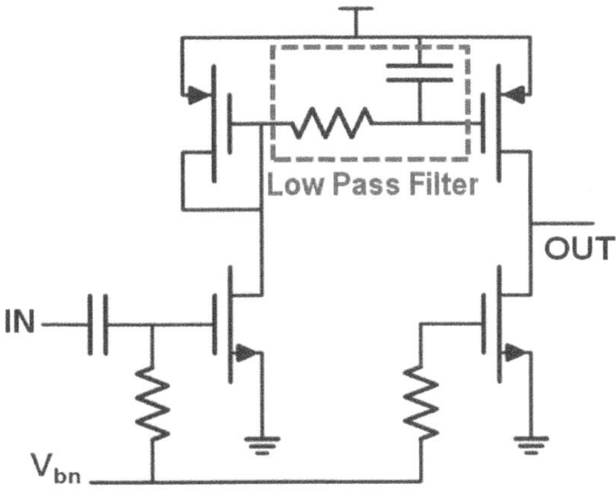

Figure 7.18: Designed single-ended square low power detector.

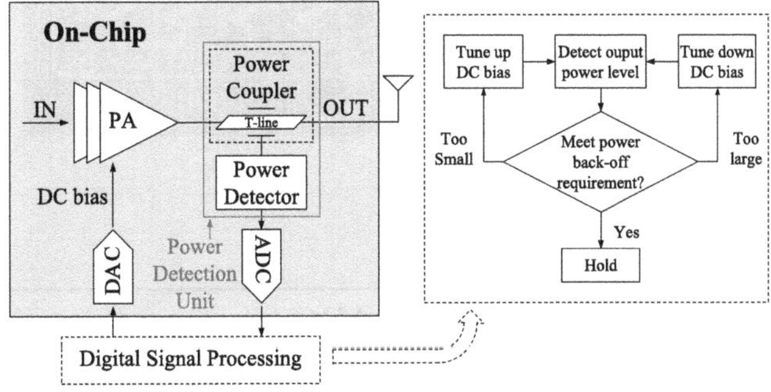

Figure 7.19: Designed digital control system.

Power Detection Unit

The design shown in Figure 7.16 is used for power detection with minimized degradation of the PA output power performance.

3-Bit ADC

A flash ADC topology is adopted in this work for its simple topology. As Figure 7.20(a) shows, the 3-bit flash ADC contains a resistor-array to generate reference voltages, 7 comparators to convert the analog input to digital signal, and a 8-to-3 encoder to convert the 7-bit thermometer code (D7D6D5D4D3D2D1) to 3-bit digital output (Q2Q1Q0).

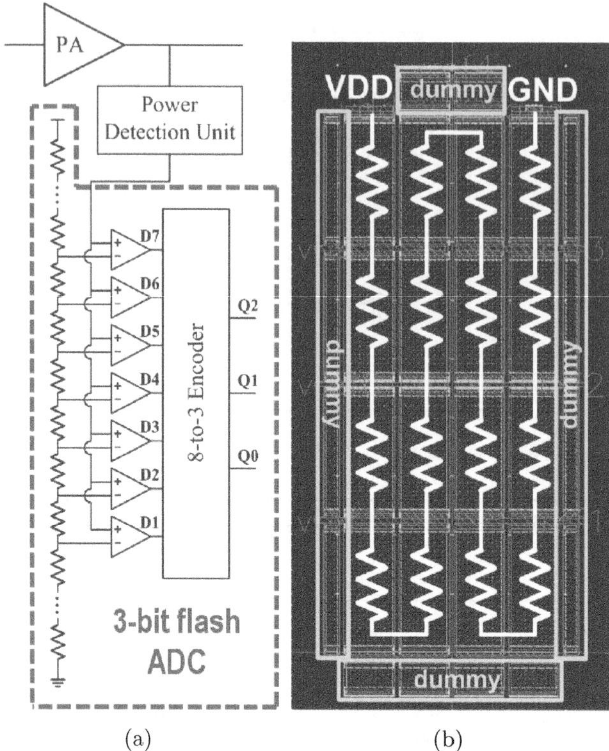

Figure 7.20: ADC design: (a) flash ADC topology; (b) resistor array to generate reference voltage.

The layout for the resistor array is shown in Figure 7.20(b), with 16 serial-connected resistors to generate 7 specific reference voltages from given power supply. Dummy resistors are used to reduce variation between resistor values.

Seven comparators are used to compare the analog input from power detector and each reference voltage, generating a 7-bit digital thermometer code. Due to different voltage levels of reference voltages, two types of comparators are designed, as shown in Figure 7.21. N-type comparator with NMOS input transistors is used to compare higher-level inputs, while a p-type comparator with PMOS input transistors is used to compare lower level inputs.

The obtained 7-bit thermometer code (D7D6D5D4D3D2D1) is then converted to 3-bit digital output (Q2Q1Q0) with a 8-to-3 encoder. The layout is designed based on NAND gate and invertors, as shown in Figure 7.22. The formula for the encoder is as follows:

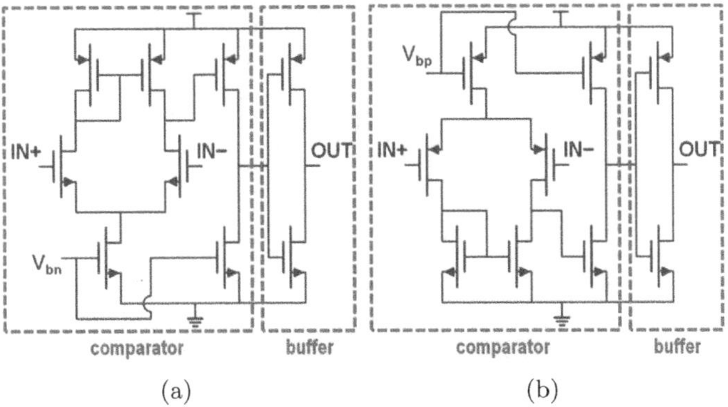

Figure 7.21: Comparator topologies for ADC design: (a) n-type; (b) p-type.

$$\begin{cases} Q0 = \overline{D6} \cdot \left(\overline{D4} \cdot \left(\overline{D2} \cdot D1 + D3\right) + D5\right) + D7 \\ Q1 = \overline{D5} \cdot \overline{D4} \cdot (D2 + D3) + D6 + D7 \\ Q2 = D4 + D5 + D6 + D7. \end{cases} \tag{7.10}$$

Note the digital inputs and their inverts $\overline{DX}$ are passed to the encoder through transmission gates and invertors to ensure a similar time delay.

3-Bit DAC

The DAC is used to control the PA's biasing current based on input digital signals. A simple comparator is designed to switch different biasing currents. As shown in Figure 7.23, by using 3 comparators, the obtained biasing current I_b can be controlled by the DAC inputs:

$$I_b = I_{ref} \times (4 \cdot DAC3 + 2 \cdot DAC2 + 1 \cdot DAC1), \tag{7.11}$$

where DAC3, DAC2, and DAC1 are the 3-bit digital input, with which the biasing current can be varied from I_{ref} to $7I_{ref}$.

7.4 Circuit Prototyping and Measurement

7.4.1 *60 GHz PA Design with Single-Ended 2×2 Power Combining*

One 60GHz Pt prototype with proposed 2D distributed power combining is implemented in UMC 65nm logic and mixed-mode low leakage low-K CMOS

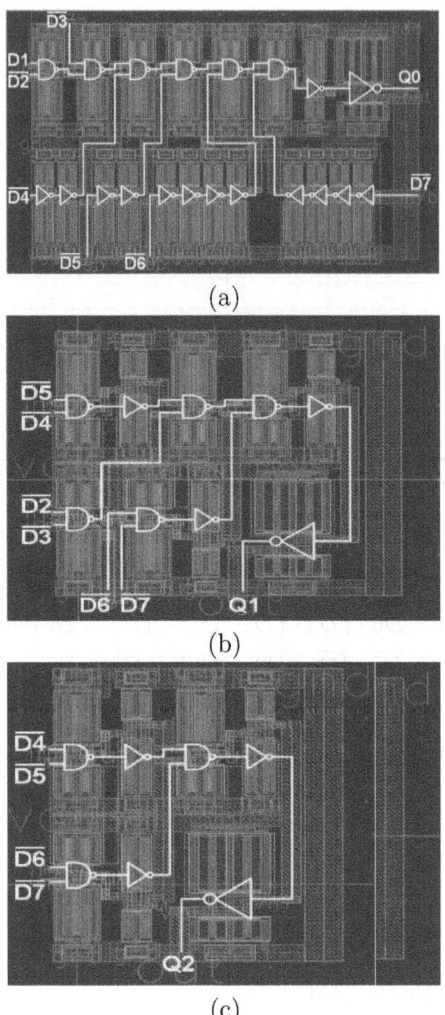

Figure 7.22: 8-to-3 encoder for ADC design: (a) Q0, (b) Q1, (c) Q2.

technology with 6-metal layers (1 thick metal layer). The circuit is designed and verified by EM simulation (ADS-Momentum) before fabrication.

7.4.1.1 60GHz PA Design

With ZPS designed and characterized, the proposed 2D distributed power combining network is implemented in a PA for demonstration [224]. As shown in Figure 7.24, a 2-stage PA is designed with a single transistor in the 1st

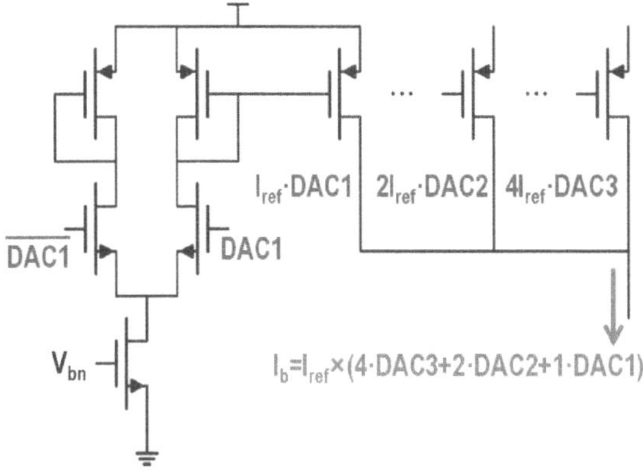

Figure 7.23: DAC topology.

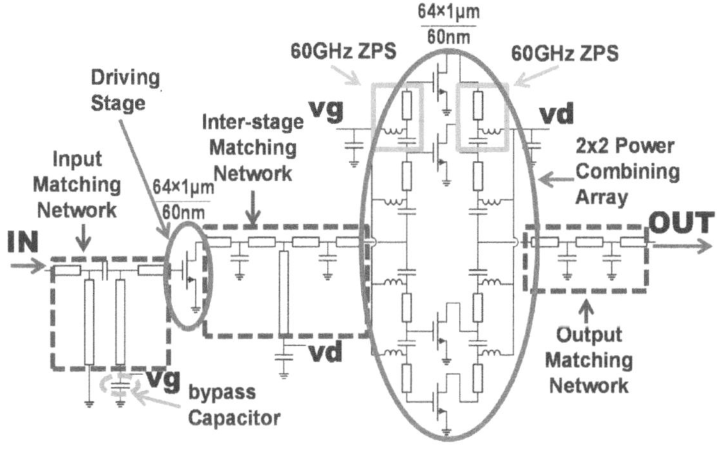

Figure 7.24: Schematic of 2-stage PA with a 2×2 distributed power combining network.

stage as a driver; and a 2×2 distributed power combining array in the 2nd stage, which has 2 power-combining branches and each branch has a 2-stage SEDFDA. All transistors are in single-ended common-source topology with transistor size of 64×1μm/60nm. With a biasing current of 22mA, the simulated f_t is 172 GHz. The parasitic capacitances from transistor gate and drain are absorbed during the ZPS design to realize the distributed amplification. As a result, the shunt inductor (L_p) in Figure 2.5(b) is resized to a single loop.

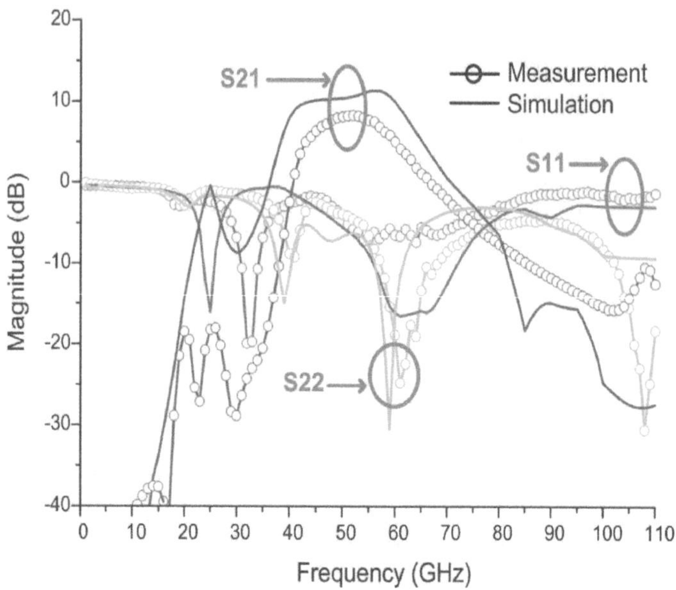

Figure 7.25: Simulated and measured S parameters of PA under 1.2 V supply.

Notice the size of L_s in the gate line is smaller than in the drain line due to a larger parasitic capacitance at transistor gate.

The power combiner implemented in the 2nd stage only has 2 branches, mainly due to limitation of the tape-out area. More branches can be used to enhance the power performance. Moreover, CPW transmission lines are used as parallel inductors for matching and DC biasing at the same time, therefore no additional biasing circuit is required.

7.4.1.2 Simulation and Measurement Results

Circuit simulation is done in both Cadence and ADS. The chip is measured on a CASCADE Microtech Elite-300 probe station and Agilent PNA-X (N5247A) with frequency-sweep up to 110GHz. Measurement for PA power performance is done at the center frequency (52GHz) with pads de-embedded.

Figure 7.25 shows the simulated and measured S parameters. An open-short de-embedding was performed to obtain the results. From simulation, the maximum gain is at 56.3 GHz with 11.3 dB. A 3-dB bandwidth of 21GHz is achieved (40.3GHz $\sim$ 61.7GHz). At 60GHz, a 9.8-dB gain is obtained. The measured gain, on the other hand, has a peak value of 8.3 dB at 52 GHz. The 3-dB BW is 16GHz (44 to 60GHz). Compared with simulation, the center fre-

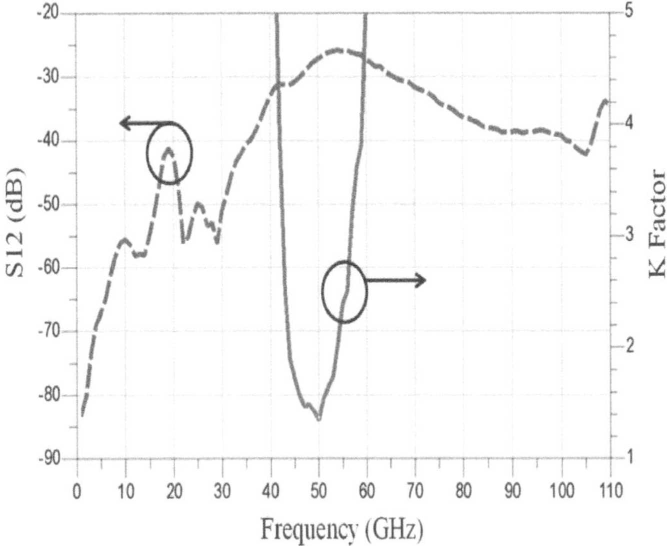

Figure 7.26: Reverse isolation and stability of PA under 1.2 V supply.

quency is not shifted much, but power gain drops 3dB and bandwidth shrinks 5 GHz. Output matching confirms with the simulation while degradation occurs at the input matching. This input mismatch may be due to lack of device modeling, and can be used to justify the reduction of power gain.

The measured reverse isolation and stability for PA are shown in Figure 7.26. The circuit is unconditionally stable from DC to 110GHz, with reverse isolation better than -25 dB over the entire range.

In addition, Figure 7.27 shows the measured power performance at center frequency (52GHz). With 1.2-V supply, OP_{1dB} of 9.7 dBm and t_{sat} of 11 dBm are achieved. PAE drops to 7.1%. Note that both PAE and output power are limited by the number of power combining branches and distributed stages, and can be further improved when a larger 2D power combining network is employed, as will be demonstrated in the following sections.

Furthermore, Table 7.1 summarizes the presented work with comparison to the state-of-the-art 2-stage CMOS PAs at 60 GHz. Comparison shows that the proposed PA can achieve the state-of-the-art performance for all FOMs.

Lastly, Figure 7.28 shows the chip micrograph. Including pads, the PA occupies an area of 0.39 mm^2, which is quite compact when compared to the traditional design with the use of T-line. Note that the upper part of the photo is the 60GHz PA with 2×2 power combining network. The lower part of the photo is the de-embedding structures used to characterize the CRLH T-line-based zero-phase-shifter.

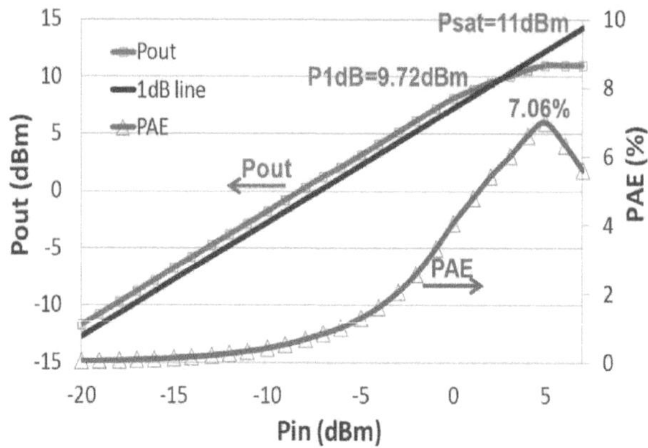

Figure 7.27: Measured power and PAE of PA at 52 GHz under 1.2 V supply.

Table 7.1: Comparison of State-of-the-Art Two-Stage 60 GHz CMOS PAs

	This Work	**[192]**	**[212]**	**[193]**	**[211]**
Tech. (CMOS)	65nm	65nm	45nm	90nm	90nm
Supply (V)	1.2	1.2	1.1	1	1
Gain (dB)	8.3	14.3	6	8.2	5.6
$\mathbf{OP}_{1dB}$ (dBm)	9.7	11	11	10.1	9
$\mathbf{P}_{sat}$ (dBm)	11	16.6	13.8	11.6	12.3
PAE (%)	7.1	4.6	7	11.5	8.8
$\mathbf{BW}_{-3dB}$ (GHz)	16	15	19	13	22
Area ($\mathbf{mm}^2$)	0.39	0.46*	0.06*	1.03	0.25

*Excluding pads

In summary, the presented simulation and measurement results have demonstrated the feasibility of the proposed 2D distributed power combining as well as the implementation of metamaterial in the mm-wave region by 65nm CMOS technology.

7.4.2 60 GHw PA Design with Differential 2×4 Power Combining

The proposed 2D power combining network with the use of CRLH T-line-based ZPS is demonstrated in the above section, proving its feasibility for 60GHz

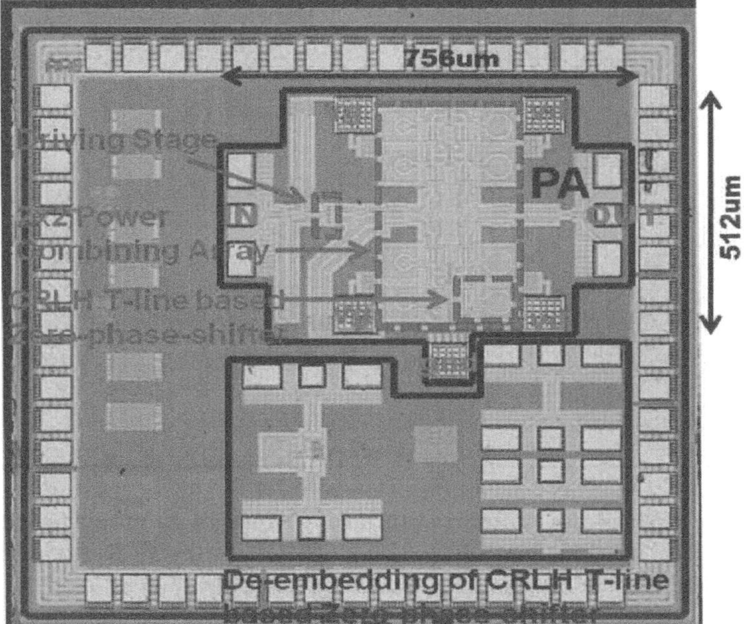

Figure 7.28: Die micrograph with block illustrations.

CMOS PA design. However, due to the single-ended topology with a large matching network deployed, the benefit to achieve wide-band and high output power density is still not fully demonstrated. In this prototype, a differential power combining network is implemented in 65nm CMOS technology with improved performances in both power density and bandwidth [225].

7.4.2.1 60GHz PA Design

Differential CRLH T-lines presented in Section 3.2.3 are first designed and implemented in both gate and drain lines in the 2D active CRLH T-line network to obtain zero-phase-shift with circuit and layout diagrams shown in Figure 7.29. The parasitic capacitances from transistor gate and drain are absorbed in ZPS design. The designed CRLH T-lines can realize zero-phase shift at 60GHz with compact size of $61\mu m \times 81\mu m$ and $76\mu m \times 81\mu m$ in gate and drain lines, respectively. Note a smaller L_p is implemented in rate line compared to drain line due to larger parasitic capacitance on transistor gate compared to transistor drain.

With the designed differential ZPS, one 3-stage PA is implemented with the central frequency at 63GHz in 65nm CMOS from Global Foundries 1P8M RF CMOS technology, as shown in Figure 7.30. The first 2 stages work as

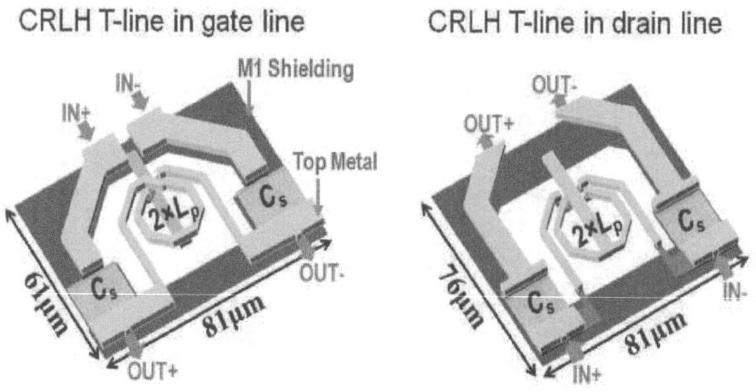

Figure 7.29: On-chip implementation of CRLH T-line (metamaterial) to realize zero-phase shift in standard CMOS technology for the 60 GHz PA prototype with differential 2×4 distributed power combining network.

drivers; and a 2×4 distributed power combining array is in the 3rd stage, which has 2 power combining branches with each branch being a differential 2-stage distributed PA. Each transistor is in a common-source (CS) topology with size of 30×1μm/60nm for the first stage; and 60x1μm/60wm for the second and third stages. With a biasing current of 14mA, the simulated f_{mai} for the 60μm transistor is 231GHz. After adjusted in-phase by ZPS, all horizontal distributed amplification branches are vertically combined by transformers, which simultaneously perform the impedance transformation. Under the differential structure, transformers are also adopted for inter-stage matching. Note one additional compact matching network is used for inter-stage matching between the 2nd and 3rd stages, which may be merged into the differential ZPS design in the gate line to further reduce area and loss. Moreover, the stabilization is realized by compact neutralization capacitors.

7.4.2.2 Simulation and Measurement Results

The design is verified by EM simulation (ADS-Momentum) before fabrication. Figure 7.31 shows the chip micrograph with an active area of 0.268 mm^2. It is measured on CASCADE Microtech Elite-300 probe station and Agilent PNA-X (N5247A) with frequency-sweep up to 110 GHz. Measurement is done at the center frequency (63 GHz) with pads de-embedded.

Figure 7.32 shows the measured S parameters with an open-short de-embedding performed. One can observe that the power gain S21 is 13.2 dB at 63 GHz with the 3-dB bandwidth of 20 GHz (53 to 73 GHz). The PA is unconditionally stable over the entire measured frequency range.

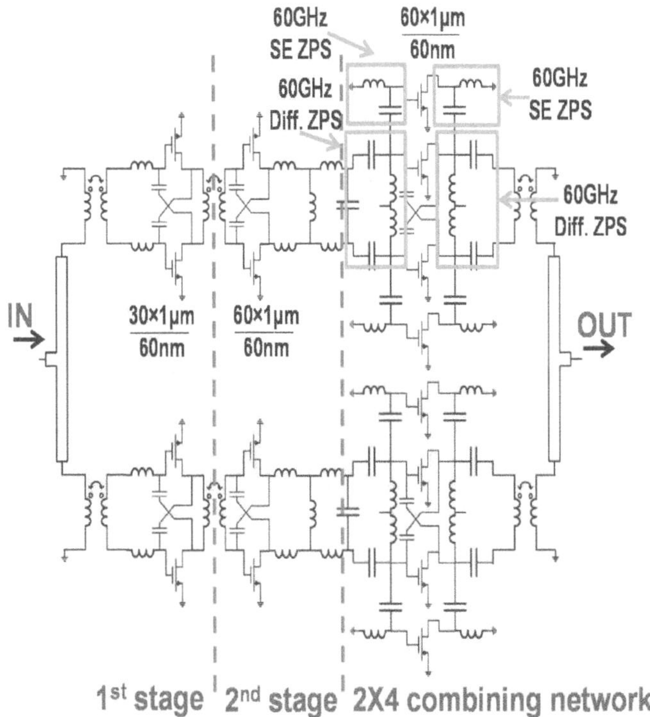

Figure 7.30: Schematic of 3-stage differential PA with differential 2×4 distributed power combining network.

Figure 7.32 shows the measured power performance at 63GHz. Output power OP_{1dB} of 13 dBm and PAE of 8.7% are achieved with 1-V supply. Note that the output power performance can be further improved with more branches combined compactly.

Table 7.2 summarizes the performance of the proposed PA, which demonstrates wide-band high-density power combining. The performance will be compared with the state-of-the-art together with the next PA prototype in the next section.

7.4.3 60 GHz PA Prototype with Differential 4×4 Power Combining and Digital Control

To further improve output power, this section presents another 60GHz PA prototype with its combining network size increased to 4×4. Though the bandwidth is reduced a bit due to much longer signal lines in the output match-

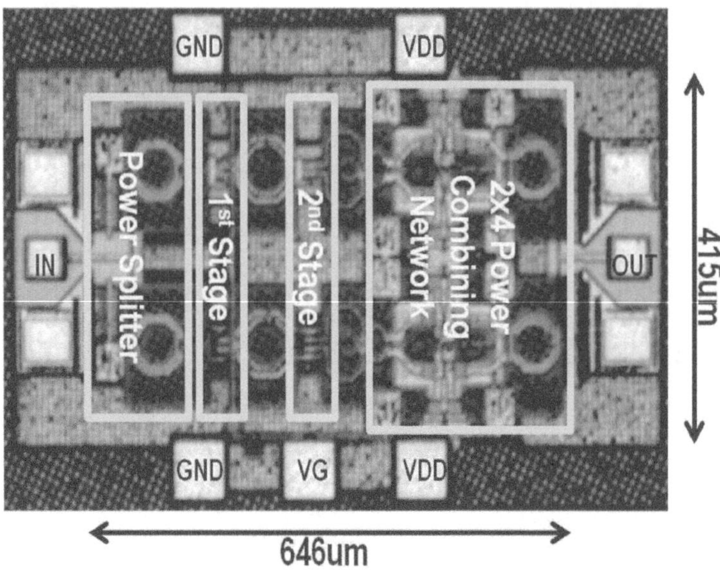

Figure 7.31: Die micrograph of PA with 2D power combining network by zero-phase-shifter.

Table 7.2: Performance Summary for the Implemented 60 GHz CMOS PA Prototype with Differential 2×4 Power Combining

Technology (nm)	65
Supply (V)	1
Gain (dB)	13.2
OP_{1dB} (dBm)	13
P_{sat} (dBm)	13.4
Peek PAE (%)	8.7
BW_{-3dB} (GHz)	20
Area (mm^2)	0.268

ing network, the 7-GHz spectrum band at 60GHz can still be fully covered. Meanwhile, the output power and output power density are further improved, achieving the state-of-the-art. Both circuits are designed and verified by EM simulation (ADS-Momentum and EMX). Furthermore, the digital control loop shown in Figure 7.19 is implemented for PA design to enhance efficiency during power back-off.

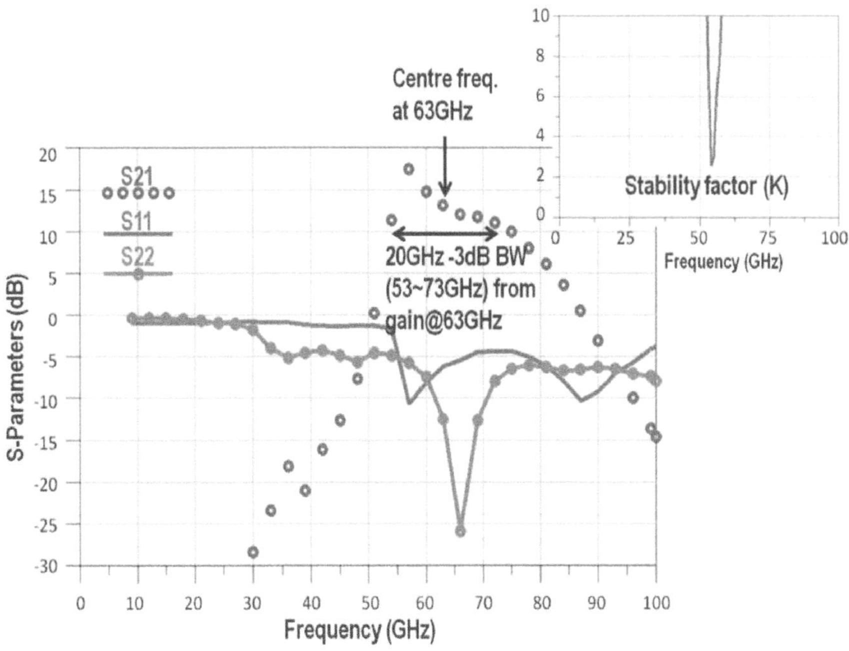

Figure 7.32: The measured S parameters of PA and its stability factor with center frequency (63 GHz) under 1 V supply.

7.4.3.1 60GHz PA Design

The designed differential CRLH T-line-based ZPSs implemented in both gate and drain lines are shown in Figure 7.34, with the parasitic capacitances from transistor late and drain absorbed in ZPS design. The designed CRLH T-lines can realize zero-phase shift at 60GHz with compact size of 49μm$\times$76μm and 50μm$\times$72μm in gate and drain lines, respectively.

Figure 7.35 further compares the performance between zero-phase CRLH T-line and traditional RH $\lambda/2$ T-line with transistor parasitic capacitance and loss absorbed into the design. As the top figure shows, as frequency changes, the phase shift in zero-phase CRLH T-line varies much slower than $\lambda/2$ T-line. For example, a phase change within $\pm 10°$ can be maintained in the 14 GHz frequency range (53 to 67 GHz) in the designed zero-phase CRLH T-line, while in $\lambda/2$ T-line it can only be maintained in the 4.5 GHz range (57.5 to 62GHz). In other words, zero-phase CRTH T-line can provide a much wider band performance than $\lambda/2$ T-line. The insertion loss is also compared in the lower figure. By absorbing parasitic capacitance and loss from transistor, the zero-phase CRLH T-lines show insertion loss below 0.9 dB and 1.4 dB in 50 GHz to 70 GHz frequency range in the gate line and drain line, respectively,

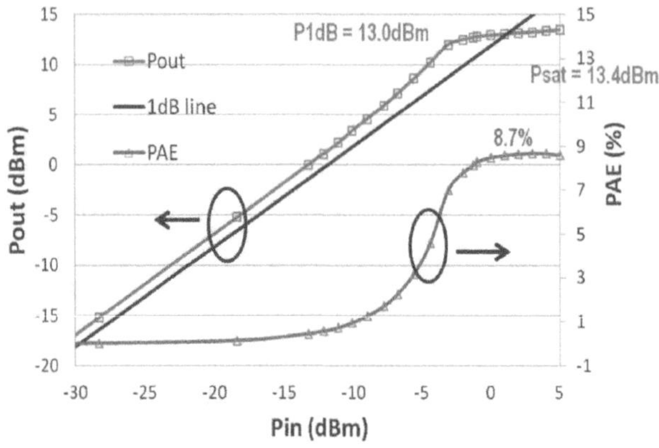

Figure 7.33: The measured output power and PAE of PA at center frequency (63 GHz) under 1 V supply.

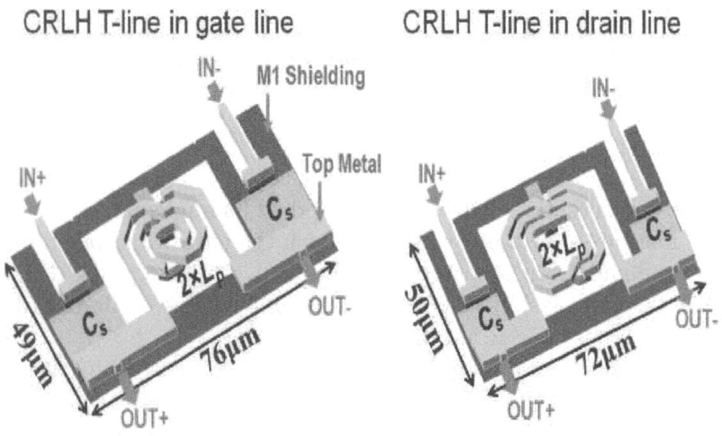

Figure 7.34: On-chip implementation of CRLH T-line (metamaterial) to realize zero-phase shift in standard CMOS technology for the 60 GHz PA prototype with differential 4×4 distributed power combining network.

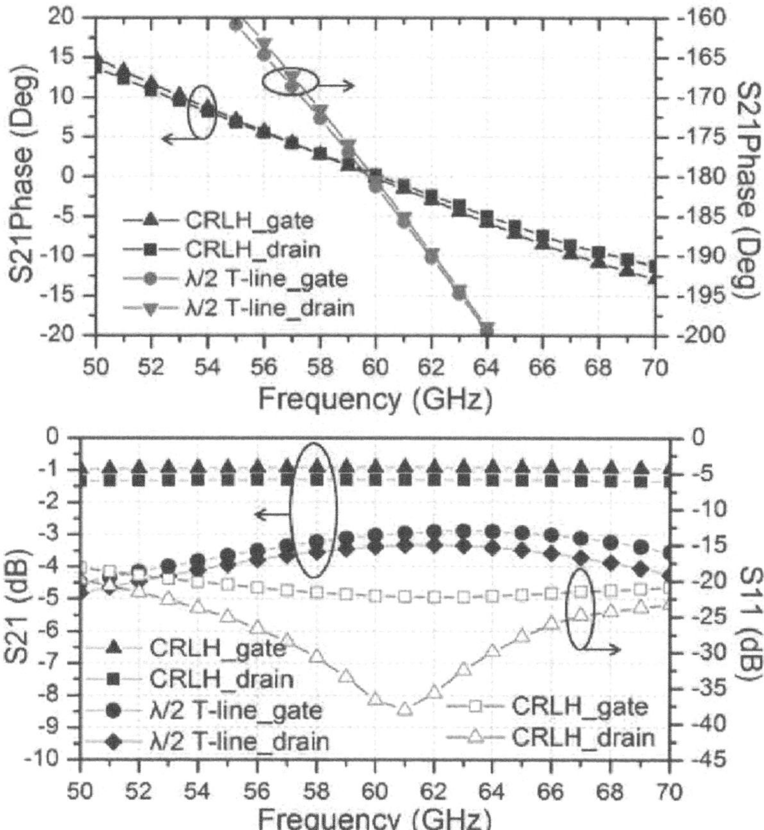

Figure 7.35: EM simulation results of both loaded CRLH T-line and loaded $\lambda/2$ T-line for comparison. Slower S21 phase change of CRLH T-line indicates wider bandwidth, while the dB(S21) plot indicates lower loss. The dB(S11) plot shows wideband matching.

while $\lambda/2$ T-line contributes more than 3dB loss in both gate and drain lines. In conclusion, the implemented on-chip differential zero-phase CRLH T-line demonstrates much more compact size, wider bandwidth and lower loss than $\lambda/2$ T-line.

The PA implementation is shown in Figure 7.36 with 3 stages and 58 GHz as the central frequency. The first 2 stages work as drivers; and a 4×4 distributed power combining array is in the 3rd stage, which has 4 power-combining branches with each branch being a differential 2-stage distributed PA. Same transistor topology, size and biasing are adopted. As 4 branches are combined in parallel at the output instead of 2 branches, matching to 50Ω at

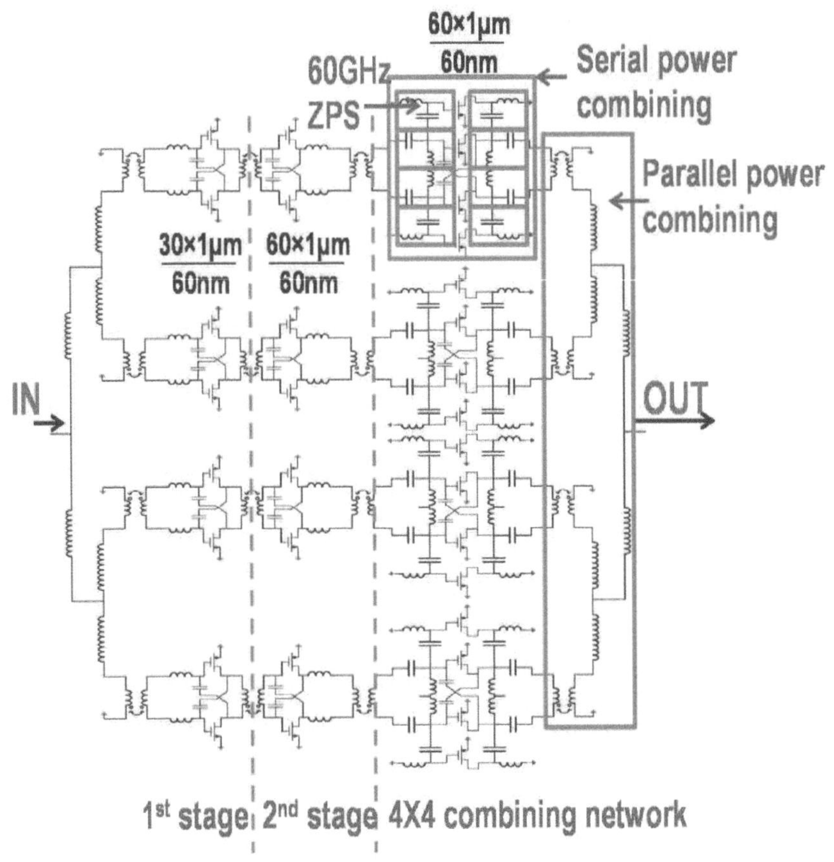

Figure 7.36: Schematic of the 60-GHz PA prototype with 3 stages and differential 4×4 distributed power combining network at 3rd stage.

the output node would require 200Ω in each branch, which cannot be provided by in-chip T-line. As a result, signal distribution lines are absorbed into the output matching network, which reduces the PA bandwidth due to its long length.

Neutralization technique is used to boost the PA's performance while ensuring stability. The risk of mismatch and performance degradation due to sensitivity of the neutralization capacitor to process variation is minimized by adopting multiple large-value capacitors connected in serial. Since the capacitance of each capacitor is much larger than a single neutralization capacitor, its sensitivity to variation can be reduced.

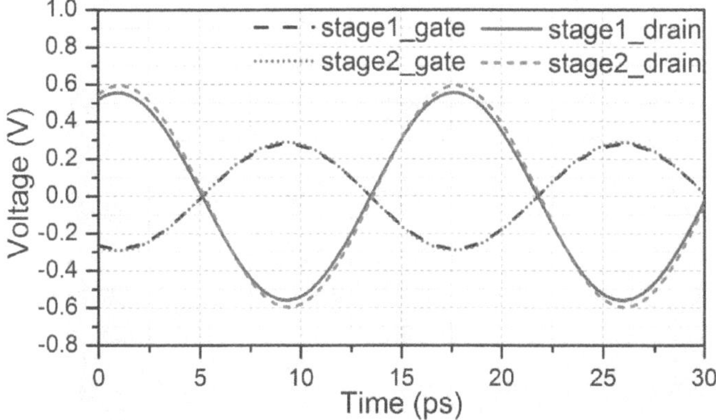

Figure 7.37: Simulated voltage swings on both distributed stages in the gate line and drain line of designed 2D distributed power combiner. Similar voltage magnitude indicates simultaneous power optimization for each transistor, while similar phase indicates in-phase power combining.

The digital control system is integrated for this PA implementation to facilitate power back-off with enhanced efficiency. The system view for the digital control loop is shown in Figure 7.19, where the output power level is sensed by a power coupler and converted to DC signal through a power detector. The detected signal is further converted to digital signal through a 3-bit ADC and passed to off-chip signal processing. The feedback digital signal is then converted to analog signal through a 3-bit DAC to control PA's biasing. The capacitive power coupler designed in Figure 7.16 is selected to minimize the effect of power detection on PA's output power performance. The single-ended square law power detector designed in Figure 7.18 is adopted to fit the single-ended PA output.

7.4.3.2 Simulation and Measurement Results

Simulation Results

Figure 7.37 shows simulated voltage swings on the transistor gate and drain of both distributed stages of the implemented differential 2D power combining network at 60GHz. As the figure shows, both gate and drain voltage swings have almost the same phase and amplitude in two distributed stages. As a result, the power performance of transistors in distributed amplifier can be optimized simultaneously and in-phase combined in series, thus improving the power gain and efficiency of the whole distributed amplifier.

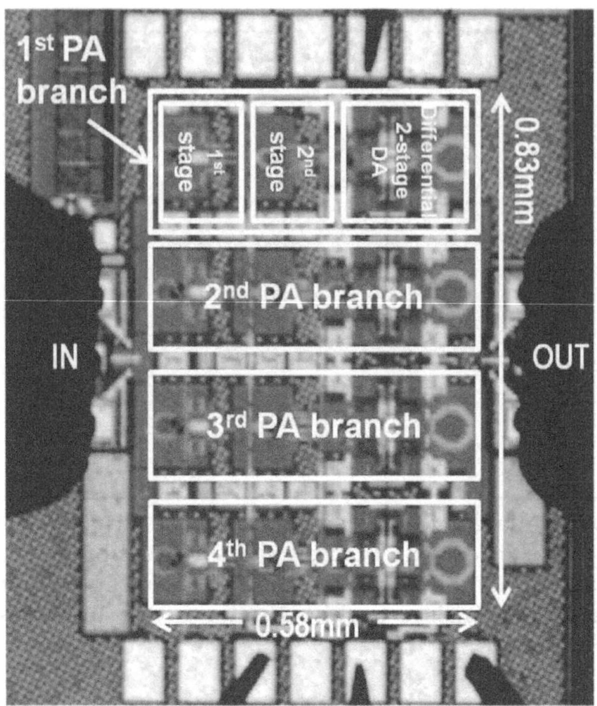

Figure 7.38: Die micrograph of the 60 GHz PA prototype with differential 4×4 distributed power combining network.

PA On-Chip Measurement Results

The fabricated PA is measured on CASCADE Microtech Elite-300 probe station and Agilent PNA-X (N5247A) with frequency-sweep up to 110 GHz. Measurement is done at the center frequency with pads de-embedded. Open-short is used for de-embedding.

Figure 7.38 shows the chip micrograph with active area of 0.48 mm^2. Figure 7.39 shows the measured S parameters. The power gain (S21) is 17.5 dB at 58.3 GHz with a 3-dB bandwidth of 8.8 GHz (54 to 62.8 GHz). The PA is unconditionally stable from DC to 110 GHz.

Figure 7.40 shows the measured power performance at center frequency (58.3 GHz). With a power supply of 1.2 V, OP_{1dB} of 15.9 dBm and P_{sat} of 16.6 dBm are achieved. The peak PAE is 9.74%. Figure 7.41 further shows the measured power performance at 60GHz band (57 $\sim$ 64 GHz). Over the entire 60GHz band, >15dBm OP_{1dB} and >16 dBm P_{sat} are observed. The peak values for OP_{1dB} and P_{sat} are 16.6 dBm and 17.2dBm, respectively. The PAE maintains above 8% for the entire 60GHz band with a peak value of 11.3%.

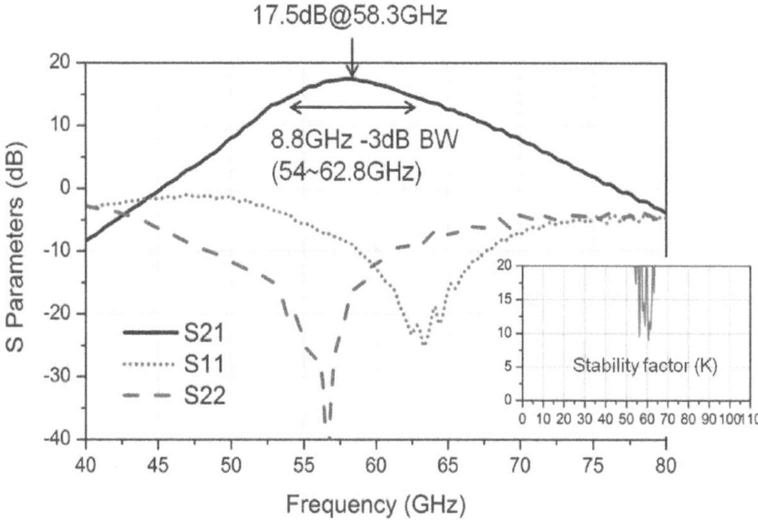

Figure 7.39: The measured S parameters of the PA prototype and its stability factor under 1.2 V supply. The PA achieves 17.5 dB power gain at 58.3 GHz with 8.8-GHz bandwidth.

For 60GHz communication, high-order modulation requires linearity, indicated by OP_{1dB}. The measured output power performance of both PA prototypes presented in this section and Section are compared with state-of-the-art in Figure 7.42 in terms of both output mower (OP_{1dB}) and also output power density (OP_{1dh}/Area). Note that the PA with a higher output power (OP_{1dB}) tends to have a lower output power density (OP_{1dB}/Area) due to extra loss and area. As Figure 7.42 shows, the proposed power combining with 4 branches can achieve the state-of-the-art power performance for both OP_{1dB} (16.6 dBm) and OP_{1dB}/Area (95.2 mW/mm^2). The work in [194] achieves a higher output power with 4-way Wilkinson power combiners that lead to a large area and hence lower output power density. The work in [226] achieves a higher output power with a combination of 16 branches by T-lines and transformers, which largely degrades the output power density. On the other hand, the work in [195] realizes higher output power density, but the distributed-active-transformer (DAT) topology limits the number of combined transistors, which leads to a lower output power.

Table 7.3 summarizes the performance of both PA prototypes presented in this section with comparison to the state-of-the-art CMOS PAs at 60 GHz with various power combining methods. Both proposed 2×4 and 4×4 distributed power combining with metamaterial-based zero-phase-shifter can

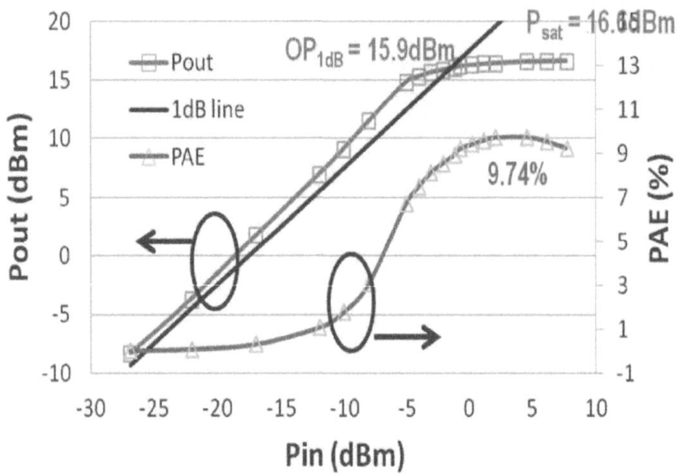

Figure 7.40: The measured output power and PAE of the PA prototype at center frequency (58.3 GHz) under 1.2-V supply. The PA achieves 15.9-dBm OP_{1dB}, 16.6-dBm P_{sat} and peak PAE of 9.74%.

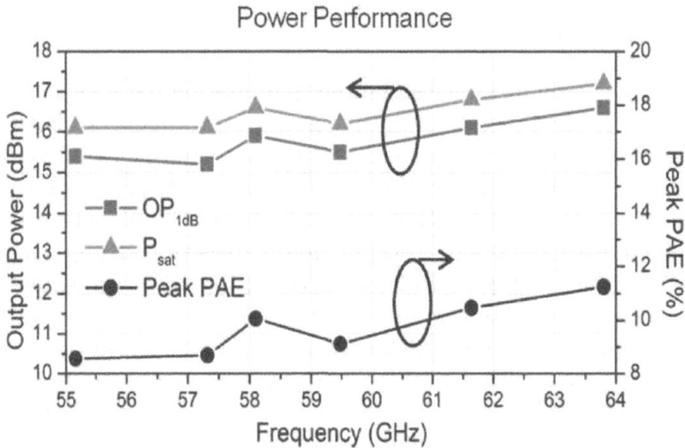

Figure 7.41: Measured power performance of the PA prototype over 60-GHz band (57 ~ 64 GHz), where >15 dBm OP_{1dB} and >16 dBm P_{sat} are observed with peak values of 16.6 dBm and 17.2 dBm, respectively. The peak PAE maintains above 8% with a peak value of 11.3%.

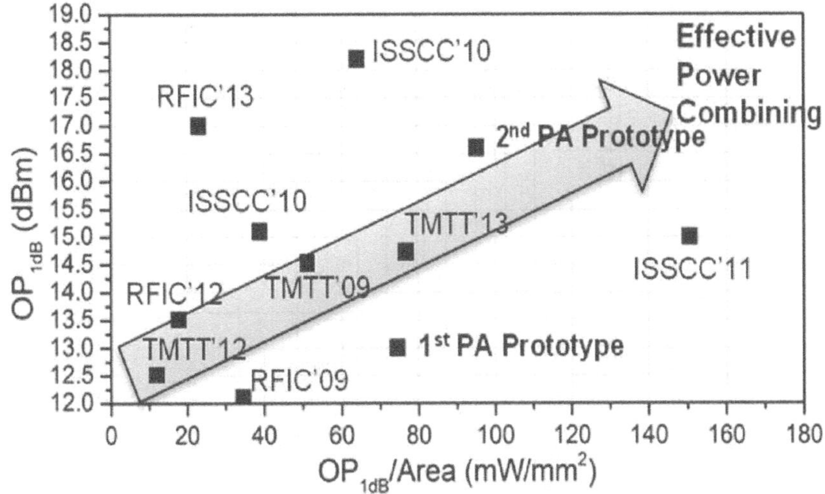

Figure 7.42: Power performance (OP_{1dB} and OP_{1dB}/Area) comparison of both differential PA prototypes with 2×4 and 4×4 power combining networks with state-of-the-art 60-GHz CMOS PAs.

achieve performance comparable to the state-of-the-art. The 2×4 PA prototype realizes 13.2-dB power gain, OP_{1dB} of 13 dBm, P_{sat} of 13.3 dBm, peak PAE of 11.3%, with a very wide 20-GHz bandwidth (53 to 73GHz). With a compact core area of 0.268 mm^2, output power density of 74.5 $dBm{\cdot}mm^{-2}$ is achieved. The 4×4 PA prototype realizes 17.5-dB power gain, 8.8-GHz bandwidth and peak PAE of 11.3%. Most importantly, the 4×4 PA prototype realizes 16.6dBm output power with 95.2-mW/mm^2 output power density, indicating the top output power performance for CMOS PA at 60GHz toward effective short-range communication.

Digital Control Loop Measurement Results on PCB

The digital control loop is also measured to test its functionality. As shown in Figure 7.43(a), the output power level of PA is controlled by a 3-bit DAC with 8 modes. Mode 0 turns off the PA completely. Modes 1 to 7 varies the PA's output power at center frequency (58.3 GHz) from 10 to 15dBm. Note 1 or 2 dB drop in output power is observed compared to on-chip PA measurement since PCB bonding is used for digital control measurement, which provides degraded ground condition with lower supplied DC current. However, the improvement in PA efficiency during power back-off is fully demonstrated. As shown in Figure 7.43(f), the drain efficiency of PA is plotted, which varies from 8% to 5% during power back-off. For a fair comparison, another drain

Table 7.3: Comparison of Both 60-GHz CMOS PA Prototypes (PA1: with 2×4 Power Combining, PA2: with 4×4 Power Combining) and State-of-the-Art CMOS PAs at 60 GHz with High Output Power by Various Power Combining Methods

	RFIC '09 [193]	**TMTT '09 [198]**	**ISSCC '10 [13]**	**ISSCC '10 [194]**	**ISSCC '11 [195]**	**TMTT '12 [227]**	**RFIC '12 [228]**	**TMTT '13 [214]**	**RFIC '13 [226]**	**PA1**	**PA2**
Technology (nm)	90	90	65	90	65	65	65	90	40	65	65
Supply (V)	1	3	1	1.8	1	1	1.2	1.2	1.2	1	1.2
Gain (dB)	4.4	26.6	19.2	20.6	20.3	20	20	15.7	29	13.2	17.5
OP_{1dB} (dBm)	12.1	14.5	15.1	18.2	15	12.5	13.5	14.7	17	**13**	**16.6**
P_{sat} (dBm)	14.2	18	17.7	19.9	18.6	16	15.6	18.5	22.6	13.4	17.2
Peak PAE (%)	5.8	12.2	11.1	14.2	15.1	6.6	6.6	10.2	7	8.7	11.3
BW_{-3dB} (GHz)	9.5	16	8	8	9	5	7	5.8	N.A.	**20**	**8.8**
Core Area (mm^2)	0.47	0.55	0.83	1.03	0.21	1.47	1.26	0.39	2.16	**0.27**	**0.48**
OP_{1de}/Area (mW/mm^2)	34.6	51.2	39	64.1	150.6	12.1	17.8	76.7	23.2	**74.5**	**95.2**
Combiner Topology	4-way SE	DAT, 2-way diff.	4-way difa.	4-way aE	DAT, 2-way wiff.	2-way Sy	DAT, 4-way difa.	4-way diff.	8-way diff.	2x4 net-work	4x4 net-work

diff.: differential; SE: single-ended

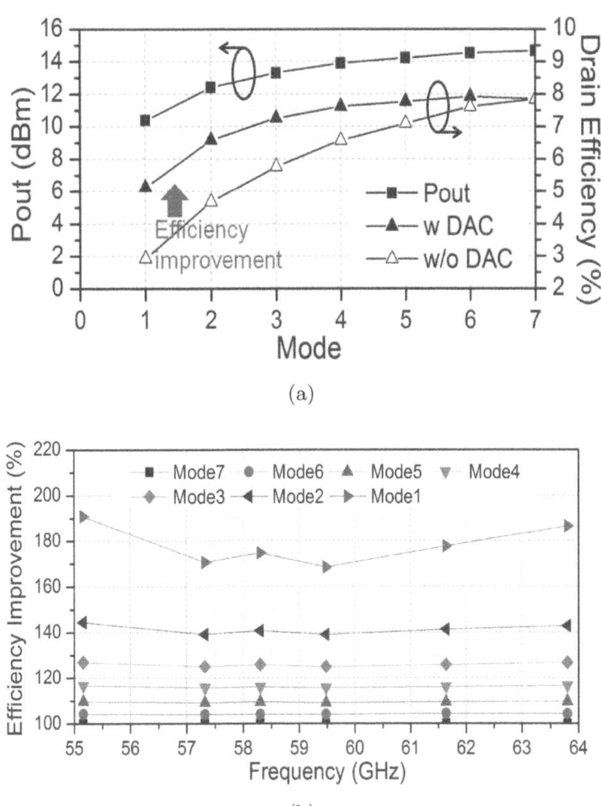

Figure 7.43: DAC control of PA output power and improved efficiency during power back-off. (a) Comparison of drain efficiency during power back-off for PA with and without DAC control to obtain the sage output power at 58.3GHz. (b) Summarized efficiency improvement for different output power level (DAC modes) at different frequencies.

efficiency curve is plotted by varying the input power to the PA with the DAC turned off to achieve the same output power level. As shown in Figure 7.43(a), though the PA with DAC control also shows degradation in efficiency during power back-off due to deviation of biasing from optimum point, the efficiency is still largely improved compared with PA without digital control. For example, an improvement of 175% (by dividing the two drain efficiency values) is achieved for PA efficiency at Mode 1. The improvement in drain efficiency at different frequencies for different DAC modes and thus different

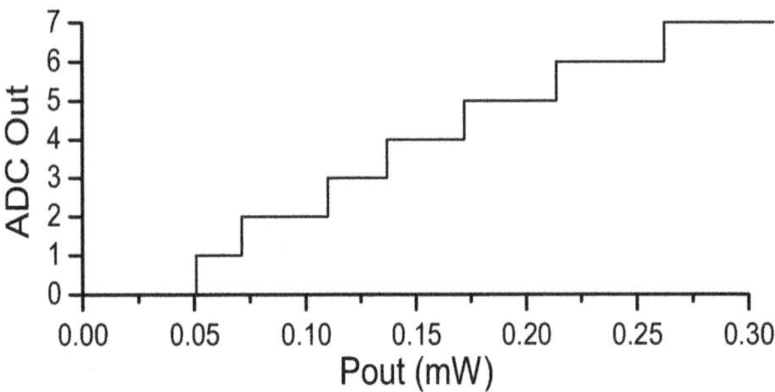

Figure 7.44: ADC outputs for PA output power detection at 58.3 GHz.

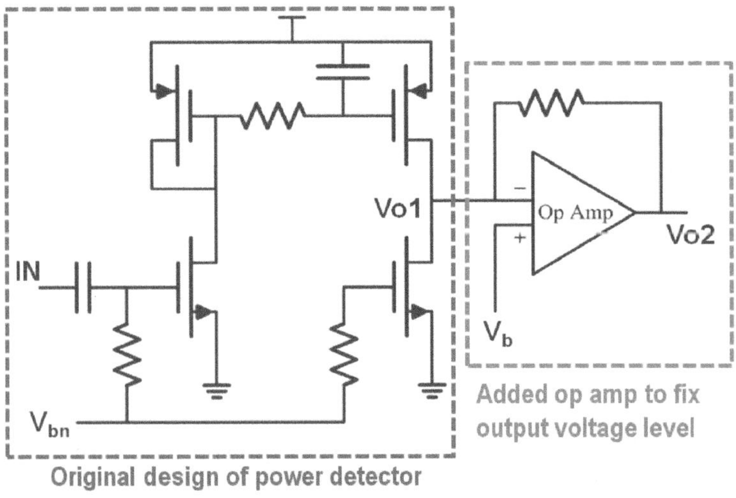

Figure 7.45: Modification for the power detector design.

back-off levels is further summarized in Figure 7.43(b). An improvement from 170% to 190% is obtained at Mode 1 for the whole 60GHz band.

The power detection for the PA's output power is further measured with the results shown in Figure 7.44. Since a square root detector is used which has output voltage proportional to the square of the signal's voltage swing, mm is used for the X-axis. Figure 7.44 shows the measurement results at center frequency (58.3GHz). The 3-bit ADC outputs 8 digital levels as the PA's output power varies from 0 to 0.3 mW.

Note the detectable power range deviates from the originally designed power range near OP_{1dB} level. This can be explained by the designed tower detector schematic shown in Figure 7.45. As the output node Vol is a high impedance point, it is sensitive to process variation. As a result, the transistor biasing (V_{bn}) needs to be adjusted to tune the Vol level back, which shifts the power detection range. This problem can be easily fixed by adding an op-amp after the originally designed power detector circuit to fix the output voltage level, as shown in Figure 7.45.

7.5 Conclusion

In this chapter, a 2D distributed power combining network is proposed by replacing the bulky RH T-line in traditional power combiners with compact metamaterial-typed CRLH T-line. Compared with the RH T-line, CRLH T-line shows unique features such as nonlinear phase-frequency dependence and zero-phase-shift capability, and thus can replace bulky RH T-line with the same functionality but much more compact area. By periodically loading transistors in a proposed 2D active in-phase CRLH T-line network, transistor outputs can be in-phase combined both in series and in parallel within a compact area in a distributed manner, thus achieving high output power, high output power density and wide-band simultaneously. Three 60GHz PA prototypes with single-ended 2×2 power combining network and differential 2×4 and 4×4 power combining networks are implemented in 65nm CMOS technology. The 1st PA prototype with single-ended 2×2 power combining shows 8.3dB gain, 7.1% PAE, and 9.7dBm OP_{1dB} with 16GHz bandwidth (44 to 60GHz) and area of 0.39mm^2. This work is further improved to have a differential topology with compact transformer matching. The 2nd PA prototype with differential 2×4 power combining shows 13.2 dB gain, 8.7% PAE, 20GHz bandwidth (53 to 73 GHz) and 13 dBm OP_{1dB} with 74.5 mw/mm^2 output power density, realizing state-of-the-art power performance and wide bandwidth simultaneously. The power performance is further improved by the 3rd PA prototype with differential 4×4 power combining, which shows 17.5-dB gain, peak PAE of 11.3%, 8.8-GHz bandwidth (54 to 62.8 GHz), and 16.6-dBm OP_{1rB} with 95.2-mw/mm^2 output power density, demonstrating the top power performance in literature. All three PA prototypes show state-of-the-art performance, demonstrating the benefit of the proposed power combining network for effective short-range communication.

Chapter 8

Antenna

8.1 Introduction

In order to compensate huge propagation loss of THz signal, and realize wideband and high sensitivity receivers, effective THz imaging/communication systems also require antenna an antenna array with high-directivity radiation pattern [229] and high efficiency with sufficient bandwidth, which imposes grand challenges for an on-chip antenna design in CMOS. Firstly, the realization of highly directive radiation is not trivial. The conventional right-handed antennas (patch, dipole and etc.) [230, 32] have a positive phase-and-length relation that usually results in non-in-phase radiation and large-sized design. Secondly, due to close distance between the top metal layer and ground, the radiation efficiency of on-chip antenna is not high. Moreover, each antenna element must be as compact as possible to form antenna array in limited chip area. The previous on-chip antenna works [32, 230, 90, 231] have either low gain or narrow bandwidth and ignored the polarization issue. For example, given the THz source with linearly polarized radiation, the longitudinal polarization may be turned into transverse direction after penetrating through the tissue [16]. If the antenna at the receiver is also linearly polarized, the detection efficiency may be largely reduced due to the mismatch in the polarization directions.

On-chip antennas have more stringent requirements on the antenna size than the off-chip ones. They are usually implemented at a frequency higher than 200GHz, for which a structure with equivalent electrical length of $\lambda/4$ or $\lambda/2$ can be fit into the chip scale with good efficiency.

In this chapter, two types of on-chip antennas are proposed to deliver both high gain and compact size. In the first part, the on-chip THz leaky wave antenna (LWA) design is explored with periodic composite right/left-handed

(CRLH) transmission-line (T-line) structure with broadside radiation under a zero phase propagation condition. Moreover, stacking a high-resistivity dielectric layer is deployed to improve efficiency. A 13-cell on-chip CRLH T-line is fabricated in the 65nm CMOS process and is characterized from 220 GHz to 325 GHz. The corresponding 1D and 2D LWA array design shows a broadside radiation pattern, 65% efficiency and 5.1-dBi gain at 280 GHz.

In the second part of this chapter, one wide-band 280-GHz on-chip circularly polarized SIW antenna is designed in the CMOS process with compact area. By creating corner slots in SIW structure, the size of the proposed SIW antenna is reduced by 15% when compared to the conventional designs. As verified by the EM simulation, the proposed antenna has -0.5-dBi antenna gain and 32.1-GHz bandwidth centered at 268 GHz.

8.2 CRLH T-Line-Based Leaky Wave Antenna

The recently explored left-handed metamaterial can provide negative phase with a nonlinear phase-and-length dependence, which can realize a zero-phase EM-wave propagation or radiation with compact area on chip [232], ideally for a broadside radiation antenna design. In this section, the CRLH T-line is studied for leaky wave antenna (LWA) design at THz with broadside radiation under a zero phase propagation condition.

CRLH T-line is a well-known metamaterial structure that can achieve positive, negative and zero phase propagation. A CRLH T-line consists of a number of periodic unit-cells. The traveling wave can be generated in the CRLH T-line-based LWA with

$$\phi(y,z) = \phi_0 e^{-jk_y y} e^{-\gamma z} \tag{8.1}$$

where $\gamma = \alpha - j\beta$ is the propagation constant of the traveling wave in the CRLH T-line; $k_y = \sqrt{k_0^2 - |\beta|^2}$ is the wave factor of radiated power along the y axial; and k_0 is the wave number in free space.

When the signal travels along the antenna surface (z axis) as shown in Figure 8.1, the energy leak-out is confined in parallel with k_0. If the phase velocity is slower than that of light, or $|\beta| > |k_0|$, the signal is attenuated exponentially along the y axial. In this case the antenna works in slow-wave region. On the other hand, if $|\beta| < |k_0|$, the antenna is in the fast-wave mode with a real k_y, which is a desired condition for LWA to operate. Note that the main beam radiation angle can be described by

$$\theta_{MB} = arcsin(|\beta|/|k_0|). \tag{8.2}$$

Therefore, the radiation pattern becomes broadside when $|\beta|$ equals zero, and beam steering can be observed along broadside radiation with high directivity for THz communication.

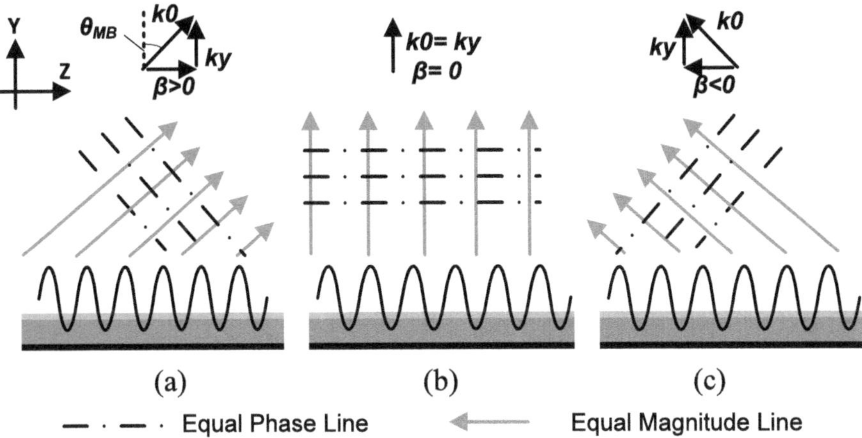

Figure 8.1: Operation diagram of leaky wave antenna: (a) $\beta > 0$, (b) $\beta = 0$, and (c) $\beta < 0$.

8.3 Circularly Polarized SIW Antenna

SIW structures have been recently explored for the design of high-quality factor (Q) passive devices in both mm-wave and sub-THz regions [233, 234, 235]. SIW can be regarded as a dielectric-filled rectangular waveguide with surrounding walls and metal layers on the top and bottom surfaces, which leverages the advantages of both planar transmission line and non-planar waveguide with lower loss and wide-band performance in a miniaturized cavity for on-chip antenna design.

SIW antennas designs are proposed in both PCB scale [233] and chip scale [234] with a wide bandwidth and a high gain. In [234], a 400GHz linear polarized on-chip SIW antenna is demonstrated in SiGe process with -0.55dBi gain and 7.8% relative bandwidth. However, its dimension has to satisfy an equivalent electrical length of $\lambda/2$, which should be further miniaturized when designed on-chip.

A compact circular-polarized SIW antenna design is designed in the CMOS process with corner slots, of which the geometrical configuration is illustrated in Figure 8.2. The operating frequency of a SIW antenna is determined by the cavity dimension. It can be approximated by the following equation by considering the cavity resonance model [236].

$$f_{mnp} = \frac{c}{2\sqrt{\mu_r \varepsilon_r}} \sqrt{\left(\frac{m}{L_{eff}}\right)^2 + \left(\frac{n}{W_{eff}}\right)^2 + \left(\frac{k}{h}\right)^2} \tag{8.3}$$

where $L_{eff} = L$ and $W_{eff} = W$ are the effective length and width of the substrate integrated cavity, c is the speed of light in free space, μ_r and ε_r

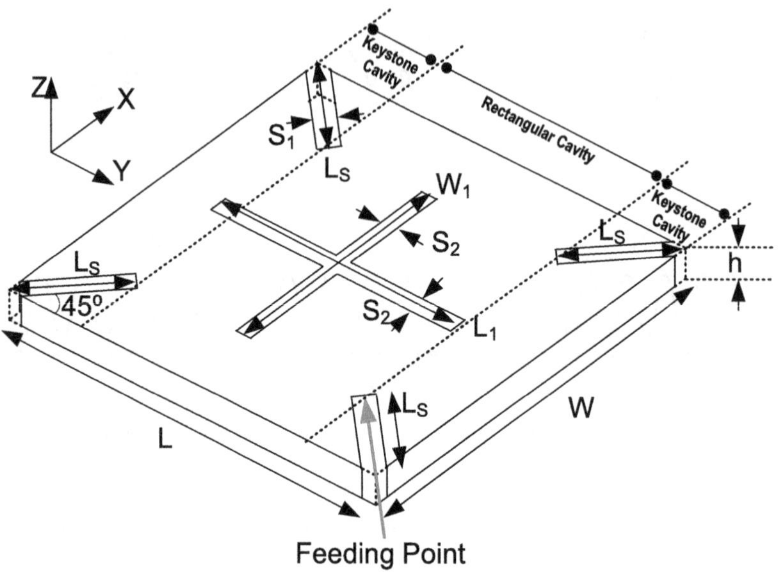

Figure 8.2: Geometrical configuration of the proposed SIW antenna with four corner slots.

are the relative permeability and permittivity of the dielectric material inside the cavity and h is the cavity height. The resonance modes with lowest order are used for a minimum antenna size, considering h is much smaller than the wavelength when designed on-chip, the available resonance frequencies left are f_{210} and f_{120} with

$$\begin{cases} f_{210} = \frac{c}{2\sqrt{\mu_r \varepsilon_r}} \sqrt{\frac{4}{L_{eff}^2} + \frac{1}{W_{eff}^2}} \\ f_{120} = \frac{c}{2\sqrt{\mu_r \varepsilon_r}} \sqrt{\frac{1}{L_{eff}^2} + \frac{4}{W_{eff}^2}} \end{cases}. \tag{8.4}$$

After introducing corner slots with 45° to the edge, both L_{eff} and W_{eff} can be approximated by the total effective length of the center rectangular cavity and two keystone cavities as shown in Figure 8.2:

$$\begin{cases} L_{eff} = L_{rectangular} + 2L_{keystone} \\ W_{eff} = W_{rectangular} + 2W_{keystone} \end{cases} \tag{8.5}$$

where $L_{rectangular} = L - \sqrt{2}L_S$, $W_{rectangular} = W - \sqrt{2}L_S$, $W_{keystone}$ and $L_{keystone}$ are the effective lengths of each keystone cavity in the X and Y directions, respectively. The effective length of keystone cavity can be approximated by the following equations [237]:

$$\begin{cases} L_{keystone} = \frac{L_S R_{tl}}{1.152} \\ W_{keystone} = \frac{L_S R_{tw}}{1.152} \end{cases} \tag{8.6}$$

with

$$\begin{cases} R_{tl} = \frac{L_S(2W-\sqrt{2}L_S)}{\sqrt{2}WL_S} \\ R_{tw} = \frac{L_S(2L-\sqrt{2}L_S)}{\sqrt{2}LL_S} \end{cases}. \tag{8.7}$$

With (8.5), (8.6) and (8.7), L_{eff} and W_{eff} can be simplified as:

$$\begin{cases} L_{eff} = L + 1.042L_s - \frac{1.737L_s^2}{W} \\ W_{eff} = W + 1.042L_s - \frac{1.737L_s^2}{L} \end{cases}. \tag{8.8}$$

As observed from (8.8), both the effective width and length are extended by a factor of L_{eff}/L or W_{eff}/W after introducing corner slots, which means the antenna size can be reduced by the same ratio at a particular frequency. However, the reduction radio is also limited by higher-order effects. As shown in (8.8), L_{eff} and W_{eff} reach their maximums of $1.15L$ and $1.15W$ when $L_s = 0.3W$ and $0.3L$, respectively, which is equivalent to a 15% size reduction in each dimension of SIW antenna.

Note that the lengths of center slots $L1$ and $W1$ can be calculated by:

$$\begin{cases} L1 = \frac{1}{2f_{L1}\sqrt{\mu_{eff}\varepsilon_{eff}}} \\ W1 = \frac{1}{2f_{W1}\sqrt{\mu_{eff}\varepsilon_{eff}}} \end{cases} \tag{8.9}$$

where f_{L1} and f_{W1} are the resonant frequencies of center slots, μ_{eff} and ε_{eff} are the equivalent permeability and permittivity in the center slots, respectively. In a conventional SIW antenna design [233], to maximize radiation efficiency, both center slots need to have the same resonant frequencies as the respective resonance mode: $f_{L1} = f_{120}$ and $f_{W1} = f_{210}$. By properly adjusting the cavity dimensions, f_{120} and f_{210} can be close to each other so that a circularly polarized radiation is generated at a frequency in between. However, the antenna designed in such method has a narrow bandwidth, because only two resonance modes exist. In this work, the radiation bandwidth is extended by introducing additional resonance modes in the antenna design, where four resonance modes are generated by designing f_{L1} and f_{W1} slightly lower and higher than f_{120} and f_{210}, respectively. Moreover, the antenna performance is further improved from the following two aspects. Firstly, the radiation efficiency is increased with the cavity height, which could be achieved by selecting a CMOS process option with a large number of stacking layers. Secondly, the metal loss of SIW walls is largely reduced by replacing metal vias with metal bars. Note that vertical connection by metal bars is an option provided in the standard CMOS process to connect many vias horizontally (Figure 8.3) if the metal density is not critical in the particular area.

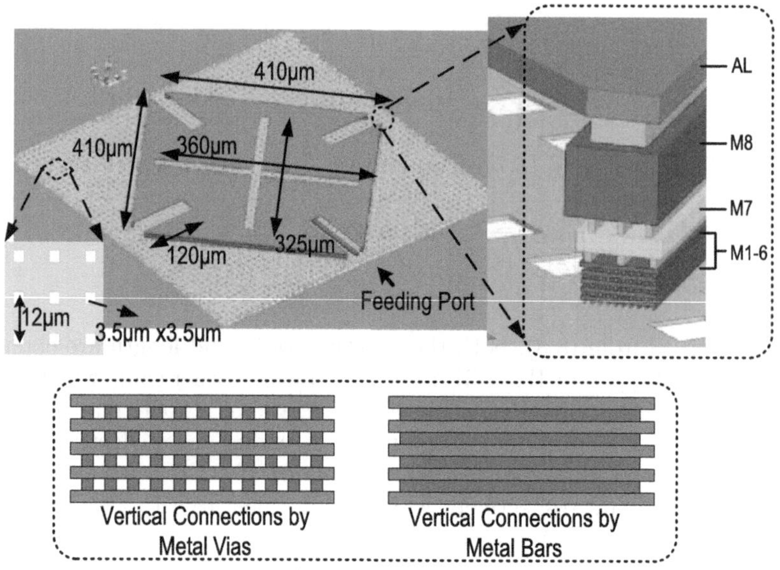

Figure 8.3: Design of on-chip integrated circular-polarized SIW antenna in CMOS 65 nm process.

8.4 Circuit Prototyping and Measurement

8.4.1 280-GHz LWA

8.4.1.1 1D Antenna Array Design

Based on the fabricated 13-cell CRLH T-line in Sec. 3.4.2, one 280-GHz LWA is also implemented in the Global Foundry 65-nm CMOS process. P1 in Figure 3.10 is selected as the antenna input, and P2 is left open circuit. As shown in Figure 8.4, a standard high-resistivity silicon layer ($750\ \Omega \cdot cm$) with a thickness of 100 μm is placed on top of the antenna surface to enhance the radiation efficiency.

8.4.1.2 2D Antenna Array Design

One single CRLH T-line (1-D)-based LWA design in CMOS has limited gain and radiation efficiency at THz. Meanwhile, a 1D leaky-wave structure produces a fan beam, narrow in the scan plane and fat in the transverse plane. As for that, a 2D phased array by combining several 1D LWAs in an array configuration naturally can lead to pencil beams and provide additional 2D scanning capability, when using frequency scanning in the plane of the LWA structures and electronic scanning (typically used in conventional array phase

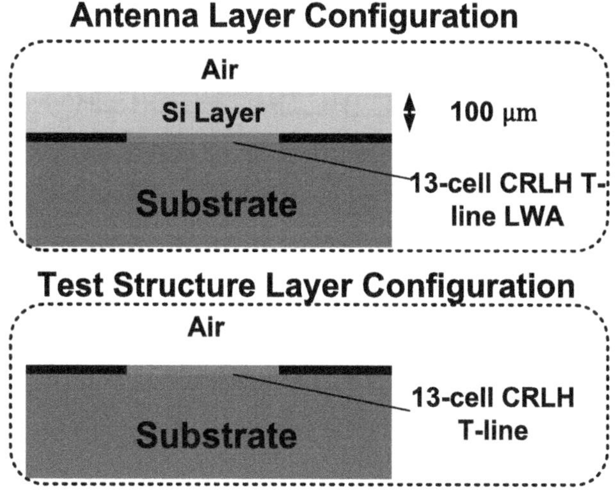

Figure 8.4: Stacking of high-resistivity Si layer on top of the LWA.

shifters) in the transverse plane as shown in Figure 8.5. The 2D array composes of a shielded 1D 13-unit-cell CRLH T-line-based power divider feeding 4 identical 1D 13-unit-cell CRLH T-line-based LWAs. The CRLH T-line-based power divider is identical to each of 4 CRLH T-line based LWAs in structure, but radiation losses are ignored due to a shielding layer on it. A THz signal source drives the power divider from one terminal and the first four unit-cells are used as matching networks to have maximized input power to multiple 1D arrays.

8.4.1.3 EM Simulation

The proposed CRLH T-line-based LWA design is verified by EM simulation in HFSS. As shown in Figure 8.6, the maximum efficiency was 6.4% in 230 $\sim$ 290 GHz, and it is enhanced to 40.5 $\sim$ 65.2% after stacking the dielectric layer with high resistivity of Si. The maximum enhancement of 26 times is achieved. After the enhancement of efficiency, the maximum antenna gain of 4.1 dBi is achieved at 280GHz. As illustrated in the radiation pattern shown in Figure 8.7, a broadside radiation is observed at 280 GHz when $\beta = 0$. Note that the zero phase propagation at 280 GHz also provides higher gain and efficiency than the negative phase ($\beta < 0$ at 290 GHz) and positive phase ($\beta > 0$ at 250 GHz) propagation with tilted radiation direction. Note that the zero-β frequency of 280GHz shown in Figure 8.7 is lower than the 303 GHz shown in Figure 3.13. This is mainly because of the increase of equivalent permittivity due to the stacking of a high-resistance silicon layer.

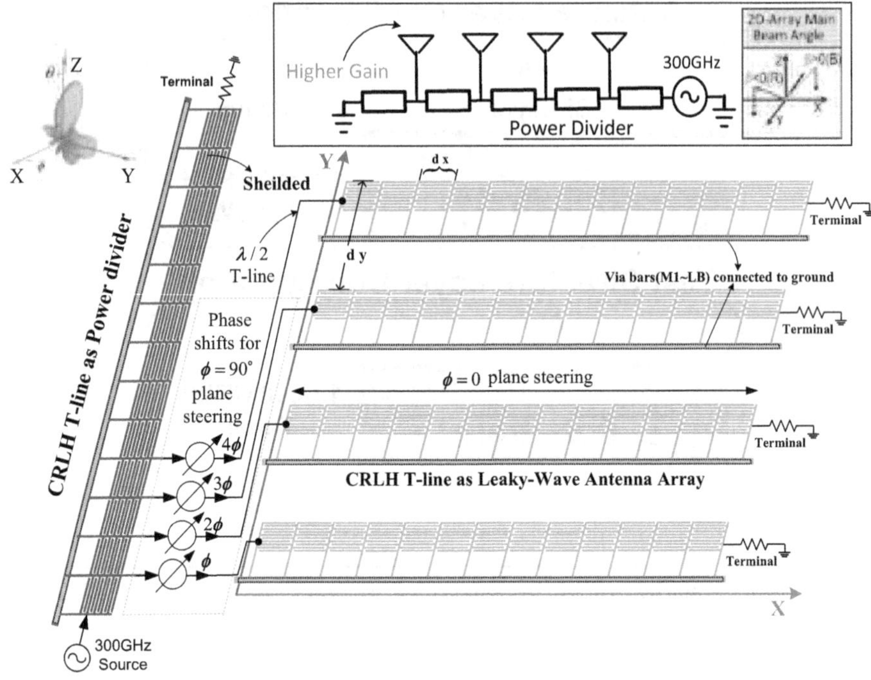

Figure 8.5: Structure of CRLH T-line-based 2D phase-arrayed array in THz.

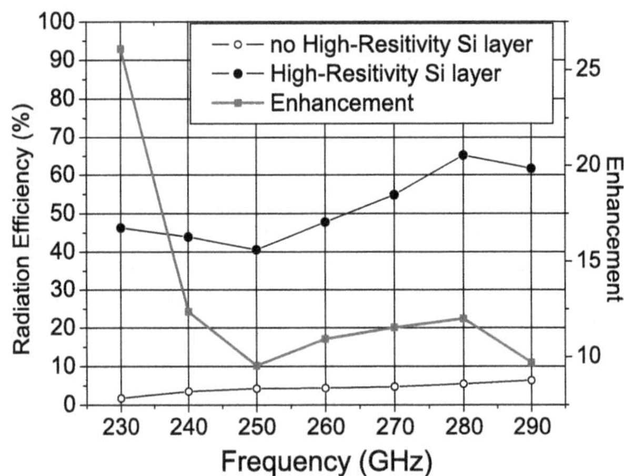

Figure 8.6: Radiation efficiency enhancement by stacking a high-resistivity Si layer.

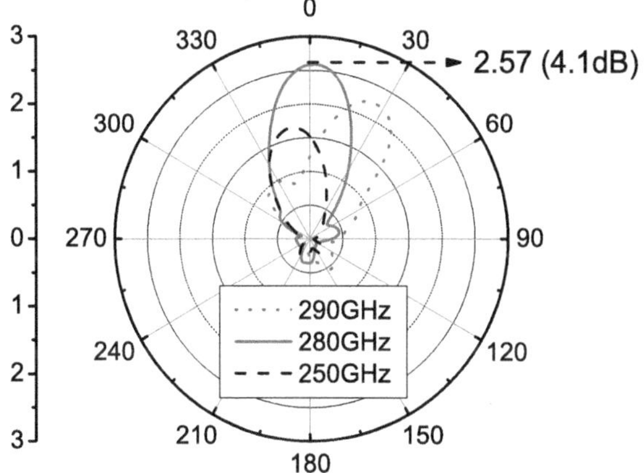

Figure 8.7: Gain radiation patterns for the proposed 1D LWA array at three frequencies: f = 250 GHz ($\beta < 0$, backward radiation), f = 280 GHz ($\beta = 0$, broadside radiation), and f = 290 GHz ($\beta > 0$, forward radiation).

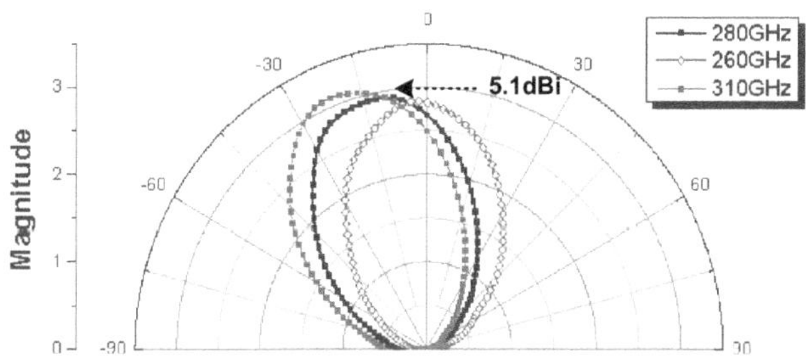

Figure 8.8: Gain radiation patterns for the proposed 2D LWA array at three frequencies: f = 260 GHz, f = 280 GHz and f = 310 GHz.

Fig. 8.8 shows the EM simulation results of the 2D phase-arrayed LWA for $\phi = 90°$ plane. The proposed 2D array achieves a gain of 5.1 dBi at 280 GHz, 1 dB higher than 1D array to support longer transmission distance. Higher gain improvement will be achieved if we can use a power divider with smaller attenuation constant α. The proposed 2D array thereby can improve the gain of antenna and also realize 2 directions for the frequency-dependent beam steering.

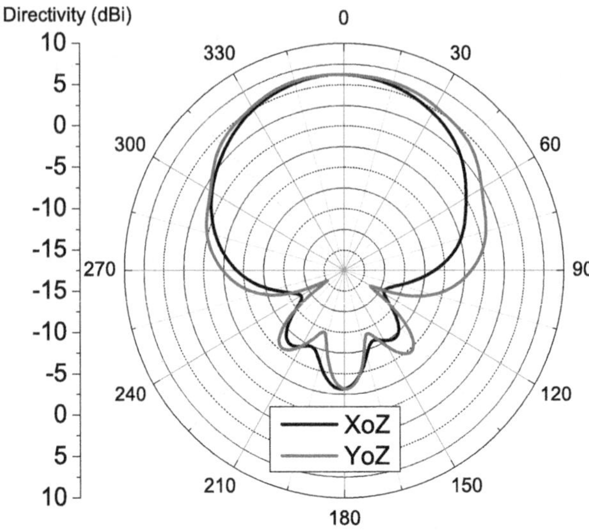

Figure 8.9: HFSS simulation results of proposed SIW antenna directivity at 270 GHz.

8.4.2 280-GHz SIW

8.4.2.1 Antenna Design

The proposed on-chip SIW antenna is designed in the 65nm CMOS process with 9 metal layers as shown in Figure 8.3. A composite dielectric material with silicon dioxide (SiO_2) and silicon nitride (Si_3N_4) is enclosed in the cuboid cavity (410 μm × 410 μm × 9 μm) formed by the topmost aluminum layer (AL), bottommost copper layer (M1) and metal walls constructed by metal layers and via bars (M1-AL). The chip area required for SIW antenna is 0.17 mm^2. Two 17-μm wide rectangular slots with different lengths (325 μm and 360 μm) are crossed at the center of the AL layer to create four resonance modes with perpendicular polarization directions at 270 GHz. A rectangular slot (120 μm × 30 μm) is created at each corner to reduce the antenna size at the desired operating frequency as discussed in Sec. 8.3. Different from the SIW design in Printed Circuit Board (PCB), a uniform metallic plane is not available in CMOS process according to the metal density rules. As such, the bottom side (M1) is implemented in mesh type with tiny square slots (3.5 × 3.5 μm^2) placed with 12-μm pitch. The antenna input is fed by a micro-strip line with characteristic impedance of 40Ω, which is implemented by M8 and M1 layers for signal and ground, respectively.

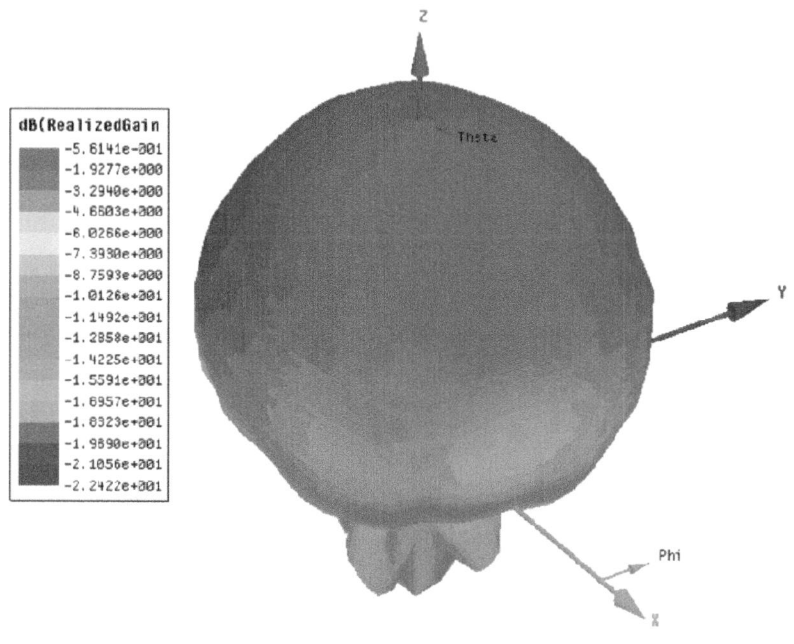

Figure 8.10: HFSS simulation results of the proposed SIW antenna radiation pattern at 270 GHz.

8.4.2.2 EM Simulation

The proposed antenna structure is verified by a full wave simulation in Ansoft HFSS. Figure 8.9 shows the simulated radiation pattern at 270 GHz. It has a broadside radiation pattern with 6.2-dB directivity and a 21.4% radiation efficiency at 270 GHz. As a result, a -0.5-dB antenna gain is obtained as illustrated in the simulated 3D radiation pattern in Figure 8.10. Figure 8.11 shows the simulated E-field distribution of SIW cavity at 270 GHz, where a circularly polarized field distribution is observed with two modes (f_{120} and f_{210}) excited with a phase difference of 90°. The simulated 3dB-axial-ratio frequency range is 265.6–274.5GHz as observed from Figure 8.12. Figure 8.12 also shows the S11 of the proposed antenna. As a result of the difference between W1 and L1, f_{120} is slightly different from f_{210}. Thereby four resonances are generated including in f_{120}, f_{210}, f_{L1} and f_{W1}, resulting in a very wide -6dB S11 bandwidth of 32.1GHz centered at 268GHz.

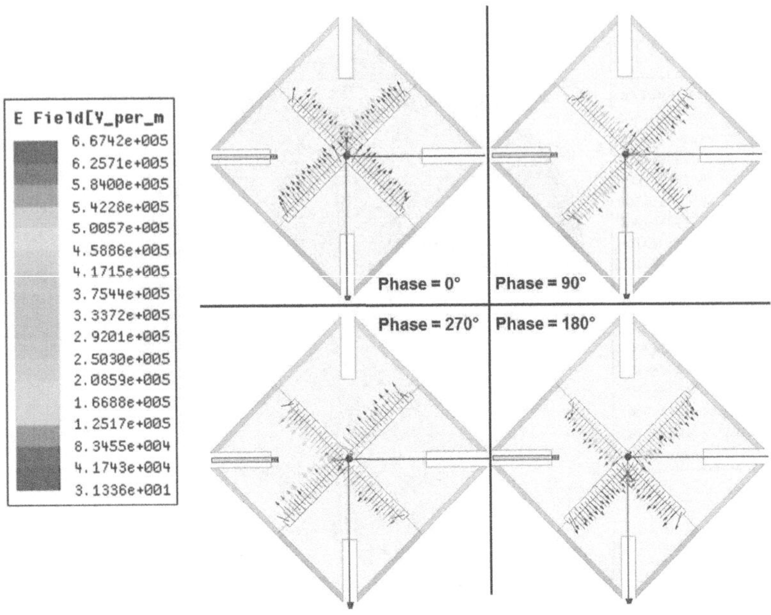

Figure 8.11: HFSS simulation results of polarized vector electric field in the slots of SIW cavity at 270 GHz.

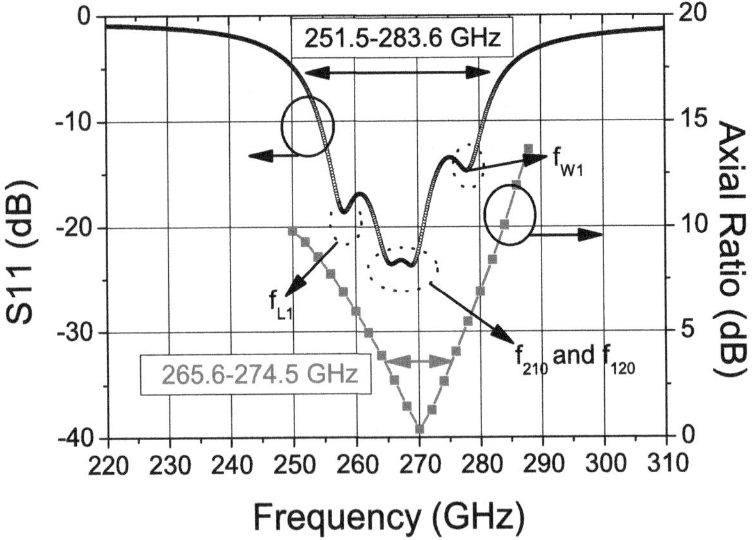

Figure 8.12: HFSS simulation results of input S11 and antenna axial ratio on broadside radiation direction.

8.5 Conclusion

The designs of THz CMOS wide-band and high-gain on-chip antennas are demonstrated in a compact area by high-Q passive structures such as substrate integrated waveguide (SIW) and metamaterial based composite right/left-handed transmission line (CRLH T-line). In the wide-band 280-GHz on-chip circularly polarized SIW antenna design in the 65nm CMOS process, by creating corner slots in SIW structure, the size of the proposed SIW antenna is reduced by 15% when compared to the conventional designs. As verified by the EM simulation, the proposed antenna has -0.5-dBi antenna gain and 32.1-GHz bandwidth centered at 268 GHz. In the CRLH T-line-based leaky wave antenna (LWA) design in the 65-nm CMOS process, stacking of dielectric layer with high resistivity of Si is utilized to improve the LWA efficiency. With correlated measurement and EM validation from 220 GHz to 325 GHz, a broadside radiation pattern is achieved at 280 GHz with 65% radiation efficiency and 4.1dBi antenna gain at 280GHz. Both antenna structures can be potentially deployed for the design of an on-chip antenna array in THz biomedical imaging systems. In the following section, CMOS-based transceiver design for THz Imaging will be discussed.

CMOS THZ SIGNAL DETECTION

Chapter 9

Resonator

9.1 Introduction

The Q factor of the LC-tank-based resonator has performance degradation at 60$\sim$100 GHz. EM-wave-based oscillators have been studied to improve the Q factor. The commonly deployed standing-wave-based oscillator (SWO) in [79, 238, 239] increases the Q of $\lambda/4$ coplanar stripline (CPS) resonators by forming an open-circuit load when the incident and reflected EM waves perfectly move in phase with each other. The primary limitations of this approach are twofold. Firstly, the open circuit condition is hard to achieve due to loss in the $\lambda/4$ CPS line; and secondly, the dimension is still large when implementing $\lambda/4$ CPS lines on chip. Placing additional floating metal shielding to form slow-wave lines may alleviate the aforementioned problems. Alternatively, metamaterial-based designs have been explored recently within the microwave community [240, 54, 241, 78]. A number of works are proposed recently for the design of a transmission line (T-line) loaded high-Q metamaterial resonator at the printed circuit board (PCB) scale. Split-ring resonator (SRR)-based or complementary split-ring resonator(CSRR)-based oscillator designs are explored at 5.5$\sim$5.8 GHz [79, 80]. As the node becomes advanced, recently, a single-ended T-line loaded with SRRs (STL-SRRs) was studied in [84]. The SRR-based open-loop multiple split-ring resonator structure was studied for a 24-GHz oscillator in a 130-nm CMOS process [79, 80]. No in-depth works are, however, performed on how to design a high-Q and low-loss metamaterial resonator in advanced node. For example, it is unknown to design differential oscillators or voltage-controlled oscillators (VCOs) with use of a metamaterial resonator at 60$\sim$100 GHz in the 65-nm CMOS process.

To demonstrate the high-Q performance of the proposed metamaterial resonator at mm-wave region and its improvement in phase noise, two MMIC

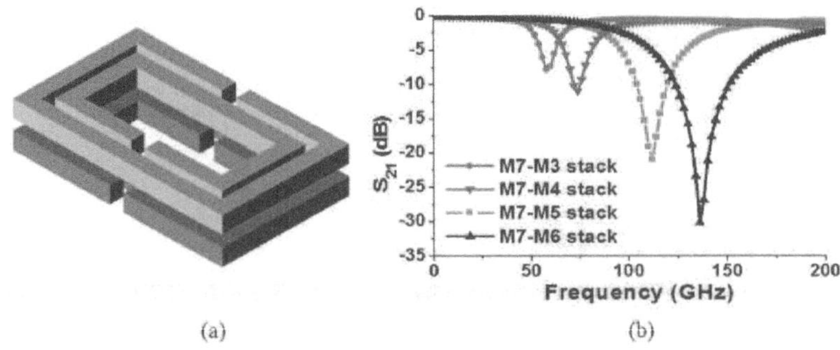

Figure 9.1: (a) Stacked SRR unit-cell designed by metal layers of M7 and M6; (b) S21 simulation results with different stacking methods.

oscillators based on metamaterial resonators have been designed in 65-nm CMOS (STM 7-metal-layer). The first one is operated at 76 GHz using the differential T-line loaded with SRR (DTL-SRR), and the second one is operated at 96 GHz using the differential T-line loaded with SRR (DTL-SRR). Note that the design of slow-wave shielding is implemented for both MMIC oscillators with loss reduction. The slow-wave shielding strips are designed by the bottom metal layer M1 with both width and pitch of 1 μm. The two MMIC oscillators are designed and verified with Agilent ADS Momentum for EM simulation and Cadence Spectre for oscillator circuit simulation.

9.2 Differential TL-SRR Resonator

9.2.1 Stacked SRR Layout

The on-chip SRR can be implemented in a stacked fashion with on-chip multilayer interconnect [84]. As shown in Figure 9.1(a), one SRR unit-cell is realized by the top two metal layers stacked alternatively, considering a trade-off among resonant frequency, area and loss. When its size is fixed, S21 of TL-SRR with different stacked layers is shown in Figure 9.1(b). It is found that more stacked layers result in lower resonant frequency, but suffer from lower Q at the same time. With the increased resonant frequency, TL-SRR reveals a steeper and higher rejection property, which means a higher Q. Thus TL-SRR shows the potential application for on-chip MMIC designs.

Figure 9.2(a) shows a differential T-line with stacked on-chip SRR (DTL-SRR) in the CMOS process, of which the cross-section is illustrated in Figure 9.2(c). The two loaded SRR unit-cells are excited by the axial magnetic field generated by the host T-line. It has the following advantages in Q improvement. Firstly, as the SRR-load is metamaterial with stop-band property, it

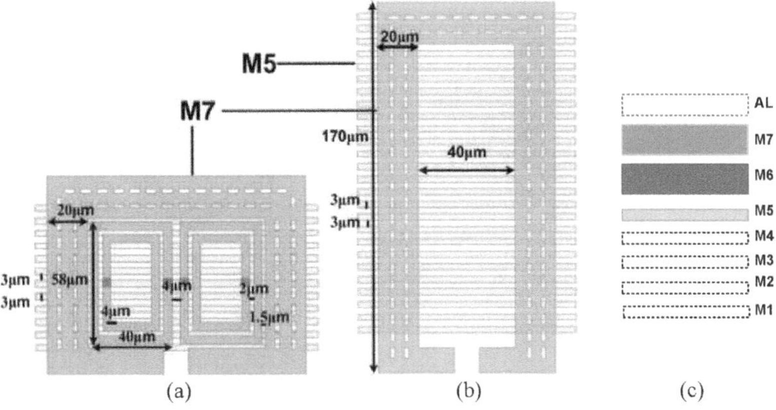

(a) (b) (c)

Figure 9.2: Geometries of resonators with slow-wave shielding: (a) differential T-line loaded with stacked SRR, (b) T-line based standing-wave resonator, and (c) cross-section of BEOL.

results in large impedance with the open circuit condition formed. Thus EM energy can be perfectly reflected in the host T-line. Secondly, the differential design provides local ground to reduce EM loss and enhance the EM-energy coupling. For example, the magnetic field generated by the differential T-line is equidirectional and superimposed when applied to the two SRR unit-cells. Thus a stronger coupling between T-line and SRR is achieved with larger mutual capacitance and mutual inductance, which can store more EM-energy with less EM-energy leakage into the substrate. Due to the stronger EM coupling, the DTL-SRR needs fewer SRR unit-cells than STL-SRR when the same rejection property is achieved. This makes the DTL-SRR achieve higher area efficiency as well. To strengthen the coupling between T-line and SRRs, a shortest distance (or gap) between SRRs and T-line is selected with the consideration of the process limitation (1.5 μm in STM 65nm CMOS). Lastly, floating metal shielding is also employed in this design to further reduce the substrate loss.

9.2.2 Comparison with Single-Ended TL-SRR Resonator

In the following, detailed analysis for the enhancement of Q factor is shown with comparison between the DTL-SRR and STL-SRR. Assuming both terminals of an SRR unit-cell observe the same characteristic impedance (Z_0). The reflection coefficient can be estimated at the position TL-SRR unit cell

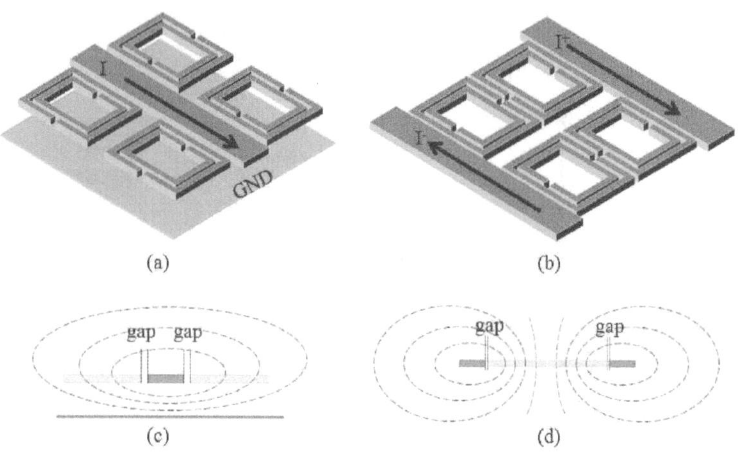

Figure 9.3: T-line-based SRR excitation: (a) single-ended approach, (b) differential approach, (c) magnetic field distribution of single-ended approach, and (d) magnetic field distribution of differential approach.

by

$$\Gamma = \frac{R_s'}{R_s' + 2Z_0} = \frac{k^2}{k^2 + \frac{2Z_0 L_s}{R_s L}}. \tag{9.1}$$

One can have two observations from (9.1). Firstly, if the Q factor of SRR is sufficiently high that $k^2 >> 2Z_0L_s/R_sL$, Γ is approaching unity, which means a perfectly reflection of EM-wave at the SRR-load. Secondly, Γ increases with k for a given SRR with a finite Q, thus improving k is the means to enhance the EM-energy reflection efficiency. Note that the coupling coefficient k is often limited by the geometry mismatch between T-line and SRR.

As a result, in order to have a high-Q DTL-SRR design, one needs to have the reflection coefficient Γ as high as possible. One can observe from (9.1) that Γ increases with the coupling coefficient k between SRRs and T-line, In the single-ended T-line as shown in Figure 9.3(a), the magnetic flux cannot be fully covered between the SRR and T-line. This is illustrated in Figure 9.3(c) as part of the magnetic flux leaked to the open space regardless of the distance between SRR and T-line. In contrast, the differential T-line shown in Figure 9.3(b) does not have this limitation. As one can see from Figure 9.3(d), it is possible to have SRR fully cover the magnetic flux generated by the differential T-line. Thus, a high EM coupling coefficient can be achieved with a high Γ for the DTL-SRR structure than the STL-SRR structure.

To further validate the high-Q of the DTL-SRR, EM simulation (Agilent ADS momentum) is performed for STL-SRR and DTL-SRR structures shown in Figure 9.3(a) and (b). The conductivity of the topmost metal layers M6 and M7 are 4.6×10^7 S/m, the metal layers M1$\sim$M5 are 4.1×10^7 S/m and the silicon substrate is 10 S/m according to the 65-nm CMOS process files. The simulation result of reflection coefficient (Γ) is plotted against different gap sizes in the Smith Chart as shown in Figure 9.4. Note that the resonance happens when the imaginary part of Γ equals zero. One can observe that the reflection coefficient of DTL-SRR at resonance frequency is much higher than that of STL-SRR. Moreover, the reflection coefficient is increased for a smaller gap size. For example, at the minimum gap of 2 μm that is allowed by the design rule, the reflection coefficient of the differential T-line is 10.6% higher than that of single-ended T-line. Since the minimum gap size is limited by the design rule, the maximum reflection coefficient one can obtain is around 0.9. The Q factor for both resonators are also compared by the reflection coefficient as shown in Figure 9.5. As discussed, a high reflection coefficient of DTL-SRR can be directly transferred into a high Q. One can observe that the Q of DTL-SRR is around 20 $\sim$ 40% higher than that of STL-SRR with the same gap size.

9.2.3 Comparison with Standing-Wave Resonator

The proposed DTL-SRR resonator is further compared with the standing-wave resonator using coplanar strip line (CPS). As shown in Figure 9.2, they are both designed under the same resonance frequency and are also provided with floating metal shielding to reduce substrate loss.

The optimization of the two structures is conducted with the full-wave EM simulator (Agilent Momentum). As for DTL-SRR-based metamaterial resonator, the stacked SRR unit-cell is designed with the top two metal layers (M7, M6). M7 and M5 are used for the design of the host T-line and the floating metal strips for shielding of the two resonators, respectively. The sizes of T-line, SRR and floating metal strips are carefully selected to obtain the desired frequency. Moreover, for the CPS-based standing-wave resonator, its Q factor also depends on the width and the separation of the T-line, the width of the floating metal strip and the spacing between two adjacent floating metal strips. Due to the parasitic capacitance of the cross-coupled NMOS transistors and the layout-dependent parasitic effect, the physical length of CPS is shorter than the ideal length of $\lambda/4$. The detailed physical sizes are shown in Figure 9.2 and one can observe that the use of SRR has 40% area reduction versus the use of CPS.

Note that the Q of one resonator can be described by

$$Q = \omega \frac{Average\_energy\_stored}{Energy\_loss/second}. \tag{9.2}$$

As such, one can compare the Q factors of the DTL-SRR with the standing-

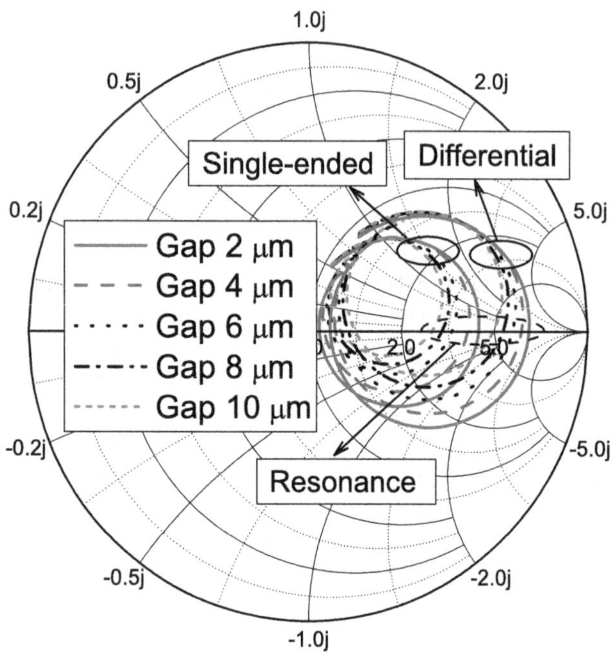

Figure 9.4: Simulated Γ plot in Smith chart of SRR/T-line unit cell at resonance.

wave resonator as follows. Firstly, the smaller size of the DTL-SRR leads to a lower substrate loss, and hence the denominator above decreases. Secondly, for the DTL-SRR, the strong EM-energy coupling between the SRR and T-line with perfect reflection can enhance the energy storage capability with the nominator in (9.2) increased. Thereby, one can expect that a higher quality factor can be achieved by DTL-SRR than the standing-wave resonator, which is further validated by the measured experiment results.

9.3 Differential TL-CSRR Resonator

It is not feasible to directly deploy the etched CSRR from ground [78] on chip due to the lossy substrate in CMOS process. To realize a low-loss and high-Q implementation for on-chip CSRR, the CSRR can be etched directly on a metal layer using signal lines as shown in Figure 2.14. Compared with the previous method [78], CSRRs on a metal layer can form much stronger coupling between T-line and CSRR because they are on the same metal layer.

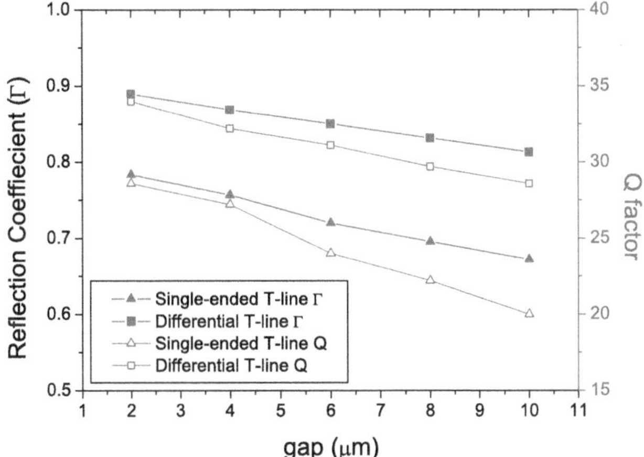

Figure 9.5: Simulated Γ and quality factor (Q) of SRR/T-line unit cell at resonance.

More EM-energy can thereby be stored in the resonator and in turn results in a higher Q-factor.

In this work, a differential CSRR structure is proposed in Figure 9.6 to provide a compact area. Both inputs are designed on the same side to provide an AC ground for easy DC supply, which further reduces the potential

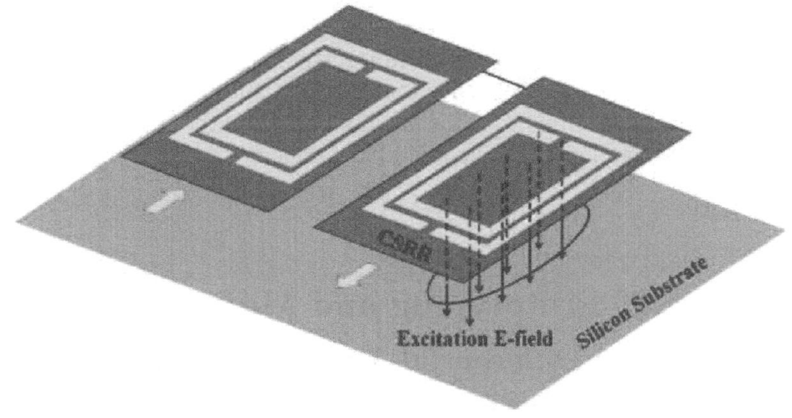

Figure 9.6: On-chip differential T-line loaded with CSRR.

coupling to the lossy substrate. Note that the metamaterial property of the proposed differential T-line-loaded CSRR and its high-Q feature can be illustrated through simulation as follows.

For example, the metamaterial property can be calculated from S-parameters by [242, 243]

$$\begin{aligned} cos(nkd) &= \frac{1 - S_{11}^2 + S_{21}^2}{2S_{21}}, \\ z &= \pm\sqrt{\frac{(1+S_{11})^2 - S_{21}^2}{(1-S_{11})^2 - S_{21}^2}}, \\ \varepsilon &= \frac{n}{z},\ \mu = nz, \end{aligned} \tag{9.3}$$

where n is the refractive index, z is the wave-impedance, k is wave-factor, and d is the physical length. Because the metamaterial is considered as a passive medium, the signs of n and z in (9.3) can be determined by two requirements: $\Im(n) \geq 0$ and $\Re(z) \geq 0$, where $\Im(n)$ and $\Re(z)$ denote the imaginary part and real part of n and z, respectively.

Based on (9.3), one can characterize the metamaterial resonator as follows. The proposed DTL-CSRR structure in Figure 9.6 is implemented on chip with resonance frequency biased around 100 GHz. ADS Momentum is used for the EM simulation to obtain the S-parameters. As shown in Figure 9.7, a negative μ can be observed within a narrow band near the resonance frequency. As stated earlier, the negative μ and positive ε create the electric plasma, where the propagating EM-waves become evanescent waves and are largely reflected backward. The deep rejection frequency band with a sharp cut-off can be viewed from S12 plot in Figure 9.7, which corresponds to a high-Q performance.

The Q-factor can be estimated from the simulation by $Q = f_0/BW_{-3dB}$, where f_0 is the resonance frequency and BW_{3dB} is the bandwidth. As such, the obtained Q-factor is 65, which is much higher than the normal Q value by a resonator composed of LC-tank at similar frequency, around 30 as indicated in [244].

9.4 Circuit Prototyping and Measurement

9.4.1 76-GHz Differential TL-SRR Resonator

Firstly, as shown in Figure 9.8, the DTL-SRR-based metamaterial oscillator has the property of position-dependent voltage-current amplitudes. If a cross-coupled transistor pair is connected to the opened ends of the two striplines in the host T-lines, an oscillation can be sustained at the specified frequency according to the length of the striplines. The incident-wave energy is injected by the cross-coupled inverters propagates in forward waves along the T-line

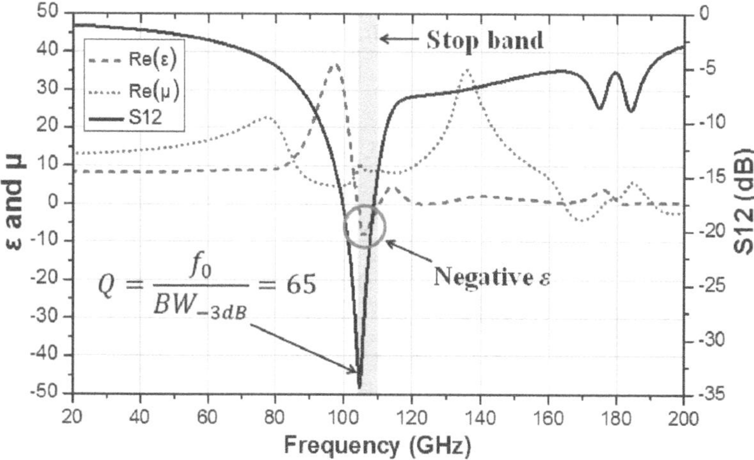

Figure 9.7: EM characterization of the proposed differential CSRR resonator.

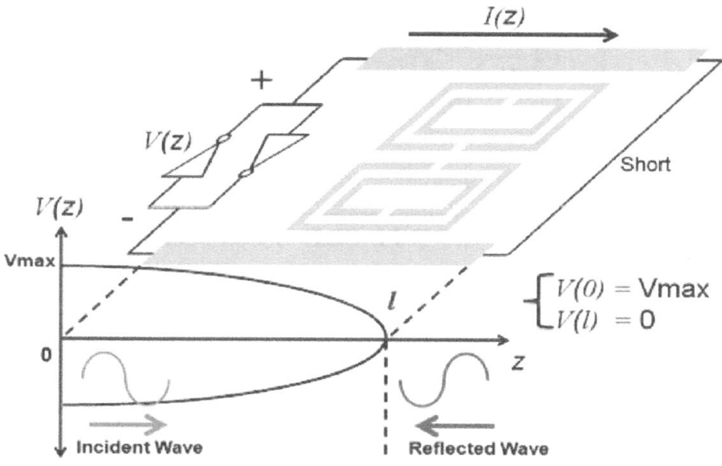

Figure 9.8: Voltage distribution of the DTL-SRR-based resonator.

toward the short point; the energy is reflected at SRR load; and the reverse-wave has a superposition of the incident-wave and leads to a resonance if in phase. Stronger wave reflection means less loss and higher Q of the resonator for oscillation.

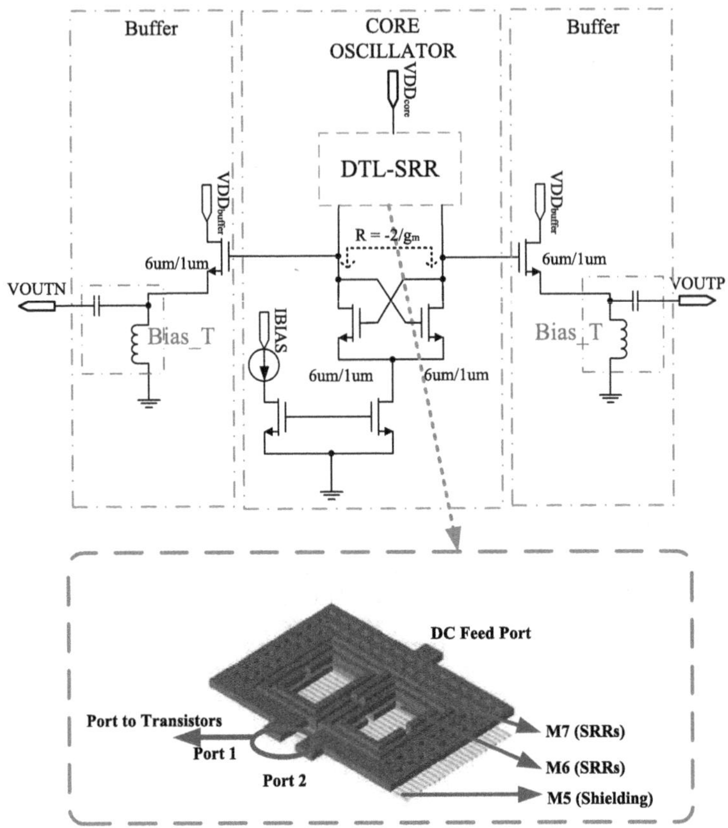

Figure 9.9: Schematic of the DTL-SRR-based oscillator.

As a result, with the use of the proposed metamaterial resonator by DTL-SRR, a 76GHz oscillator is designed. As shown in Figure 9.9, a pair of cross-coupled NMOS transistors is deployed as the negative resistor to compensate the energy loss in the resonator. Source-follower output buffers are implemented with off-chip bias T to save area. The supply-voltage for the resonator is provided from the middle point of the T-line short-circuit termination, which is a differential zero AC-voltage point. External current source is fed into the chip through a DC-PAD and mirrored to the core circuit of oscillator to control the power consumption. In addition, for comparison, the standing-wave resonator by coplanar stripline (CPS) under the same resonant frequency is also implemented in the same chip with geometries shown in Figure 9.2(b). For a fair comparison, the proposed two oscillators have the same size and layout designs of cross-coupled NMOS transistors and output buffers, except for resonators. The channel length of transistor is chosen to the minimum 60 nm allowed by the technology to reduce the parasitic effects, while the width is 6 μm (each finger width is 1 μm) for both the cross-coupled pair and the source-follower output buffers. The detailed physical sizes in Figure 9.2 show that the use of SRR has 40% area reduction versus the use of CPS.

9.4.2 96-GHz Differential TL-CSRR Resonator

Next, a 96GHz oscillator is also implemented in the same CMOS 65nm process with the use of metamaterial resonator by DTL-CSRR. Similarly, the loss from the resonator is compensated by a cross-coupled pair of NMOS transistors, as shown in Figure 9.10. To obtain the maximum f_{MAX} of NMOS transistors, the individual finger width is designed to be 1 μm [245], and the total finger number is designed to be 8 to sustain the oscillation on slow-corner while minimizing parasitic capacitance. In order to isolate the oscillator from the peripheral circuits and also to provide enough output power, the output is designed together with on-chip buffer and RF choke. It is composed of a quarter-wavelength slow-wave T-line and de-coupling capacitor. All four transistors in the circuit are self-biased. The DC-supply voltages for the core oscillator and buffer-stage are provided separately to identify the individual current consumption. Note that the 1-metal-layer design of resonator used for demonstration in Figure 2.14 is modified to be a 2-metal-layer design for oscillator implementation. Other than the benefit of size reduction, the stacked structure is also expected to improve the Q-factor. Because the stacked two CSRRs are in the opposite direction, they are excited in the odd mode at resonance by the E-field in between, which avoids the E-field to penetrate through the substrate. As such, the impact of the lossy substrate to the resonator Q-factor can be further reduced.

9.4.3 Measurements

The proposed 76-GHz SRR and 96-GHz CSRR oscillators were both is implemented in the STM 65-nm CMOS RF process with f_T/f_{MAX} of 170/230 GHz. As shown in Figure 9.11, the RF and DC signals are connected through a CASCADE Microtech Elite-300 probe station. The single-ended output of the chip is connected to a phase-noise analyzer FSU-P50 from Rohde & Schwarz (R&S) for the phase noise measurement at millimeter-wave frequency region. To measure the signal frequency in 75 $\sim$ 110 GHz, a W-band harmonic mixer FS-WR10 is used for down-conversion. The external Bias-T is required in the measurement for DTL-SRR and SWO-based oscillators at 76 GHz.

9.4.3.1 Results of 76GHz Oscillator with DTL-SRR

As shown by the die photo in Figure 9.12, both the DTL-SRR-based oscillator and the standing-wave-oscillator (SWO) by coplanar stripline are implemented side by side on the same chip with the same resonant frequency. The sizes excluding RF-PADs is 310 $\times$ 210 μm^2 (0.06 mm^2) for DTL-SRR, and 310 $\times$

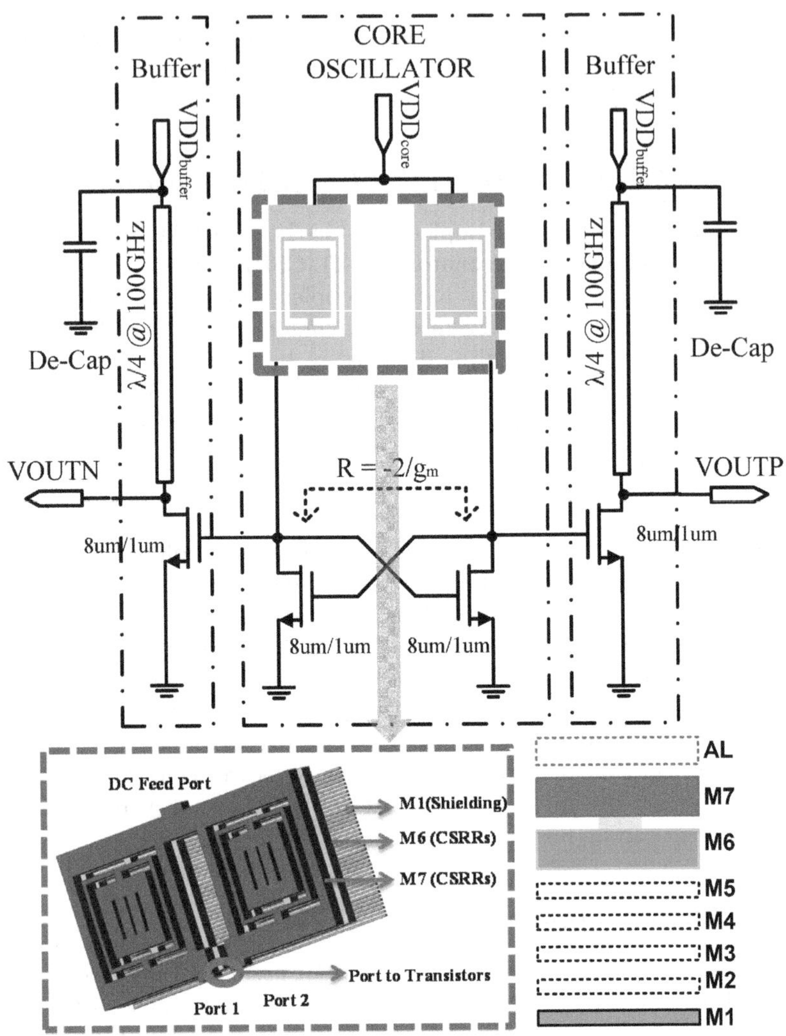

Figure 9.10: Circuit diagram of the 96 GHz CMOS oscillator with the use of the proposed metamaterial resonator by CSRR structure.

270 μm^2 (0.08 mm^2) for SWO. The proposed DTL-SRR oscillator consumes only 2.7 mW from a 1-V power supply, which is slightly higher than the power consumption of SWO of 2.63 mW from the same 1-V power supply. The measured oscillation frequency of the DTL-SRR and SWO oscillators are both observed at 76.1 GHz as shown in the spectrum diagram in Figures 9.13 and 9.14, where one spur contributed by the harmonic mixer can be observed at 200 MHz away from the oscillation frequency. Here a signal identification

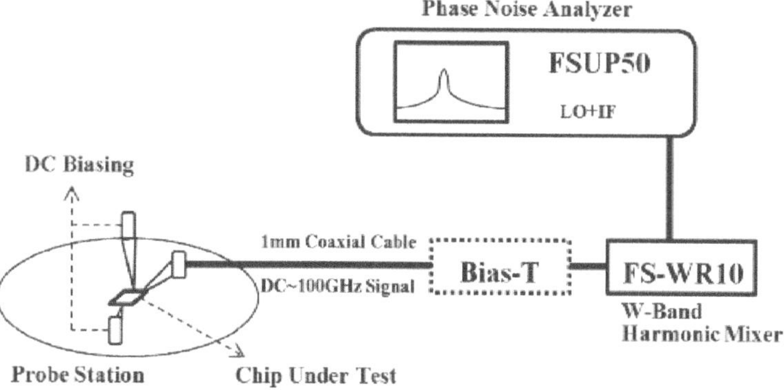

Figure 9.11: Equipment setup for W-band 75∼110 GHz phase noise measurement.

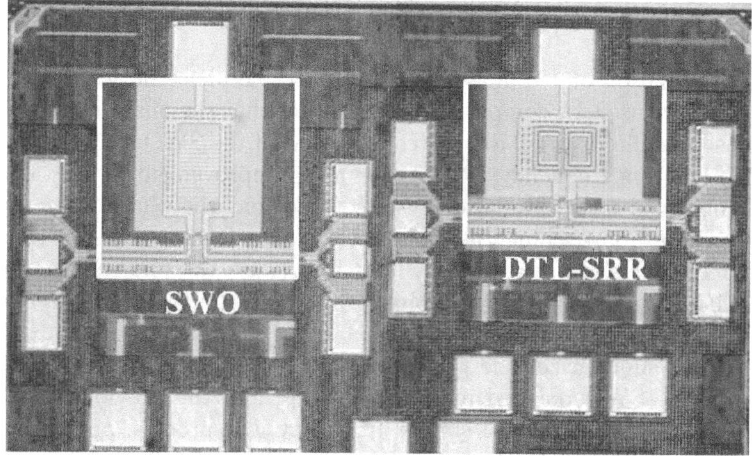

Figure 9.12: Chip photo of the DTL-SRR-based oscillator and SWO.

function of spectrum analyzer is used to verify the source of spurs. However, the signal power level could be distorted by such identification function, which should be turned off when capturing the measurement results. The output power is −16 dBm by subtracting the loss of cable and Bias-T.

Figure 9.15 shows the phase noise measurement and simulation results of the DTL-SRR and SWO-based oscillators. It can be observed that the variation of phase noise becomes worse near the oscillation frequency, induced

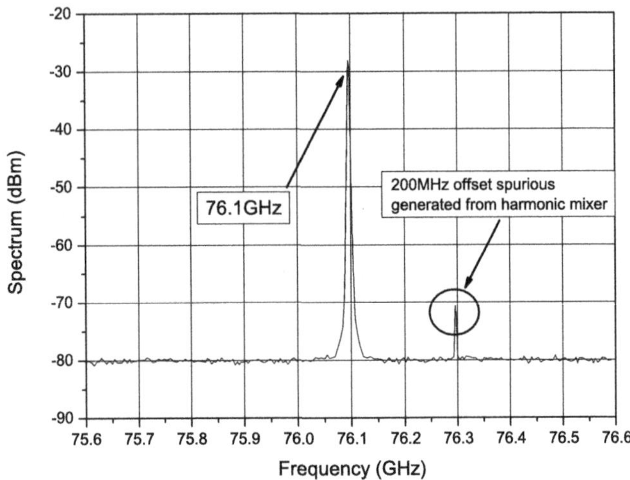

Figure 9.13: Spectrum of the 76 GHz DTL-SRR oscillator.

by the modulation of $1/f$ noise. Thus more stable phase noise results at 10 MHz offset are used for comparison. One can see that the phase noise of DTL-SRR-based oscillator is 4.2 dB better than that of the SWO at 10 MHz offset at the oscillation frequency. This phase noise improvement is very close to 2.6 dB observed from simulation results. Note that the phase noise of both oscillators are approaching the same level (around -116 dBc/Hz) from 10-MHz to 100-MHz frequency offset. This is because the phase noise level of the oscillator is lower than the noise level of the spectrum analyzer in the measurement.

Table 9.1 summarizes the performance of the proposed DTL-SRR-based oscillator, the SWO realized in the same chip, and the previous oscillators by LC-tank or SWOs at the similar frequency and process, and achieves a phase noise of -108.8 dBc/Hz at 10 MHz offset and a FOM of -182.1 dBc/Hz. Note that the energy loss is reduced due to the higher power efficiency, thus the power consumption of DTL-SRR-based oscillator is much smaller than the SWO-based oscillator while the phase noise is minimized. As a summary, when compared to the existing LC-tank or standing-wave resonator-based oscillator [246, 238, 239], the phase noise and FOM are improved by 2.7 dB and 7.6 dB on average, respectively. When compared to the standing-wave resonator-based oscillator implemented on the same chip, the phase noise and FOM are improved by 4.2 dB and 4.1 dB, respectively.

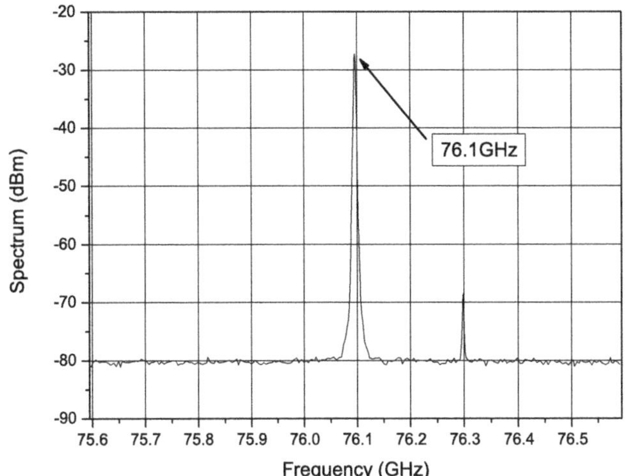

Figure 9.14: Spectrum of the 76 GHz SWO.

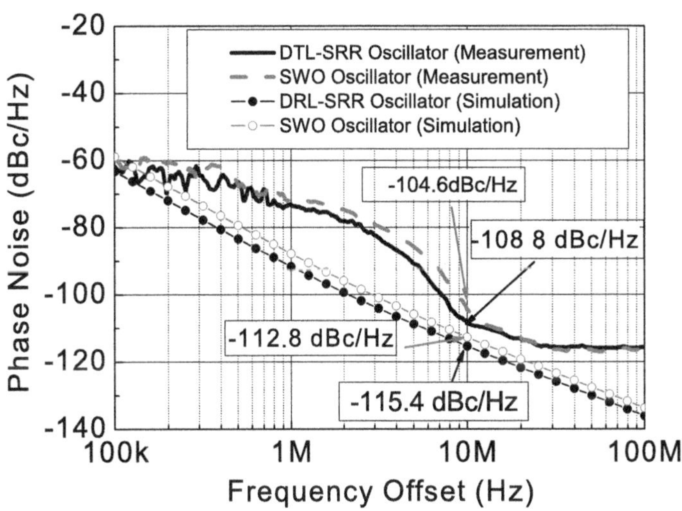

Figure 9.15: Phase noise measurement and simulation results of the 76 GHz DTL-SRR oscillator and SWO.

9.4.3.2 Results of 96-GHz Oscillator with DTL-CSRR

The die photo of the 96-GHz Oscillator with DTL-CSRR is shown in Figure 9.16 with area of 430 × 320 μm^2 ($0.14mm^2$) excluding RF-PADs. Both the

Table 9.1: Performance Comparison of State-of-the-Art Oscillator Designs around 70 GHz

Parameters	[246]	[238]	[239]	This work	This work
Oscillator Design	LC-tank	SWO	SWO	SWO	DTL-SRR
f_{osc} (GHz)	70.2	71.1	76.5	76.1	76.1
Power Supply (V)	1.2	1.2	1.5	1.0	1.0
$Power_{core}$ (mW)	5.4	6	14.3	2.63	2.7
Phase Noise @ 10-MHz offset (dBc/Hz)	-106.1	-104	-108.4	-104.6	-108.8
FOM (dBc/Hz)	-175.8	-173.2	-174.5	-178	-182.1
Technology	65-nm CMOS	65-nm CMOS	65-nm CMOS	65-nm CMOS	65-nm CMOS

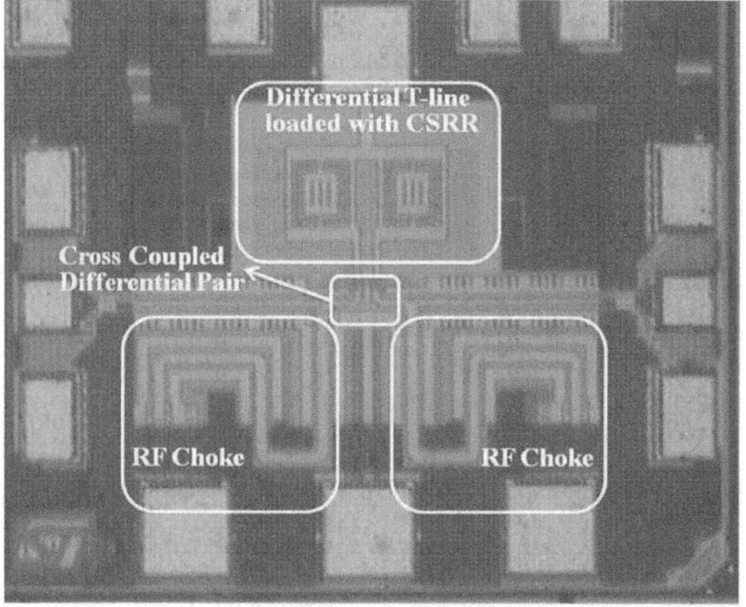

Figure 9.16: Chip photo of the DTL-CSRR-based oscillator.

oscillator core and output buffer are supplied with a 1.2-V power supply, of which the current consumption is 6.24 mA and 6.53 mA, respectively. Thus the power consumption for the oscillator core circuit is 7.5 mW. Figure 9.17 shows the measured spectrum when the output frequency is 96.36 GHz. Same as the oscillator with DTL-SRR, there is a 200 MHz offset spur generated

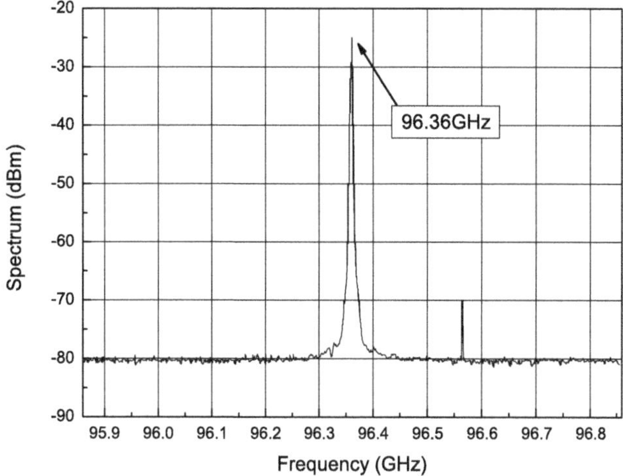

Figure 9.17: Spectrum of the 96-GHz oscillator with DTL-CSRR.

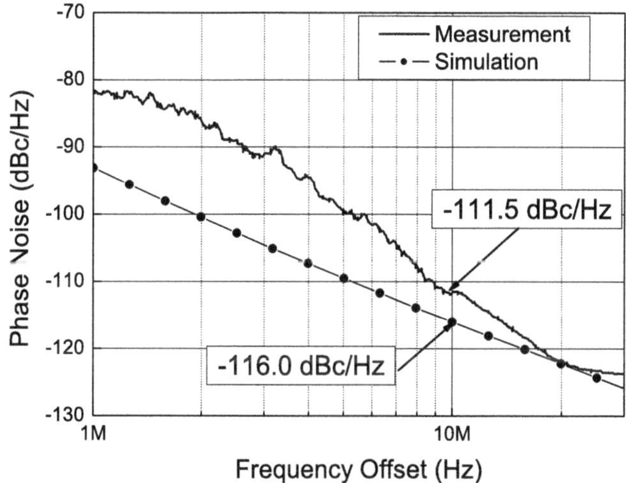

Figure 9.18: Phase noise measurement and simulation results of 96 GHz oscillator with DTL-CSRR.

by the harmonic mixer. Figure 9.18 shows the measured phase noise at this frequency of -111.5 dBc/Hz at 10-MHz offset, which is 4.5dB higher than the simulation results. This is probably due to the noise coupled from the DC power supply.

Table 9.2: Performance Comparison of State-of-the-Art Oscillator Designs around 100 GHz

Parameters	[247]	[248]	[249]	This Work
Oscillator Design	SWO	LC-tank	LC-tank	DTL-CSRR
f_{osc} (GHz)	104	128	100	96
Power Supply (V)	1.48	1.2	1	1.2
$Power_{core}$ (mW)	25.3	9	30	7.5
Phase Noise @10-MHz offset (dBc/Hz)	-105	-105	-85	-111.5
FOM (dBc/Hz)	-171.3	-177.6	-150.2	-182.4
Technology	130-nm CMOS	90-nm CMOS	90-nm CMOS	65-nm CMOS

As described in Table 9.2, the measurement results of the proposed 96-GHz oscillator by DTL-CSRR resonator show state-of-the-art performance when compared to the recent oscillators designed at 100 GHz using the traditional on-chip LC-tank resonators. Clearly, the proposed high-Q metamaterial resonator structure shows the best phase noise result of -111.5 dBc/Hz at 10-MHz offset and FOM of -182.4 dBc/Hz at 96 GHz. As a summary, when compared to the existing designs by LC-tank or standing-wave resonator-based oscillator [247, 248, 249], the phase noise and FOM are improved by 13 dB and 16 dB on average, respectively.

9.5 Conclusion

High-Q oscillation can be achieved by metamaterial resonators such as DTL-SRR and DTL-CSSR. As demonstrated in this section, Both DTL-SRR and DTL-CSSR can be applied in the oscillator design with low phase noise, low power, and compact chip. The 76GHz oscillator by the DTL-SRR is fabricated with a compact area of $0.06mm^2$ and measured with -108.8 dBc/Hz phase noise at 10MHz offset, -182.1 dBc/Hz FOM and 2.7mW core power consumption. The 96GHz oscillator by the DTL-CSRR is fabricated with a compact area of $0.14mm^2$ and measured with -111.5 dBc/Hz phase noise at 10MHz offset, -182.4 dBc/Hz FOM and 6.24mW core power consumption. Both oscillators have 4~6dB better phase noise than that of the standing-wave oscillator by a CPS with similar operating frequencies.

Chapter 10

Super-Regenerative Detection

10.1 Introduction

Recently, CMOS-based THz detectors have been developed [250, 89, 31, 32, 33, 251]. One can thereby develop a low-cost, portable and large-arrayed THz imaging system in CMOS. One transmission-type design is shown in Figure 10.1, where each THz image pixel consists of a receiver and an antenna. However, the THz radiation signal strength is usually weak when generated by CMOS and it will be further attenuated by absorption and diffraction during the propagation. The main challenge is to design a high-sensitivity receiver that can compensate the weak signal source and the path propagation loss with both narrow-band or wide-band approaches. Moreover, a large-arrayed receiver is desired with improved spatial resolution and also image capturing speed, requiring a compact design of each THz image pixel [252].

The recent super-regenerative receiver (SRX) [89, 90] topology can achieve high sensitivity within a narrow band, which is desired for a THz imager that has a relatively low data rate. As depicted in Figure 10.2(a), the core of a SRX is a quench-controlled oscillator, which consists of a resonator with a positive feedback network to realize an oscillatory amplification. When a periodic quench-control signal is applied, the average of detected signal envelope is amplified for the injected RF signal from LNA. One compact and high-sensitivity SRX for a THz imager requires a compact and high quality factor (Q) resonator. Note that the Q of the traditional LC-tank-based resonator [253] has significant performance degradation with large area at THz frequency region.

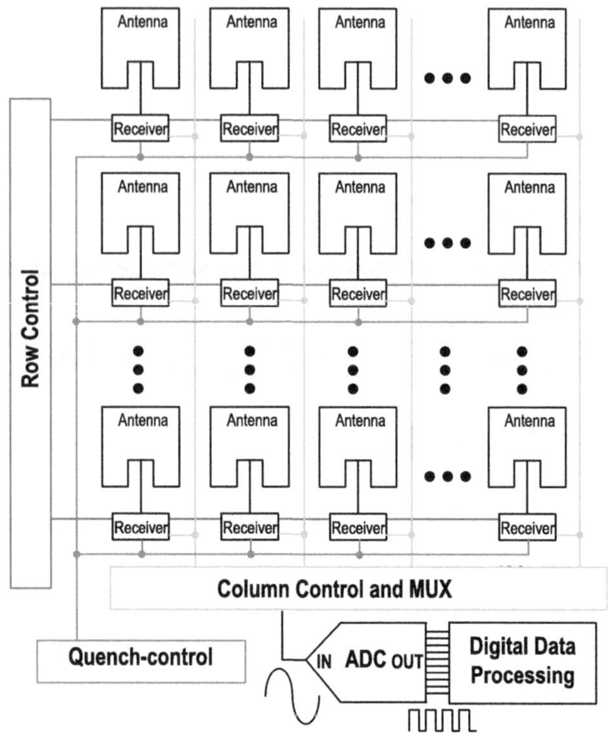

Figure 10.1: CMOS THz imager array.

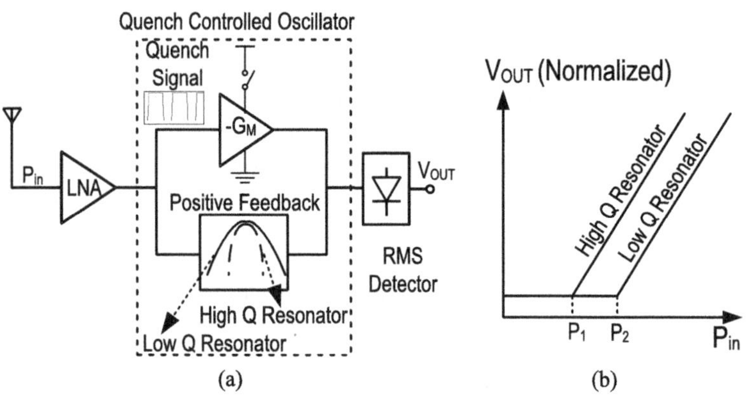

Figure 10.2: (a) Block diagram of super-regenerative receiver; (b) impact of resonator Q-factor to receiver sensitivity.

Recently, a metamaterial-based resonator has been explored in [254] to improve the Q with compact area at the mm-wave frequency region. A split-ring-resonator (SRR) can be designed in the CMOS process top-metal layer to provide negative permeability (μ) for mm-wave propagation. When loading SRR to a host transmission-line (TL-SRR), the integrated structure becomes a non-transmission medium with single-negative property ($\mu \cdot \varepsilon < 0$) in the vicinity of resonance frequency. A sharp stop-band is thereby formed such that the incident mm-wave can be perfectly reflected at SRR load with a stable standing-wave established in the host T-line [254]. Compared to the traditional LC-tank-based resonator, TL-SRR has stable EM-energy storage within a compact area, which results in a much higher Q factor. As such, it becomes relevant to study the CMOS on-chip SRR for the compact and high-sensitivity SRX design of the THz imager.

In this chapter, firstly, the design of on-chip metamaterial resonators is explored based on differential T-line loaded with SRR and CSRR beyond 70 GHz. As a demonstration of the idea, two oscillators based on SRR and CSRR resonators are implemented with 65nm CMOS process at 76 GHz and 96 GHz, respectively. The state-of-the-art performance shows that the phase noise and FOM of SRR achieves -108.8 dBc/Hz and -182.1 dBc/Hz (@10 MHz offset), respectively. The power is reduced dramatically to 2.7 mW compared to the existing designs on SWOs [246, 238, 239]. And the CSRR oscillator shows a state-of-the-art phase noise of -111.5 dBc/Hz (@10-MHz offset) and FOM of -182.4 dBc/Hz. Secondly, two super-regenerative receivers with quench-controlled metamaterial high-Q oscillators by TL-CSRR and TL-SRR are demonstrated with improved sensitivity over traditional LC-tank resonator-based designs at 96 GHz and 135 GHz, respectively. With a sharp stop-band introduced by the metamaterial resonators, high-Q oscillatory amplifications are achieved. The 96-GHz DTL-CSRR-based SRX has a compact core chip area of 0.014 mm^2, and it is measured with power consumption of 2.8 mW, sensitivity of -79 dBm, noise figure (NF) of 8.5 dB, and noise equivalent power (NEP) of 0.67 fW/$\sqrt{Hz}$. The 135-GHz DTL-SRR-based SRX has a compact core chip area of 0.0085 mm^2, and it is measured with power consumption of 6.2 mW, sensitivity of -76.8 dBm, NF of 9.7 dB, and NEP of 0.9 fW/$\sqrt{Hz}$. The proposed SRXs have 2.8-4 dB sensitivity improvement and 60% smaller core chip area when compared to the conventional SRX with LC-tank-based resonator at similar frequencies.

10.2 Fundamentals of Super-Regenerative Amplification

Generally, a SRX consists of a quench-controlled oscillator injected by an external signal and an envelope detector. The process of injecting an external signal into a quench-controlled oscillator is firstly reviewed to understand the operation of SRX, called super-regenerative amplification (SRA).

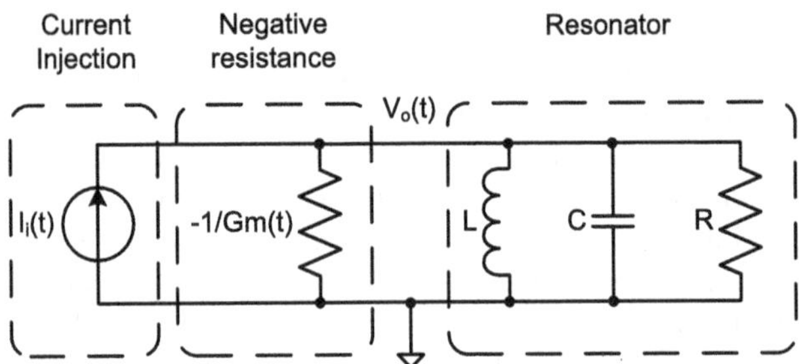

Figure 10.3: Simplified equivalent circuit model of super-regenerative amplifier.

10.2.1 Equivalent Circuit of SRA

A simplified circuit model of SRA is shown in Figure 10.3. The resonator is modeled by RLC block, and its oscillation is quench-controlled by a time-dependent negative resistance $-1/G_m(t)$, where G_m is the equivalent conductance determined by the associated active devices. The external signal injected is modeled as a time-dependent current source $I_i(t)$. $V_o(t)$ is the output voltage. The resonance frequency is $\omega_0 = 1/\sqrt{LC}$; the quality factor is $Q_0 = R/Z_0 = 0.5\zeta_0^{-1}$; Z_0 and ζ_0 are the characteristic impedance and quiescent damping factor, respectively.

Assuming $G_m(t)$ varies much slower than ω_0 such that a quasi-static condition holds in the system to have a time-varying transfer function in s-domain by

$$\frac{V_o(s,t)}{I_i(s)} = \frac{Z_0\omega_0 s}{s^2 + 2\zeta(t)\omega_0 s + \omega_0^2}, \tag{10.1}$$

where $\zeta(t) = \zeta_0[1 - G_m(t)R]$ is the instantaneous damping factor.

A second-order linear time variant system can be observed from (10.1). By varying $\zeta(t)$, the pole can be shifted between left and right sides of the s-plane periodically. In other words, the oscillation starts in SRA when $\zeta(t)$ is negative, and stops when $\zeta(t)$ is positive. Note that (10.1) is only valid when SRA works in linear mode, such that $V_o(s,t)$ is small enough to prevent significant distortion in each quench cycle. Generally, SRA working in linear mode is preferred in the application of millimeter-wave imaging since it has a better sensitivity than that in the logarithmic mode [255, 256].

After a Laplace transform, (10.1) can be written as a second-order differential equation in the time domain:

$$v_o''(t) + 2\zeta(t)\omega_0 v_o'(t) + \omega_0^2 v_o(t) = Z_0\omega_0 I_i'(t). \tag{10.2}$$

Assuming the oscillation is fully quenched in each cycle, such that $v_o(t)$ is independent of the previous ones. For a particular quench cycle $t \in (t_a, t_b]$ with $t_a < 0 < t_b$, if $\zeta(t)$ is positive for $t \in (t_a, 0]$ and negative for $t \in (0, t_b]$,

(10.2) can be written as [256]:

$$v_o(t) = \frac{Z_0}{s(t)} \int_{t_a}^{t} I_i'(\tau)s(\tau)sin[\omega_0(t-\tau)]d\tau \tag{10.3}$$

where $s(t) = e^{\omega_0 \int_0^t \zeta(\lambda)d\lambda}$ is called the sensitivity function, and it reaches maximum when t=0; and decays rapidly with t. As a result, the SRA is only sensitive to the input $I_i'(t)$ in the time window centered at t=0 when $\zeta(t)$ turns from positive to negative.

10.2.2 Frequency Response of SRA

The frequency response of SRA can be analyzed with a convolution model [257]. For an AC input with $I_i(t) = I_0 sin(\omega_i t + \phi_i)$, the output waveform can be approximated by

$$v_o(t) \approx \frac{Z_0 \omega_i I_0}{2s(t)} |S(\Delta\omega)| sin(\omega_0 t + \phi_i) \tag{10.4}$$

where $\Delta\omega = \omega_0 - \omega_i$ and $S(\omega)$ is the Fourier transform of $s(t)$. In the application of millimeter-wave imaging, we are more interested in the envelope of v_o, which is

$$Env[v_o(t)] = \frac{Z_0 \omega_i I_0}{2s(t)} |S(\Delta\omega)|. \tag{10.5}$$

Assuming ω_i is very close to ω_0 ($\Delta\omega << \omega_i$), a quasi-static condition holds in (10.5) that the frequency response of $Env(v_o(t))$ is determined by $|S(\Delta\omega)|$.

For a typical ramping quench signal with time variant conductance $G_m = \frac{1}{R}(kt+1)$, where k is the normalized ramping slope of G_m with the unit of $1/s$, the instantaneous damping factor is $\zeta(t) = -\frac{k}{2Q_0}t$. Thus the envelope of $v_o(t)$ can be solved by

$$Env[v_o(t)]_{ramp} = \frac{\sqrt{\pi} Z_0 \omega_i I_0}{\Omega_0} e^{\frac{\Omega_0^2}{4}t^2} e^{-\frac{\Delta\omega^2}{\Omega_0^2}}, \tag{10.6}$$

where $\Omega_0 = \sqrt{k\omega_0/Q_0}$ is a constant that determines the frequency response of SRA, e.g., the 3-dB bandwidth of SRA equals $1.177\Omega_0$. As such, one can observe that for the given k and ω_0, the bandwidth is inversely proportional to Q_0.

10.2.3 Sensitivity of SRA

The sensitivity of SRA is defined as the minimum detected power, which means the induced output signal power is the same as its variance:

$$S_{SRA} = P_{min}|_{I_x^2=\sigma_x^2} = \frac{I_0^2 R}{2}|_{I_x^2=\sigma_x^2} \tag{10.7}$$

where I_x is the equivalent induced AC in SRA in response to the AC input I_i, and σ_x^2 is the variance of I_x.

As discussed in [257], for a typical ramp-damping function with normalized ramping slope of k, we have

$$I_x = \frac{I_0 \omega_0 \sigma_s}{2}, \sigma_x^2 = \frac{N\omega_0^2 E_g}{2} \tag{10.8}$$

where $\sigma_s = \sqrt{\frac{2Q_0}{\omega_0 k}}$ is the SRA time constant with a unit of $s/\sqrt{rad}$, $E_g = \sigma_s\sqrt{\pi}$ is the energy of density function, and N is the noise power density with $N = 4K \cdot T \cdot F/R$. Note that K and F denote the Boltzmann constant and noise factor of SRA contributed by active devices, respectively.

As such, the sensitivity of SRX can be found by substituting (10.8) into (10.7):

$$S = 2KTF\sqrt{\frac{k\omega_0}{\pi Q_0}}. \tag{10.9}$$

Note that the receiver noise figure (NF) can be approximated as [89]:

$$NF = \frac{S}{K \cdot T \cdot B}. \tag{10.10}$$

Note that the NF of an SRX is independent of quench signal. For a typical 3-dB bandwidth of the SRX ($B = 1.177\Omega_0$), the NF becomes 0.958 F. In addition, the noise equivalent power (NEP) can be calculated by $S/\sqrt{B}$:

$$NEP = 1.38KTF\sqrt[4]{\frac{k\omega_0}{\pi Q_0}}. \tag{10.11}$$

Note that k is usually determined by the frequency of the quench signal and the sampling rate of one SRA. Therefore, it can be observed from (10.9) and (10.11) that, for a given ω_0 and k, the sensitivity and NEP are inversely proportional to the square-root and the fourth-root of Q_0, respectively. So the resonator with higher Q will significantly improve the sensitivity within the interested bandwidth for imaging application.

10.3 Super-Regenerative Receiver by SRR/CSRR Resonator

Two SRXs working at 96 GHz and 135 GHz are implemented in the CMOS process to demonstrate the advantages of applying quench-controlled oscillators with metamaterial resonators in super-regenerative receivers (SRX). The fundamentals of quench-controlled oscillator design is introduced first.

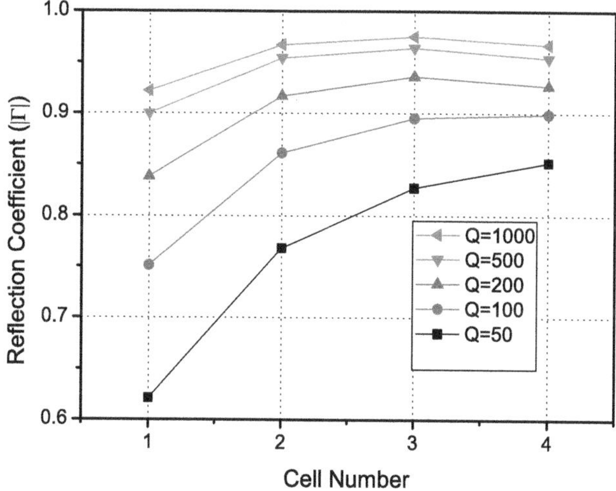

Figure 10.4: Reflection coefficient of T-line loaded with CSRR unit-cells.

10.3.1 Quench-Controlled Oscillation

10.3.1.1 High-Q Resonance with Standing Wave

In the practical on-chip resonator design with finite Q of SRR or CSRR, the reflection coefficient ($|\Gamma|$) depends on the number of cascading TL-SRR or TL-CSRR unit-cells. Figure 10.4 shows the circuit-level simulation of TL-CSRR at 96-GHz resonance frequency with following observations. First, the reflection coefficient $|\Gamma|$ is more sensitive to the cells number when Q is below 200. Second, $|\Gamma|$ can be improved by cascading more unit-cells.

10.3.1.2 Voltage Controlled Negative Resistance

The oscillation can be sustained by compensating the reflection loss ($|\Gamma| < 1$) with a negative resistance. Similarly, a quench-controlled oscillation can be achieved by controlling voltage controlled negative resistance (VCNR), which determines the instantaneous damping factor ($\zeta(t)$) of (10.1) as discussed in Section II. The sensitivity of SRX is also a function of $\zeta(t)$ that is determined by VCNR. Usually a cross-coupled NMOS pair is applied for the differential negative resistance design as depicted in Figure 10.5, where the tail current of the cross-coupled NMOS pair (I_D) can be quench-controlled by another NMOS biased in the saturation region. The equivalent differential negative conductance between nodes "a" and "b" can be expressed as below by ne-

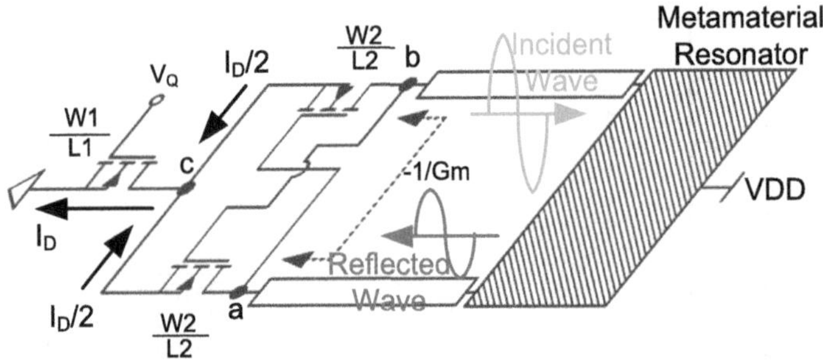

Figure 10.5: Reflection loss compensation by cross-coupled NMOS pair with controlled tail current.

glecting the channel-length modulation

$$G_m = \frac{gm_2}{2} = \frac{I_D}{2V_{od2}} \tag{10.12}$$

where gm_2 and V_{od2} are the transconductance and overdrive voltage of cross-coupled NMOS FETs, respectively. Note that I_D can be obtained by

$$I_D = \frac{W_1}{2L_1}\mu_n C_{ox} V_{od1}^2 = \frac{W_2}{L_2}\mu_n C_{ox} V_{od2}^2 \tag{10.13}$$

where W_1, L_1 and $V_{od1} = V_Q - V_T$ are the channel width, length and overdrive voltage of tail NMOS; W_2 and L_2 and V_{od2} are the channel width, length and overdrive voltage of the cross-coupled NMOS pair; $\mu_n C_{ox}$ and V_T are the process related parameters. As such, (10.12) can be written as a function of V_Q by

$$G_m = \frac{\mu_n C_{ox}(V_Q - V_T)}{4}\sqrt{\frac{2W_1 W_2}{L_1 L_2}}. \tag{10.14}$$

One can observe from (10.14) that G_m is linearly controlled by V_Q, of which the slope is determined by the product of W_1/L_1 and W_2/L_2. Note that the oscillation starts when $1/G_m < R$ and stops when $1/G_m > R$. As such, $(W_1/L_1)(W_2/L_2)$ must be large enough to satisfy the oscillation start conduction ($1/G_m < R$). However, large W_2/L_2 will introduce additional parasitic capacitance, which will be counted into the resonator rank and reduce the oscillation frequency. Moreover, in order to provide sufficient head room for the cross-coupled NMOS pair, $W1/L1$ is selected several times larger than $W2/L2$.

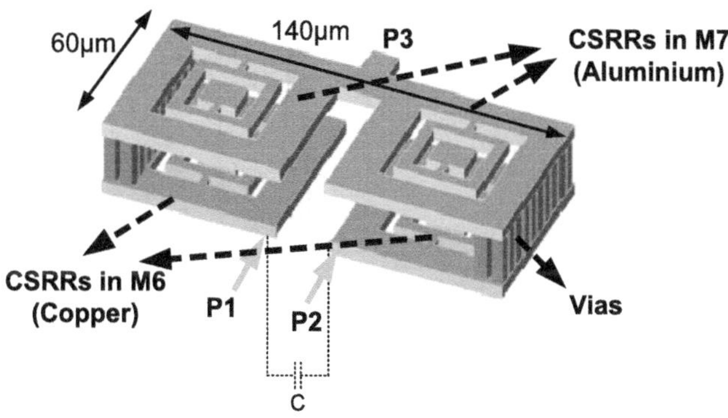

Figure 10.6: Layout for CMOS on-chip implementation of DTL-CSRR for 96 GHz SRX.

10.3.2 SRX Design by TL-CSRR

10.3.2.1 Folded Differential T-Line Loaded with CSRR

TL-CSRR structure cannot be directly employed for the SRX design. Firstly, the single-ended approach will bring large common-mode noise in the oscillator; secondly, cascading more unit-cells will increase area overhead. A folded differential T-line loaded with CSRR (DTL-CSRR) structure is proposed to reduce area by half while doubling the number of unit-cells [258]. As shown in Figure 10.6, two cascaded TL-CSRR unit-cells (with CSRR size of 60 ×60 μm^2) are folded in the two topmost metal layers (M6 and M7).

The S-parameters of the proposed DTL-CSRR structure is verified by EM simulation tool EMX with a parasitic capacitance of 40 fF from transistors. Both ε and μ of DTL-CSRR are extracted from the simulation results according to (9.3), which both become complex numbers due to the existence of loss factor induced imaginary parts. The metamaterial property is illustrated by the real parts of ε and μ in Figure 10.7. At the vicinity of 105-GHz resonance frequency, an electric plasmonic medium is formed with $\varepsilon < 0$ and $\mu > 0$. A stop-band is thereby formed within a narrow bandwidth of 1.8 GHz, where the Q factor is found to be 58 by $Q = \omega_0/\omega_{3dB}$ from the differential impedance (Z_{diff}) between P1 and P2.

10.3.2.2 96-GHz DTL-CSRR-Based SRX

Figure 10.8 depicts the schematic of DTL-CSRR-based SRX. DTL-CSRR is firstly connected to a differential negative resistance formed by cross-coupled NMOS (M2 and M3). To further improve the detection efficiency, a virtual ground at 96 GHz is formed by two $\lambda/4$ stubs. The size of M4 is designed as 4 times of that M2 and M3. Note that W_{Total} and W_{Single} are the total

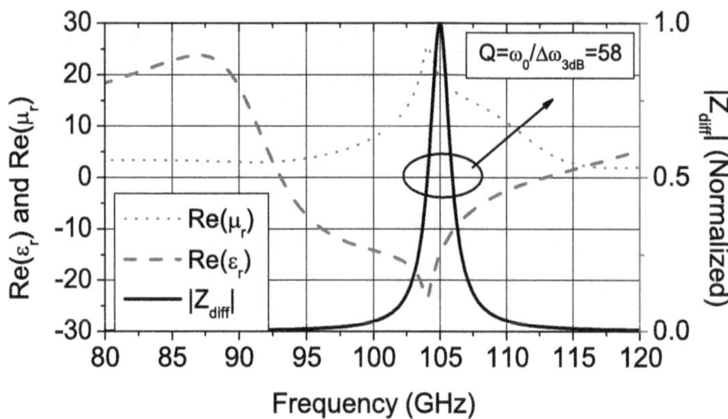

Figure 10.7: EM-simulation-based comparison of DTL-CSRR and LC-tank resonator for CMOS 96 GHz SRX design.

and individual finger width of transistors in Figure 10.8, respectively. And the channel length of every active device is 60nm. The remaining circuit consists of a common source input buffer (M1) for current injection and an envelope detector formed by M5 and M6. The common source stage (M1) is designed for input signal injection and also reverse isolation from the oscillator to the input. The size of M1 is optimized with consideration of minimized parasitic capacitance as well as the input matching. Similarly, M5 and M6 also need to be minimized but doing so will reduce the detection efficiency. To solve this problem, a capacitance coupling by C1 and C2 is introduced between the outputs of the oscillator tank and the envelope detection. Firstly, the capacitance loading from M5 and M6 is reduced by series connection of the coupling capacitors; secondly, M5 and M6 are biased externally by large resistors (R1, R2) to optimize the detection; thirdly, 1/f noise from M5 and M6 is also isolated.

10.3.3 SRX Design by TL-SRR

10.3.3.1 Differential T-Line Loaded with SRR

The TL-SRR structure with horizontal placement of SRRs (Figure 2.13) is also not suitable for the practical implementation for SRX, mainly due to the large area overhead. Compared to TL-CSRR, TL-SRR inherently has better layout flexibility because SRRs can be vertically stacked within a compact area. One differential T-line loaded with stacked SRRs (DTL-SRR) is proposed in this work for the application of 135 GHz SRX design in the 65nm CMOS RF process.

As shown in Figure 10.9(a), the DTL-SRR is designed by stacked SRRs with the same dimensions of $24 \times 24\ \mu m^2$ in 4 metal layers (M5 to M8). All

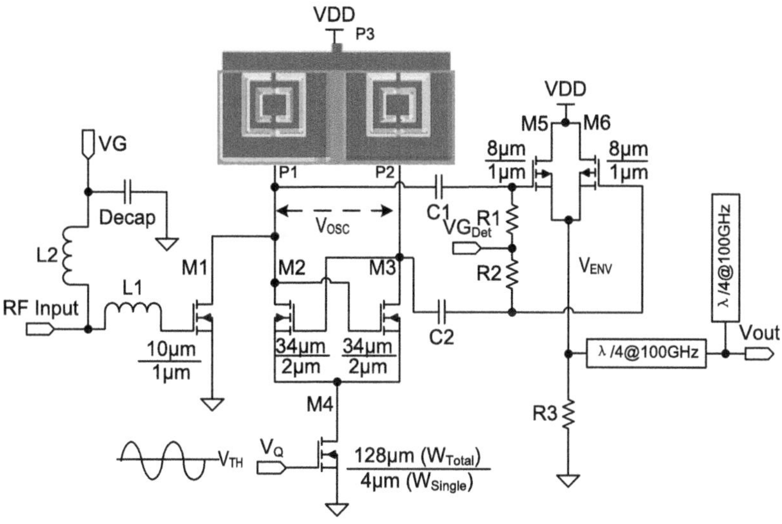

Figure 10.8: Schematic of CMOS 96 GHz SRX with DTL-CSRR.

SRRs are closely coupled to the same host T-line implemented in the topmost metal layer (M8). The overall size of the proposed DTL-SRR is 35 × 34 μm^2. For the purpose of comparison, a traditional LC-tank resonator is designed in the M8 metal layer as shown in Figure 10.9(b), which has the same resonance frequency of 135GHz. The S-parameters of both structures are also verified by EMX with the same parasitic capacitance of 16fF. As shown in Figure 10.10, at the vicinity of 140-GHz resonance, $\varepsilon > 0$ and $\mu < 0$, and a magnetic plasmonic medium is formed. As a result, a stop-band is formed at 140 GHz within a narrow bandwidth of 3.5 GHz. The Q factor of the DTL-SRR resonator is 40, which is more than 2 times the Q of the LC-tank resonator. Moreover, the DTL-SRR resonator layout area (1190 μm^2) is less than half of the LC-tank resonator (2500 μm^2).

Such a Q factor enhancement effect can also be explained by the strong phase non-linearity in the frequency range closed to SRRs resonance. Note that the Q factor can also be obtained by phase-based method:

$$Q = \frac{\omega_0}{2} \cdot |\frac{d\angle Z(j\omega)}{d\omega}|, \tag{10.15}$$

where $\angle Z(j\omega)$ is the phase of resonator impedance. Figure 10.11(a) shows the impedance diagram of both DTL-SRR and LC-Tank without any capacitor loading. A resonance generated by the SRR loadings is observed at 167 GHz for DTL-SRR. Such resonance causes non-linear phase shift at 140 GHz. Figure 10.11(b) shows that DTL-SRR has much stronger phase non-linearity than that of LC-Tank around 140 GHz. As shown in Figure 10.11(c), both

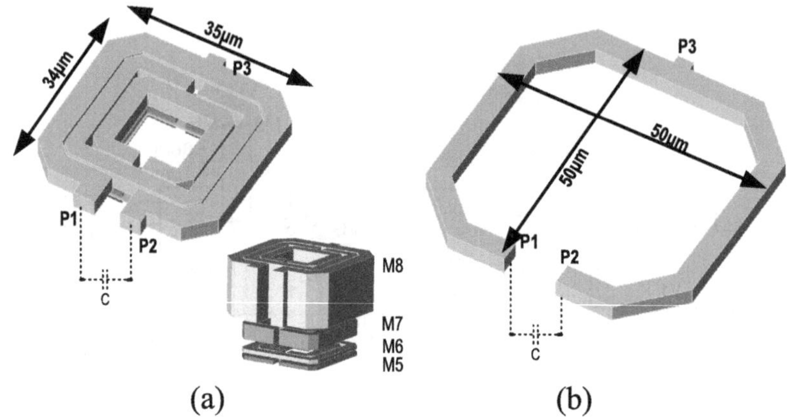

Figure 10.9: Layout for CMOS on-chip implementation of DTL-SRR for 135 GHz SRX.

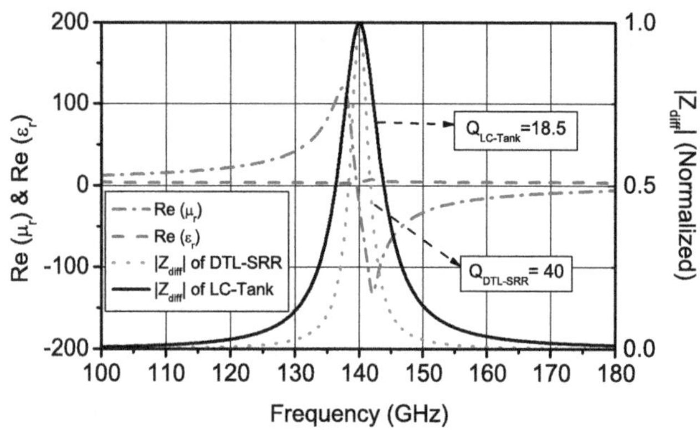

Figure 10.10: EM-simulation-based comparison of DTL-SRR and LC-tank resonator for CMOS 135 GHz SRX design.

structures have the same resonance frequency of 140 GHz after including the ideal capacitance (C = 16 fF). The phase non-linearity in DTL-SRRs increases the phase gradient of Z_{Diff} at 140 GHz, resulting in a higher Q according to (10.15).

10.3.3.2 135-GHz DTL-SRR-Based SRX

Figure 10.12 depicts the schematic of 135-GHz DTL-SRR-based SRX. Firstly, a transformer-based matching network is applied to the input matching for

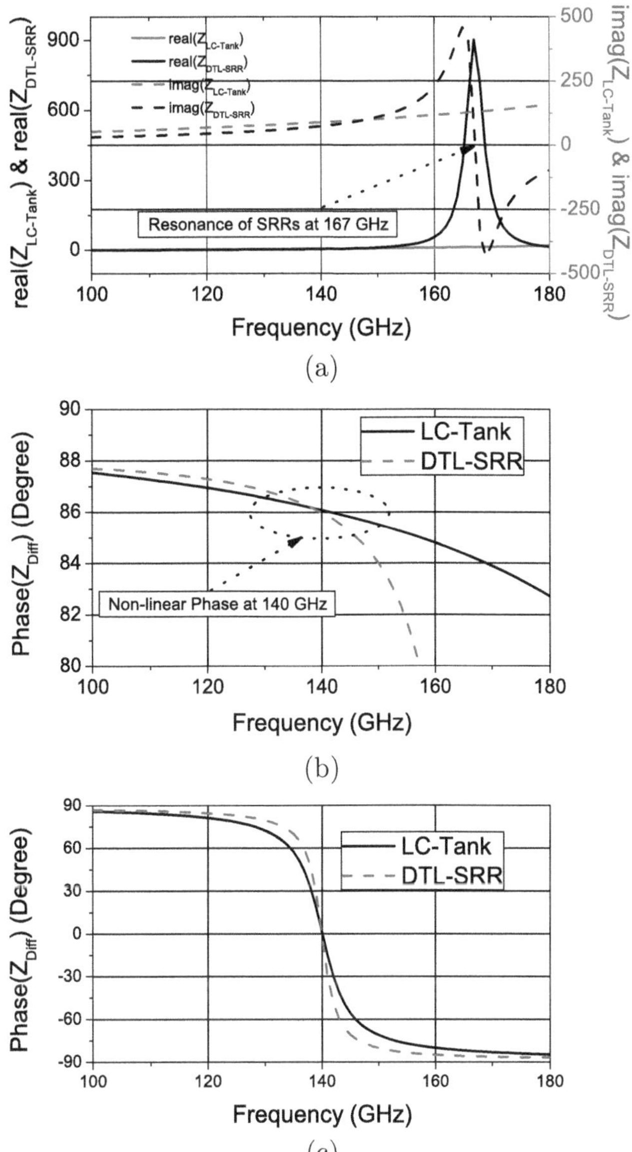

Figure 10.11: Impedance diagram of DTL-SRR and LC-tank in Global Foundries 65-nm CMOS process. (a) real and imaginary parts of Z_{Diff}, (b) phase of Z_{Diff}, (c) phase of Z_{Diff} when the ideal 16-fF capacitor is included.

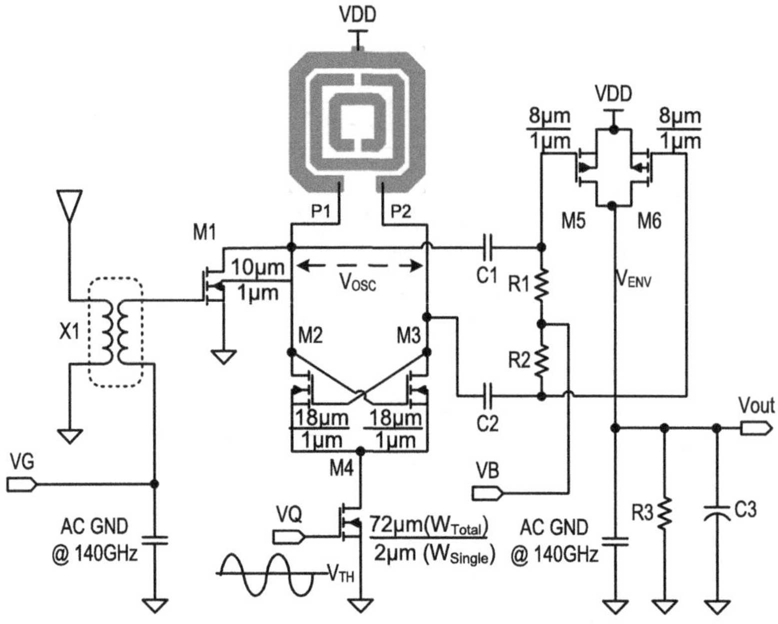

Figure 10.12: Schematic of CMOS 135 GHz SRX with DTL-SRR.

M1 for the electrostatic discharge (ESD) protection when integrating with the antenna; secondly, the virtual ground formed by two $\lambda/4$ T-lines is replaced by the high-Q MOM capacitor to further reduce the chip area; thirdly, the detected envelope signal V_{ENV} is directly averaged by an on-chip low-pass filter formed by R3 and C3 at the output.

10.4 Circuit Prototyping and Measurement

10.4.1 DTL-CSRR-Based SRX at 96 GHz

As shown in Figure 10.13(a), the proposed DTL-CSRR-based SRX is implemented in the UMC 65-nm CMOS process with f_T/f_{MAX} of 170/190 GHz. The total die area is 500 × 440 μm^2 including a core area of 0.014 mm^2 with resonator and active devices. The SRX is measured on probe station (CASCADE Microtech Elite-300) with RF input signal provided by Agilent PNA-X (N5247A) with T/R modules (N5260), of which the output power is calibrated in the range of -85 ~ -10 dBm by Agilent Spectrum Analyzer E4407B with a W-band waveguide harmonic mixer (11970W). Note that the output power of the T/R module can be controlled by N5247A, but its minimum output power

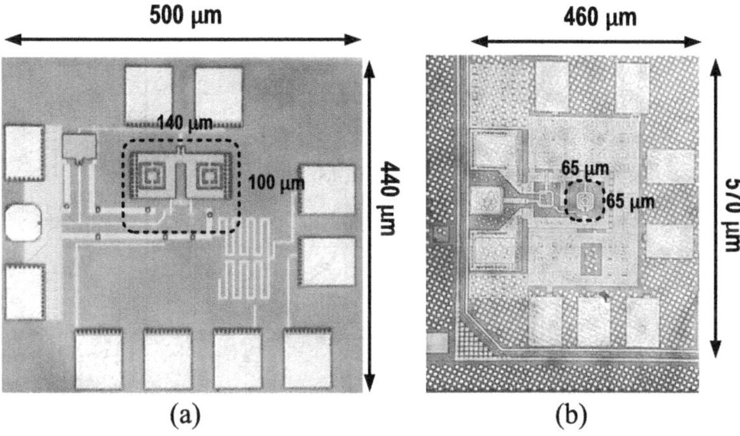

Figure 10.13: Die micrographs: (a) CMOS 96 GHz SRX with DTL-CSRR, and (b) CMOS 135 GHz SRX with DTL-SRR.

level that can be calibrated is limited by the sensitivity of spectrum analyzer. A 12.5MHz sinusoid quench-control signal is applied by function generator (AFG3022) with voltage swept in 0 $\sim$ 250 mV. The receiver operates under 1-V power supply with a power consumption of 2.8 mW.

The receiver gain is defined as $Gain(dB) = 20\log V_{out} - P_{in}$, where V_{out} is the normalized output voltage of receiver and P_{in} is the input power level of proposed SRX in dBm. The actual gain of SRX is not totally independent of P_{in} as discussed in (10.6) in Sec. 10.2. A relative higher P_{in} of -20 dBm is applied to have sufficient V_{out} at the frequency outside the bandwidth. Figure 10.14(a) shows the measured and simulated gain and input S11, where the maximum gain of proposed SRX at -20-dBm P_{in} is 21 dB at 95.5 GHz and a 3-dB bandwidth of 560 MHz is observed. The measured gain is quite close to the postlayout simulation result. A good input match is also observed with S11 smaller than -14 dB from 94.6 GHz to 96.6 GHz. Figure 10.14(b) shows the normalized V_{out} against P_{in} as well as the responsivity, where an almost linear response is observed with a sensitivity of -78 dBm and a maximum responsivity of 6.02 MV/W. Note that responsivity is calculated by V_{out}/P_{in}. The measured responsivity is very close to the simulation results especially when the input power level is below -70dBm. The noise equivalent power (NEP) of proposed SRX is 0.67 fW/$\sqrt{Hz}$, which is calculated by $S/\sqrt{B}$, where S is the sensitivity and B is the 3-dB bandwidth [89]. Finally, the noise figure (NF) is found to be 8.5 dB by $S/(K \cdot T \cdot B)$ at room temperature of 290K.

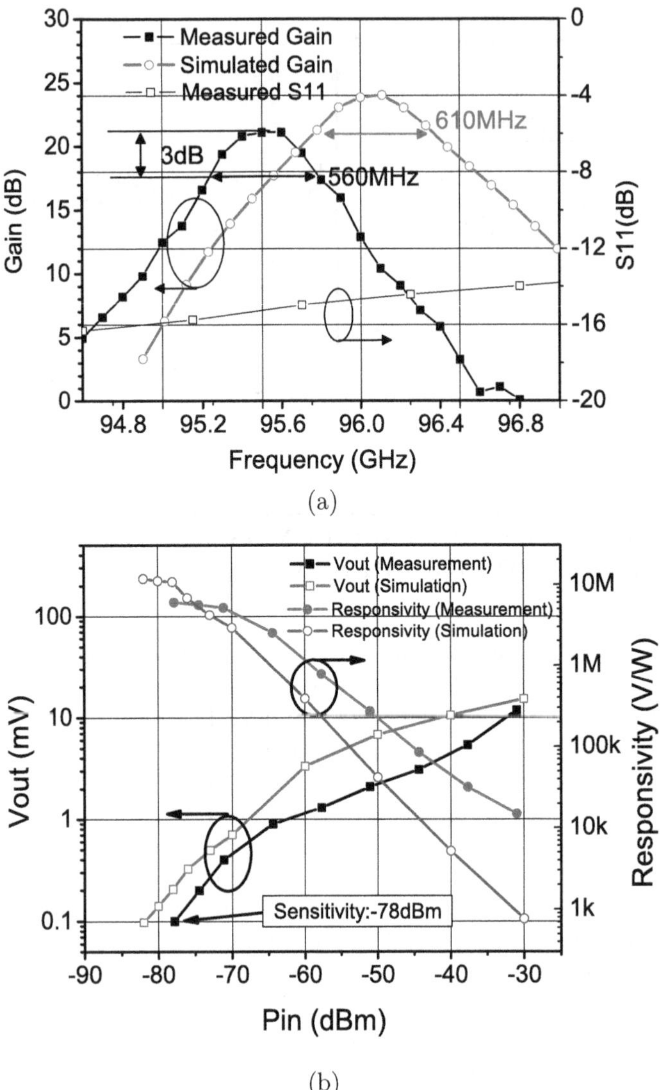

Figure 10.14: Measurement and simulation results of CMOS 96 GHz SRX. (a) gain and input S11, and (b) output voltage (V_{out}) and responsivity vs. input power (P_{in}).

10.4.2 DTL-SRR-Based SRX at 135 GHz

As shown in Figure 10.13(b), the proposed DTL-SRR-based SRX is implemented in Global Foundries 65-nm CMOS RF process with f_T/f_{MAX} of

180/530 GHz. It has a total die area of 570 $\times$460 μm^2, and a core area of 0.0085 mm^2. For the purpose of imaging system integration, the receiver chip is firstly attached to a test board (FR4, 1.6-mm thickness). As shown in Figure 10.15, the whole test board is placed on a probe station for SRX measurement. As such, the SRX can be easily integrated with an imaging system by replacing the GSG probe with bonding wires connected to a 135GHz antenna. The RF input signal is provided by a VDI D-Band signal generator, for which the output power is calibrated in the range of -85 $\sim$ -10 dBm by the R&S FSUP signal source analyzer with a D-band waveguide harmonic mixer. A 12.5-MHz sinusoid quench-control signal is applied from function generator (Agilent 33250a) with voltage sweep-range of 0$\sim$400mV. Operating from a 1-V power supply, the receiver consumes 6.2 mW.

Figure 10.16(a) shows the measured gain when P_{in} is -18 dBm, where the maximum gain of proposed SRX is 15.5dB at 134.8GHz and the 3-dB bandwidth is 530 MHz. The measured gain is also quite close to the postlayout simulation result, but the center frequency of measurement results are 5-GHz lower than that from simulation, which is probably due to the inaccurate transistor model above 100 GHz. Figure 10.16(b) shows normalized V_{out} against P_{in} as well as the responsivity, where the receiver sensitivity (S) and the maximum responsivity are observed as -76.8 dBm and 4.82 MV/W, respectively. Note that the measured responsivity is very close to the simulation results especially when the input power level is below -50dBm. And the NEP is calculated to be 0.9 fW/$\sqrt{Hz}$. A near-linear relationship between V_{out} and P_{in} is observed when the input power is below -40 dBm, which can be utilized in post-data processing to generate THz images.

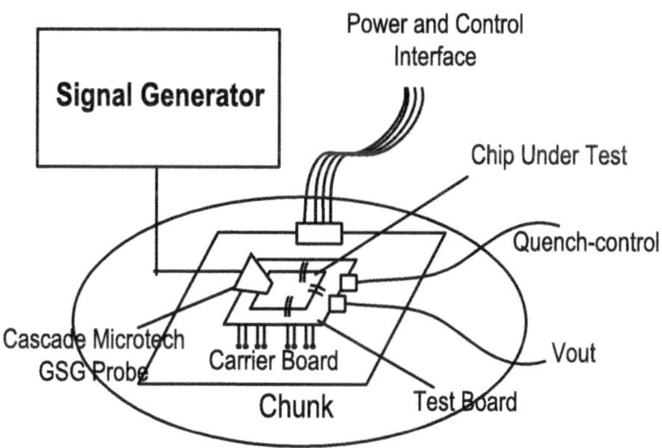

Figure 10.15: Measurement setup of CMOS 135 GHz SRX with DTL-SRR.

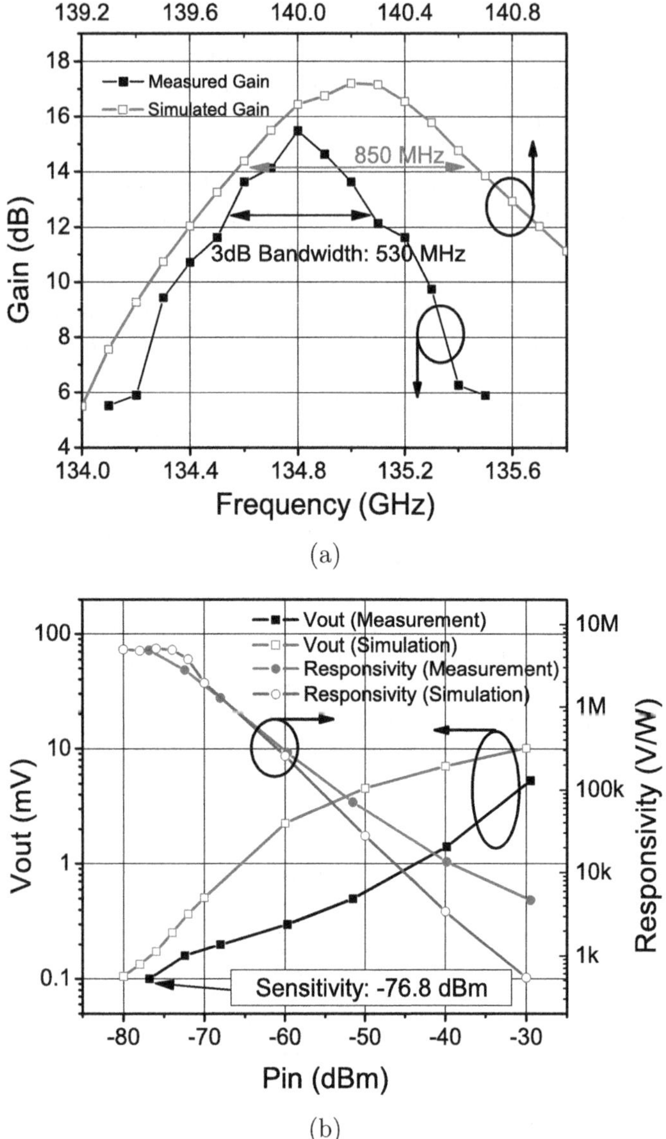

Figure 10.16: Measurement and simulation results of CMOS 135 GHz SRX. (a) gain, and (b) output voltage (V_{out}) and responsivity vs. input power (P_{in}).

Table 10.1: Performance Comparison of State-of-the-Art Receivers for Imaging Application

Parameters	[89]	[90]	[259]	**DTL-CSRR**	**DTL-SRR**
Topology	SRX	SRX	DC	**SRX**	**SRX**
Resonator Type	LC-tank	LC-tank	—	**TL-CSRR**	**TL-SRR**
Technology Node	65-nm CMOS	65-nm CMOS	180-nm BiCMOS	**65-nm CMOS**	**65-nm CMOS**
f_{osc} (GHz)	144	183	103	**95.5**	**135**
Power (mW)	2.5	13.5	225	**2.8**	**6.2**
Sensitivity (dBm)	-74	-72.5	-56	**-78**	**-76.8**
Bandwidth (GHz)	0.94	1.4	20	**0.56**	**0.53**
NF (dB)	10.2	9.9	15	**8.5**	**9.7**
NEP (fW/$\sqrt{Hz}$)	1.3	1.5	17.8	**0.67**	**0.9**
Core Area (mm^2)	0.021	0.013	0.75	**0.014**	**0.0085**

10.4.3 Comparison and Discussion

The performance of the measurement results of proposed SRXs is summarized in Table 10.1 as well as the previous state-of-the-art receiver designs. Compared to the direct conversion receiver [259], SRXs have a 16 $\sim$ 22 dB better sensitivity due to a narrower receiver bandwidth. Compared to the traditional SRX designs with LC-tank resonator [89, 90], the proposed SRXs show 30% $\sim$ 50% reduced NEP, 2.8 $\sim$ 4dB better sensitivity and 60% area reduction, which makes them well suited to the portable THz imaging with a large sensor array.

10.5 Conclusion

As demonstrated in this section, both DTL-SRR and DTL-CSRR can also be applied in the super-regenerative receiver design with quench-controlled oscillators to achieve better sensitivities. When compared to the conventional SRX design with LC-tank resonator at the similar frequency, both proposed SRXs at 96 GHz and 135 GHz show 2.8 $\sim$ 4 dB improved sensitivity. Especially, the proposed SRXs at 135 GHz has 60% reduced core chip area. In the following section, CMOS-based THz antenna design will be discussed.

Chapter 11

In-Phase Detection

11.1 Introduction

In this section, an in-phase coupled CON architecture is proposed to improve the sensitivity of SRX. As shown in Figure 11.1, the input power is amplified by two oscillators, which are coupled in phase in a positive feed-back loop. Then, the output voltage envelope is detected, indicating the input power level. The main design challenge is how to realize in-phase coupling between two oscillators.

The key idea of this paper is using a zero phase shifter (ZPS) to couple two quench-controlled oscillators in phase. Compared to the transformer-coupling method [95], the ZPS approach does not introduce the extra phase between two oscillators, as shown in Figure 11.1(a). As a result, the SRX sensitivity can be improved in terms of both reduced noise figure (NF) and increased oscillatory amplification.

The proposed SRX with ZPS-coupled CON is designed in 65nm CMOS at 131.5GHz with a core area of 0.06mm^2. The circuit measurement shows that the receiver features a sensitivity of -84dBm, a noise equivalent power (NEP) of $0.615\text{fW/Hz}^{0.5}$, a NF of 7.26dB and a power of 8.1mW.

11.2 SRX Sensitivity Enhancement by ZPS-Coupled CON

In this section, the fundamentals of the SRX circuit are described at first and then, the sensitivity enhancement by the ZPS-coupled CON is discussed.

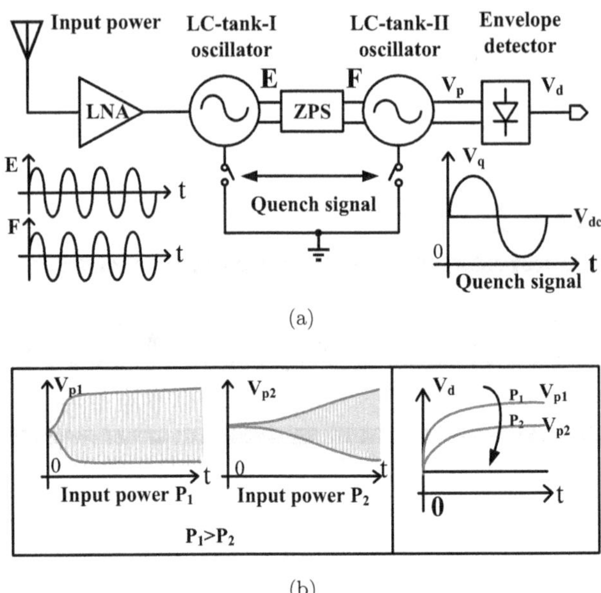

Figure 11.1: (a) Proposed SRX structure, in-phase output (E,F), and sin-wave quench signal; (b) envelope shape response (V_P) of oscillator under different input power, and envelope detector output (V_d).

In order to understand the sensitivity enhancement from the coupling of two quench-controlled oscillators, one can apply the feedback model in a linear time variant (LTV) analysis of SRX [94]. A simplified circuit model as well as its feedback model are shown in Figure 11.2 (a) for conventional SRXs with a single quench-controlled oscillator. Its time-varying transfer function is

$$Z_{TV}(s,t) = \frac{Z_0\omega_0 s}{s^2 + 2\zeta(t)\omega_0 s + \omega_0^2} \tag{11.1}$$

where ω_0 is $1/\sqrt{LC}$, $Z_0$is $\sqrt{L/C}$, and is damping function:

$$\zeta(\mathrm{t}) = \zeta_0 (1 - \mathrm{G_m}(\mathrm{t})\,\mathrm{R}) = \zeta_{\mathrm{dc}} + \zeta_{\mathrm{ac}} \tag{11.2}$$

where ζ_0 is a constant.

Note that the receiver's behavior is mainly determined by AC characteristics of the damping function [94].

When the damping signal $\zeta(\mathrm{t})$ in each quench cycle is a ramping signal $\zeta_{\mathrm{ac}}(\mathrm{t}) = -\beta t$, the gain function and the sensitivity function $\mathrm{g}(\mathrm{t})$ of the SRX become

$$\mu(\mathrm{t}) = \kappa e^{\frac{1}{2}\omega_0 \beta t^2} \tag{11.3}$$

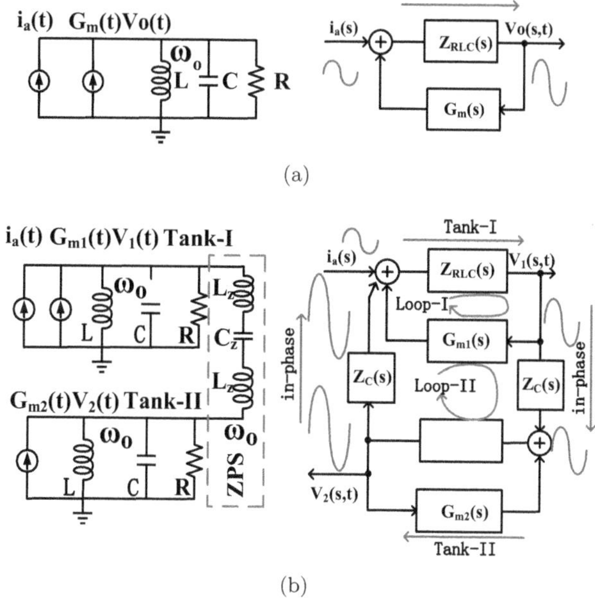

Figure 11.2: Traditional SRX circuit model and its feedback model; (b) proposed SRX circuit model and its feedback model.

$$g\left(t\right) = \kappa e^{-\frac{1}{2}\omega_0\beta t^2} \tag{11.4}$$

where β is the slope ($G_m R$), and κ is a constant.

The simplified circuit and feedback loop model of the SRX with two coupled quench-controlled oscillators is shown in Figure 11.2 (b). Its transfer function can be simplified as follows:

$$Z_{NTV}\left(s,t\right) = \frac{Z_{RLC}(s)Z_{RLC}(s)Z_C(s)}{\left[1 - G_{m1}\left(t\right)Z_{RLC}\left(s\right)\right]\left[1 - G_{m2}\left(t\right)Z_{RLC}\left(s\right)\right]Z_c^2(s)} \tag{11.5}$$

where $Z_{RLC}(s)$ is the impedance of the parallel resonator (or RLC), and $Z_C\left(s\right)$ is the impedance of serial resonator (or ZPS).

Note that $G_{m1}\left(t\right)$ and $G_{m2}\left(t\right)$ are determined by the phase difference of the injected signal between the two oscillators [89]. At the interested frequency around ω_0, the impedance of serial resonator (or ZPS) is much smaller than the parallel resonator (or RLC). As such, equation (11.5) can be further simplified as

$$Z_{NTV}\left(s,t\right) = \frac{Z_{RLC}(s)}{1 - \left[G_{m1}\left(t\right) + G_{m2}\left(t\right)\right]Z_{RLC}(s)} \tag{11.6}$$

where high-order terms are neglected due to small value at the beginning of the start-up.

Substituting $Z_{RLC}(s)$ into equation (11.6), the transfer function of the proposed SRX can be expressed as

$$Z_{NTV}(s,t) = \frac{Z_0\omega_0 s}{s^2 + 2\zeta_n(t)\omega_0 s + \omega_0^2} \tag{11.7}$$

where the new damping function $\zeta_n(t)$ becomes

$$\zeta_n(t) = \zeta_0[1 - G_{m1}(t) R (1 + e^{j\varphi})]. \tag{11.8}$$

Note that the absolute value $G_{m2}(t)$ is equal to $G_{m1}(t)$, and a phase difference φ is introduced due to the phase difference from the injected signals. Therefore, when the damping signal is a ramping signal with slope β, the damping function becomes

$$\zeta_n(t) = 1 - (1 + e^{j\varphi})\beta t.$$

As a result, the gain function $\mu_n(t)$ and the sensitivity function $g_n(t)$ become

$$\mu_n(t) = \kappa e^{\frac{1}{2}\omega_0\beta(1+e^{j\varphi})t^2} \tag{11.9}$$

$$\mathrm{g_n}(\mathrm{t}) = \kappa e^{-\frac{1}{2}\omega_0\beta(1+e^{j\varphi})t^2}. \tag{11.10}$$

One can observe that the gain and sensitivity functions are both influenced by the phase difference of the injected signal between two oscillators. When the phase difference becomes zero, both the gain and the sensitivity functions can be optimized.

We further compare the gain function and sensitivity function of the conventional SRX with that of the proposed ZPS-coupled SRX by

$$U_C = \frac{\mu_n(t)}{\mu(t)} = e^{\frac{1}{2}\omega_0\beta t^2} \tag{11.11}$$

$$\mathrm{G_C} = \frac{\mathrm{g_n}(\mathrm{t})}{\mathrm{g}(\mathrm{t})} = \mathrm{e}^{-\frac{1}{2}\omega_0\beta \mathrm{t}^2}. \tag{11.12}$$

One can observe that the gain of the SRX enhancement is exponential with ω_0. When a signal frequency around ω_0 is injected into LC-tank-I, it is amplified and injected into LC-tank-II in phase. Then, it is further amplified by LC-tank-II and re-injected into LC-tank-I. Thus, a positive feedback loop is established when in-phase coupling is realized by the ZPS, where the oscillator amplification gain is increased with the improved detection sensitivity.

11.3 Circuit Prototyping and Measurement

11.3.1 SRX Circuit Design

The schematic of the proposed SRX is shown in Figure 11.3. It consists of two ZPS-coupled LC-tank resonators, one common source input buffer and

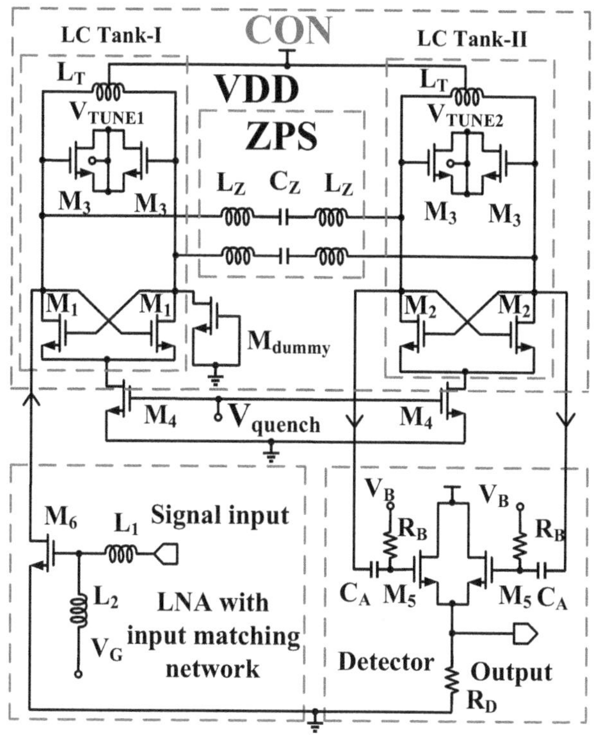

Figure 11.3: Circuit diagram of proposed SRX with ZPS-coupled oscillators.

one output envelope detector. Relatively small sized (2μm/100nm) NMOS transistors (M3) are connected in both oscillator tanks, working as varactors for frequency tuning. By tuning control voltages VTUNE1 and VTUNE2, the process mismatch in two LC tanks is well cancelled to make sure that the free-running frequencies of two tanks are the same. As a result, CON synchronization mainly depends on the coupling network, which is ensured by the ZPS given in this paper. The quench-controlled transconductances are implemented by cross-coupled transistor pairs (M_1 and M_2), of which the tail current is controlled by M_4. Note that M_1 and M_2 have an identical size of 60nm length and 12μm width, and M4 has a size of 60nm length and 60μm width. The input of LC-tank-I is connected to a common source buffer (M_6), of which the input is matched to 50Ω by L_1 and L_2. A dummy transistor (M_{dummy}) is introduced to compensate parasitic capacitor unbalance. The output of LC-tank-II is connected to a differential envelope detector (M_5).

The design of a passive part such as ZPS [163] is shown in Figure 11.4. The inductor is implemented in the top metal layer. The radius of the inductor

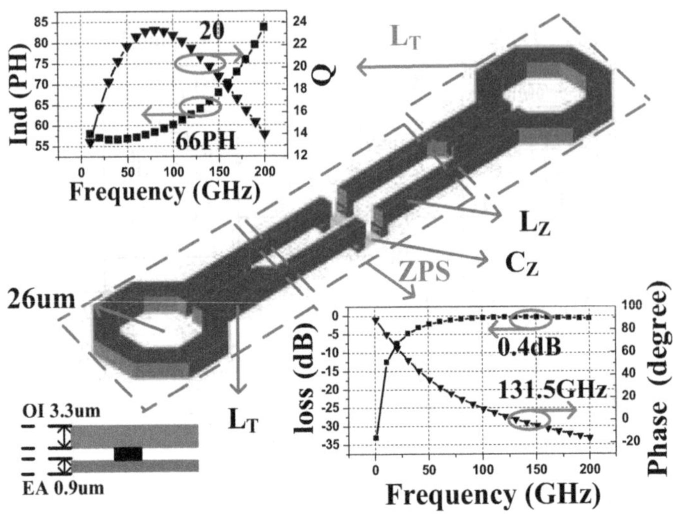

Figure 11.4: Layout of ZPS and simulation results of inductor and ZPS.

is 26μm and the width is 10μm. The simulated inductance is 66pH, and the quality factor is 20. The ZPS is implemented by a serial connection of two inductors L_Z and one capacitor C_Z [163]. An EM simulation shows a zero-phase-shift at 131.5 GHz with a small insertion loss of 0.4dB.

11.3.2 Measurements

The proposed SSR is fabricated in 65nm CMOS process, and the die micrograph is shown in Figure 11.5 (a). The core area is 0.06 mm^2, and total area is 600 μm $\times$ 500 μm including input and output pads. The receiver is measured on a probe station with RF signal provided by a microwave signal generator through GSG probe. A 12-MHz sinusoid quenching signal is applied by a function generator with 0.6-V DC level and peak-to-DC voltage swing is swept in a range of 0 $\sim$ 300 mV. The receiver operates under 1-V power supply. The current consumption of each LC-tank is 3.8 mA, while the one of LNA is 0.5 mA.

The operating frequency of the SRX is measured at 131.74 GHz, which is also the self-oscillation frequency, as shown in Figure 11.5 (b). A tuning range of 1 GHz is observed when sweeping V_{TUNE} in a range of 0 $\sim$ 1 V. Good input power matching is also achieved for NF reduction and sensitivity improvement. As shown in Figure 11.6, S_{11} is below -10dB from 122 GHz to 140 GHz. The bandwidth is around 680 MHz. Note that the maximum gain is 41 dB, which is almost 13 dB higher than conventional SRX design [90].

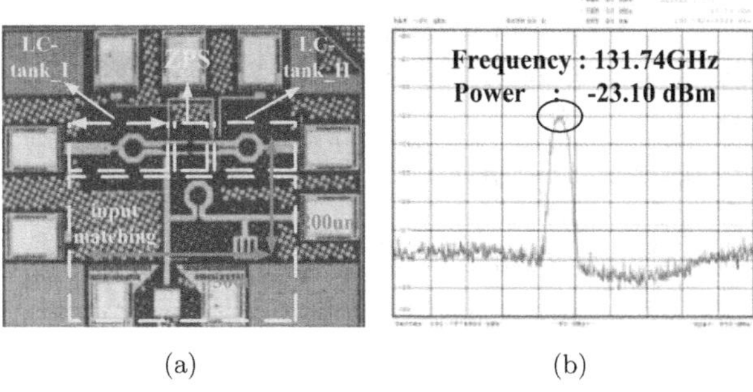

Figure 11.5: (a) Chip photo of 131.5 GHz SRX in 65 nm CMOS; (b) measured self-oscillation frequency of 131.74 GHz and output power of −23.10 dBm.

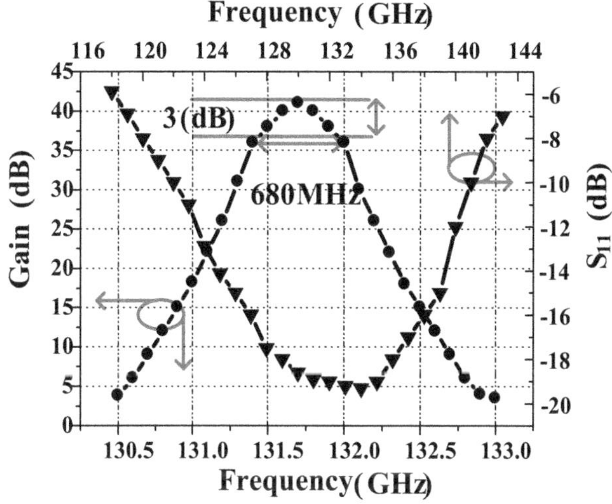

Figure 11.6: Measurement results: i) the maximum gain of 41 mB; and ii) input S_{11} parameter.

In addition, as shown in Figure 11.7, the sensitivity of the receiver is measured as -84 dBm. NEP is defined as the signal power in 1Hz bandwidth of unity signal-to-noise ratio, equivalent to $S/\sqrt{B}$, and measured as 0.615 fW/Hz$^{0.5}$. Finally, NF is measured as 7.26 dB by S/KTB at a room temperature. As shown in Table 11.1, the measurement results of the proposed receiver are compared to recently published mm-wave imaging receivers

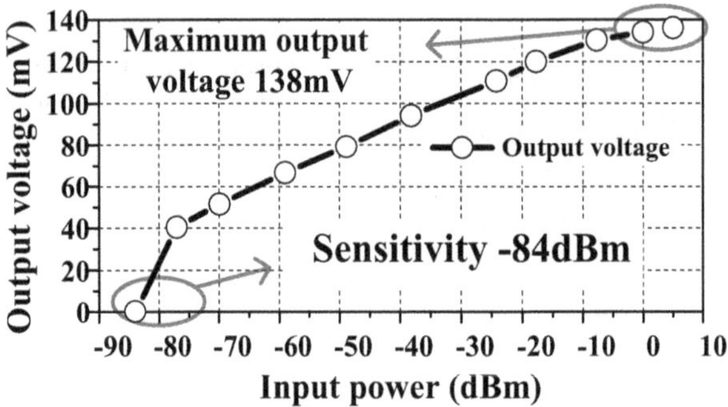

Figure 11.7: Measured sensitivity of −84 dBm and the maximum output voltage of 138 mV.

Table 11.1: Performance Comparison with Recent mm-Wave Receivers

	[91]	[92]	[89]	[90]	[93]	**This work**
Technology	65-nm CMOS	65-nm BiCMOS	65-nm CMOS	65-nm CMOS	65-nm CMOS	65-nm CMOS
Supply (V)	1.2	1	1.2	1	1.2	**1**
Frequency (GHz)	94	94	144	183	95.5	**131.5**
Sensitivity (dBm)	-66	-57	-74	-72.5	-78	**-84**
Noise Figure(dB)	N/A	12	10.2	9.9	8.5	**7.26**
Bandwidth(GHz)	23	26	0.94	1.4	0.56	**0.68**
NEP ($fW/Hz^{0.5}$)	N/A	10.4	1.3	1.51	0.67	**0.615**
Power (mW)	93	200	2.5	13.5	2.8	**8.1**
Core Area (mm^2)	0.31	1.25	0.021	0.013	0.014	**0.06**

[89, 90, 91, 92, 93]. The proposed receiver achieves better sensitivity, noise figure and NEP.

11.4 Conclusion

A CMOS super-regenerative receiver is demonstrated based on ZPS-coupled oscillators for 131 GHz. Compared to traditional SRX designs, the receiver shows an improved sensitivity by 10 dBm due to the additional positive feedback loop introduced between the two in-phase-coupled oscillators. The chip is implemented in 65nm CMOS with 0.06-mm^2 area. Measurement results show that the receiver has achieved -84-dBm sensitivity, 0.615-fW/Hz$0^{.5}$ NEP, 7.26-dB NF and 8.1-mW power consumption. The compact size with improved sensitivity is ideal for the application of large-arrayed mm-wave imaging applications.

APPLICATIONS V

Chapter 12

CMOS THz Imaging

12.1 Introduction

High performance THz imaging systems can be constructed by the proposed on-chip metamaterial-based signal sources, receivers and antennas in the previous sections. As illustrated in Figure 12.1, A high power THz signal firstly generated by MPW-based zero-phase CON and then radiated by the CRLH T-line-based on-chip LWA. After penetrating through the sample under test, the resulting THz signal is received by a high sensitivity super-regenerative receivers by TL-SRR/TL-CSRR-based quench-controlled oscillators. With the proposed transmitter and receiver designs, both narrow-band and wide-band THz imaging systems can be demonstrated at 135 GHz and 280 GHz, respectively.

In this chapter, firstly, a narrow-band transmission type THz imager is demonstrated at 135 GHz with various pharmacy and security applications. To further enhance a wide-band CMOS THz imaging system at 280 GHz with high sensitivity, and high spectrum resolution, a heterodyne receiver architecture is required [260]. As shown in Figure 12.2, a high-sensitivity CMOS wide-band transmission-type THz imager is also demonstrated by integrating the circular polarized substrate integrated waveguide (SIW) antenna introduced in Sec. 8.3 with a heterodyne receiver, which consists of a down-conversion mixer and a power gain amplifier (PGA). The down-conversion mixer with single-gate topology can achieve 80-GHz bandwidth with a conversion gain of -19 dB. The three-stage PGA achieves 150-MHz bandwidth for the detection resolution. The entire imager is measured with -2-dBi conversion gain over 42-GHz bandwidth, -54.4-dBm sensitivity at 100-MHz detection resolution bandwidth, 6.6-mW power consumption and 0.99-mm^2 chip area with high-contrast images measured.

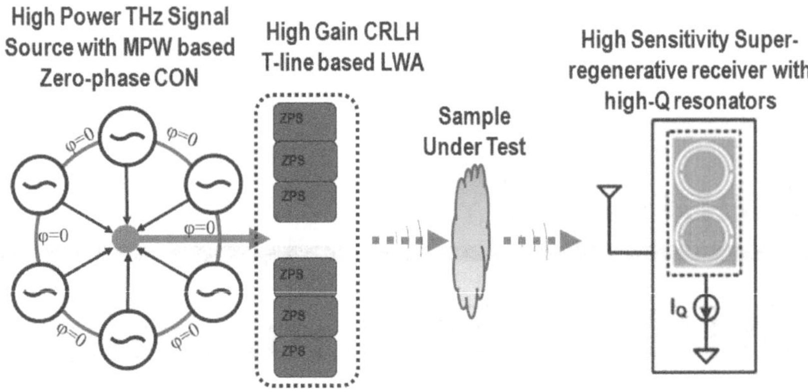

Figure 12.1: Metamaterial-based THz imaging system.

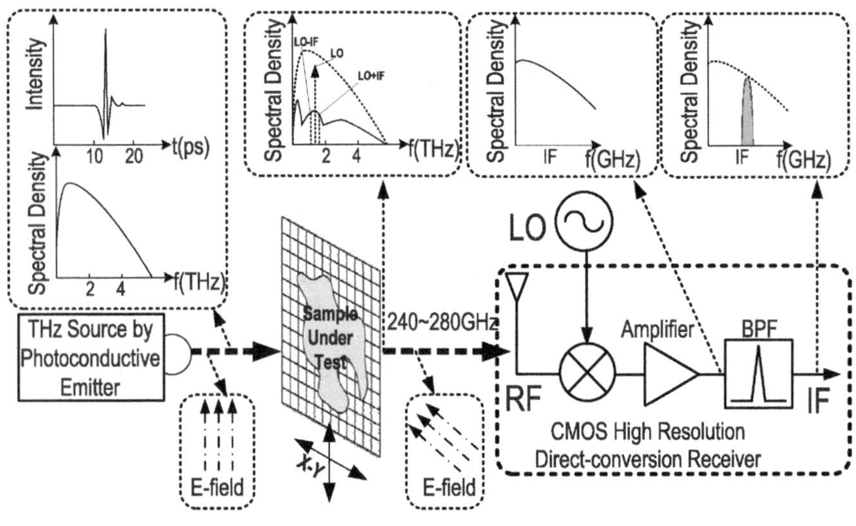

Figure 12.2: THz image system with heterodyne receiver for high spectrum resolution detection and circular-polarized antenna for the tolerance of depolarization effect.

In addition, a reflection-based THz imager is also required for in-vivo skin cancer diagnosis. Compared to the transmissive imaging system, the reflective type has a higher requirement for transmitter power, receiver sensitivity and the control of path of incident and reflected signal. As such, a reflective CMOS THz imaging system is also proposed based on simulation results in this work with on-chip integrated THz transceivers, which has been constructed by a differential heterodyne receiver the on-chip CRLH-TL leaky wave antenna (LWA), and zero-phase CON-based signal source demonstrated in previous sections.

12.2 135-GHz Narrow-Band Imager by DTL-SRR-Based SRX

12.2.1 THz Imaging by SRA Detection

THz radiation is usually attenuated due to absorption and scattering during the propagation [261], which can be modeled by

$$I_{\gamma_1} = I_{\gamma_0} e^{-\int_{\gamma_0}^{\gamma_1} \alpha_e(z)dz} \tag{12.1}$$

where I_{γ_0} and I_{γ_1} are the incoming and outgoing radiance intensity along the path (γ_0, γ_1); and $\alpha_e(z)$ is the extinction coefficient, which is the summation of absorption (α_a) and scattering (α_s) coefficients. For a homogeneous material placed between (γ_0, γ_1), α_a is a constant. The scattering only happens at the interface with scattering coefficients of $\alpha_s(\gamma_0)$ and $\alpha_s(\gamma_1)$. The received power (P_R) in a transmissive-type THz imaging system is [262]

$$\begin{aligned} P_R(dBm) &= P_T(dBm) + G_R(dBi) - L(dB) \\ &\quad - 8.686[\Delta\gamma\alpha_a + \alpha_s(\gamma_0) + \alpha_s(\gamma_1)](dB) \end{aligned} \tag{12.2}$$

where P_T is the effective isotropic radiated power (EIRP) of the transmitter, G_R is the receiver antenna gain, and L is the path loss without any objects placed in the propagation path, including both the free space path loss (FSPL) and atmosphere absorption.

As shown in (10.5), the envelope of receiver output is proportional to the injected current or the square root of input power. A DC output can be obtained by averaging $Env[v_o(t)]$ in each periodic quenching cycle.

$$V_{DC} = \frac{\omega_i Z_0 |S(\Delta\omega)| \sqrt{P_R}}{\sqrt{2R}(t_b - t_a)} \int_0^{t_b} \frac{1}{s(t)} dt \tag{12.3}$$

As such, the received power could be detected by measuring V_{DC} from the SRA output. As a result, the THz image of an object can be further obtained by the 2D scanning of V_{DC} with fixed P_T, G_R and L. Moreover, by analyzing V_{DC} as well as P_R with various object thickness $(\Delta\gamma)$, one can further find the absorption coefficient of the object under test.

12.2.2 Narrow-Band Imaging Results

The SRX can be integrated with the THz imaging system by replacing the GSG probe with bonding wires connected to an 135-GHz antenna. It is demon-

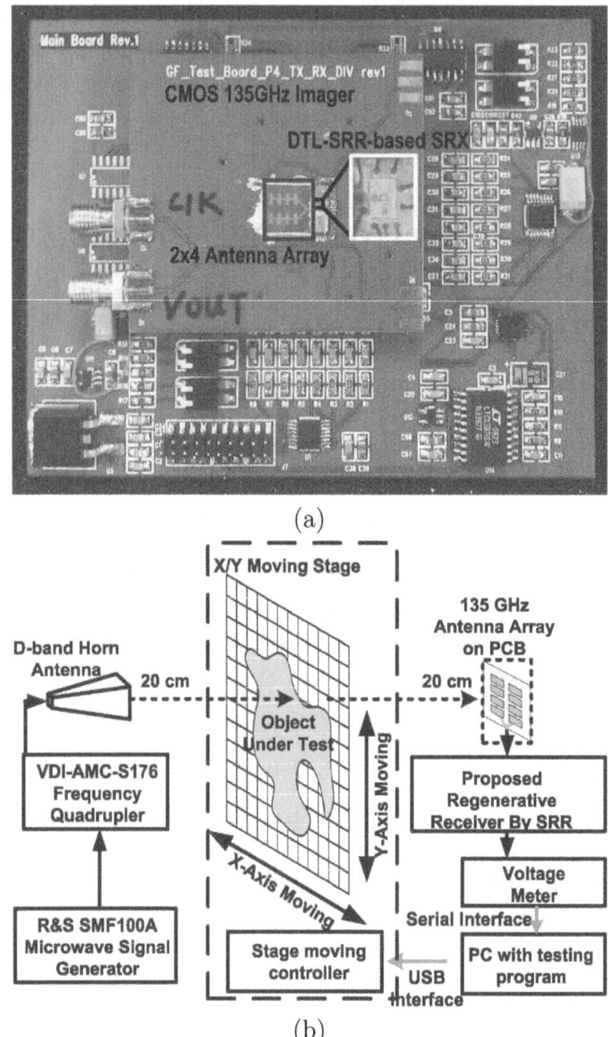

Figure 12.3: (a) PCB integration of CMOS 135-GHz SRX with antenna; (b) THz imaging measurement setup with the proposed receiver chip integrated on PCB and object under test fixed on an X-Y moving stage.

strated by wires bonding from the input of the proposed 135-GHz SRX to a 2×4 antenna array with hybrid series/parallel feeding network as shown in Figure 12.3(a). The receiver and antenna must be well aligned to minimize the connection loss, which is estimated to be 3~5dB according to the EM simula-

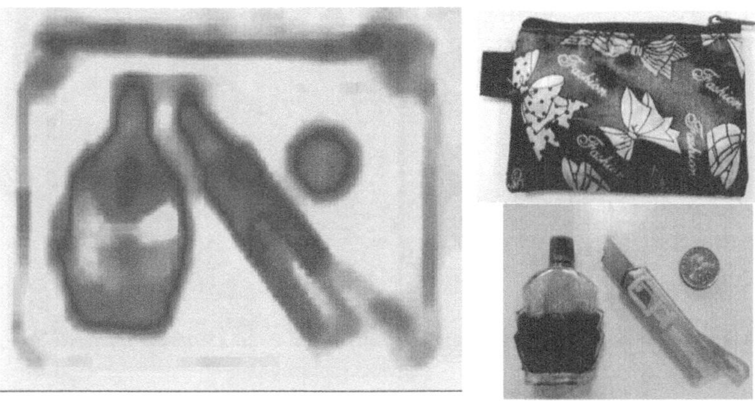

Figure 12.4: Images captured by imaging system with the proposed 135-GHz SRX receiver: knife, perfume, and coin in handbag.

tion in Ansoft HFSS. A 2x4 antenna array using hybrid series/parallel feed is designed and fabricated in Roger RT5880 with size of 8 ×8 mm^2. The antenna has 15.4dBi simulated gain at 135 GHz. Its input is matched to 50ohm with measured S11 below -10dB from 124 to 139GHz. Detailed information of the antenna array design is shown in [263]. The entire THz imaging setup is also shown in Figure 12.3(b). The 135-GHz radiation from a VDI source (0-dBm output power) is received by proposed SRX after propagating through the objects under test, which is held by an X-Y moving stage (STANDA) placed in the middle. Although a substantial portion of the object is illuminated due to the divergent beam from the source antenna, only the power propagating in the direction of the receiver is detected. As such, a high-resolution image can be obtained without a focus lens. The resulting V_{out} at each X-Y stage position is recorded into a 2D matrix, which can be plotted in colored image in MATLAB® with JET colormap.

Figure 12.18 shows the imaging results by the proposed CMOS THz image system. Figure 12.4 demonstrates the detection of a knife, perfume, and a coin inside a hand-bag. These items can be clearly identified in the image, because different material types like metal, plastic and liquid have different absorption and reflection properties to the THz radiation. Figure 12.5 shows that one can differentiate between a moisturized Panadol pill and a dry one. Due to the strong water absorption at THz frequencies, a moisturized Panadol has higher absorption than the dry one. Figure 12.6 shows the imaging of various types of food oil including sunflower, olive, fresh soybean and soybean that has been used once. Note that four petri dishes are used to hold the oil samples.

The imaging system can also be applied in transmission analysis to characterize the material in the propagation path. The absorption ratio of each oil

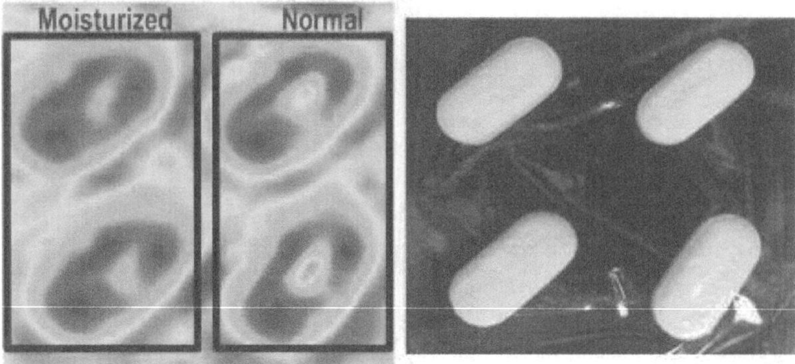

Figure 12.5: Images captured by imaging system with the proposed 135-GHz SRX receiver: moisturized and normal Panadol pills.

Figure 12.6: Images captured by imaging system with the proposed 135-GHz SRX receiver: various types of oil.

type can be identified by comparing the received power under different sample volume with the help of (12.2) in Section II, and it is depicted in the box chart in Figure 12.7. It is interesting to observe that the soybean oil that has been used once has higher absorption of the 135-GHz energy than the fresh one. With the significantly improved receiver sensitivity, the proposed CMOS THz imager results in high-contrast images and it can be further utilized in the analysis of moisture level as well as the identification of particular liquid content.

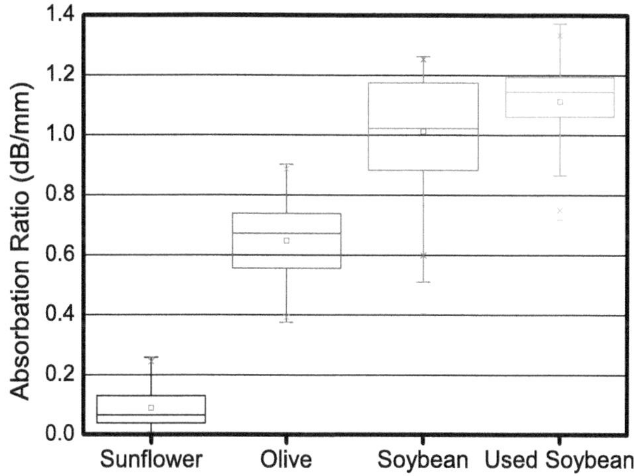

Figure 12.7: Absorption ratio of various types of oil detected at 135 GHz.

12.3 240 ~ 280-GHz Wide-Band Imager with Heterodyne Receiver

Since THz radiation is highly sensitive to the crystal lattice vibration, hydrogen-bond as well as intermolecular interactions, it results in unique spectroscopy fingerprints for many materials. There are two design targets for the receiver to enable the spectroscopy analysis in a sub-THz imaging: high spectrum selectivity and wide frequency range of operation. Diode detection-based receivers [230, 32, 259] can achieve the latter target, but not the former one; while super-regenerative-based receivers [90, 231] can achieve the former target, but not the latter one. In order to satisfy both of the two targets in the receiver design, one needs to deploy either heterodyne [264] or direct-conversion receivers. Compared to direct-conversion architecture with a zero IF, heterodyne architecture with a near-zero IF is more flexible in the system design with both magnitude and phase detection capability. The magnitude detection in an sub-THz imaging system can be achieved by either heterodyne or direct-conversion architecture, but only heterodyne architecture is able to retain the phase information of sub-THz signal, which is very useful to analyze the complex refractive index of the sample under test. As such, this paper focuses on the design of heterodyne receivers with a near-zero IF.

12.3.1 Architecture and System Specification

The design of a CMOS heterodyne receiver in THz has to be conducted in a scenario without any low noise amplifiers (LNA) as illustrated in Figure 12.2, because hardly any amplifiers can be designed at a frequency close to or above the f_{max}. For example, the f_{max} in a typical CMOS 65nm process is around 300 GHz [265],

The receiver gain (G_{tot}) in such case can be calculated as

$$G_{tot} = G_{ant} G_{mix} G_{pga} \tag{12.4}$$

where G_{ant}, G_{mix} and G_{pga} denote the gain of antenna, mixer and power gain amplifier (PGA), respectively. Also, the total receiver noise figure (NF_{tot}) becomes

$$NF_{tot} = NF_{mix} + \frac{NF_{pga} - 1}{G_{mix}} \tag{12.5}$$

where NF_{mix} and NF_{pga} denote the NF of the mixer and VGA, respectively. Eq. (12.4) denotes that the total receiver gain can be improved from antenna, mixer and PGA, while (12.5) denotes that the noise contributed by each stage decreases as the total gain of preceding stages. The noise contributions from mixer and PGA are no longer negligible without LNA, so the NF of the receiver has to be improved by increasing the conversion gain of the mixer and minimizing the noise figure of PGA. In the following sections, the designs of the mixer and PGA in a THz CMOS heterodyne receiver are introduced.

12.3.2 Down-Conversion Mixer

As the first active building block connected to the antenna, the design of the down-conversion mixer largely affects the performance of heterodyne receiver, including conversion gain and NF. Conventionally there are two types of mixers that are commonly used in the mm-wave region: Gilbert-cell mixer and single-gate mixer [266, 267]. Gilbert-cell mixer [266] has a compact size and low implementation loss, and it generates the cross-modulation product of LO and RF signals. However, the conversion gain of the Gilbert-cell mixer largely depends on the transconductance of transistors in the saturation region, which will be heavily reduced when the signal frequency is approaching f_{max}. On the other hand, the single-gate mixer [267] utilized the nonlinearity of transistors when biased in the subthreshold region, which is less frequency dependent compared to the Gilbert-cell mixer, and is able to work at a higher frequency in THz. Moreover, compared to the subharmonic mixer working with 1/3-LO [234], the conversion loss could be largely reduced when directly mixing the RF and LO signal in fundamental tones. In this work, a single-gate mixer is designed to down-convert the RF signal in 220 $\sim$ 300 GHz to the baseband by the fundamental tone of LO signal.

Figure 12.8 shows the schematic of a proposed down-conversion mixer design. A Wilkinson combiner implemented by coplanar waveguide (CPW)

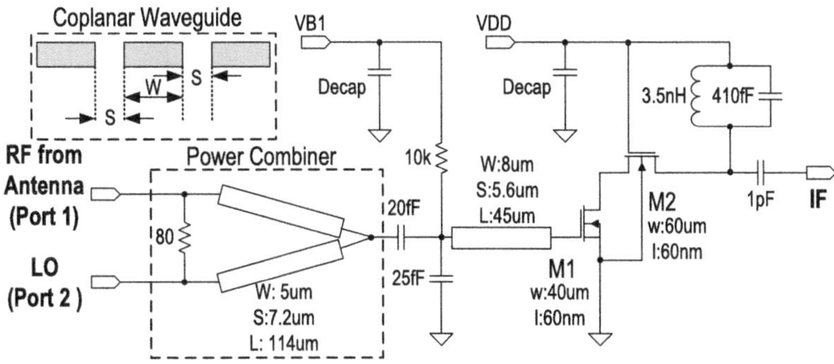

Figure 12.8: Schematic of THz down-conversion mixer at 280 GHz.

is deployed to combine the RF signal from the antenna and the LO signal, and also to provide isolation in between. The combined output is connected to the input of the common-source stage (M1) biased in the subthreshold region (0.4-V V_{GS}) by a compact composite CPW and lump components matching network. The following common-gate stage is applied to improve the conversion efficiency as well as the reverse isolation. One LC resonator is connected between the VDD and the mixer output to filter out the unwanted harmonics of the IF signal.

A post-layout simulation is performed to the proposed mixer design with passive devices simulated in an EMX environment, including power combiner, matching network and inductors. A maximum conversion gain of -19 dB is demonstrated by proposed mixer in Figure 12.9(a) when the power of LO is 0 dBm. Note that the on-chip generation of 0 dBm LO power by 65nm CMOS has been recently demonstrated in [176]. Compared to the subharmonic mixer design in [234], the conversion gain is improved by more than 10 dB. Also, the proposed mixer has a wide operation frequency range with a gain of $-19 \sim -22$dB from 220 GHz to 300 GHz. Moreover, a good input matching and LO-RF isolation is achieved with S11, S22 and S12 smaller than -10 dB in 220 $\sim$ 300 GHz. Note that the conversion gain of the proposed mixer is also determined by the available LO power at mixer input. As shown in Figure 12.9(a), the conversion gain will drop to -37 dB when LO power is reduced to -20 dBm.

12.3.3 Power Gain Amplifier

There are two major objectives in the PGA design in a THz heterodyne receiver. First, sufficient gain must be provided to the targeted IF frequency with a low noise figure. Compared to the common-source amplification topology, cascode is more preferred with higher gain and stability. Second, a narrow frequency response is required to increase the selectivity of the receiver

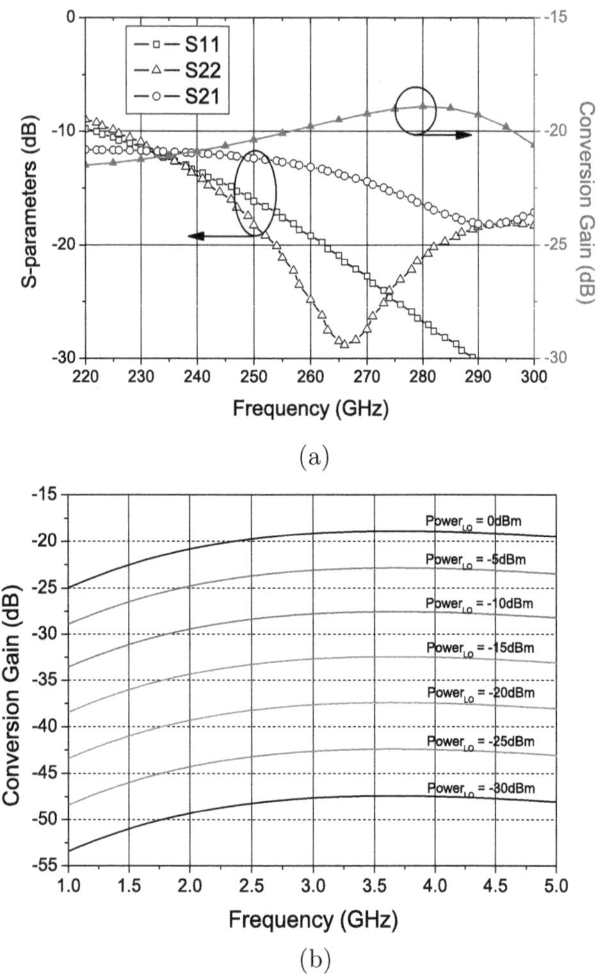

Figure 12.9: Simulation results of proposed mixer. (a) S-parameters and conversion gain when sweeping RF and LO frequencies with $F_{LO} = F_{RF} + 3GHz$; (b) conversion gain at different LO power level when sweeping RF frequency with $F_{IF} = F_{RF} - 280GHz$.

for the purpose of THz imaging. Generally, a narrow frequency response can be achieved by a resonator tank with a high quality factor, which is mainly determined by the inductor for on-chip implementation. However, since the inductor size is inversely proportional to the resonating frequency for a given Q factor, it will generate large chip area overhead when the resonant frequency is too small. As such, an optimized resonant frequency of 3GHz is selected in the PGA design.

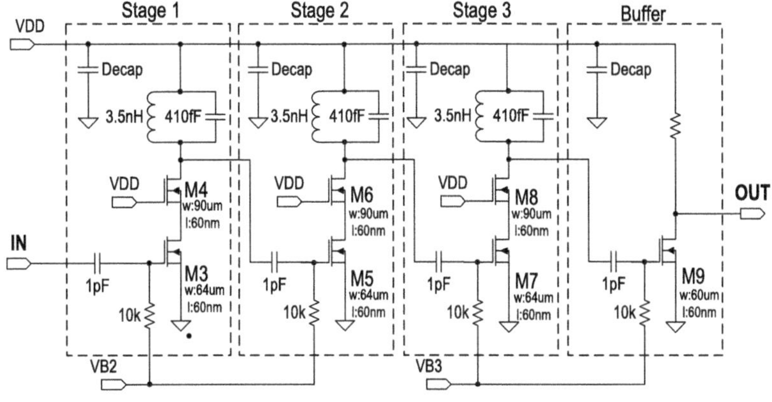

Figure 12.10: Schematic of the three-stage power gain amplifier and the output buffer.

Figure 12.10 shows the schematic of the proposed PGA, which is implemented by three stages of cascode amplifiers followed by a common-source output buffer. In each cascode stage, both transistors are biased in the saturation region (0.6-V V_G for M3, M5 and M7, V_G is connected to VDD for M4, M6 and M8.) The resonator is implemented by a 410-fF metal-insulator-metal capacitor and a 3.5nH spiral inductor. A common-source output buffer is used to drive a 50-Ohm output impedance for the purpose of measurement. The post-layout simulation is also performed on the proposed PGA design. As shown in Figure 12.11, a maximum gain of 33dB is obtained at a center frequency of 3 GHz, and the 3-dB bandwidth is 150 MHz. Moreover, the proposed PGA has a noise figure lower than 4 dB from 2.5 GHz to 3.5 GHz.

12.3.4 Wide-Band Imaging Results

The proposed wide-band CMOS imager is fabricated in Global Foundries (GF) 65-nm CMOS RF process after integrating the heterodyne receiver with the circular polarized substrate integrated waveguide (SIW) antenna introduced in Sec. 8.3. The die micrograph is shown in Figure 12.12 with a chip area of 0.99 mm^2. The fabricated receiver chip is firstly measured alone followed by the applications in the THz imaging system.

12.3.4.1 Receiver Measurements

The receiver operates under 0.8-V power supply with overall power consumption of 6.6 mW. As shown in Figure 12.13, the receiver chip is firstly measured on a probe station (CASCADE Microtech Elite-300). An LO-signal (VDI) is

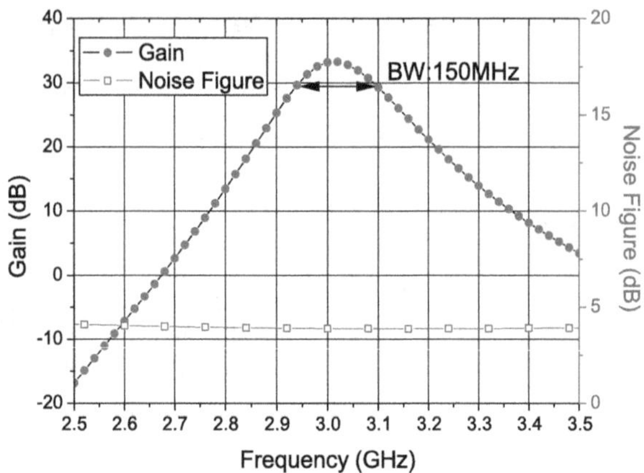

Figure 12.11: Simulation results of the three-stage power gain amplifier with output buffer.

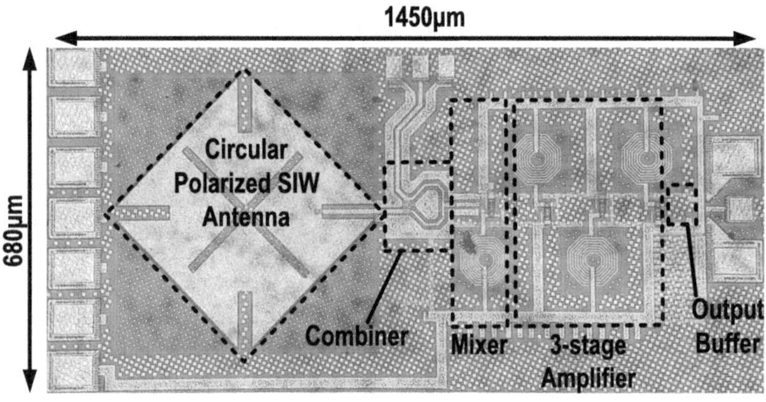

Figure 12.12: Chip micro photograph of the proposed CMOS 280-GHz heterodyne receiver with on-chip integrated circular polarized SIW antenna.

directly injected via a waveguide GSG probe with 50-μm pitch from 220 GHz to 330 GHz, and a RF signal is emitted by a 20-dB gain horn antenna placed right above the chip under-test by 10-cm distance. The output IF signal is connected to another low-frequency GSG probe with 100-μm pitch.

The receiver output power is measured by a spectrum analyzer (Agilent E4408b) when the power of the RF source (VDI) is pushed to the maximum power level ($\sim$ -10 dBm). The receiver gain in (12.4) can be obtained by

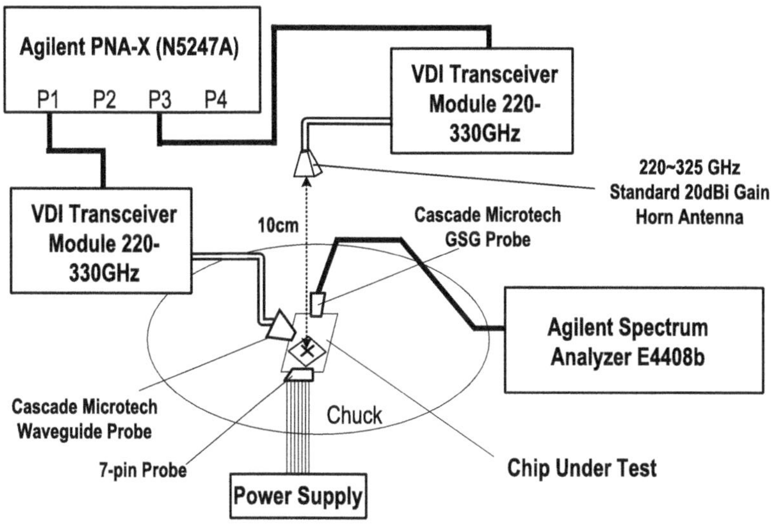

Figure 12.13: Equipment setup for 280-GHz receiver measurement.

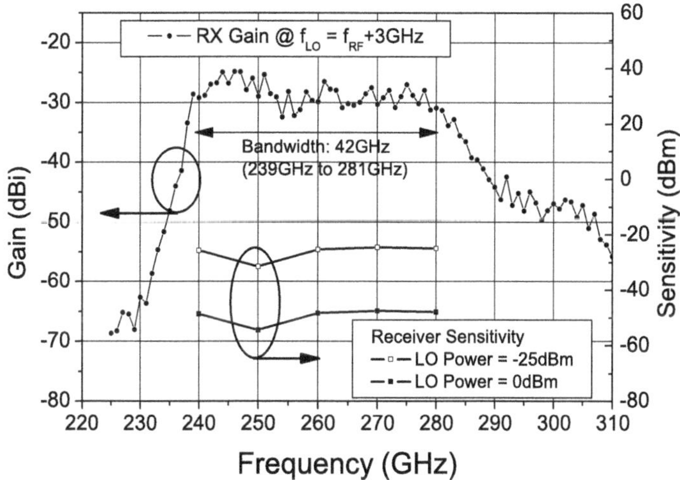

Figure 12.14: Gain and sensitivity measurement results when sweeping RF and LO frequencies with $F_{LO} = F_{RF} + 3GHz$.

$G_{tot}(dBi) = P_{IF} - ERIP_{RF} + L(d)$, where P_{IF} is the output power of the receiver in dBm, $ERIP$ is the equivalent isotropically radiated power of the signal source in dBm, $L(d)$ is signal propagation loss in dB and d is the

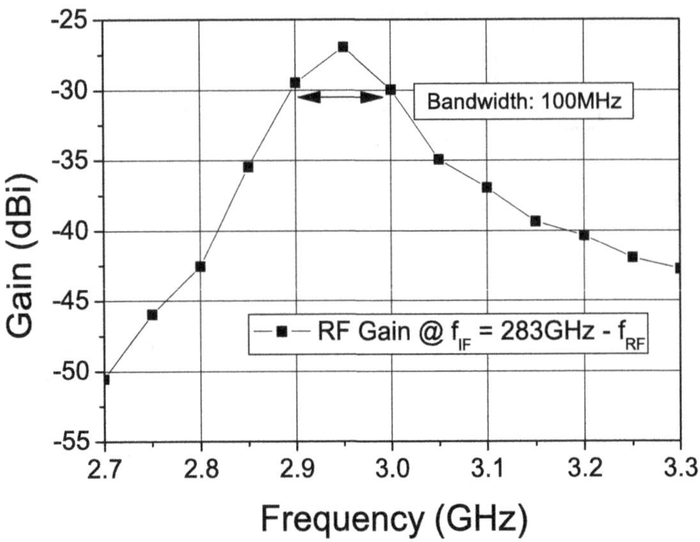

Figure 12.15: Gain measurement results when sweeping RF and LO frequencies with $F_{IF} = F_{LO} + 280GHz$.

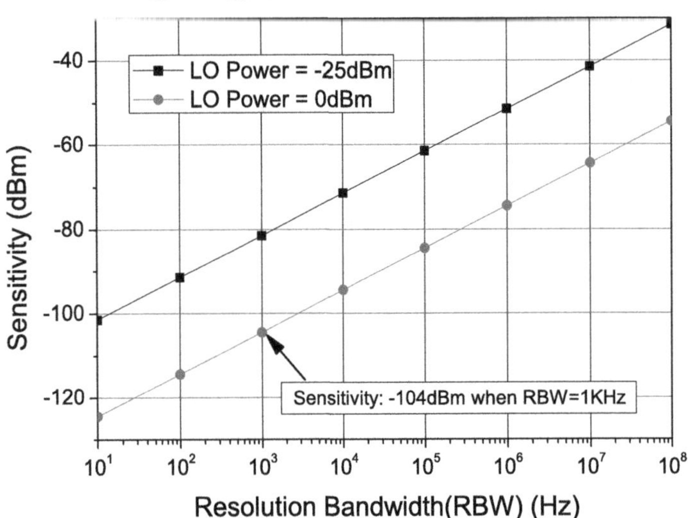

Figure 12.16: Receiver sensitivity at 250 GHz versus receiver resolution bandwidth.

distance between the horn antenna and the SIW antenna in the receiver. Note that $ERIP_{RF}$ and $L(d)$ can be obtained by the following equations:

$$\begin{cases} ERIP_{RF} = P_{TX} + G_{TX} \\ L(d) = 20\log\left(\frac{c}{4\pi fd}\right) + 4.343\alpha d \end{cases} \tag{12.6}$$

where P_{TX} is the source power, G_{TX} is the horn antenna gain, and α is the attenuation factor due to the atmospheric absorption, which is almost negligible for an in door environment. The wide-band gain response is measured by fixing IF output frequency (f_{IF}) at 3GHz and sweeping RF and LO frequencies (f_{RF} and f_{LO}) simultaneously with $f_{LO} = f_{RF} + f_{IF}$. As shown in Figure 12.14, the proposed receiver is measured with an operating bandwidth of 42 GHz from 239 GHz to 281 GHz and a maximum conversion gain of -25 dBi. The narrow-band selectivity response is measured by fixing f_{LO} at 283GHz and sweeping f_{RF} with $f_{IF} = f_{LO} - f_{RF}$. As shown in Figure 12.15, a 100-MHz resolution bandwidth is observed. This is slightly lower than the simulated bandwidth of PGA because of an additional LC resonator in the down-conversion mixer. The best sensitivity (S) is found to be -31.4 dBm at 250 GHz as illustrated in Figure 12.14, where S is calculated by $PSD_{noise} \cdot B/G$, PSD_{noise} is the measured output noise power spectrum density from spectrum analyzer, B and G are the receiver resolution bandwidth and conversion gain, respectively. Due to the loss of waveguide and probe ($\sim$15dB) at LO input, the maximum LO power allowed at the mixer input is about -25dBm, which largely affects the receiver performance in terms of conversion gain and sensitivity. According to the relation between conversion gain and LO power illustrated in Figure 12.9(b), the compensated receiver gain is -2 dB when LO power is increased to 0 dBm. Similarly, the receiver sensitivity in the 0-dBm LO condition is improved to -54.4 dBm as illustrated in Figure 12.14. Moreover, the receiver sensitivity can be further improved by introducing off-chip filters with even smaller resolution bandwidth. For example, as shown in Figure 12.16, a -104 dBm sensitivity can be achieved at 250 GHz when the resolution bandwidth is reduced to 1kHz. Note that the maximum imager data rate is determined by the integration time of each pixel, and can be derived from the resolution bandwidth (RBW) based on the selected low pass filtering response. For example, the integration time of a single RC low pass filter is $0.35/RBW(1/Hz)$.

The receiver performance is summarized in Table 12.1 and compared to other recent state-of-the-art CMOS THz image receivers. For the first time, a CMOS-based THz image system is demonstrated by the heterodyne receiver with on-chip integrated circular-polarized SIW antenna. The proposed receiver has much smaller detection resolution bandwidth when compared to the other detection method. Especially when comparing to the super-regenerative-based receiver designs with resonant-type narrow-band detection, the resolution bandwidth is further increased by 15 times, while the system bandwidth is improved by 30 times. Moreover, the sensitivity of the proposed receiver

Table 12.1: State-of-the-Art CMOS THz Image Receivers Performance Comparison

Parameters	Unit	This Work	[32]	[230]	[259]	[90]	[231]
Technology	—	65-nm CMOS	130-nm CMOS	130-nm CMOS	180-nm SiGe BiCMOS	65-nm CMOS	65-nm CMOS
Frequency	GHz	239 ∼ 281	280	280	93-113	183	201
Detection Method	—	Heterodyne	Diode-detection	Diode-detection	Diode-detection	Super-regenerative	Super-regenerative
Detection Polarization	—	Circular	Linear	Linear	Linear	Linear	Linear
System Bandwidth	GHz	42	7	700	20	1.4	1.5
Resolution Bandwidth	GHz	0.1	7	700	20	1.4	1.5
Gain	dB	-25/-2*	—	31	39	—	—
Sensitivity	dBm	-31.4/-54.4*	-26.9	—	-56	-72.5	-59.6
Power	mW/pixel	6.6	2.5	0.1	225	13.5	18.2
Chip Area	mm^2/pixel	0.03	3.8	0.25	0.29	0.45	0.99

*Calculated results when 0-dBm LO power is applied to the mixer.

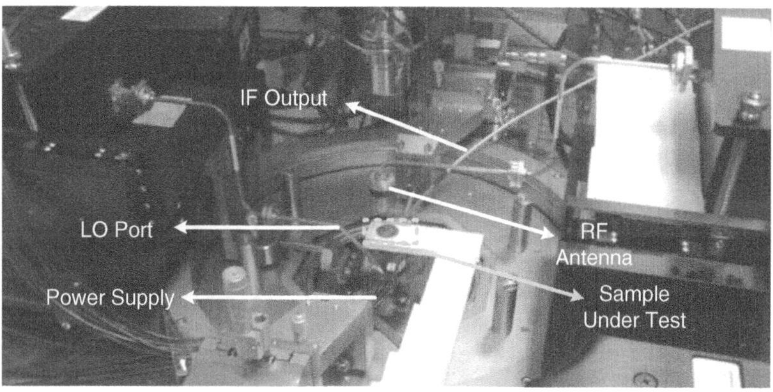

Figure 12.17: Measurement setup of THz image system.

is comparable to the designs in other receiving topologies [259, 231] when a 0-dBm LO power is applied.

12.3.5 Wide-Band THz Imaging

The THz image system is set up as shown in Figure 12.17 with samples placed between the horn antenna and receiver chip. The samples under test are held by an X-Y moving stage, controlled by the testing program. The proposed THz image system shown is applied to study Panadol pills and animal skin sample in dry and moisturized conditions at 240 GHz and 280 GHz, respectively. The samples are placed between the antenna of the transmitter and receiver chip. The samples are held by an X-Y moving stage controlled by the testing program. Figure 12.18 shows two imaging cases for the biomedical applications. The first case shows that one can differentiate between a moisturized Panadol pill and a dry one because of strong water absorption at THz frequencies. In the second case, the moisturized area in the animal skin sample can be clearly identified from the surrounding dry area. Moreover, different images are obtained at 240 GHz and 280 GHz with different absorption ratios.

12.4 280-GHz Reflective Imaging System

Figure 12.19 shows the block diagram of the proposed CMOS-based THz reflective imaging system. The entire system consists of two identical transceivers with on-chip antennas that each of them can either generate or detect a THz signal.

When the transceiver works as a signal source, the signal generated from

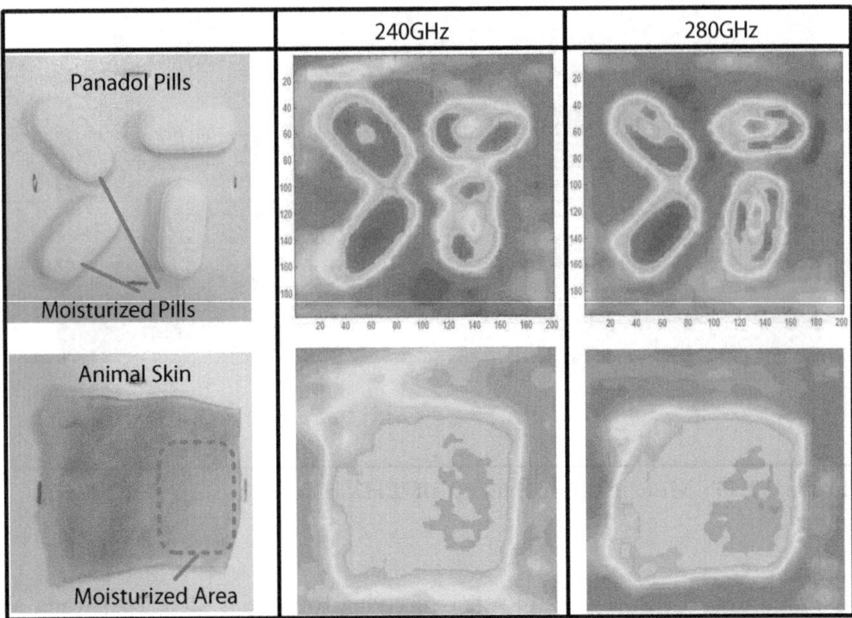

Figure 12.18: Captured THz image results of Panadol pills and skin samples under 240 GHz and 280 GHz radiation.

the CMOS local oscillator (LO) is directly fed to the on-chip antenna by a T-line network with high characteristic impedance (high-Z_0). The application of a high-Z_0 T-line has two advantages compared to the conventional T-line with 50 Ω impedance. Firstly, for the signals traveling in the T-line with the same power level, higher Z_0 generates larger voltage magnitude, which can drive the gate of the mixer more effectively. Secondly, the signal propagation loss can be effectively reduced due to a smaller current magnitude in the high-Z_0 T-line.

When the transceiver works as a signal detector, the incoming THz signal (RF) is firstly received by the on-chip antenna, then it is down-converted by the single-gate mixers attached to both ends of the T-line network. Because both the LO and RF signals travel in opposite directions with 90° phase shift in the T-line, a differential IF signal results. Note that the LO frequency is usually slightly different from the RF frequency to have an IF output in the mixer. Compared to the single-ended mixer design introduced in Sec. 12.3.2, a differential mixer output in the base-band provide stronger immunity to the EM interference as well as common noise rejection. After further amplification by variable gain amplifier (VGA), both magnitude and phase information of the resulting differential IF signal can be detected and processed for imaging applications.

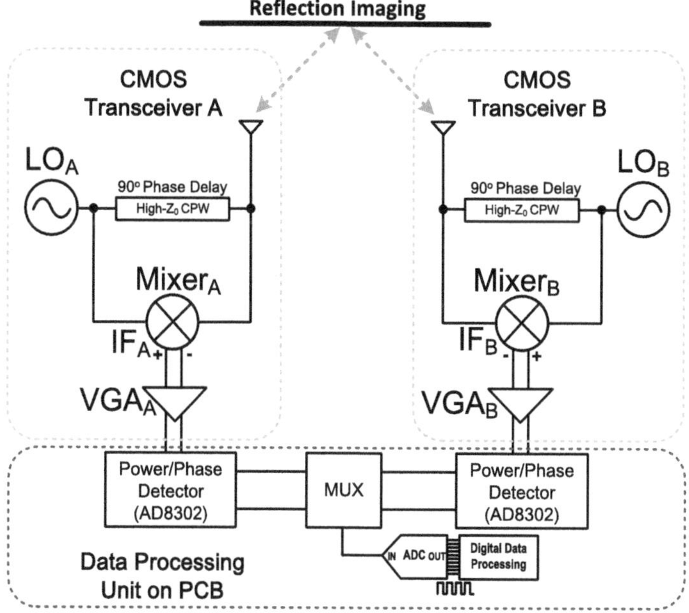

Figure 12.19: The block diagram of CMOS-based THz reflective imaging system.

In the following sections, the design of each building block in the 280-GHz CMOS transceiver is discussed, including a high-power CON-based signal source, a high-gain 2D CRLH T-line-based LWA array and a differential down-conversion mixer with VGA.

12.4.1 Differential Down-Conversion Receiver

12.4.1.1 Differential Down-Conversion Mixer with Bidirectional Hybrid Coupler

Figure 12.20 shows the schematic of the proposed 280 GHz differential down-conversion mixer. A 90° phase shifter is designed for both LO and RF signals with high-Z_0 T-lines implemented by coplanar waveguide (CPW) as well as the parasitics capacitances contributed by M1, M2 and R1. The size of both M1 and M2 is optimized between the down-conversion efficiency and the capacitance loadings to the high-Z_0 T-line. For instance, a smaller size of M1 and M2 helps reduce the loaded capacitance to the high-Z_0 T-line, but it also reduces the output currents of mixing products. Moreover, they are biased in the subthreshold region (0.4-V V_{GS}) by a diode-connected NMOS transistor

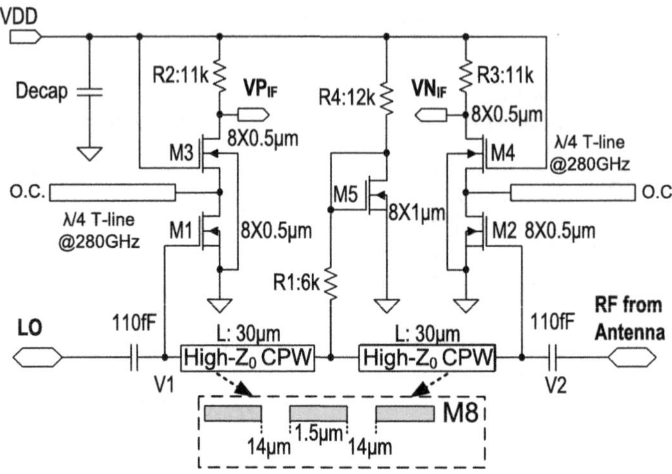

Figure 12.20: Schematic of proposed differential down-conversion mixer with an input network of 90° high-Z$_0$ T-line.

(M5) to maximize the nonlinearity. Two $\lambda/4$ T-line open stubs at 280 GHz are connected to the drains of M1 and M2 to improve the down-conversion efficiency by reducing the LO leakage to the following common-gate stages (M3 and M4).

Assuming the frequencies of both RF and LO signals are closed to each other, both of them have 90° phase shift without any signal loss, and an equal amount of LO or RF voltages are applied to the gate of M1 and M2 with a 90° delayed version of each other that can be expressed as:

$$\begin{cases} V_{M1} = V_{RF} \cdot \cos(\omega_{RF}t + \phi_{RF} + 90^\circ) + V_{LO} \cdot \cos(\omega_{LO}t + \phi_{LO}) \\ V_{M2} = V_{RF} \cdot \cos(\omega_{RF}t + \phi_{RF}) + V_{LO} \cdot \cos(\omega_{LO}t + \phi_{LO} + 90^\circ) \end{cases} \tag{12.7}$$

where $[V_{RF}, \omega_{RF}, \phi_{RF}]$ and $[V_{LO}, \omega_{LO}, \phi_{LO}]$ are the [input voltage magnitude, frequency, initial phase] of RF and LO signal, respectively.

Note that the output voltage of a single-gate mixer can be expressed as

$$\begin{cases} V_{IF}(t) = R_0 g_m(t) V_{RF}(t) \\ g_m(t) = a_0 + \sum_{n=1}^{\infty} a_n cos(n\omega_{LO}t) \end{cases} \tag{12.8}$$

where a$_n$, n=(0,1,2...) are the Fourier coefficients of g$_m$ with respect to ω_{LO}. It can be shown that a$_0$ and a$_1$ represent the fundamental transconductance and the first-order mixing product of (ω_{RF} - ω_{LO}), respectively. As such, by substituting (12.7) into (12.8), the first-order mixing product at IF outputs

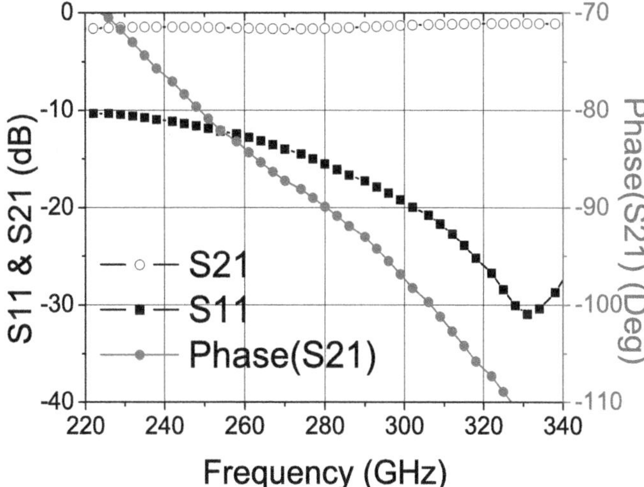

Figure 12.21: Post-layout simulation results of the high-Z_0 T-line network with 90° phase delay.

become:

$$\begin{cases} VP_{IF} = a_1 \cdot V_{RF} R_0 \cos\left[\omega_{IF} t + (\phi_{RF} - \phi_{LO}) + 90°\right] \\ VN_{IF} = a_1 \cdot V_{RF} R_0 \cos\left[\omega_{IF} t + (\phi_{RF} - \phi_{LO}) - 90°\right] \end{cases} \tag{12.9}$$

where $\omega_{IF} = \omega_{RF} - \omega_{LO}$ is the IF frequency. A differential IF output is observed from (12.9) that VP_{IF} and VN_{IF} have the same magnitude and opposite phase. As a result, the total output voltage of mixer (V_{IF}) is

$$V_{IF} = VP_{IF} - VN_{IF} = 2a_1 \cdot V_{RF} R_0 \cos\left[\omega_{IF} t + (\phi_{RF} - \phi_{LO}) + 90°\right]. \tag{12.10}$$

Equation (12.10) indicates that both magnitude and phase information of the RF signal can be obtained by the proposed down-conversion mixer, which are very useful in the refractive index measurement by a THz imaging system.

A post-layout simulation is performed to study the proposed differential mixer design. Figure 12.21 shows the 2-port S-parameter analysis of the high-Z_0 T-line network under 76Ω system impedance. A good input matching is observed with S11 smaller than -10dB in 220–340GHz. The maximum insertion loss (S21) in 220 ∼ 340 GHz is 1.6dB. A wide-band 90° phase shift is observed with ±10 degrees bandwidth of 55 GHz centered at 280 GHz. Figure 12.22(a) shows the post-layout simulation results of the 280-GHz differential mixer from 260 GHz to 320 GHz under the following conditions: the power of LO signal is fixed at 0 dBm; the frequency of the RF signal is 1GHz above

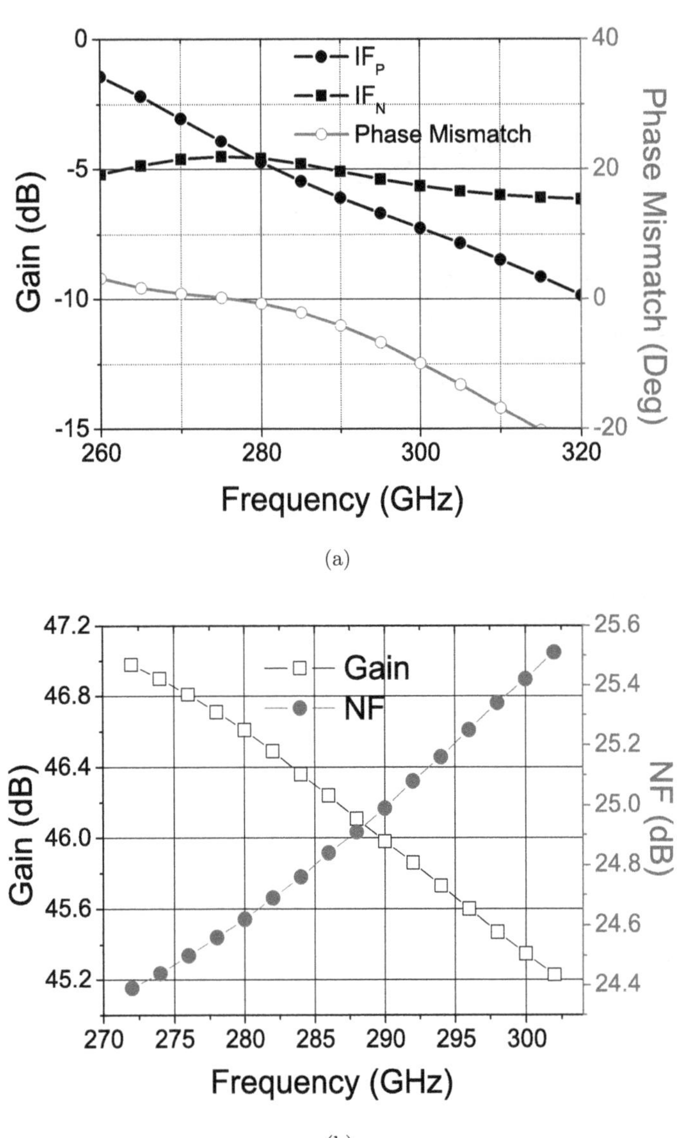

Figure 12.22: Post-layout simulation results. (a) the conversion gain and output phase mismatch of the 280-GHz differential mixer; (b) the conversion gain and NF of the 280-GHz receiver with differential mixer and VGA from [14].

the frequency LO signal. An averaged conversion gain of -4.6 dB is observed at 280GHz for VP_{IF} and VN_{IF}, which have magnitude and phase mismatch of 0.2 dB and -0.7 degrees, respectively. Note that the phase mismatch has already been normalized to 180 degrees.

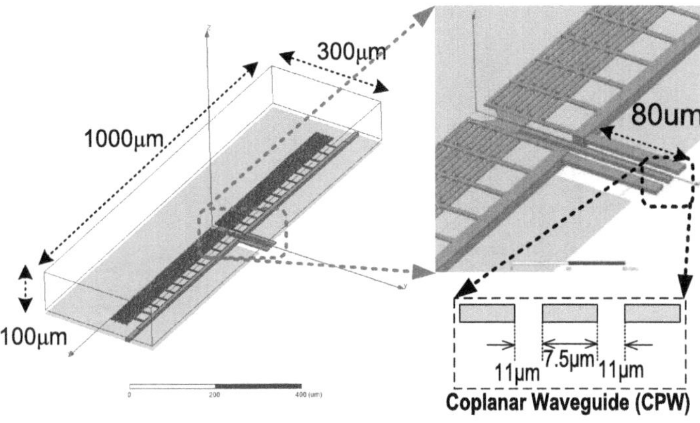

Figure 12.23: 2D LWA array with 2×13 unit cells.

12.4.1.2 Variable Gain Amplifier

In this work, a modified Cherry–Hooper amplifier-based VGA [14] is employed to boost the power of IF signals from mixer outputs with low power consumption, compact design size as well as large gain control range. Figure 12.22(b) shows the post-layout simulation results of the entire receiving part after integrating mixer and VGA under the following conditions: the power of the LO signal is fixed at 0 dBm; the frequency of RF signal is 1GHz above the frequency LO signal. The gain and noise figure (NF) observed at 280GHz is 46.6 dB and 24.6 dB, respectively. And the variations of gain and NF are both less than 2dB in 272 $\sim$ 302 GHz. The 3dB IF bandwidth is 1.1 GHz, which is mainly determined by VGA [14].

12.4.2 2D On-Chip Leaky Wave Antenna Array

A 2D antenna array with on-chip LWA with 2 $\times$ 13 CRLH T-line unit-cells is designed in the 65-nm CMOS process as shown in Figure 12.23. Two 1D CRLH T-line-based LWAs introduced in Sec. 8.2 are connected in parallel by a T-junction to further increase the broadside antenna gain as well as reduce the end-fire leakage. The antenna input is matched to the system characteristic impedance of 76 Ω by connecting a coplanar waveguide (CPW) with a length of 80 μm, which is implemented in layer M8. A standard high-resistivity silicon layer (1000 $\times$ 300 μm^2) with a thickness of 100 μm is also placed on top of the antenna surface to enhance the radiation efficiency of antenna array.

The proposed 2D LWA array is verified by a full wave simulation in Ansoft HFSS. Figure 12.24(a) shows the simulated radiation pattern at 280 GHz. It has a broadside radiation pattern with a directivity of 9.1 dBi and a radiation

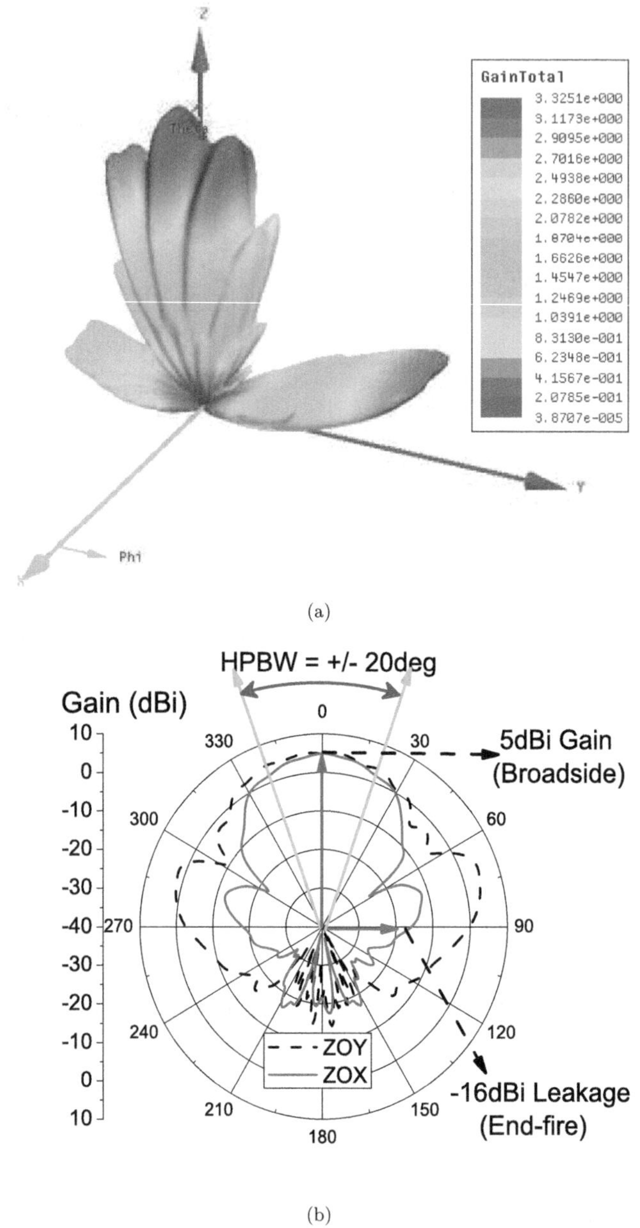

(a)

(b)

Figure 12.24: HFSS simulated radiation pattern of the 2D LWA array at 280 GHz in (a) 3D plot, and (b) polar plots in ZOX and ZOY planes.

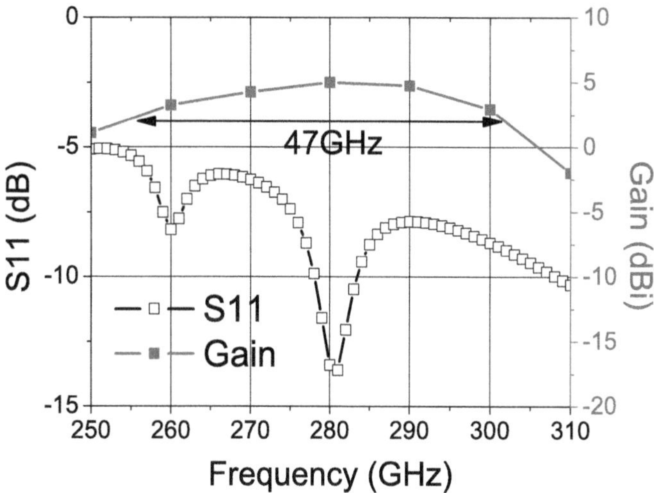

Figure 12.25: Simulated antenna input S11 and gain at broadside direction (Z-axis).

efficiency of 41%. As a result, the half-power bandwidth (HPBW) is ±20 degrees in the ZOX plane as illustrated in Figure 12.24(b); and a broadside radiation gain of 5 dBi (in Z direction) as well as an end-fire leakage of -16 dBi (in X direction) are obtained. Compared to the 1D LWA demonstrated in Sec. 8.2, 2D LWA has 0.9 dB higher gain at 280 GHz. This improvement is lower than the ideal value of 3dB because of the additional loss introduced by the matching network as well as the T-junction. Figure 12.25 shows the simulation results of input S11 as well as the wide-band antenna gain on the broadside direction. The S11 is observed to be smaller than -6 dB from 256 GHz to 310 GHz; a 47-GHz 3-dB bandwidth centered at 279 GHz is observed from 255 GHz to 302 GHz.

12.4.3 Transceiver Integration

The proposed 280-GHz CMOS transceiver design is implemented in the 65-nm CMOS RF process with the Cadence layout shown in Figure 12.26. It has a total area of 1000 × 1010 μm^2. Note that there are no measurements for the proposed 280-GHz transceiver, and the performance of transceiver is verified by post-layout and EM simulation. Operating from a 1.2-V power supply, the whole transceiver consumes 298.6 mW, including 3.5 mW contributed by the 280 GHz differential mixer and VGA.

The performance of the proposed THz source is summarized in Table 12.2 with comparison to the recent state-of-the-art THz transmitters and receivers

Table 12.2: Performance Comparison with Recently Published THz Transmitters and Receivers

Transmitters					
Parameters	Unit	[31]	[269]	[178]	**This Work**
Technology	—	CMOS 45nm SOI	CMOS 65nm	CMOS 65nm	**CMOS 65nm**
Center Frequency	GHz	280	260	288	**286**
P_{OUT}	dBm/Pixel	-7.2	0.5	-4.1	**1.3**
Broadside P_{EIRP}	dBm	9.4	15.7	14.2	**6.3**
FTR	%	3.2	9.5	1.7	**10.5**
DC Power	mW/Pixel	52.25	800	275	**295.6**
Power Efficiency	%	0.37	0.14	0.14	**0.46**
Transmitter Size* (A_{TX})	mm^2	2.7×2.7	78.5	12.56	**1×1.01**
P_{EIRP}/A_{TX}	mw/mm^2	1.19	0.47	2.09	**4.27**
Receivers					
Parameters	Unit	[230]	[268]	Receiver in Sec. 12.3	**This Work**
Technology	—	CMOS 0.13μm	CMOS 65nm	CMOS 65nm	**CMOS 65nm**
Center Frequency	GHz	280	201	260	**286**
Detection Method	—	Diode-detection	Super-regenerative	Heterodyne with Single-ended output	**Heterodyne with Differential output**
Gain	dBi	31	—	-2	**54**
NF	dB	—	-	38.6	**25**
System Bandwidth	GHz	700	1.5	42	**30**
Resolution Bandwidth	GHz	700	1.5	0.1	1.1
DC Power	mW/Pixel	0.1	18.2	6.6	**3.5**
Receiver Size	mm^2	3.8	0.45	0.99	**1.01**

*The area of silicon lens is included in the transmitter size calculation.

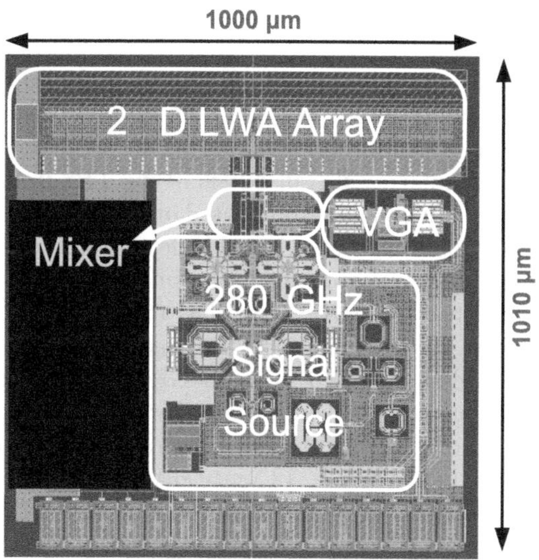

Figure 12.26: Cadence layout of the proposed 280 GHz transceiver in CMOS.

in CMOS. It can be observed that the proposed 280 GHz transmitter has the highest output power and power efficiency. A transmitter with very high equivalent isotropically radiated power (EIRP) density is developed by the integration of the 280GHz CON-based signal source with high power density and the compact CRLH T-line-based LWA with high gain. Note that the EIRP density is defined by the EIRP power generated in the unit chip area of the transmitter (P_{EIRP}/A_{TX}). The proposed transmitter has an EIRP density of 4.27 mW/mm^2, which is more than twice the best result in the literature [178].

Moreover, the proposed 280 GHz receiver with differential output has a 53 dB higher gain, 13.6 dB smaller NF and a more than twice smaller power consumption when compared to the single-ended receiver proposed in Sec. 12.3. As a result of the compact differential mixer and VGA designs, a high-power signal source is integrated in the receiver without increasing the chip size. The sensitivity of the proposed receiver is -57.6 dBm, which is quite close to the result of the super-regenerative receiver design in [268]. Note that the sensitivity can be further improved by additional off-chip IF filters with smaller bandwidth.

12.5 Conclusion

CMOS-based imaging systems are demonstrated in this chapter. The proposed 135-GHz SRX is integrated in a sub-THz imaging system with various demonstrated imaging diagnosis applications. It has great potential to be utilized for the future large-arrayed transmission-type THz imaging system. In addition, a wide-band THz image system based on direct-conversion receiver is demonstrated in the CMOS process with wide detection frequency range. The proposed THz image system is able to capture images in 239 $\sim$ 281 GHz with a resolution bandwidth of 100MHz, which has many applications in the detection of tissue with species-specific spectral absorption. An integrated THz CMOS transceiver is demonstrated for a 280GHz reflection imaging system with high power transmitter, high sensitivity receiver and high-gain on-chip in simulation. The 2D on-chip high-gain LWA array is designed by connecting two 1D LWAs in parallel with 2 $\times$ 13 unit-cells, and it is simulated with a broadside radiation pattern with 9.1-dBi directivity and 41% radiation efficiency at 280 GHz. The differential down-conversion receiver is designed by integrating a differential single-gate mixer with one modified Cherry–Hooper amplifier-based variable-gain amplifier with compact size, and it is simulated with a conversion gain of 46.6 dB, and an NF of 24.6 dB at 280GHz. The entire transceiver has a compact size of 1 mm^2, and consumes 298.6 mW power operating under 1.2V power supply. The transmitter is simulated with an equivalent isotropically radiated power (EIRP) of 6.3 dBm, an EIRP density of 4.27 mW/mm^2; the receiver is simulated with a maximum gain of 51dB and a sensitivity of -57.6 dBm.

Chapter 13

CMOS THz Wireless Communication

13.1 Introduction

Due to the significant increase of mobile data in recent years, there is an emerging demand for capacity and speed for the next generation of wireless network to provide wireless data rate of several tens of gigabit/s [270]. It requires developing more spectrum-efficient wireless transmission with large bandwidth. A depiction of the evolution of data rate achieved by wireless system, known as Edholm's law of data rates [271], is shown in Figure 13.1. It can be observed that around the year of 2020 the wireless data rate will reach around 100 gps.

A wireless communication system with gigabyte data rate can only be achieved with an advanced transmission scheme and a modulation method having a spectrum efficiency of at least 14 bit/s/Hz, which is extremely challenging for the existing RF or microwave technologies [15]. One approach to reach that high data rate with a spectrum efficiency of few bit/s/Hz is to employ ultra-high carrier frequency far beyond 10 GHz. Wireless links with data rates of 2Gbps have been recently explored at 60 GHz [272, 39] for wireless HD but still cannot reach the scalability for the future demand of ultra-high-definition (UHD) video. Consequently, an alternative unregulated spectrum to achieve ultra-high bandwidth can be found in the sub-THz frequency range (up to 300GHz). The short-range (or near-field) sub-THz wireless communication is currently studied by various research groups such as UC-Berkeley, Caltech and Qualcomm [273, 274]. The Terahertz Interest Group (IGthz) under IEEE 802.15 WPAN was founded in 2008 to develop standards for THz

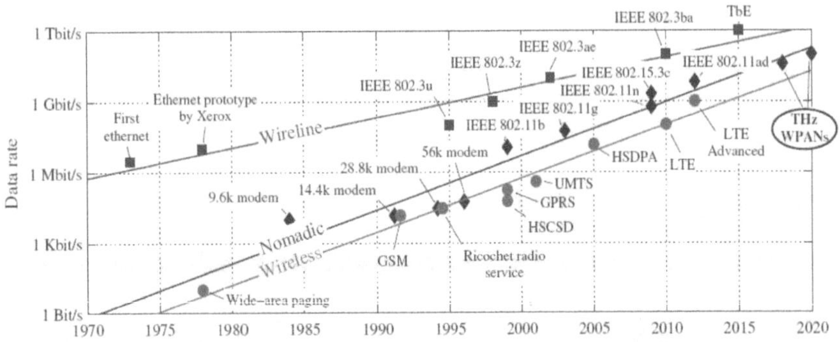

Figure 13.1: Development of data rates in wireline, nomadic and wireless systems [15].

communications. The main task of the group is working on the spectrum evaluation and standard draw-up for potential application, such as ultra-high speed and capacity backhaul for cellular communication, THz Nano Cells, Board-to-Board Communication, etc.

Recently, much attention has come to focus on point-to-point local-area wireless technologies within the office or home as well as human-area wireless communication technologies within human reach. The most successful and popular near-field (close proximity) wireless technology is IC-card and Bluetooth which operate at microwave frequency range with limited data rate. As shown in Figure 13.2(a), many advanced applications, such as UHD video downloading and sharing, ultra-high speed wireless USB, etc., push the data volume of transmission toward gigabytes and even terabytes. Meanwhile, the transmitting time is required within seconds for better user experience. This can be only achieved by operating in sub-THz regime which offers ultra-wide bandwidth and a high-speed data rate. The potential applications by such a near-field THz wireless link are illustrated in Figure 13.2 (b).

For the current experimental THz communication system, the conventional approaches to generate and detect THz-band radiation include the utilization of a photonic device. For example, from a THz signal generation perspective, photodiodes and Quantum Cascade Lasers (QCLs, e.g., GaN, GaAs) [275] have been proposed as high-power THz local oscillators (LO) in a heterodyne transceiver architecture. Note that QCLs operate at very low (almost cryogenic) temperatures, and is also limited by the need for an external laser for optical electron pumping with lots of mirrors and lenses for optical path adjustment. The whole system is usually bulky, expensive (SGD 400K $\sim$ 600K) and hence difficult for extensive deployment. From the signal detection point of view, among others, Schottky diodes and bolometric detectors have been investigated for direct detection of terahertz radiation. These devices are able

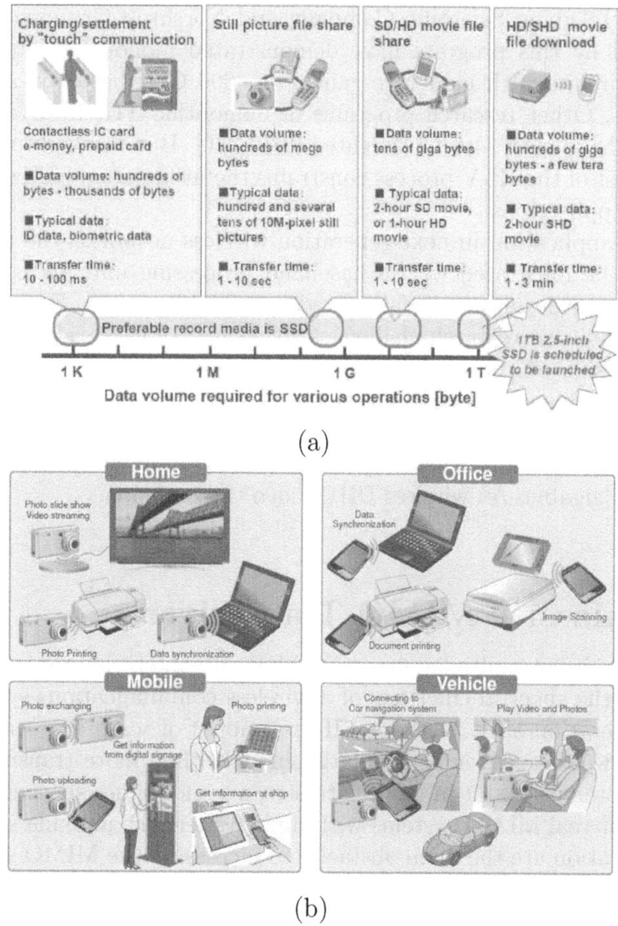

Figure 13.2: (a) Need of near-field wireless communication classified by data column; (b) potential appellations of a near-field THz big data rate wireless link.

to detect very low power signals with a modulation bandwidth up to GHz. Unfortunately, their performance is always degraded when operating at room temperature. The other approach to generate and detect THz-band radiation includes the utilization of nonlinear optics such as optical rectification and the linear electro-optic effect, mainly utilized for spectroscopy application [276].

With the rapid development of semiconductor technology, III-V process (such as GaAs, InP)-based electronic THz system has the advantage of compact size compared to photonic solutions. A typical program funded by DARPA-USA is aimed to achieve terahertz monolithic integrated circuit

[277, 278]. Teledyne Scientific Company and Northrop Grumman Corporation funded by this program have demonstrated monolithic integrated PA and LNA circuits with moderate gain up to 600 GHz based on a sub-50nm InP process. Other research programs of monolithic THz-MMIC in Europe and Japan have been also investigated [279, 280]. But the high performance and high cost of the III-V process constrains the utilization of THz electronics to limited applications.

For the application in next-generation wireless networks, the radio front-end should be integrated with a baseband processing unit and storage unit [50], which can be massively fabricated by CMOS process. However, it also imposes significant research challenges to push CMOS-based integrated circuit (IC) design at such an extreme high frequency of THz, such as signal generation, propagation and detection. As such, it is aimed to research on CMOS-based THz electronics for wireless MIMO communication. The targeted application is for near-field point-to-point communication such as ultra-high speed (gigabyte/s) wireless UHD video transmission.

13.2 Massive MIMO Transceiver

The multiple-input multiple-output (MIMO) antenna technique is well known to increase the spectral efficiency of a wireless communications system [281], with consideration of the path loss. If the amount of scattering and reflection in the multi-path environment is large enough, then more transmitting and receiving antennas result in more data streams and higher spectral efficiency. However, for real MIMO systems with limited area, the antenna size and antenna separation are the main obstacles to increasing the MIMO scale, which is difficult to solve when carrier frequency is in the GHz range. In the THz regime, on-chip antenna integrated with transceiver in CMOS technology can motivate a massive MIMO wireless communication system. With the further utilization of a metamaterial-based LWA phase-array, one can have a more compact and low-cost implementation of the MIMO on-chip in CMOS.

Figure 13.3 shows a block diagram of the proposed sub-THz MIMO phase-arrayed transceiver with the radio front-end (TX) of each module containing an I/Q modulator/demodulator. The transceiver chip consists of quadrature VCO, which provides two pairs of 0° and 90° phase-shift carrier signal, transmission/receiving antenna and I/Q modulator and demodulator. The variable gain amplifier (VGA) is designed following the output of the demodulator to dynamically provide gain for proper ADC operating range.

The MIMO algorithm should be developed to program the radiation direction of transmit antennas to increase the capacity of the system. In this work, the dual-mode MIMO (spatial diversity and spatial multiplexing) is applied for near-field THz big data rate wireless communication. Both LOS and NLOS transmission scenarios should be handled by the system. The MIMO mode control algorithm will be developed based on the channel estimation.

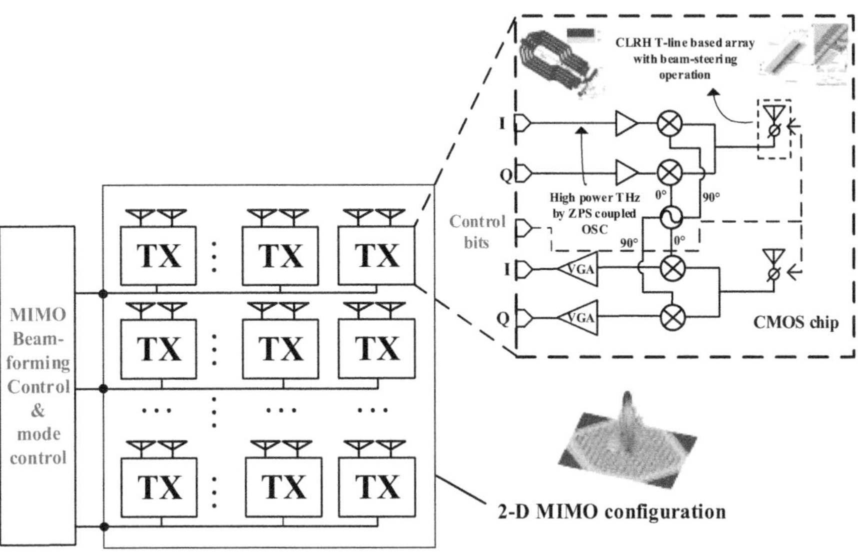

Figure 13.3: Block diagram of the proposed sub-THz MIMO phased array transceiver architecture and transceiver (TX) front-end structure.

In the LOS scenario, transmission capacity will be enhanced by spatial multiplexing MIMO, and the algorithm will switch the transceiver to work in the spatial multiplexing mode. The transmitter will transmit the data of multiple users simultaneously, and the algorithm will control both the transmitter and receiver antenna to form a directive beam pointed to each other.

In the NLOS scenario, the transmission signal suffers from server path loss and multiple-path reflection. The multiple signals arriving at the receiver side can be constructive or destructive combining, which presents a decadency in the channel. In order to solve this problem, the algorithm will switch the transceiver to work in the spatial diversity mode. We will develop an algorithm to program the antenna radiation direction dynamically to accommodate multi-path effect in a near-field THz wireless link. This mechanism can improve the range of coverage effectively with the maintenance of the big data transmission.

Table 13.1 presents the key specification comparison of the proposed approach with other works. As the link budget presented previously in Table 13.1, the key factor of high performance near-field big-data-rate wireless link is proposing a system design to accommodate high path loss and multiple-path transmission channel. Previous works shown in Table 13.1 demonstrate a variety approach for high data rate (~10 Gbps) wireless transmission beyond 0.1 THz. The work in [158] only proposed a transmitter without on-chip

Table 13.1: Comparison with Previous Works

	[158]	[282]	[29]	Proposed work
Technology	65nm LP	65nm	40nm	40nm
Frequency range (GHz)	116	260	135	280
Data Rate(Gbps)	10	10	10	>20
Modulation	BPSK /QPSK /8QAM	ASK	ASK	BPQK /SPSK
Phase-arrayed MIMO	No	No	No	Yes
DC Power (mW)	200	688	98	<300
Transmitter Output power (dBm)	-5	5 (EIPR)	-9.7∼-8.1	>-9
System integration	Only Transmitter	Only Transmitter	Transceiver with embedded OSC	Transceiver with embedded antenna and OSC

LO generation. Besides, the antenna is not integrated with the transmitter. Thus this approach constrains the degree of integration. For work in [29], a more advanced 40nm CMOS process is utilized. However, the signal generator approach is not efficient for high-power THz signal generation. Besides, the antenna is not integrated with the transceiver and thus has a limitation degree of integration. For work in [282], a transceiver with on-chip approach is proposed. However, this approach does not contain a beam-forming operation thus limiting the range of communication.

The highlight of our approach, compared to the previous works, is in the following aspects. The proposed new circuit design technique is based on a metamaterial device. Metamaterial-based zero-phase-shift T-line and coupler will be invented for a high-power THz signal generator and on-chip leaky wave antenna array design, which can be deployed for compact MIMO design. Furthermore, the dual-mode massive THz MIMO is proposed to enhance the range and capacity of near-field THz big data rate transmission with the beam-forming control.

13.3 Conclusion

A concept of massive THz MIMO for ultra-high-speed and high-capacity wireless communication is introduced in this chapter. In order to fulfill the demand of the next-generation high-volume wireless data transmission application, communication system working at the THz range with high spectrum resource can be proposed. To address the issues of high path loss and attenuation due to rain, foliage and atmospheric absorption in THz region, a phased array MIMO architecture is proposed for THz wireless communication. Exemplary link budget at the THz range is calculated to evaluate the possibility of ultra-high-speed wireless communication in the short-range scale. Meanwhile, both space multiplexing for LOS and space diversity for NLOS scenarios are proposed for mode operation of THz massive MIMO. Finally, an RF architecture for THz massive MIMO wireless communication based on CMOS technology is proposed.

Chapter 14

CMOS THz Wireline Communication

14.1 Introduction

Future high-performance computers require wide-band on-chip communication between memory and microprocessor cores. The global interconnect by top-layer metal in present CMOS technology has limited bandwidth and large crosstalk ratio [283, 284]. The lossy substrate with typical 10-Ω/cm resistivity introduces a low-impedance path between metal and substrate, resulting in narrow bandwidth and high loss. Moreover, at high operating frequency the current flow tends to crowd toward the surface of metal due to proximity effect, which leads to not only higher ohmic loss but also large electromagnetic coupling. As such, the CMOS metal-based interconnect is not scalable to provide wide bandwidth for on-chip communication beyond gigabit per second (Gbps) for one channel.

Though the optical interconnect has shown great potential to replace electrical interconnects [285, 286], its source, transmission and detection are all difficult to be implemented in silicon. Terahertz (THz) bands have recently attracted great interest because all components can be realized in CMOS technology [93, 287]. However, highly integrated on-chip high-speed interconnects by traditional transmission lines (T-lines) have the limitation of crosstalk between two adjacent channels.

Due to the negative permittivity behavior [288, 289, 290], surface plasmon polariton (SPP) is one special electromagnetic wave locally confined on the metal/dielectric interface, propagating in parallel to the interface and exponentially decaying in the direction perpendicular to the interface

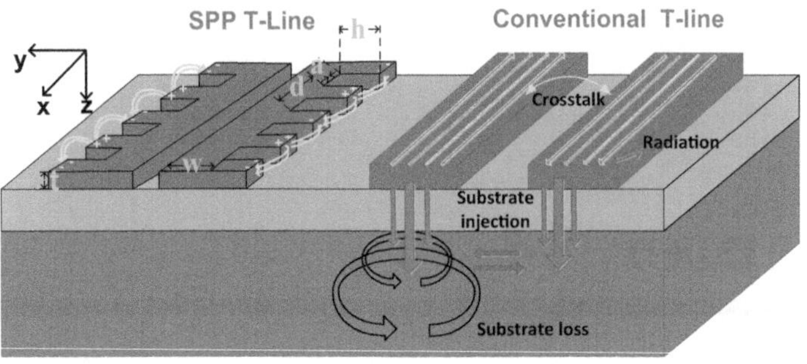

Figure 14.1: The layout and E-field distribution of the on-chip SPP/conventional T-line in lossy substrate environment, d, h, a, w denotes the periodic pitch, groove depth, groove width and line width off SPP T-line, respectively. The magnetic field of SPP T-line is directed to the x direction while the electrical field is guided by the grooves in the *y*-*z* plane.

[291, 292, 293]. By introducing sub-wavelength periodic corrugation structure onto the T-line, SPPs can be established to propagate signals with strongly localized surface-wave in the metal/dielectric interface at frequency up to THz. Such a surface-wave can be supported with propagation adapted to the curvature or holes of the surface [294, 169, 295, 296, 297, 298, 299, 300, 301]. Previous works have demonstrated GHz SPP T-lines on board level with bulky size and loss [294, 169, 295, 296, 297, 298]. In this work, SPP T-line is investigated at the THz region in the standard CMOS process that shows great potential for system-on-chip integration with other components in CMOS for on-chip THz communication.

The physical layout of the proposed structure is illustrated in Figure 14.1. Two on-chip SPP T-lines are placed back-to-back to form a broadband low-loss, low-crosstalk coupler. Such a plasmonic metamaterial consists of a metal strip with thin film thickness, in which a 1D periodical array of grooves is drilled. The propagation of surface-confined mode is adapted to the curvature of the surface, and the resulting crosstalk between the two back-to-back placed SPP T-lines will be reduced significantly. For comparison, two traditional quasi-TEM T-lines are also realized to form an on-chip coupler with line space of 2.4 μm in standard 65 nm CMOS process, which shows large loss and strong crosstalk at THz. Measurement results show that the SPP T-lines achieve wide-band reflection coefficient lower than -14 dB and the crosstalk ratio better than -24 dB, which is 19 dB lower on average than the traditional T-lines from 220 GHz to 325 GHz. The compact and wide-band SPP T-lines have shown great potential for on-chip THz communication.

14.2 Surface Plasmon Polariton T-Line

The surface plasmon polariton (SPP) propagating at the flat interface between a real metal and a dielectric are naturally 2D electromagnetic waves. Confinement of EM wave is realized since the propagation constant is greater than the wave vector k within the dielectric, resulting in evanescent decay on both sides of the interface. Essentially, because the SPP dispersion curve lies to the right of the light line of the dielectric (given by $\omega = ck$) [302], among optical applications the SPPs excited by 3D light beams is impossible unless special techniques for phase-matching are utilized. Various optical techniques have been proposed to fulfill phase matching, including grating coupling and excitation with highly focused beams. Normally, for geometries exhibiting strong field-localization below the diffraction limit, the overlap between the excitation beam and the coupled SPP mode is small, leading to low excitation efficiency.

While those optical excitation schemes are suitable for the development of SPP propagation and functional plasmonic structures, in practice the SPPs used in the design of integrated circuits will normally require high conversion efficiency (and hence large-bandwidth) coupling schemes. In order to make full use of the benefit of wide bandwidth in optics designs, the plasmonic structures should allow for efficient matching with conventional optical waveguides or fibers, which would be used in such a scenario to guide energy over long distance onto plasmon transmission lines and cavities with broad bandwidth. However, in on-chip electronic communication, the on-chip interconnect is generally connected to CMOS transistors or other passive devices which in fact have narrower bandwidth than optical devices. At the same time, the converter with exponentially grading CPW reported in Ref [294], is difficult to be integrated on chip. As such, it is more important to first investigate the impedance matching and resulting return loss for the realization of the on-chip SPP T-line. Normally, there are two major lossy mechanisms contributing to the guiding loss of SPP T-lines: the return loss and the insertion loss (or transmission loss). While the insertion loss can be improved over other traditional T-line structures due to the confinement of EM energy, the return loss begins to dominate as long as the periodical array decouples the incident beam into the propagating SPPs. To understand how the mismatch affects the excitation, Figure 14.2(a) shows the input reflection coefficient of the designed on-chip SPP T-line as a function of groove depth h. A plane TEM wave is injected from one end of the structure while the other end is terminated. As observed, the designed structure cannot maintain highly efficient coupling from 3–6 THz, which confirms the limited bandwidth of the input matching. On the other hand, the SPP coupling efficiency trades off the confinement of the surface wave. In general, the tight confinement can be achieved by merely increasing the groove depth for this structure, which will be discussed later. However, this does not necessarily bring about the same amount of improvement if the coupling efficiency is taken into account: the

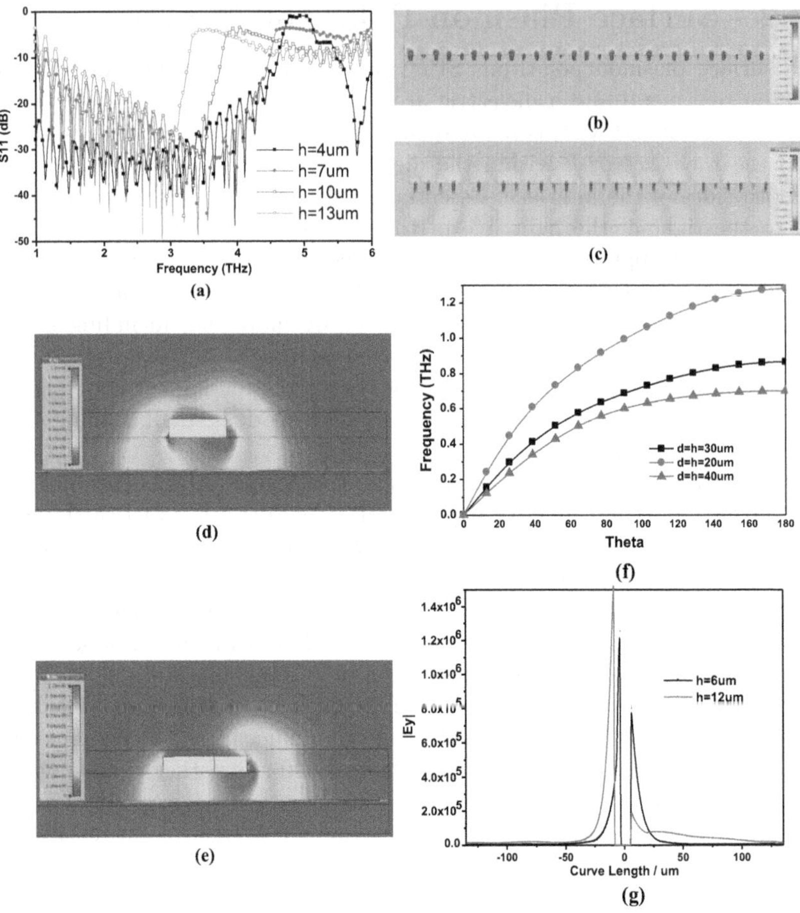

Figure 14.2: (a) Simulated input reflection coefficient of the designed on-chip SPP T-line for different groove depth h with d = 15 μm, a = 2.4 μm, w = 5 μm. (b–c) The simulated amplitude of E-field distribution of the designed SPP T-line (a: h = 6 μm, b: h = 12 μm) evaluated at the xy plane using the CMOS process. (d–e) E-field distribution on the cross-section of the corrugated metal strip: h = 6 μm, d: h = 12 μm) at *yz* plane, also at 3 THz, and (f) the simulated dispersion diagram with different periodic pitch d and groove depth h ranged from 20 μm to 40 μm. (g) E-field enhancement along the vertical cut for h = 6 μm and h = 12 μm, respectively.

higher the confinement, the lower the bandwidth of efficient coupling. Physically, due to the momentum mismatch at the interface, only a small fraction of the incident TEM wave can be converted to SPPs mode and coupled to the periodical structure, leading to strong reflection of incident wave and energy

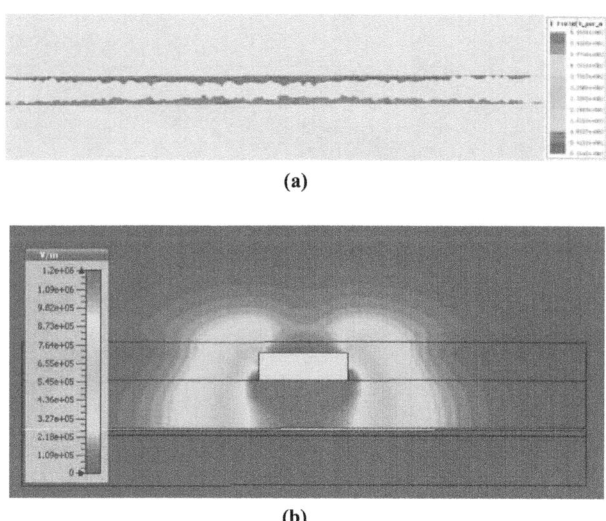

(a)

(b)

Figure 14.3: (a) The simulated amplitude of E-field distribution of the conventional transmission line evaluated at the xy plane using the same process, and (b) E-field distribution on the cross-section of the corrugated metal strip (yz plane) also at 3 THz. The width of T-line is 11 μm with wideband impedance matching up to above 3 THz.

loss. As a conclusion, the loss of SPP T-line cannot be reduced by rendering the structure when only to obtain a tight confinement.

Recall that for a compact SPP T-line structure, the return loss is pretty high at several terahertz due to the low coupling efficiency of the incident beam to propagating SPPs. It appears lower than -10 dB at around 1 THz, along with the penalty of weaker field-localization below the diffraction limit. This does not necessarily mean that the coupling efficiency becomes more effective at lower frequencies. In this case, the dispersion diagram of propagating SPPs starts to bend with respect to the light line but the bending degree is lower than that of strong field-localization, which indicates that part of EM energy maintains their polarization property when being injected into the structure. In fact, the confinement of surface mode can be evaluated through the dispersion diagram [294, 169], and the SPP T-line behaves in purely propagating surface mode only if it operates close to the plasma asymptotic frequency (several terahertz for the dimension given in Figure 14.2(a)), which is difficult for CMOS on-chip transmission since the physical dimension becomes pretty large. This scenario is apparently different from the case of board-level implementation in the microwave region [294, 169, 295, 296, 297, 298], in which the substrate can be either made by an insulation layer or even removed. Instead,

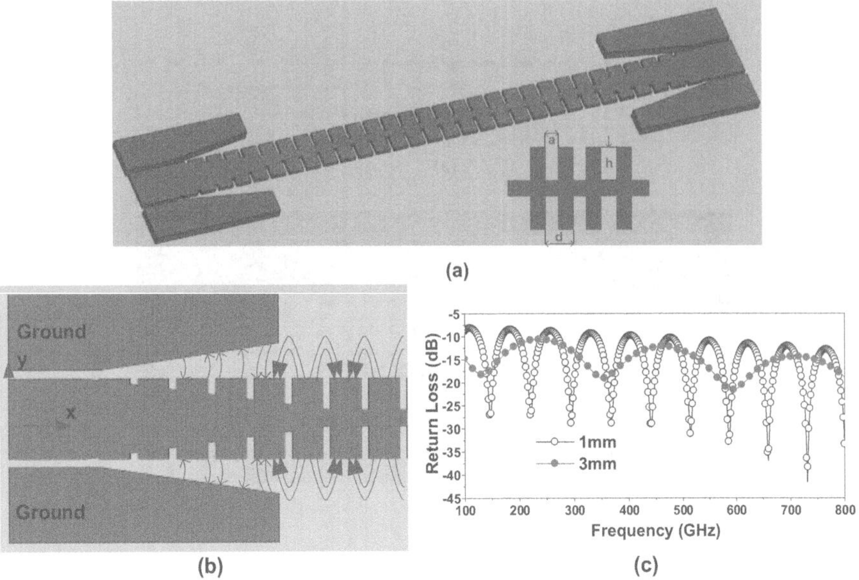

Figure 14.4: (a) The layout of SPP T-line including EM wave to surface wave (or vice versa) converter and with M1 as ground, (b) converter design and conceptual E-field distribution, and (c) the simulated result of reflection coefficient (S_{11}).

in the following, we investigate the SPP property by designing a compact SPP T-line structure operating at frequencies that are away from the plasma asymptotic frequency region.

The CMOS-based SPP T-line structure is designed as shown in Figure 14.1. The period pitch d is chosen to be 15 μm which is far less than the operation wavelength ($\lambda = 1$ mm), and the line width w is 5 μm. Note that the conventional microstrip line with $w = 5$ μm has a characteristic impedance of 50 Ω from 10 GHz to 3 THz in this process. As the line is structured, the SPP modes are generated, which can be confirmed by the full-wave near-field simulation using FDTD with the boundary condition set as open to simulate the real space. The boundaries are at a large distance from the metal structure to avoid significant reflections. With the surface mode confined by the corrugated strip, we are now in a position to evaluate the E-field distribution of the guiding structure.

Figures 14.2(b) and (c) illustrate the simulated E-fields (E_x components) evaluated at the top of corrugated strips with different corrugation depth at 3 THz. The gray-scale from highest to lowest density indicates the tight confinement of EM wave within the comb-shaped metal strip. In this experiment, instead of defining a monopole excitation, the TEM wave is injected from one terminal of this periodical T-line with the other terminal loaded with 50Ω impedances. Due to a non-perfect transition from the TEM wave to the surface wave at the injection interface, the excited surface mode is not completely restricted within the groove. However, one can still observe that part of the EM field is strongly localized within the comb-shaped metal structure and decays at the metal/dielectric interface. We observe that the surface EM waves are tightly confined and propagate along the SPP T-line with small losses at 3 THz as well. In addition, the confinement of the surface mode can be effectively improved by solely increasing the groove depth, which can be further confirmed by the observation of corresponding E-field distribution shown in Figures 14.2(d) and (e) at the yz plane, in compliance with the findings in the microwave region using the similar structure [294, 169]. A ground plane realized by the bottom copper metal is implemented to ensure that the E-field is mainly restricted between the two conductors. Without the ground, a great portion of energy will be absorbed by the lossy substrate, and the resulting confinement by the designed structure becomes less effective. Again, the dispersion diagram is re-simulated with the consideration of ground. It shows that the asymptotic frequency is still clearly bending away from the light line except that it slightly increases. The dispersion relation is further examined by varying the groove depth h as shown in Figure 14.2(f).

Clearly, the asymptotic frequency decreases with deeper grooves, consistent with the case without ground beneath the SPP T-line. When both the periodical pitch d and groove depth h are equal to 40 μm, the asymptotic frequency is down to approximately 0.6 THz, presenting stronger confinement in the sub-THz region. As such, the ground plane inherently has negligible influence on the SPP property while it helps to further reduce radiation loss. The details of confinement can be clearly observed from E-field enhancement in the cross-sections perpendicular to the strips, as illustrated in Figure 14.2(g). The field clearly decays exponentially along the orthogonally lateral y direction, illustrating the typical feature of SPP mode. In summary, the above study reveals the feasibility of confining surface mode with the periodical groove structured T-line in the CMOS process.

In contrast to TM polarization in the SPP T-line, the conventional transmission line propagates TEM mode along the structure. As shown in Figure 14.3(a), the current intensity of the microstrip line tends to crowd on the metal surface. Note that in such a scenario the effective metal resistance will be increased and in return degrades the signal transmission. Given that the E-field is dominating near the metal surface, more energy would be radiated out in the form of radiation loss and crosstalk to adjacent conductors. Even though most of the E-field is restricted to the metal surfaces between T-line and ground as illustrated in E-field distribution at the yz plane, as shown in Figure 14.3(b), the radiation outside of T-line remains strong, leading to more energy penetration into the dielectric medium and hence results in larger radiation loss. Similarly, despite the fact that ground plane has considerable

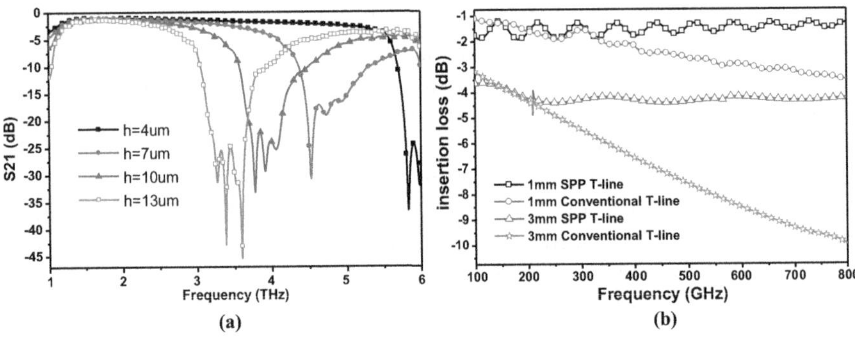

Figure 14.5: (a) Simulated transmission coefficient of the SPP guided wave as a function of the groove depth h with $a = 2.4$ μm, $w = 5$ μm, $d = 15$ μm, (b) comparison of simulated insertion loss for both SPP T-line and conventional T-line with different length.

effect on the shielding of E-field from T-line to the substrate, it inherently introduces significant crosstalk into the nearby conductors through the current flowing onto the ground surface, which will be even worse as frequency rises. All these features manifest the T-line as an unsuitable candidate for on-chip interconnects in a high-speed wireline system.

To obtain low reflection, a bending coplanar waveguide (CPW) converter using the gradient corrugation grooves and flaring ground [294] is employed to realize momentum matching between SPP interconnect and other devices, such as a transformer or modulator, as illustrated in Figures 14.4(a) and (b). Note that in the plasmonic waveguide only SPP modes are supported with E_z component remaining strong along the x direction, leading to a momentum mismatch ($k_x \neq k_0$) at the interface. As a result, a gradient CPW, which guides and confines the quasi-TEM wave along the y direction between signal trace and ground, gradually transforms the guided wave to SPP mode, or vice versa. The E-field distribution of such conversion is conceptually illustrated in Figure 14.4(b). Due to limitation of the CMOS process, a linearly gradient model is used. Figure 14.4 (c) shows the input reflection coefficient (S_{11}) of the SPP T-line with converter loaded by 50 Ω resistance at both sides, which indicates wide-band impedance matching for different lengths of wire. The gap of CPW and the gradient factor are both optimized during the design phase of the I/O transceiver for maximum matching efficiency between functional blocks.

Next, we examine the transmission property of on-chip SPP T-line with comparison to that of conventional T-line structure. While the bandwidth of conventional T-line is largely affected by the highly conductive substrate at THz, the asymptotic frequency of surface plasma is mainly determined by the metal structure. To verify this, we begin by examining the spectral transmission properties of designed SPP T-line up to several THz. In Figure 14.5(a), we show the simulated wide-band transmission spectra with h = 4, 7, 10 and 13 μm. There are a few of notable characteristics in these spectra. As observed, when the grooves are very shallow (i.e., 7μm deep or less), despite an obvious high-frequency cutoff, the SPP T-line transmission spectra appear to be relatively broadband. As the groove depth begins to increase, both the line width and cut-off frequency of this resonance decrease. As the groove depth further increases, the single wide-band transmission resonance is replaced by multiple narrowband transmission resonances. In the theoretical limit of transmission by guided SPPs, there are no modes appearing at frequencies above the Bragg frequency $f_B = c/2d$, where c is the speed of light. Here, the anti-resonance (AR) frequency, which is used to characterize the frequency corresponding to the signal being sharply attenuated, can be applied to explain the transmission properties of the periodical curvature structures due to Fano-interference phenomenon [303]. Even so, the transmission maintains low loss and wide band at the frequency far below the AR frequency. We then compare the transmission for both T-line structures at frequencies less than 1 THz, where the advanced integrated circuits normally operate. With low return loss, the loss of the SPP T-line is mainly contributed by the metal resistive loss. Figure 14.5 (b) shows the comparison results. Clearly, the transmission of SPP T-line has very wide bandwidth with low loss, whereas the conventional T-line suffers from strong attenuation in THz. This observation confirms the insensitivity of guided wave to the low-resistive substrate profile. Specifically, the 3-mm long SPP T-line is almost 3 times that of its 1 mm counterpart across a very wide band, similar to cascading of three 1-mm unit-cells. However, the 3-mm-long traditional T-line has much larger attenuation than the loss added by three 1-mm unit-cells, illustrating its vulnerability to lossy substrate. As a result, by properly structuring the top metal, the loss of SPP T-line can be minimized across the wide band, which cannot be achieved by a bare T-line in CMOS at THz. We then estimate how long the on-chip SPP T-line can support the THz signal by transforming the S parameters to the attenuation constant. The resulting propagation length of the lowest-order mode can be readily obtained. It shows that the attenuation constant along the pointing vector is around 1 cm^{-1}, leading to about 1 $\sim$ 2 cm e^{-1}-decay length for propagation, which satisfies most on-chip wireline communication. Simulations further reveal that an increase of groove depth brings about longer propagation length, in consistent with the observation that the propagating modes are now more restricted to propagating only along the corrugated surface of interconnect. In other words, more energy is conserved by reinforcing the confinement of the guided mode. Note that this experiment has not incorporated the plane wave-to-surface wave converter design, which is bulky and hence not suitable for on-chip realization. In the design without a converter, the resulting transmission bandwidth will be reduced, as stated before. Fortunately, the advance mm-wave circuitries operate at frequencies far away from the asymptotic frequency, which provides great margin to consider only the low frequency region.

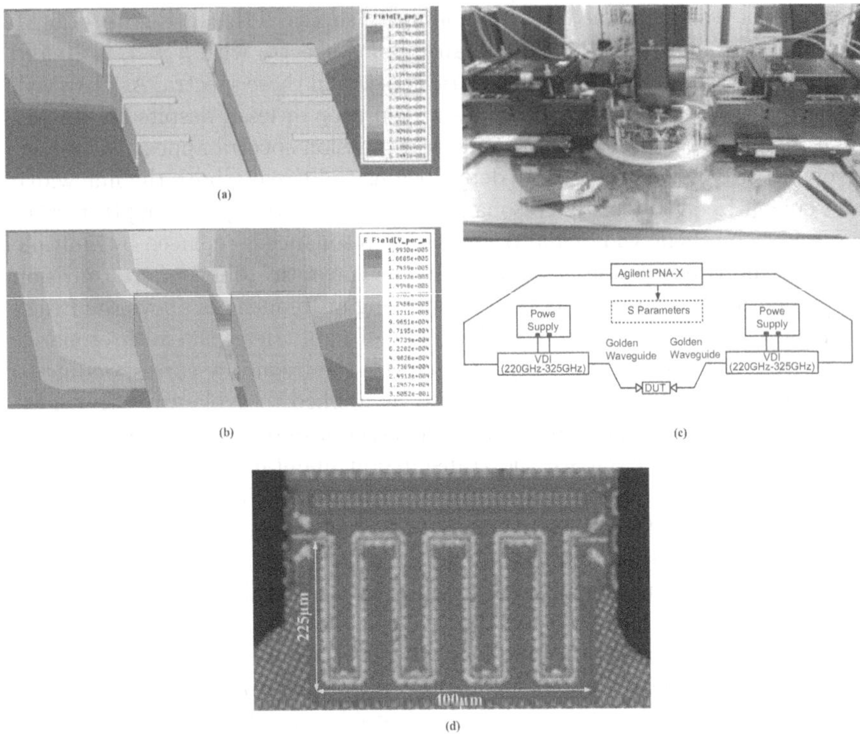

Figure 14.6: (a and b) The simulated electrical field distribution on the cross-section for both SPP and T-line coupler in 65 nm CMOS technology, the parameters configuration is the same as in Figure 14.2. The left-handed side T-line is the aggressor with EM filed excitation at one terminal with the other termination loaded with 50 Ω impedances, and the right hand side T-line is the victim trace with both ends terminated by 50 Ω impedances, (c) measurement setup for the THz SPP coupler, (d) die micrograph of the SPP-based coupler in 65 nm CMOS for Terahertzes applications.

For this reason, the converter is not necessary, and the design of on-chip SPP interconnections becomes much more relaxed.

Crosstalk arises from the interaction of EM fields generated by adjacent data signals when they propagate through T-lines and connectors. For example, wiring capacitances of on-chip interconnect tend to dominate crosstalk and backplane connectors induce multi-pin crosstalk. Recent work has addressed crosstalk equalization issues between neighboring serial links by an effort of crosstalk neutralization techniques [304]. Crosstalk considerations also affect the performance of integrated digital circuits, which can be partially alleviated by equalizing the crosstalk-induced timing jitter. However, all these methods consume considerable power with the data rate only limited to multi-gigabit per second. Owing to the advantage to control the propagation property of EM energy, we expect that interconnects realized by SPP T-line present less crosstalk. Recall that for a guided wave structure, the energy associated with the guide mode was highly confined near the surface, with the field decaying evanescently within the apertures. While the guided mode is excited along the metal surface, electromagnetic couplings to both substrate and adjacent conductors are strongly attenuated. As such, the complexity of circuit implementations can be relaxed. To verify this, two SPP T-lines are placed closely back-to-back to form an on-chip SPP-based coupler. All physical dimensions are the same as before with spacing as 2.4 μm. Figure 14.6(a) shows the E-field distribution and the conventional coupler realized by T-line with 2.4μm spacing is shown in Figure 14.6(b) for comparison. In this experiment, the left-hand side T-line is the aggressor with 300 GHz TEM wave excitation at one terminal, and the right-hand side T-line is the victim. The other three ports are terminated by 50 Ω impedances. As predicted, the local E-field intensity $|E_{tntal}|$ is locally confined by the corrugation structure with only small portion of energy to spread out, while it strongly radiates out in the case of the traditional T-line coupler. As a result, the SPP coupler confines more energy and has less coupling to the victim trace, leading to significant crosstalk reduction. The measurement results with respect to the crosstalk reduction will be given in the next section.

To demonstrate the superior performance in crosstalk reduction by the SPP-based coupler, the measured S-parameters are shown in Figure 14.6. First of all, to have a fair comparison with the directional coupler realized by conventional T-line, the simulation results of the SPP coupler are fit to the measurement ones (S_{11} and S_{41}). After the parameter fitting is done, the conventional T-line coupler is simulated using the same substrate profile. The T-line coupler also has a meandering shape that resembles the structure shown in Figure 14.6(d). The measured and simulated reflection coefficient (S_{11}) is shown in Figure 14.7(a) with comparison to the T-line coupler. The measured S_{11} is below -14 dB over 220–325 GHz, showing wide-band reflection coefficient. The fitting of S_{11} is below -14 dB over 220–325 GHz, showing wide-band reflection coefficient. The fitting of S_{11} is also presented, which has only a small deviation from the measurement result. As a comparison, the S_{11} of the traditional T-line coupler becomes poor in the vicinity of 300 GHz which is almost -5 dB, resulting in the reflection of over 30% of the electromagnetic waves. Considering that the T-line is naturally wide-band, the reason for impedance mismatches is due to the strong coupling, which is further verified by Figure 14.7(b). As shown, the measured crosstalk (S_{41}) of the proposed structure is lower than -24 dB which is on average 19 dB better than that of the traditional T-line coupler across 220–325 GHz, illustrating great improvement in crosstalk reduction. In addition, the crosstalk is not

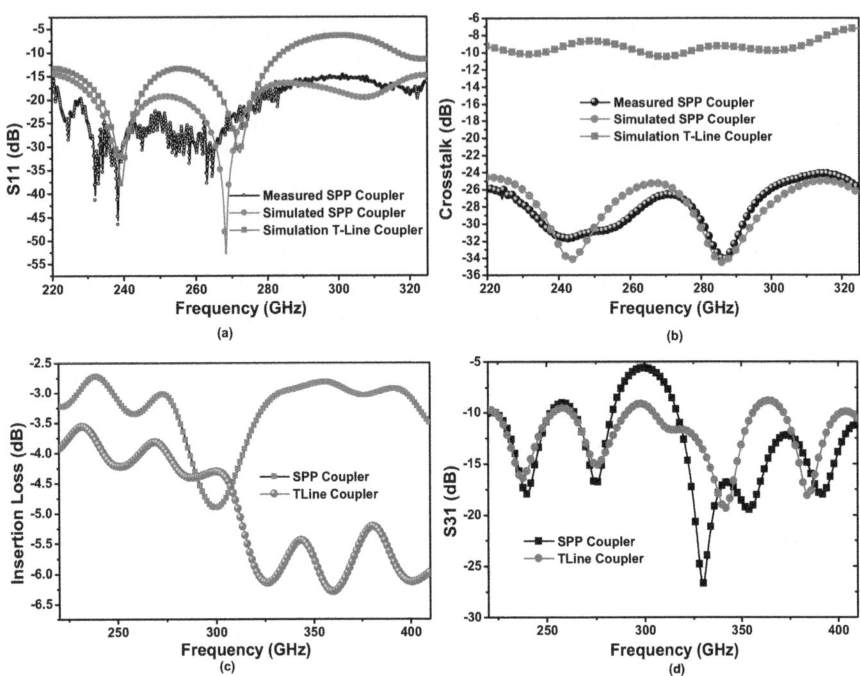

Figure 14.7: (a) The measured and simulated results of the input reflection coefficient (S_{11}) for the SPP coupler, and the simulated S_{11} of the T-line coupler. The S parameter extraction for the T-line coupler is performed after the parameter fitting is done, (b) the measured and simulated result of the crosstalk (S_{41}) for the SPP coupler, and the simulation result for the conventional T-line coupler as a comparison, (c) the simulated insertion loss (S_{21}) for both SPP/T-line couplers, and (d) the simulated near-ended coupling (S_{31}) for both SPP/T-line coupler.

obviously degraded as the frequency goes up while it becomes significantly worse for the traditional T-line coupler, implying wider bandwidth achieved by the SPP-based coupler. For example, the crosstalk is only -25 dB obtained by the SPP-based coupler at 325 GHz but it rises to -7 dB by the T-line counterpart. That is to say, about 20% of the EM energy is coupled to the victim in the traditional T-line coupler but only 0.3% energy leaks to the victim in the SPP-based coupler. The simulated crosstalk of the SPP-based coupler is given in the same figure as well which shows good agreement with the measurement result. The small discrepancy may be due to the 10% dummy fill or process variation that have not been taken into account during the simulation setup. Combined with Figure 14.7(a), we can observe that the surface wave is excited and confined by the sub-wavelength SPPs T-line, resulting in much higher efficiency in restraining crosstalk than the traditional T-line at THz frequency with wider bandwidth. The insertion loss (S_{21}) of both couplers is further simulated as shown in Figure 14.7(c). The proposed coupler has 3 dB improvements in transmission coefficient over the traditional counterpart as frequency beyond 300 GHz. There is a valley in 270 GHz possibly due to the resonances between meandering wires. Figure 14.7(d) shows the simulated near-ended coupling (S_{31}) remains lower than -10 dB for most frequencies across wide-band, indicating low near-ended coupling. Note that in this design, the line spacing is 2.4 μm with an attempt only to show the great advantages by the proposed SPP T-line. During the circuit design phase this spacing is not necessary to be so narrow.

Recent state-of-the-art on-chip implementations of interconnects using conventional transmission lines exhibit great attenuation and crosstalk at high frequency, which in turn demands more complex equalization techniques that consume considerably more power and silicon area. For instance, Ref [305] reported an interconnect model by assuming the Manhattan routing style in 0.18-μm CMOS technology. This model employs metal 5 as the interconnect to construct a BUS with 10-mm length onto a lossy substrate. It shows that, due to strong coupling between adjacent conductors the transfer function |H| drops to below -150 dB for all loadings at frequencies higher than 100 GHz, inhibiting most applications of THz on-chip communications. At the same time, the crosstalk in multi-channel series link is quantized in Ref [306] for a 10-mm interconnect in 0.13 μm CMOS, in which both the adjacent crosstalk-to-signal ratio (ACSR) and distant crosstalk-to-signal ratio (DCSR) dramatically increase as frequency goes up. This tendency is apparently caused by the coupling capacitance that is inversely proportional to the spacing. All of the above observations again confirm the significant crosstalk induced by TEM mode propagation along the long T-line. While the lower-layer metals can partially alleviate the crosstalk (the thickness of lower-layer metals are over 2–3 times smaller than that of the top copper metal, and the resulting coupling capacitance is reduced), the resistive loss will be proportionally higher. Similarly, even though the crosstalk can be much reduced by increasing the distance among wirings, in order to support ultrahigh aggregate bandwidth between modules/chips, silicon carrier channels must have very high wiring density. Consequently, fine-pitch carrier wiring is required. These wiring dimensions normally result in significant resistive losses when the on-carrier channel is long, e.g., over 5 mm [307]. Furthermore, as in the case of commonly used backplane channels [308], silicon carrier channels have very limited channel bandwidth, so the silicon carrier channel presents higher losses at higher frequencies. As a result, when high-frequency data is transmitted over long carrier channels, channel losses and limited channel bandwidth make the recovery of received data difficult. In sum, all these studies have shown great difficulty of efficiently realizing ultra-high speed on-chip data transmission by conventional T-line.

To overcome all these fundamental limits by conventional transmission line in THz frequencies, an on-chip surface plasmon polariton (SPP) T-line with sub-wavelength comb-shape onto the metal strip is demonstrated in sub-THz region by CMOS technology. The dispersion characteristics and field distribution are investigated from the design perspective toward on-chip THz communication. It shows that such a structure can tightly confine the surface wave at the metal/dielectric interface, resulting in less loss and small crosstalk. A SPP-based coupler is further fabricated in standard 65 nm CMOS with great improvement on crosstalk reduction with wide-band for on-chip interconnection. Measurement results show that the SPP coupler can guide the surface wave with lower than -15 dB reflection coefficient and the crosstalk improvement is on average 19 dB across 220 $\sim$ 325 GHz, which leads to nearly 3 dB lower transmission loss compared to the traditional T-line-based design. Therefore, such a SPP T-line is very promising in highly dense on-chip communication at THz in CMOS technology.

To verify the above design observations, a SPP-based coupler was fabricated by 1P9M bulk 65 nm CMOS process with the die micrograph shown in Figure 14.6 (d). The area occupation is 400 μm $\times$ 225 μm. Due to limited area, the coupler is designed with a meandering shape such that the equivalent physical length of the coupler is approximated 2 mm to provide a long coupling length. The spacing between the two SPP T-line is 2.4 μm which is the minimum metal gap allowed by the design rule. Such a close spacing is supposed to create a strong coupling for the long coupler, which would provide us a straight insight to evaluate the crosstalk reduction by the proposed structure. The topmost copper layer (Metal 8) with thickness of 3.3 μm is exclusively employed for the design as a low-loss coupler, and the top aluminum layer (Metal 9) with 1.325 μm thicknesses is used to form the Ground-Signal-Ground (GSG) Pad which has measured characteristic impedance around 50 Ω across the 220 $\sim$ 325 GHz frequency range. Note that the thickness of metal has very limited influence on the dispersion relation of SPPs because the sub-wavelength nature still maintains (the H-field remains unquantized in the x direction.) [169], while the resistive loss can be much improved for a thicker metal. It is important to know that for the SPP T-line the resistive loss cannot be reduced by realizing better confinement. Two terminals of the coupler are directly connected to the signal trace of Pads and the other two parts are terminated by P+ while the resistive loss can be much improved for a thicker metal. It is important to know that for the SPP T-line the resistive loss cannot be reduced by realizing better confinement. Two terminals of the coupler are directly connected to the signal trace of Pads and the other two ports are terminated by P+ polysilicon resistors that were simulated having 50 ω impedances around 300 GHz. A lumped-element model was created to fit the measurement result of Pad over wide-band, which is also an important part of the coupler design. Considering the Pad as part of the design, the SPP-based coupler is designed and optimized for the best crosstalk reduction before fabrication. The fabricated on-chip SPP-based coupler has the following design geometries: the periodic pitch d = 15 μm, groove width a = 2.4 μm, line width w =5 μm, and the groove depth h = 6 μm. Their geometry meanings are presented in Figure 14.1.

The capability of confining EM fields and crosstalk reduction can be evaluated by measuring the reflection coefficient S_{11} and the crosstalk S_{41}. The THz signal is injected from one port into the directional coupler, and the resulting S_{41} will present the coupling. The SPP interconnect is measured on CASCADE Microtech Elite-300 probe station and Agilent PNA-X (N5247A) with the VDI providing signal source from 220 $\sim$ 325 GHz. Connectors, probe, waveguides and cable loss are well calibrated before the on-wafer probe testing. The measurement setup is shown in Figure 14.6 (c).

14.3 SRR Modulator

Future high-performance computers require wide-band on-chip communication between memory and microprocessor cores. Demand is increasing for tens of gigabits per second (>10Gbps) wireline communication, and the carrier frequency has been pushed up to terahertz (THz) due to the ultra-wide bandwidth utilization at this region [309]. Recently, millimeter-wave and THz transceiver building blocks in CMOS have been reported [310]. Compared to optical on-chip communication by optical I/O link, all components of THz I/O link can be realized in CMOS. One critical block for on-chip communication is the modulator whose implementation is conventionally realized by active MOS transistors with inductive loadings [311, 312, 313]. The switching speed is, however, ultimately limited by the capacitive latency in the oscillator tank. On the other hand, the optical ring modulator with active switching region [286] is also hard to tune and is susceptible under temperature fluctuation.

Recently, the split ring resonator (SRR) is demonstrated to realize on-chip high-Q resonator [310]. Such a very compact magnetic metamaterial resonator is conventionally realized as shown in Figure 14.8 along with equivalent circuits. As the magnetic resonance frequency can be tuned by configuring the inner rings of SRR (Figure 14.8(b)) with switches, modulation becomes possible. The modulated signal will be strongly rejected at normal resonation region when the data bit is low with MOS switches turned off, while it can propagate through the structure with low loss when the resonation is shifted to other frequency. In this case the data bit is high with MOS switches turned on, and the inner rings are shorted to ground. However, directly incorporating CMOS switches in the SRR ring will result in poor isolation with high loss.

In this work, we introduce a SRR-based sub-THz modulator with two SRR unit-cells oppositely coupled as shown in Figure 14.9. As revealed in EM-field analysis, the induced residue current in the SRR loop contributes dominant radiation loss at THz, which can be effectively attenuated by the stacked SRR configuration without scarifying additional area. Moreover, multiple CMOS switches are incorporated into the inner ring. As the switches

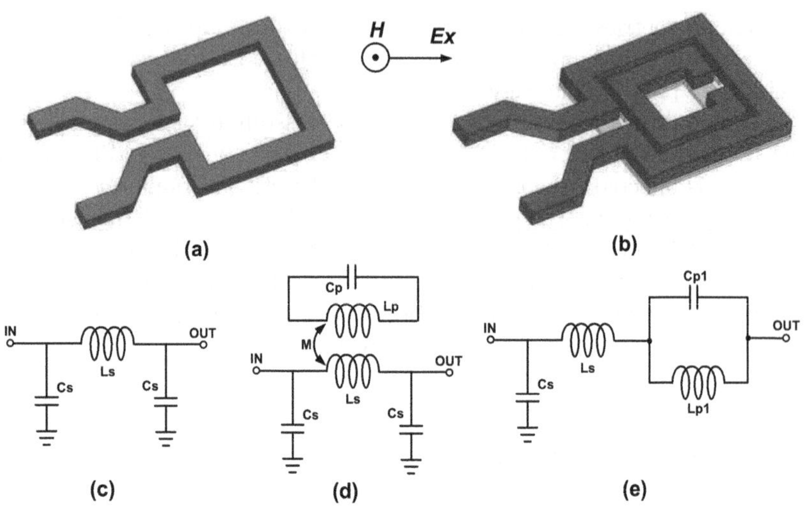

Figure 14.8: The schematic of (a) conventional single SRR and (b) stacking SRR structure; the equivalent circuit of (c) the single SRR, (d) stacking SRR, and (e) the simplified version of (d).

are now isolative from the signal path, their capacitive influence as well as distortion are minimized. As such, the data rate is now largely dependent on the performance of the SRR modulator instead of active devices.

The single SRR shown in Figure 14.8(a) is a common design to achieve the negative permeability when the H-field is perpendicular to the SRR plane. In traditional oscillator design, this structure is also referred to as the LC tank, owing to its ability to store magnetic energy. Compared to other LC tank structures in which transmission lines are employed, the single SRR provides higher quality factor, lower loss with much compact area occupation. The equivalent circuit is illustrated in Figure 14.8 (c). Here, components L_s, C_s denote the serial inductance and parasitic capacitance at the two terminals. The magnetic resonance frequency is therefore determined by $1/\sqrt{L_s C_s}$. One critical drawback in single SRR is the radiation loss, which becomes dominating especially at THz frequency. To verify this, a single SRR structure is simulated in the standard 65-nm CMOS environment. Two 40-fF capacitors (C_s) are incorporated to reduce the resonance frequency down to our concern (140GHz). The simulated body current (J_{vol}) is shown in Figure 14.10. One can observe that the induced current distribution on the SRR loop is not uniform. To be specific, the body current tends to crowd toward the metal surface, in much the same way resembling the proximity effect. Note that this crowding gives an increase in the effective resistance of the loop and introduces

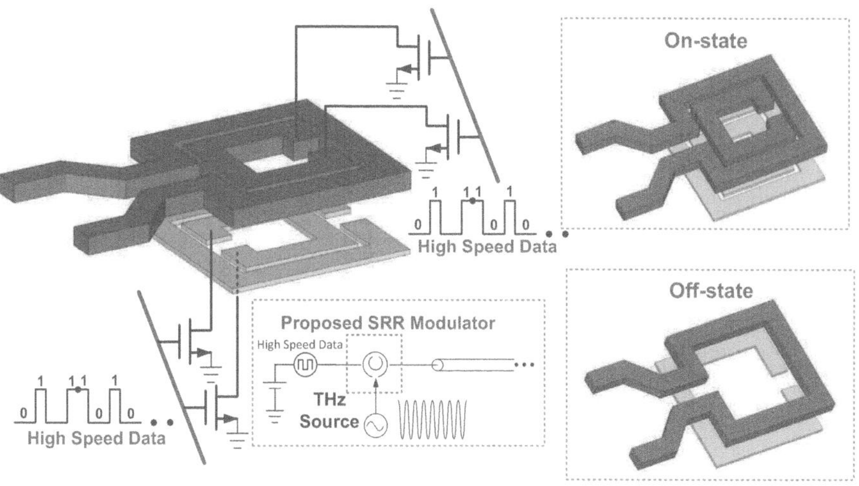

Figure 14.9: The proposed modulator evolved from the stacked SRR shown in Figure 14.1(b). Four MOS switches are incorporated connecting to the opening shape of both the two inner rings and achieve the functionality of modulation by a single data generator. The equivalent views of the on/off state are also illustrated.

stronger electromagnetic interference to adjacent conductive mediums, resulting in higher radiation loss which increases with frequency in a $\sqrt{f}$ manner. As such, single SRR has limited improvements at THz frequencies.

To further improve the quality factor of SRR structure, multiple layers of SRR unit-cell can be periodically arranged or using the interleaving architecture at the same metal plane. Due to more efficient area usage, the interleaving structure is considered in this work to form a SRR unit-cell. In fact, more SRR unit-cells can be stacked to achieve stronger isolation at magnetic resonation frequency. Here, we analyze the merit of stacking SRR from the perspective of its underlying physics. Note that in the case of a single SRR structure, the electric dipole moment is excited, accompanying the excitation of the magnetic dipole moment, leading to considerably high radiation loss [314]. Although the magnetic dipole has radiation losses as well, the radiation losses of the magnetic dipole are much lower than those of the corresponding electric dipole. As such, to implement the low-loss magnetic metamaterial, the induced current residing toward the metal surface should be strongly attenuated, i.e., the electric dipole moment induced by residual currents should be greatly suppressed. To achieve this, an additional SRR unit-cell whose placement is opposite with respect to the exiting SRR can be stacked to provide opposite current. Such a twisted SRR excites the opposite direction of induced currents for the existing SRR, and thus the induced currents of two twisted

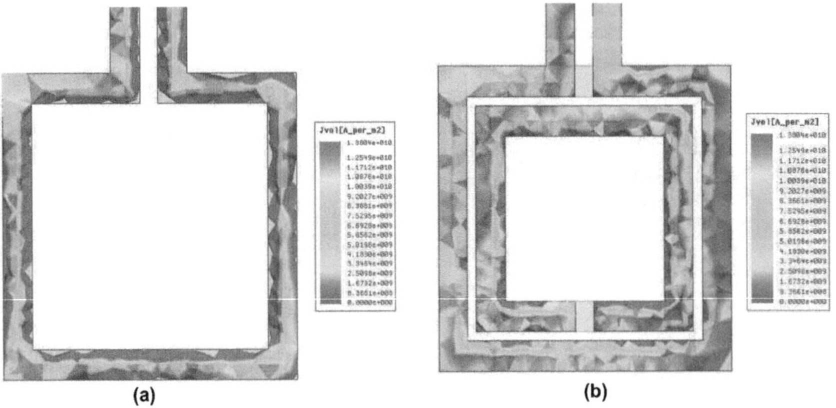

Figure 14.10: (a) The simulated body current distribution of the single SRR resonator at magnetic resonance frequency (140 GHz), and (b) the simulated body current distribution of the stacked SRR resonator at magnetic resonance frequency (140 GHz).

SRRs neutralize each other. As such, the EM energy in this case is mainly stored by the magnetic dipole, which inherently has much lower loss than an electric dipole at THz.

The layout of stacking SRR is shown in Figure 14.8 (b), in which the interleaving SRR is realized by the same metal layer to form an SRR unit-cell, while such two unit-cells are further stacked using the topmost two metal layers. The equivalent circuit is illustrated in Figure 14.8 (d), where components L_s, C_s denote the serial inductance of the outer ring and parasitic capacitance at the two terminals, while L_p, C_p represent the parallel inductance and capacitance (due to opening) of the inner ring. The interaction between the two rings is evaluated by mutual coupling factor M, which is mainly governed by their gap. The magnetic plasma region can be obtained by simplifying the equivalent circuit of Figure 14.8 (d) and (e):

$$\sqrt{\frac{1}{L_{p1}C_{p1}}} < \omega < \sqrt{\frac{1 + L_{p1}/L_s}{L_{p1}C_{p1}}}. \tag{14.1}$$

Specifically, when the EM wave travels into the medium with SRR structure the magnetic plasma will be excited within the region defined by (14.1). In this case, the EM energy cannot propagate through the SRR and is almost perfectly reflected back with an equivalent open circuit established.

With the strong attenuation obtained by the stacking SRR, the SRR-based modulator is further proposed. Recall that while SRR naturally has a high quality factor over other resonator structures, its stop band is sharper especially for the stacking structure. Carrier signal can thus propagate through SRR at frequencies slightly away from the magnetic resonance frequency. As such, by instantaneously altering the magnetic resonance frequency, the functionality of modulation can be achieved. Figure 14.9 illustrates such a novel concept. Here, the stacking SRR is employed owing to its higher quality factor. The openings of the two inner rings are connected to multiple MOS transistors whose gates are controlled to high speed data. The equivalent circuit of the proposed modulator is also illustrated at Figure 14.8(d), in which the parallel inductances of inner rings L_p is now modulated. According to (14.1), the magnetic plasma region is alternatively changed as well, leading to the modulation of resonance frequency. Physically, in the off state, the SRR acts as a normal resonator and serves to isolate the incoming carrier signal, while in the on state its resonance is shifted to the other frequency and the carrier signal can propagate through the structure with low loss.

There are several merits owing to this structure. Firstly, the MOS switches are now isolated from the signal path, resulting in less propagation loss since the finite on-resistance of switches tend to degrade the insertion loss at high frequency. Secondly, any parasitics of switches have been absorbed into the inner rings and thus minimizes the influence on the signal transmission. Thirdly, the distortions due to the nonlinear behavior of MOS switches during on/off switching are strongly attenuated by SRR as well. Finally, the purely passive structure is scalable to provide similar performance at higher carrier frequency ranges (>300GHz), in which MOS transistors only have high loss with large parasitics. All these features manifest the novel design of a potential candidate to be suitable for ultra-high speed communications. Note that the bandwidth of the modulator will increase by adding a transistor into the inner ring. This can be verified by (14.1), in which the parallel capacitance C_{s1} is increased due to the incorporation of parasitics from MOS transistor. While the enlarged bandwidth accommodates higher data rate transmission, the isolation of the proposed SRR modulator will be degraded due to weaker magnetic plasma resonation. As such, the dimension of MOS switches cannot be arbitrarily large.

To verify the conjectures, an SRR-based modulator is designed as shown in Figure 14.9 with silicon area of 40μm×67μe. Figure 14.9 also shows the simplified view of the modulator in the on state. Now the SRR unit-cell has been evolved to a single SRR, while such two unit-cells are further stacked. Therefore, the induced current can still be effectively neutralized as well, and the resulting resonance frequency will be increased. The induced current neutralization will be presented in the next section. On the other hand, in the off state the modulator evolves to a stacked SRR, as shown in Figure 14.9 as well. Four MOS transistors with 40μm width are incorporated to form switches.

Extinction ratio plays a key role in ultra-high-speed communication since the on/off state must be effectively distinguished. Conventional methods utilize various equalization techniques to enlarge the eye opening by sacrificing

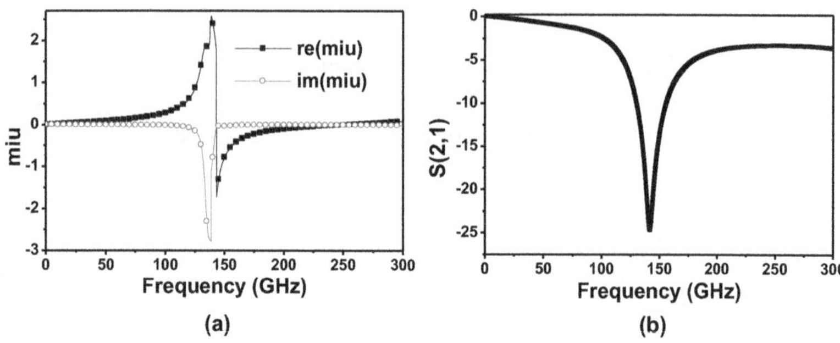

Figure 14.11: (a) The simulated body current distribution of the single SRR resonator at magnetic resonance frequency (140 GHz), and (b) Figure 14.4: the simulated body current distribution of the stacked SRR resonator at magnetic resonance frequency (140 GHz).

large power at the receiver side, but their data rates are only limited to multi-Gbps. The performance of the proposed SRR-based modulator will be evaluated by modulation of 20Gbps data in the next section.

The stacked SRR and the SRR-based modulator are designed in standard 65nm 1P9M CMOS technology. The silicon substrate is lossy with 70-S/m conductivity, while the stacking SRR and the proposed modulator are constructed using the top-most two copper metals owing a thickness of 0.9μm and 3.3μm, respectively. Here, the EM software HFSS is used for simulation. An incident EM wave polarized to the x direction (shown in Figure 14.8) excites the structure, and the boundary condition set as open to simulate the real space. The boundary conditions are at large distance from the metal structure to avoid significant reflections.

To investigate how the induced current is suppressed, Figure 14.10(b) illustrates the body current distribution in the upper SRR unit-cell. Now the currents on two stacking SRR unit-cells flow in the clockwise direction. Thus, the overall magnetic field is perpendicular to the SRR structure is reinforced by the summation of the magnetic field generated in each SRR unit-cell, which leads to a significant increase of the negative permeability effect. Meanwhile, the induced currents in each unit-cell are mutually compensated and the resulting current density is strongly suppressed as compared to the case of single SRR shown in Figure 14.10(a). As a result, the current crowding effect is omitted, and the radiation loss is significantly suppressed as well. The magnetic metamaterial property is further confirmed by Figure 14.11. The parameter extraction is done by the conversion from S parameters [315]. It shows that near the magnetic resonance frequency, the effective permeability has a narrow negative region, at which a sharp attenuation takes place. Note that while incorporating SRR unit-cell into a stack, the magnetic resonance frequency decreases as well, in return leads to a much more compact design.

Figure 14.12(a) illustrated the insertion loss (isolation) at on (off) state, respectively. It shows that the modulator has an insertion loss of 5dB and 28dB isolation at point 1 (140 GHz), leading to 23dB extinction ration, which is hardly achieved by MOS-based modulator at the same frequency. As the structure is compact, the insertion loss is mainly attributed to the energy coupling into the inner rings as well as the input reflection in the on state. Even though the inner rings have not been shown in Figure 14.9, they cannot be omitted in real design. A possible solution is to increase the gap between the inner/outer rings. However, the corresponding coupling factor will be reduced, in return degrades the magnetic resonation. As such, there is a trade-off between the insertion loss and isolation. In fact, from Figure 14.12(a) one can choose an other operation frequency, e.g., point 2 ($\sim$126GHz) in which the insertion loss is only 2.5 dB while the isolation is 15 dB. It can also achieve an extinction ratio of 12.5dB. It can also be observed that the operation bandwidth of the proposed modulator is wider than that of the pure stacking SRR structure (Figure 14.11(b)). The bandwidth of achieving over 10dB extinction ratio is larger than 20GHz. Owing to the high extinction ratio by the proposed modulator, a transient communication with data rate up to 20Gbps is conducted as shown in Figure 14.12(b). A buffer chain is designed first to mimic more real IO design, and its output swing can cover from rail (0 V) to rail (1.2 V) with clean eye. A 140-GHz continuous wave is applied to the RF input and the modulator is controlled by the random bit stream generator. The rising and falling times of the applied baseband signal are 4ps, and the minimum pulse width of data is 54ps. Figure 14.12(b) shows the modulated signal. It can be observed that the data patterns can be clearly distinguished. Here, the on/off amplitude ratio is at least 10 which coincides with the over 20-dB extinction ratio. Different from the optical scenario in which a pulse generator is used to drive the ring modulator with large output swing (>10V) [313, 286], the improved extinction ratio here can be achieved by nominal voltage level. All parasitics, including the driver chain output capacitances and loading capacitances should be included in the overall design iteration to further increase the data speed. As a comparison, recent works show the data rates are limited not higher than 13 Gbps [310, 311, 312, 313, 316, 317, 318] with large area. The performance summary and comparison are given in Table 14.1. In sum, the proposed passive modulator can adapt to a higher data rate with much more compact area than recent modulator designs.

14.4 Multi-Channel I/O Transceiver

The increasing demand for higher data rates in wireline communication systems has created the urge to seek for innovative high-bandwidth channels capable of supporting tens of gigabits per second (>10Gbps) communication

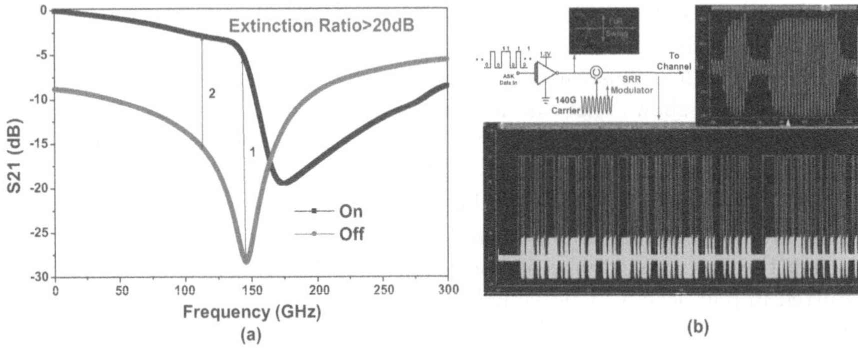

Figure 14.12: (a) The insertion loss (isolation) at on (off) state of the proposed modulator and the resulting extinction ratio, (b) the transient waveform of the modulated signal after the proposed modulator.

Table 14.1: Performances Summary and Comparison

Ref.	[311]	[313]	[319]	[317]	[318]	This work
Freq.(GHz)	46	optics	optics	60	122.5	>140
Extinction Ratio (dB)	>50	8	8.1	26.6	18.2	23
Data Rate (Gbps)	0.15	12.5	10	8	10	25
Bandwidth (GHz)	1	>25	>20	20	25	>50
Area (mm^2)	0.18	—	1.8mm long	0.18	0.11*	<0.003
CMOS Process	0.13μm	SOI	—	90nm	40nm	65nm

*: With oscillator embedded.

with high energy efficiency. Continuous scaling of CMOS technology has encouraged it as a potential mm-wave and THz implementations [52], and with great integration possibilities. This high frequency enables the use of a high available bandwidth and data rate, with limited system complexity. However, the high operation frequency also leads to a degraded performance of the MOS transistors, making the design extremely challenging.

Recent researches have demonstrated multi-channel I/O data links [307] leveraging much larger bandwidth utilization with achievement of a high data rate (~10 Gbps) compared to one channel serial link with power-consuming MUX/DEMUX. However, the CMOS top metals used in fine-pitch silicon interconnects are typically narrow and thin, leading to high channel loss with strong crosstalk among channels especially at high frequencies. Special equalization techniques such as the decision feedback equalizer (DFE) must be

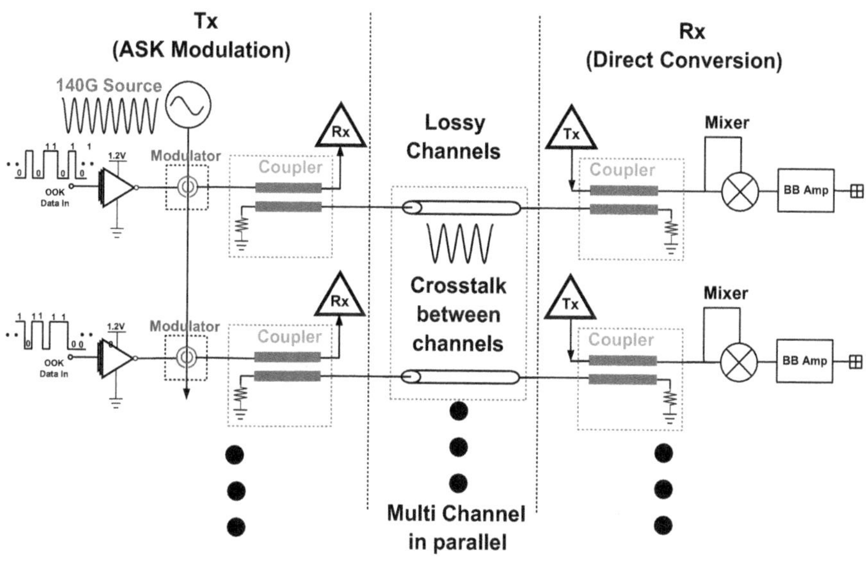

Figure 14.13: (a) The insertion loss (isolation) at on (off) state of the proposed modulator and the resulting extinction ratio, (b) the transient waveform of the modulated signal after the proposed modulator.

incorporated into the receiving side to compensate the induced inter-symbol interference (ISI) with large power overhead. Simultaneous bi-directional multi (Base+RF)-band signaling [284] is also demonstrated for high data rate transmission between controller and DRAM. However, to fulfill certain BER requirements, the data rate will be ultimately limited by the low extinction ratio of on-chip modulator as well as high channel loss. In sum, exciting I/O designs have faced great challenges due to the poor channel bandwidth along with the low extinction ratio of active modulator.

This work explores the realization of bi-directional multi-channel I/O by novel SPP interconnect (coupler and channels) and SRR-based modulator, to achieve a high data rate with high energy efficiency. The 140GHz I/O transceiver architecture is shown in Figure 14.13, which accommodates multiple RF TRx links. The SPP T-line is a kind of plasmonic metamaterial consisting of a metal strip with thin film thickness, in which a 1D periodical array of grooves is drilled. As such, the propagation of surface-confined mode is adapted to the curvature of the surface. Therefore, the resulting crosstalk between the two back-to-back placed SPP T-lines (channels) will be significantly attenuated, while the two face-to-face placed SPP T-lines (coupler) has strong wide-band coupling between their respective grooves. In addition,

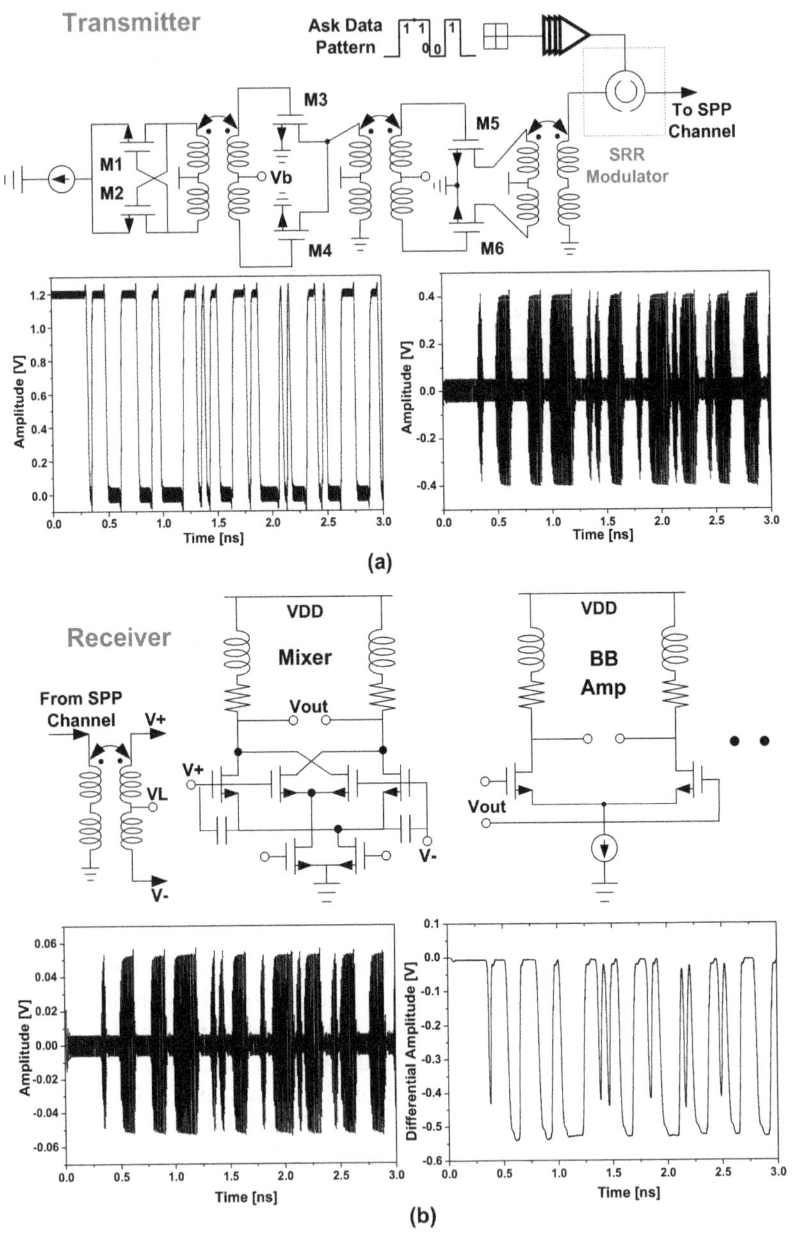

Figure 14.14: (a) The insertion loss (isolation) at on (off) state of the proposed modulator and the resulting extinction ratio, (b) the transient waveform of the modulated signal after the proposed modulator.

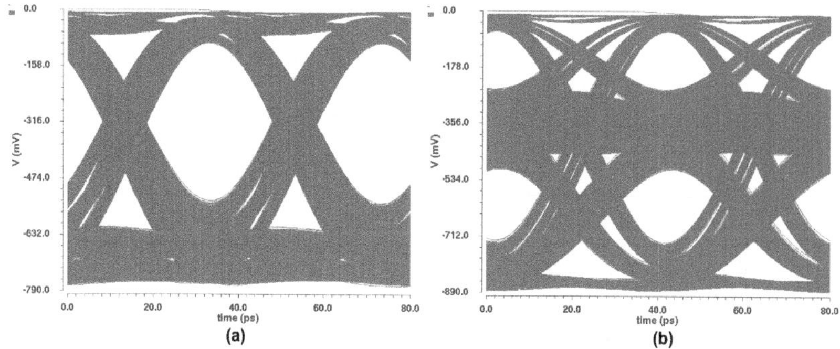

Figure 14.15: The eye-diagrams of 25Gb/s data rate communication for two I/O transceivers. (a) one is with proposed SPP T-line based channels as well as SPP coupler, and (b) the other one is with conventional T-line channels along with T-line coupler.

the proposed modulator evolves from a stacked SRR structure with MOS switches connected to the inner ring of SRR unit-cells. The carrier signal will be strongly rejected at the normal resonation region when the data bit is low with MOS switches turned off, while it can modulate the data with low loss when the resonation is shifted to other frequencies. As such, with strong crosstalk reduction of the channel, high coupling factor of the coupler, and high extinction ratio of the modulator, the IO transceiver is designed with higher than 20Gbps data communication.

The multi-channel bi-directional I/O transceiver architecture is presented in Figure 14.13. Such an I/O architecture accommodates a large number of peer-to-peer on-chip high-speed interconnects with capabilities of multi-drop arbitration, to meet the requirement of future network-on-chip (NoC). At each side only either Tx or Rx can work at a time. The non-working block will be shut down to save power. With strong crosstalk reduction by the SPP channels, the ISI neutralization equalizers are not necessary at the receiving side, saving considerable power with more design margin to further increase the data rate. In contrast to conventional I/O design, since the modulator is no longer constrains the data rate at the transmitter side, the Rx can be designed with wider bandwidth by removing the low-noise amplifier (LNA). Note that at mm-wave or THz, the wide-band LNA features a cascading of multiple amplification stages, which is not area efficient but consumes high DC power. Instead, to maintain a high SNR for one channel, high power/efficient THz source [52] can be readily utilized as a global clock for transmission. Due to the non-coherent nature of ASK modulation, the clock synthesizer is not necessary, and the wide-band self-mixing mixer can be employed to demodulate the data buffered by low-power baseband amplifiers. In this design, the SPP channel

Table 14.2: Summary and Comparison of State-of-the-Art Wireline Transceiver

-	[320]	[307]	[321]	[284]	[312]	[322]	This work
Category	Optical	Electrical	Electrical	Guided	Guided	Electrical	Guided
Duplex	FDD	Simplex	Simplex	Duplex (FDD)	Full-Duplex (TDD)	Simplex	Simplex
Carrier Frequency (Hz)	Optical	Baseband	Baseband	23GHz+ Base-Band	60GHz	Baseband	140G
Transmission Medium	Polymer waveguide	Silicon Channel	PCB Copper line	PCB T-line (Microstrip, FR-4)	On-chip T-line	Organic substrate channel	On-chip surface-wave waveguide
EM-wave	Optics	TEM	TEM	TEM	TEM	Optics	Confined-mode
Data rate (Gbps)	10 (@ $< 10^{-12}$) (per link)	10 (@BER $< 10^{-11}$) (per link)	6 (@ $< 10^{-12}$) (per link)	8.4 (RF+BB merged) (@BER $< 10^{-12}$)	5 (@BER $< 10^{-12}$) (per link)	20 (@BER $< 10^{-12}$)	25 (simulation) (per link)
Modulation	Optical Amplitude modulation	Non	Non	ASK (noncoherent)	ASK (noncoherent)	ASK (coherent)	ASK (coherent)
Transmission Distance	100mm	40mm	50mm	100mm	12mm	4.5mm	20mm
Channel Loss	0.001dB /mm	1dB/ mm@10GHz	N.A	-0.1dB/ mm@23GHz	1.2dB/ mm@60GHz	2.4dB/ mm@40GHz	0.75dB/ mm@ 140GHz
Crosstalk Ratio	N.A	-6dB/ mm@10GHz	N.A	N.A	-5dB/ mm@60GHz	-10dB/ mm@40GHz	-20dB/ mm@ 140GHz
Equalization	DFE	DFE	N/R	N.A	Self-Mixing	N/R	Self-Mixing
DC power consumption	172.8mW (all)	17mW/ link	95mW	11mW(BB) 10mW(RF)	9.4mW (Tx) 5mW (Rx) (total 14.4mW /link)	10.8mW/ link	8mW/ link
Energy efficiency (pJ/bit)	9.6	1.9	15.8	2.5	2.88	0.54	0.32
Energy efficiency per distance (pJ/bit/mm)	0.096	0.0475	0.32	0.025	0.24	0.12	0.016
Process	90nm CMOS	65nm CMOS	130nm CMOS	65nm CMOS	65nm CMOS	28nm CMOS	65nm CMOS

length is 2 mm while the channel gap is only 2.4 μm which is the minimum top metal distance allowed by the foundry. Given that the channel bandwidth is higher than 20GHz while the input/output matching is achieved by the transformer with about 3dB loss at each side, the minimum signal power required at the input of the receiver side can be calculated by:

$$\begin{aligned} P_{SIG.IN} &= -174\,(dBm) + 10\log(BW) + NF + SNR_{OUT} \\ &= -174dBm + 103dBm + 13dB + 18dB = -40dBm \quad (14.2) \end{aligned}$$

which has over 30dB of noise margin for $< 10^{-12}$ BER.

Figure 14.14 shows the TRx implementation in 65nm CMOS. The Tx contains a 70GHz fundamental LC-tank VCO, a push-push frequency doubler, an LO buffer and the proposed SRR modulator. Transformers are extensively employed to save silicon area, and impedance transformation while providing individual biasing for each functional block. The push-push doubler is realized by transistors M_3 and M_4, and the 2nd harmonic is extracted at their shared drain junction. For strong harmonic generation the voltage bias w_b should be closed to the transistor threshold region. Fundamental tone and other harmonics are inherently canceled or filtered out by the matching network. The Rx side contains a self-mixing mixer and three-stage baseband amplifier. Mm-wave technique such as inductive peaking is deployed for wider bandwidth so that sharp data transition can be detected. The simulated Tx/Rx waveform of the modulated/demodulated data is shown in Figure 14.14 as well. Though only two channels are presented here, more channels can be readily applied for higher data rate in future design. The recovered data and the corresponding eye diagram of 25Gbps communication are shown in Figure 14.15, which presents clearly the horizontal/vertical eye opening. Recent state-of-the-art ASK I/O interfaces are summarized in Table 14.2 with comparison.

14.5 Conclusion

Firstly, a low-loss and low-crosstalk surface-wave transmission line (T-line) is demonstrated at sub-THz in CMOS. By introducing sub-wavelength periodic corrugation structure onto the T-line (by top-layer metal), surface plasmon polariton (SPP) is established to propagate signals with a strongly localized surface-wave. Two coupled SPP T-lines and two quasi-TEM T-lines are both fabricated on chip with space of 2.4 μm in the standard 65 nm CMOS process. Measurement results show that the SPP T-lines achieve a wide-band reflection coefficient lower than -14 dB and crosstalk ratio better than -24 dB, which is 19 dB lower on average than the traditional T-lines from 220GHz to 325GHz. The demonstrated compact and wide-band SPP T-lines have shown great potential for on-chip THz communication. Secondly, the CMOS split ring resonator (SRR)-based modulator is investigated in this work toward on-chip THz communication. The field distribution and induced current of SRR structures are analyzed. It shows that the stacked SRR structure can neutralize the induced current at each SRR unit-cell, resulting in much less radiation loss at THz. What is more, when the stacked-SRR is deployed for the modulator design, CMOS switches can be added to the inner ring out of the signal path such that high isolation and low distortion can be achieved as well. As verified by the standard 65nm CMOS, results reveal that the proposed modulator can be effectively modulated by 20Gbps high-speed data with 5-dB insertion loss and 28-dB isolation, which leads to 23dB extinction ratio by occupying only a $40\mu m \times 67\mu m$ silicon area. Therefore, such a proposed modulator is very promising for on-chip THz communication in CMOS technology. Lastly, using the SPP interconnect and stacked SRR-based modulator, a 140-GHz carrier multi-channel bi-directional I/O interface is designed in 65-nm CMOS technology. The SPP interconnect, which consists of channels and a coupler, is able to localize EM energy into the periodical groove by exciting the surface wave. Thus the SPP channels can strongly attenuate mutual crosstalk. The modulator is based on the stacked SRR structure with MOS switches connected to the inner rings. Modulation can be thereby obtained by tuning the magnetic resonation frequency with a 23-dB extinction ratio. Results show that the proposed I/O can communicate at 25 Gbps with 1.6-pJ/bit energy efficiency, exhibiting potential for the future high-performance NoC.

References

[1] W. Momose, H. Yoshino, Y. Katakawa, K. Yamashita, K. Imai, K. Sako, E. Kato, A. Irisawa, E. Yonemochi, and K. Terada, "Applying Terahertz technology for non-destructive detection of crack initiation in a film-coated layer on a swelling tablet," *Results in Pharma Sciences*, vol. 2, pp. 29–37, 2012.

[2] T. Arikawa, M. Nagai, and K. Tanaka, "Characterizing hydration state in solution using terahertz time-domain attenuated total reflection spectroscopy," *Chemical Physics Letters*, vol. 457, no. 1–3, pp. 12–17, 2008.

[3] P. C. Ashworth, E. Pickwell-MacPherson, E. Provenzano, S. E. Pinder, A. D. Purushotham, M. Pepper, and V. P. Wallace, "Terahertz pulsed spectroscopy of freshly excised human breast cancer," *Optics Express*, vol. 17, no. 15, pp. 12 444–12 454, July 2009.

[4] R. Woodward, V. Wallace, D. Arnone, E. Linfield, and M. Pepper, "Terahertz pulsed imaging of skin cancer in the time and frequency domain," *Journal of Biological Physics*, vol. 29, no. 2–3, pp. 257–261, June 2003.

[5] Wigig white paper: "Defining the future of multi-gigabit wireless communication." http://wilocity.com/resources/WiGigWhitepaper_FINAL5.pdf.

[6] F. Schwierz, "Graphene transistors," *Nature Nanotechnology*, vol. 5, no. 7, pp. 487–496, July 2010.

[7] J. Chen and A. Niknejad, "A stage-scaled distributed power amplifier achieving 110ghz bandwidth and 17.5dbm peak output power," in *IEEE Radio Frequency Integrated Circuits Symposium*, May 2010, pp. 347–350.

[8] C. Aitchison, N. Bukhari, C. Law, and N. Nazoa-Ruiz, "The dual-fed distributed amplifier," in *IEEE MTT-S International Microwave Symposium*, May 1988, pp. 911–914 vol. 2.

[9] M. Moazzam and C. Aitchison, "A high gain dual-fed single stage distributed amplifier," in *IEEE MTT-S International Microwave Symposium*, May 1994, pp. 1409–1412 vol. 3.

[10] U. Pfeiffer and D. Goren, "A 20 dbm fully-integrated 60 ghz sige power amplifier with automatic level control," *IEEE Journal of Solid-State Circuits*, vol. 42, no. 7, pp. 1455–1463, July 2007.

[11] J. Gorisse, A. Cathelin, A. Kaiser, and E. Kerherve, "A 60ghz 65nm CMOS rms power detector for antenna impedance mismatch detection," in *IEEE European Solid-State Circuits Conference*, Sept 2009, pp. 172–175.

[12] O. Inac, S. Kim, D. Shin, C. Kim, and G. Rebeiz, "Built-in self-test systems for silicon-based phased arrays," in *IEEE MTT-S International Microwave Symposium*, June 2012, pp. 1–3.

[13] J.-W. Lai and A. Valdes-Garcia, "A 1v 17.9dbm 60ghz power amplifier in standard 65nm CMOS," in *IEEE International Solid-State Circuits Conference*, Feb 2010, pp. 424–425.

[14] D. Cai, Y. Shang, H. Yu, and J. Ren, "Design of ultra-low-power 60-GHz direct-conversion receivers in 65-nm CMOS," *IEEE Transactions on Microwave Theory and Techniques*, vol. 61, no. 9, pp. 3360–3372, Sept. 2013.

[15] A. Behzad, K. A. Carter, H.-M. Chien, S. Wu, M.-A. Pan, C. P. Lee, Q. Li, J. C. Leete, S. Au, M. S. Kappes *et al.*, "A fully integrated MIMO multiband direct conversion CMOS transceiver for WLAN applications (802.11 n)," *IEEE Journal of Solid-State Circuits*, vol. 42, no. 12, pp. 2795–2808, 2007.

[16] M. Tonouchi, "Cutting-edge terahertz technology," *Nature Photonics*, vol. 1, pp. 97–105, Feb. 2007.

[17] D. Arnone, C. Ciesla, and M. Pepper, "Terahertz imaging comes into view," *Physics World*, vol. 13, no. 4, pp. 35–40, April 2000.

[18] Y. Sun, M. Y. Sy, Y. X. Wang, A. T. Ahuja, Y. T. Zhang, and E. Pickwell-Macpherson, "A promising diagnostic method: Terahertz pulsed imaging and spectroscopy," *World Journal of Radiology*, vol. 3, no. 3, pp. 55–65, March 2011.

[19] R. Han, Y. Zhang, Y. Kim, D. Y. Kim, H. Shichijo, and K. Kenneth, "Terahertz image sensors using CMOS Schottky barrier diodes," in *International SoC Design Conference*, Nov. 2012, pp. 254–257.

[20] H.-J. Song and T. Nagatsuma, "Present and future of terahertz communications," *IEEE Transactions on Terahertz Science and Technology*, vol. 1, no. 1, pp. 256–263, Sept. 2011.

[21] K. Kawase, Y. Ogawa, Y. Watanabe, and H. Inoue, "Non-destructive terahertz imaging of illicit drugs using spectral fingerprints," *Opt. Express*, vol. 11, no. 20, pp. 2549–2554, Oct. 2003.

[22] L. Zhang, H. Zhong, C. Deng, C. Zhang, and Y. Zhao, "Terahertz wave reference-free phase imaging for identification of explosives," *Applied Physics Letters*, vol. 92, no. 9, 2008.

[23] Terahertz Detection of Skin, Mouth and Epithelial Cancers. [Online]. Available: http://www.teraview.com/applications/medical/ oncology.html

[24] T. Nagatsuma, H.-J. Song, Y. Fujimoto, K. Miyake, A. Hirata, K. Ajito, A. Wakatsuki, T. Furuta, N. Kukutsu, and Y. Kado, "Giga-bit wireless link using 300-400 GHz bands," in *International Topical Meeting on Microwave Photonics*, Oct. 2009, pp. 1–4.

[25] L. Moeller, J. Federici, and K. Su, "THz wireless communications: 2.5 Gb/s error-free transmission at 625 GHz using a narrow-bandwidth 1 mW THz source," in *30th URSI General Assembly and Scientific Symposium*, Aug. 2011, pp. 1–4.

[26] M.-C. Chang, V. Roychowdhury, L. Zhang, H. Shin, and Y. Qian, "RF/wireless interconnect for inter- and intra-chip communications," *Proceedings of the IEEE*, vol. 89, no. 4, pp. 456–466, April 2001.

[27] I. Kallfass, J. Antes, T. Schneider, F. Kurz, D. Lopez-Diaz, S. Diebold, H. Massler, A. Leuther, and A. Tessmann, "All active MMIC-based wireless communication at 220 GHz," *IEEE Transactions on Terahertz Science and Technology*, vol. 1, no. 2, pp. 477–487, Nov. 2011.

[28] Z. Xu, Q. Gu, Y.-C. Wu, A. Tang, Y.-L. Lin, H.-H. Chen, C. Jou, and M.-C. Chang, "D-band CMOS transmitter and receiver for multi-giga-bit/sec wireless data link," in *2010 IEEE Custom Integrated Circuits Conference*, Sept. 2010, pp. 1–4.

[29] N. Ono, M. Motoyoshi, K. Takano, K. Katayama, R. Fujimoto, and M. Fujishima, "135 GHz 98 mW 10 Gbps ASK transmitter and receiver chipset in 40 nm CMOS," in *2012 Symposium on VLSI Circuits*, June 2012, pp. 50–51.

[30] A. Nahata, A. Weling, and T. Heinz, "A wideband coherent terahertz spectroscopy system using optical rectification and electro-optic sampling," *Applied Physics Letters*, vol. 69, no. 16, pp. 2321–2323, Oct. 1996.

[31] K. Sengupta and A. Hajimiri, "A 0.28 THz power-generation and beam-steering array in CMOS based on distributed active radiators," *IEEE Journal of Solid-State Circuits*, vol. 47, no. 12, pp. 3013–3031, Dec. 2012.

[32] R. Han, Y. Zhang, Y. Kim, D. Y. Kim, H. Shichijo, E. Afshari, and O. Kenneth, "280GHz and 860GHz image sensors using Schottky-barrier diodes in 0.13 μm digital CMOS," in *IEEE International Solid-State Circuits Conference*, Feb. 2012, pp. 254–256.

[33] B. Khamaisi, S. Jameson, and E. Socher, "A 210–227 GHz transmitter with integrated on-chip antenna in 90 nm CMOS technology," *IEEE Transactions on Terahertz Science and Technology*, vol. 3, no. 2, pp. 141–150, March 2013.

[34] Y. Shang, H. Yu, C. Yang, Y. Liang, and W. M. Lim, "A 239–281ghz sub-thz imager with 100mhz resolution by CMOS direct-conversion receiver with on-chip circular-polarized SIW antenna," in *Custom Integrated Circuits Conference (CICC), 2014 IEEE Proceedings of the*, Sept 2014, pp. 1–4.

[35] W. Fei, H. Yu, Y. Shang, D. Cai, and J. Ren, "A 96-ghz oscillator by high-q differential transmission line loaded with complementary split-ring resonator in 65-nm CMOS," *Circuits and Systems II: Express Briefs, IEEE Transactions on*, vol. 60, no. 3, pp. 127–131, March 2013.

[36] A. Tomkins, R. Aroca, T. Yamamoto, S. Nicolson, Y. Doi, and S. Voinigescu, "A zero-if 60 ghz 65 nm CMOS transceiver with direct bpsk modulation demonstrating up to 6 gb/s data rates over a 2 m wireless link," *IEEE Journal of Solid-State Circuits*, vol. 44, no. 8, pp. 2085–2099, Aug 2009.

[37] C. Marcu, D. Chowdhury, C. Thakkar, J.-D. Park, L.-K. Kong, M. Tabesh, Y. Wang, B. Afshar, A. Gupta, A. Arbabian, S. Gambini, R. Zamani, E. Alon, and A. Niknejad, "A 90 nm CMOS low-power 60 GHz transceiver with integrated baseband circuitry," *IEEE Journal of Solid-State Circuits*, vol. 44, no. 12, pp. 3434–3447, Dec. 2009.

[38] W. Chan and J. Long, "A 60-ghz band 2 × 2 phased-array transmitter in 65-nm CMOS," *IEEE Journal of Solid-State Circuits*, vol. 45, no. 12, pp. 2682–2695, Dec 2010.

[39] K. Okada, N. Li, K. Matsushita, K. Bunsen, R. Murakami, A. Musa, T. Sato, H. Asada, N. Takayama, S. Ito, W. Chaivipas, R. Minami, T. Yamaguchi, Y. Takeuchi, H. Yamagishi, M. Noda, and A. Matsuzawa, "A 60-ghz 16qam/8psk/qpsk/bpsk direct-conversion transceiver for IEEE 802.15.3c," *IEEE Journal of Solid-State Circuits*, vol. 46, no. 12, pp. 2988–3004, Dec 2011.

[40] S. Shahramian, Y. Baeyens, N. Kaneda, and Y.-K. Chen, "A 70–100 ghz direct-conversion transmitter and receiver phased array chipset demonstrating 10 gb/s wireless link," *IEEE Journal of Solid-State Circuits*, vol. 48, no. 5, pp. 1113–1125, May 2013.

[41] D. Cai, Y. Shang, H. Yu, J. Ren, and K. S. Yeo, "A 76 ghz oscillator by high-q differential transmission line loaded with split ring resonator in 65-nm CMOS," in *Silicon Monolithic Integrated Circuits in RF Systems (SiRF), 2013 IEEE 13th Topical Meeting on*, Jan 2013, pp. 111–113.

[42] S. Ma, H. Yu, and J. Ren, "A 32.5-gs/s sampler with time-interleaved track-and-hold amplifier in 65-nm CMOS," *Microwave Theory and Techniques, IEEE Transactions on*, vol. 62, no. 12, pp. 3500–3511, Dec 2014.

[43] Y. Shang, H. Yu, S. Hu, Y. Liang, X. Bi, and M. Arasu, "High-sensitivity CMOS super-regenerative receiver with quench-controlled high-q metamaterial resonator for millimeter-wave imaging at 96 and 135 ghz," *IEEE Transactions on Microwave Theory and Techniques*, vol. 62, no. 12, pp. 3095–3106, Dec 2014.

[44] Y. Shang, D. Cai, W. Fei, H. Yu, and J. Ren, "An 8mw ultra low power 60ghz direct-conversion receiver with 55db gain and 4.9db noise figure in 65nm CMOS," in *Radio-Frequency Integration Technology (RFIT), 2012 IEEE International Symposium on*, Nov 2012, pp. 47–49.

[45] Y. Shang, H. Yu, D. Cai, J. Ren, and K. S. Yeo, "Design of high-q millimeter-wave oscillator by differential transmission line loaded with metamaterial resonator in 65-nm CMOS," *IEEE Transactions on Microwave Theory and Techniques*, vol. 61, no. 5, pp. 1892–1902, May 2013.

[46] H. Fu, W. Fei, H. Yu, and J. Ren, "A 60.8-67ghz and 6.3mw injection-locked frequency divider with switching-inductor loaded transformer in 65nm CMOS," in *Microwave Symposium (IMS), 2014 IEEE MTT-S International*, June 2014, pp. 1–4.

[47] W. Fei, H. Yu, Y. Liang, and W. M. Lim, "A 54 to 62.8ghz pa with 95.2mw/mm2 output power density by 4×4 distributed in-phase power combining in 65nm CMOS," in *Microwave Symposium (IMS), 2014 IEEE MTT-S International*, June 2014, pp. 1–4.

[48] K. Okada, K. Matsushita, K. Bunsen, R. Murakami, A. Musa, T. Sato, H. Asada, N. Takayama, N. Li, S. Ito, W. Chaivipas, R. Minami, and A. Matsuzawa, "A 60ghz 16qam/8psk/qpsk/bpsk direct-conversion transceiver for ieee 802.15.3c," in *IEEE International Solid-State Circuits Conference*, Feb 2011, pp. 160–162.

[49] T. Nagatsuma, S. Horiguchi, Y. Minamikata, Y. Yoshimizu, S. Hisatake, S. Kuwano, N. Yoshimoto, J. Terada, and H. Takahashi, "Terahertz wireless communications based on photonics technologies," *Optics express*, vol. 21, no. 20, pp. 23 736–23 747, 2013.

[50] I. F. Akyildiz, J. M. Jornet, and C. Han, "Terahertz band: Next frontier for wireless communications," *Physical Communication*, vol. 12, pp. 16–32, 2014.

[51] Y. Shang, H. Yu, P. Li, Y. Liang, and C. Yang, "A 280GHz CMOS on-chip composite right/left handed transmission line based leaky wave antenna with broadside radiation," in *IEEE MTT-S International Microwave Symposium*, June 2014, pp. 1–3.

[52] Y. Shang, H. Yu, P. Li, X. Bi, and M. Je, "A 127-140GHz injection-locked signal source with 3.5mW peak output power by zero-phase coupled oscillator network in 65nm CMOS," in *IEEE Custom Integrated Circuits Conference*, Sept. 2014, pp. 1–4.

[53] J. Paramesh, R. Bishop, K. Soumyanath, and D. J. Allstot, "A four-antenna receiver in 90-nm CMOS for beamforming and spatial diversity," *IEEE Journal of Solid-State Circuits*, vol. 40, no. 12, pp. 2515–2524, 2005.

[54] R. A. Shelby, D. R. Smith, and S. Schultz, "Experimental verification of a negative index of refraction," *Science*, vol. 292, no. 5514, pp. 77–79, 2001.

[55] T. J. Cui, D. R. Smith, and R. Liu, *Metamaterials: Theory, Design, and Applications.* Springer, 2009.

[56] S. B. Cohn, "Parallel-coupled transmission-line-resonator filters," *IRE Transactions on Microwave Theory and Techniques*, vol. 6, no. 2, pp. 223–231, April 1958.

[57] J.-S. Hong and M. Lancaster, "Couplings of microstrip square open-loop resonators for cross-coupled planar microwave filters," *IEEE Transactions on Microwave Theory and Techniques*, vol. 44, no. 11, pp. 2099–2109, Nov. 1996.

[58] E. Shamonina, V. Kalinin, K. Ringhofer, and L. Solymar, "Magneto-inductive waveguide," *Electronics Letters*, vol. 38, no. 8, pp. 371–373, April 2002.

[59] A. Sample, D. Meyer, and J. Smith, "Analysis, experimental results, and range adaptation of magnetically coupled resonators for wireless power transfer," *IEEE Transactions on Industrial Electronics*, vol. 58, no. 2, pp. 544–554, Feb. 2011.

[60] C.-W. Yang and C.-L. Yang, "Analysis of inductive coupling coils for extending distances of efficient wireless power transmission," in *IEEE MTT-S International Microwave Workshop Series on RF and Wireless Technologies for Biomedical and Healthcare Applications*, Dec. 2013, pp. 1–3.

[61] C. Caloz, T. Itoh, and A. Rennings, "CRLH metamaterial leaky-wave and resonant antennas," *IEEE Antennas and Propagation Magazine*, vol. 50, no. 5, pp. 25–39, Oct 2008.

[62] C.-J. Lee, K. M. K. H. Leong, and T. Itoh, "Metamaterial transmission line based bandstop and bandpass filter designs using broadband phase cancellation," in *IEEE MTT-S International Microwave Symposium*, June 2006, pp. 935–938.

[63] C.-J. Lee, K. M. K. Leong, and T. Itoh, "Broadband quadrature hybrid design using metamaterial transmission line and its application in the broadband continuous phase shifter," in *IEEE MTT-S International Microwave Symposium*, June 2007, pp. 1745–1748.

[64] C. Liu and W. Menzel, "Broadband via-free microstrip balun using metamaterial transmission lines," *IEEE Microwave and Wireless Components Letters*, vol. 18, no. 7, pp. 437–439, July 2008.

[65] F. Bongard, J. Perruisseau-Carrier, and J. Mosig, "Enhanced CRLH transmission line performances using a lattice network unit cell," *IEEE Microwave and Wireless Components Letters*, vol. 19, no. 7, pp. 431–433, July 2009.

[66] P.-P. Ding, X. Chen, and K. Agarwal, "A novel ultra-wideband electromagnetic bandgap structure for ssn suppression," in *IEEE Asia-Pacific Conference on Antennas and Propagation*, Aug. 2012, pp. 149–150.

[67] F. Ng-Molina, T. Martin-Guerrero, and C. Camacho-Penalosa, "Power and gain considerations in distributed amplifiers based on composite right/left-handed transmission lines," *IET Microwaves, Antennas Propagation*, vol. 4, no. 8, pp. 1000–1006, Aug. 2010.

[68] C.-T. M. Wu and T. Itoh, "Dual-fed distributed amplifier-based CRLH-leaky wave antenna for gain-enhanced power combining," in *IEEE MTT-S International Microwave Workshop Series on Innovative Wireless Power Transmission: Technologies, Systems, and Applications*, May 2012, pp. 87–90.

[69] D. Cai, Y. Shang, H. Yu, and J. Ren, "80 ghz on-chip metamaterial resonator by differential transmission line loaded with split ring resonator," *Electronics Letters*, vol. 48, no. 18, pp. 1128–1130, August 2012.

[70] A. Lai, T. Itoh, and C. Caloz, "Composite right/left-handed transmission line metamaterials," *IEEE Microwave Magazine*, vol. 5, no. 3, pp. 34–50, Sept 2004.

[71] T. Cui, D. Smith, and R. Liu, *Metamaterials: Theory, Design, and Applications*. Springer, 2009. [Online]. Available: http://books.google.com.sg/books?id=rX7qBqsZWtoC

[72] M. Boers, "A 60ghz transformer coupled amplifier in 65nm digital CMOS," in *IEEE Radio Frequency Integrated Circuits Symposium*, May 2010, pp. 343–346.

[73] J. Gao and L. Zhu, "Characterization of infinite- and finite-extent coplanar waveguide metamaterials with varied left- and right-handed passbands," *IEEE Microwave and Wireless Components Letters*, vol. 15, no. 11, pp. 805–807, Nov 2005.

[74] W. Fei, H. Yu, K. S. Yeo, and W. M. Lim, "A 60ghz vco with 25.8% tuning range by switching return-path in 65nm CMOS," in *IEEE Asian Solid State Circuits Conference*, Nov 2012, pp. 277–280.

[75] S.-W. Tam, H.-T. Yu, Y. Kim, E. Socher, M. C. F. Chang, and T. Itoh, "A dual band mm-wave CMOS oscillator with left-handed resonator," in *IEEE Radio Frequency Integrated Circuits Symposium*, June 2009, pp. 477–480.

[76] T. Jiang, K. Chang, L.-M. Si, L. Ran, and H. Xin, "Active microwave negative-index metamaterial transmission line with gain," *Phys. Rev. Lett.*, vol. 107, p. 205503, Nov 2011. [Online]. Available: http://link.aps.org/doi/10.1103/PhysRevLett.107.205503

[77] M. Lont, R. Mahmoudi, E. van der Heijden, A. de Graauw, P. Sakian, P. Baltus, and A. van Roermund, "A 60GHz miller effect based VCO in 65nm CMOS with 10.5% tuning range," in *IEEE Topical Meeting on Silicon Monolithic Integrated Circuits in RF Systems*, Jan. 2009, pp. 1–4.

[78] F. Falcone, T. Lopetegi, J. Baena, R. Marques, F. Martin, and M. Sorolla, "Effective negative- ε stopband microstrip lines based on complementary split ring resonators," *IEEE Microwave and Wireless Components Letters*, vol. 14, no. 6, pp. 280 – 282, June 2004.

[79] D. Huang, W. Hant, N.-Y. Wang, T. Ku, Q. Gu, R. Wong, and M.-C. Chang, "A 60GHz CMOS VCO using on-chip resonator with embedded artificial dielectric for size, loss and noise reduction," in *IEEE International Solid-State Circuits Conference*, Feb. 2006, pp. 1218–1227.

[80] C. Lee, D. Jung, and C. Seo, "Design of low phase noise VCO using complimentary split ring resonator," in *Asia Pacific Microwave Conference*, Dec. 2008, pp. 1–4.

[81] D. Cai, Y. Shang, H. Yu, and J. Ren, "80 ghz on-chip metamaterial resonator by differential transmission line loaded with split ring resonator," *Electronics Letters*, vol. 48, no. 18, pp. 1128–1130, August 2012.

[82] A. Velez, J. Bonache, and F. Martin, "Varactor-loaded complementary split ring resonators (VLCSRR) and their application to tunable metamaterial transmission lines," *IEEE Microwave and Wireless Components Letters*, vol. 18, no. 1, pp. 28–30, Jan. 2008.

[83] J. Choi and C. Seo, "Microstrip square open-loop multiple split-ring resonator for low-phase-noise VCO," *IEEE Transactions on Microwave Theory and Techniques*, vol. 56, no. 12, pp. 3245–3252, Dec. 2008.

[84] A. Tsuchiya and H. Onodera, "On-chip metamaterial transmission-line based on stacked split-ring resonator for millimeter-wave LSIs," in *Asia Pacific Microwave Conference*, Dec. 2009, pp. 1458–1461.

[85] S. Ko, H. Kim, J. Choi, B. Lee, J. Cho, and C. Seo, "24 GHz CMOS voltage controlled oscillator based on the open loop multiple split ring resonator," in *Asia Pacific Microwave Conference*, Dec. 2010, pp. 558–561.

[86] A. Lai, T. Itoh, and C. Caloz, "Composite right/left-handed transmission line metamaterials," *IEEE Microwave Magazine*, vol. 5, no. 3, pp. 34–50, Sept. 2004.

[87] H.-C. Chang, X. Cao, U. Mishra, and R. York, "Phase noise in coupled oscillators: Theory and experiment," *IEEE Transactions on Microwave Theory and Techniques*, vol. 45, no. 5, pp. 604–615, May 1997.

[88] G. L. G. de Mercey, "18GHz–36GHz rotary traveling wave voltage controlled oscillator in a CMOS technology," Ph.D. dissertation, Bundeswehr Universitat, Aug. 2004.

[89] A. Tang, Z. Xu, Q. Gu, Y.-C. Wu, and M. Chang, "A 144 GHz 2.5mW multi-stage regenerative receiver for mm-wave imaging in 65nm CMOS," in *IEEE Radio Frequency Integrated Circuits Symposium*, June 2011, pp. 1–4.

[90] A. Tang and M.-C. Chang, "183GHz 13.5mW/pixel CMOS regenerative receiver for mm-wave imaging applications," in *IEEE International Solid-State Circuits Conference*, Feb. 2011, pp. 296–298.

[91] K. Tang, M. Khanpour, P. Garcia, C. Gamier, and S. Voinigescu, "65-nm CMOS, W-band receivers for imaging applications," in *IEEE Custom Integrated Circuits Conference*, Sept. 2007, pp. 749–752.

[92] L. Gilreath, V. Jain, H.-C. Yao, L. Zheng, and P. Heydari, "A 94-ghz passive imaging receiver using a balanced lna with embedded Dicke switch," in *IEEE Radio Frequency Integrated Circuits Symposium*, May 2010, pp. 79–82.

[93] Y. Shang, H. Fu, H. Yu, and J. Ren, "A -78dBm sensitivity super-regenerative receiver at 96 GHz with quench-controlled metamaterial oscillator in 65nm CMOS," in *IEEE Radio Frequency Integrated Circuits Symposium*, June 2013, pp. 447–450.

[94] J. Bohorquez, A. Chandrakasan, and J. Dawson, "Frequency-domain analysis of super-regenerative amplifiers," *IEEE Transactions on Microwave Theory and Techniques*, vol. 57, no. 12, pp. 2882–2894, Dec. 2009.

[95] Z. Deng and A. Niknejad, "A 4-port-inductor-based VCO coupling method for phase noise reduction," *IEEE Journal of Solid-State Circuits*, vol. 46, no. 8, pp. 1772–1781, Aug. 2011.

[96] T. C. Haba, G. Ablart, T. Camps, and F. Oliviec, "Influence of the electrical parameters on the input impedance of a fractal structure realised on silicon," *Chaos, Solitons & Fractals*, vol. 24, no. 2, pp. 479–490, April 2005.

[97] G. L. L. T. Cisse Haba and G. Ablart, "An analytical expression for the input impedance of a fractal tree obtained by a microelectronical process and experimental measurements of its non-integral dimension," *Chaos, Solitons & Fractals*, vol. 33, no. 2, pp. 364–373, July 2007.

[98] *Star-HSPICE Manual, HSPICE, ch.18.* Fremont, CA, 2001.

[99] (2001, July) Modeling Coilcraft RF Inductors, Document 158. [Online]. Available: http://www.coilcraft.com/.

[100] C.-S. Yen, Z. Fazarinc, and R. Wheeler, "Time-domain skin-effect model for transient analysis of lossy transmission lines," *Proceedings of the IEEE*, vol. 70, no. 7, pp. 750–757, July 1982.

[101] S. Cho, K. R. Kim, B.-G. Park, and I. M. Kang, "Non-quasi-static modeling of silicon nanowire metal–oxide–semiconductor field-effect transistor and its model verification up to 1THz," *Japanese Journal of Applied Physics*, vol. 49, no. 11, p. 110206, Nov. 2010.

[102] J. Bechhoefer, "Kramers–Kronig, Bode, and the meaning of zero," *American Journal of Physics*, vol. 79, no. 10, pp. 1053–1059, 2011.

[103] S. Westerlund and L. Ekstam, "Capacitor theory," *IEEE Transactions on Dielectrics and Electrical Insulation*, vol. 1, no. 5, pp. 826–839, Oct. 1994.

[104] I. Schäfer and K. Krüger, "Modelling of lossy coils using fractional derivatives," *Journal of Physics D: Applied Physics*, vol. 41, p. 045001, Jan. 2008.

[105] Y. Shang, W. Fei, and H. Yu, "A fractional-order RLGC model for terahertz transmission line," in *IEEE MTT-S International Microwave Symposium*, June 2013, pp. 1–3.

[106] J. Lanoe, S. Le Maguer, and M. Ney, "A fractional derivative operator for surface impedance TLM modeling," *IEEE Microwave and Wireless Components Letters*, vol. 17, no. 9, pp. 625–627, Sept. 2007.

[107] Z. Yanzhu and X. Dingyu, "Modeling and simulating transmission lines using fractional calculus," in *International Conference on Wireless Communications, Networking and Mobile Computing*, Sept. 2007, pp. 3115–3118.

[108] A. Shamim, A. Radwan, and K. Salama, "Fractional Smith chart theory," *IEEE Microwave and Wireless Components Letters*, vol. 21, no. 3, pp. 117–119, March 2011.

[109] A. Radwan, A. Shamim, and K. Salama, "Theory of fractional order elements based impedance matching networks," *IEEE Microwave and Wireless Components Letters*, vol. 21, no. 3, pp. 120–122, March 2011.

[110] A. Radwan and K. Salama, "Passive and active elements using fractional $L_{\beta}C_{\alpha}$ circuit," *IEEE Transactions on Circuits and Systems I*, vol. 58, no. 10, pp. 2388–2397, Oct 2011.

[111] A. Elwakil, "Fractional-order circuits and systems: An emerging interdisciplinary research area," *IEEE Circuits and Systems Magazine*, vol. 10, no. 4, pp. 40–50, Fourth quarter 2010.

[112] I. Sch*ä*fer and K. Kr*ü*ger, "Modelling of lossy coils using fractional derivatives," *Journal of Physics D: Applied Physics*, vol. 41, no. 4, p. 045001, 2008.

[113] J. C. Wang, "Realizations of generalized warburg impedance with RC ladder networks and transmission lines," *Journal of The Electrochemical Society*, vol. 134, no. 8, pp. 1915–1920, Aug. 1987.

[114] N. Engheia, "On the role of fractional calculus in electromagnetic theory," *IEEE Antennas and Propagation Magazine*, vol. 39, no. 4, pp. 35–46, Aug. 1997.

[115] S. W. Wheatcraft and M. M. Meerschaert, "Fractional conservation of mass," *Advances in Water Resources*, vol. 31, no. 10, pp. 1377–1381, 2008.

[116] B. Nolte, S. Kempfle, and I. Schfer, "Does a real material behave fractionally? Applications of fractional differential operators to the damped structure borne sound in viscoelastic solids," *Journal of Computational Acoustics*, vol. 11, no. 03, pp. 451–489, 2003.

[117] N. Laskin, "Fractional quantum mechanics and Lévy path integrals," *Physics Letters A*, vol. 268, no. 4, pp. 298–305, 2000.

[118] M. A. E. Herzallah and D. Baleanu, "Fractional-order Euler–Lagrange Equations and formulation of hamiltonian equations," *Nonlinear Dynamics*, vol. 58, no. 1-2, pp. 385–391, Oct. 2009.

[119] I. Petráš, *Fractional-Order Nonlinear Systems, Modeling, Analysis and Simulation.* Springer, 2011.

[120] J. Zhang, J. Drewniak, D. Pommerenke, M. Koledintseva, R. DuBroff, W. Cheng, Z. Yang, Q. Chen, and A. Orlandi, "Causal RLGC(f) models for transmission lines from measured S-parameters," *IEEE Transactions on Electromagnetic Compatibility*, vol. 52, no. 1, pp. 189–198, Feb. 2010.

[121] M. Degerstrom, B. Gilbert, and E. Daniel, "Accurate resistance, inductance, capacitance, and conductance (RLCG) from uniform transmission line measurements," in *IEEE Electrical Performance of Electronic Packaging*, Oct. 2008, pp. 77–80.

[122] B. Gustavsen and A. Semlyen, "Rational approximation of frequency domain responses by vector fitting," *IEEE Transactions on Power Delivery*, vol. 14, no. 3, pp. 1052–1061, July 1999.

[123] M. R. Wohlers, *Lumped and Distributed Passive Networks.* New York: Academic, 1969.

[124] V. Lucarini, Y. Ino, K.-E. Peiponen, and M. Kuwata-Gonokami, "Detection and correction of the misplacement error in terahertz spectroscopy by application of singly subtractive Kramers–Kronig relations," *Phys. Rev. B*, vol. 72, p. 125107, Sep. 2005.

[125] P. Triverio and S. Grivet-Talocia, "Robust causality characterization via generalized dispersion relations," *IEEE Transactions on Advanced Packaging*, vol. 31, no. 3, pp. 579–593, Aug. 2008.

[126] A. V. Oppenheim and R. W. Schafer, *Discrete-Time Signal Processing*, 3rd ed. Prentice-Hall, 2009.

[127] H. Bode, *Network Analysis and Feedback Amplifier Design.* New York: Van Nostrand, 1945.

[128] N. Nahman, "A Discussion on the Transient Analysis of Coaxial Cables Considering High-Frequency Losses," *IRE Transactions on Circuit Theory*, vol. 9, no. 2, pp. 144–152, June 1962.

[129] B. Heydari, "CMOS circuits and devices beyond 100 GHz," PHD Thesis, UC-Berkeley, 2008.

[130] W. Fei, H. Yu, Y. Shang, and K. S. Yeo, "A 2-d distributed power combining by metamaterial-based zero phase shifter for 60-ghz power amplifier in 65-nm CMOS," *IEEE Transactions on Microwave Theory and Techniques*, vol. 61, no. 1, pp. 505–516, Jan 2013.

[131] T.-Y. Lu, C.-Y. Yu, W.-Z. Chen, and C.-Y. Wu, "Wide tuning range 60 ghz VCO and 40 ghz DCO using single variable inductor," *IEEE Transactions on Circuits and Systems I: Regular Papers*, vol. 60, no. 2, pp. 257–267, Feb 2013.

[132] J. Yin and H. Luong, "A 57.5-to-90.1ghz magnetically-tuned multi-mode CMOS VCO," in *IEEE Custom Integrated Circuits Conference*, Sept 2012, pp. 1–4.

[133] J. Gonzalez, F. Badets, B. Martineau, and D. Belot, "A 56-ghz lc-tank vco with 17% tuning range in 65-nm bulk CMOS for wireless HDMI," *IEEE Transactions on Microwave Theory and Techniques*, vol. 58, no. 5, pp. 1359–1366, May 2010.

[134] D. Kim, J. Kim, J.-O. Plouchart, C. Cho, W. Li, D. Lim, R. Trzcinski, M. Kumar, C. Norris, and D. Ahlgren, "A 70ghz manufacturable complementary LC-VCO with 6.14ghz tuning range in 65nm SOI CMOS," in *IEEE International Solid-State Circuits Conference*, Feb 2007, pp. 540–620.

[135] K. Ishibashi, M. Motoyoshi, N. Kobayashi, and M. Fujishima, "76ghz CMOS voltage-controlled oscillator with 7% frequency tuning range," in *IEEE Symposium on VLSI Circuits*, June 2007, pp. 176–177.

[136] V. Trivedi, K.-H. To, and W. Huang, "A 77ghz CMOS vco with 11.3ghz tuning range, 6dbm output power, and competitive phase noise in 65nm bulk CMOS," in *IEEE Radio Frequency Integrated Circuits Symposium*, June 2011, pp. 1–4.

[137] J. Borremans, M. Dehan, K. Scheir, M. Kuijk, and P. Wambacq, "VCO design for 60 ghz applications using differential shielded inductors in 0.13um CMOS," in *IEEE Radio Frequency Integrated Circuits Symposium*, June 2008, pp. 135–138.

[138] A. Mazzanti, E. Monaco, M. Pozzoni, and F. Svelto, "A 13.1115ghz frequency generator based on an injection-locked frequency doubler in 65nm CMOS," in *IEEE International Solid-State Circuits Conference*, Feb 2010, pp. 422–423.

[139] N. Zhang and K. O, "94 ghz voltage controlled oscillator with 5.8% tuning range in bulk CMOS," *Microwave and Wireless Components Letters, IEEE*, vol. 18, no. 8, pp. 548–550, Aug 2008.

[140] X. Yi, C. C. Boon, J. F. Lin, and W. M. Lim, "A 100 ghz transformer-based varactor-less vco with 11.2% tuning range in 65nm CMOS technology," in *IEEE European Solid-State Circuits Conference*, Sept 2012, pp. 293–296.

[141] F. Ben Abdeljelil, W. Tatinian, L. Carpineto, and G. Jacquemod, "Design of a CMOS 12 ghz rotary travelling wave oscillator with switched capacitor tuning," in *IEEE Radio Frequency Integrated Circuits Symposium*, June 2009, pp. 579–582.

[142] N. Nouri and J. Buckwalter, "A 45-ghz rotary-wave voltage-controlled oscillator," *IEEE Transactions on Microwave Theory and Techniques*, vol. 59, no. 2, pp. 383–392, Feb 2011.

[143] A. Moroni, R. Genesi, and D. Manstretta, "A distributed 'hybrid' wave oscillator array for millimeter-wave phased-arrays," in *IEEE Custom Integrated Circuits Conference*, Sept. 2012, pp. 1–4.

[144] G. Li and E. Afshari, "A low-phase-noise multi-phase oscillator based on left-handed lc-ring," *IEEE Journal of Solid-State Circuits*, vol. 45, no. 9, pp. 1822–1833, Sept 2010.

[145] M. Demirkan, S. Bruss, and R. Spencer, "Design of wide tuning-range CMOS VCOs using switched coupled-inductors," *IEEE Journal of Solid-State Circuits*, vol. 43, no. 5, pp. 1156–1163, May 2008.

[146] E. Mammei, E. Monaco, A. Mazzanti, and F. Svelto, "A 33.6-to-46.2ghz 32nm CMOS VCO with 177.5dbc/hz minimum noise fom using inductor splitting for tuning extension," in *IEEE International Solid-State Circuits Conference*, Feb 2013, pp. 350–351.

[147] Y. Takigawa, H. Ohta, Q. Liu, S. Kurachi, N. Itoh, and T. Yoshimasu, "A 92.6 tuning range vco utilizing simultaneously controlling of transformers and mos varactors in 0.13um CMOS technology," in *IEEE Radio Frequency Integrated Circuits Symposium*, June 2009, pp. 83–86.

[148] A. Hajimiri and T. Lee, "A general theory of phase noise in electrical oscillators," *IEEE Journal of Solid-State Circuits*, vol. 33, no. 2, pp. 179–194, Feb 1998.

[149] D. Ham and A. Hajimiri, "Virtual damping and Einstein relation in oscillators," *IEEE Journal of Solid-State Circuits*, vol. 38, no. 3, pp. 407–418, Mar 2003.

[150] R. Kubo, "A stochastic theory of line shape," *Stochastic Processes in Chemical Physics*, vol. 15, p. 105, 1969.

[151] W. Fei, H. Yu, H. Fu, J. Ren, and K. S. Yeo, "Design and analysis of wide frequency-tuning-range CMOS 60 ghz vco by switching inductor loaded

transformer," *IEEE Transactions on Circuits and Systems I*, vol. 61, no. 3, pp. 699–711, March 2014.

[152] D. Ham and A. Hajimiri, "Concepts and methods in optimization of integrated LC VCOs," *IEEE Journal of Solid-State Circuits*, vol. 36, no. 6, pp. 896–909, Jun 2001.

[153] W. Badalawa, S. Lim, and M. Fujishima, "115GHz CMOS VCO with 4.4% tuning range," in *Microwave Integrated Circuits Conference*, Sept. 2009, pp. 128–131.

[154] D. Kim, J. Kim, C. Cho, J.-O. Plouchart, M. Kumar, W.-H. Lee, and K. Rim, "An array of 4 complementary LC-VCOs with 51.4% W-Band Coverage in 32nm SOI CMOS," in *IEEE International Solid-State Circuits Conference*, Feb. 2009, pp. 278–279.

[155] W. Volkaerts, M. Steyaert, and P. Reynaert, "118GHz fundamental VCO with 7.8% tuning range in 65nm CMOS," in *IEEE Radio Frequency Integrated Circuits Symposium*, June 2011, pp. 1–4.

[156] M. Jahn, K. Aufinger, T. Meister, and A. Stelzer, "125 to 181 GHz fundamental-wave VCO chips in SiGe technology," in *IEEE Radio Frequency Integrated Circuits Symposium*, June 2012, pp. 87–90.

[157] F. Golcuk, O. Gurbuz, and G. Rebeiz, "A 0.39–0.44 THz 2 × 4 amplifier-quadrupler array with peak EIRP of 3–4 dBm," *IEEE Transactions on Microwave Theory and Techniques*, vol. 61, no. 12, pp. 4483–4491, Dec. 2013.

[158] N. Deferm and P. Reynaert, "Design, implementation and measurement of a 120GHz 10Gb/s phase-modulating transmitter in 65nm LP CMOS," *Analog Integrated Circuits and Signal Processing*, vol. 75, no. 1, pp. 1–19, 2013.

[159] W. Shin, B.-H. Ku, O. Inac, Y.-C. Ou, and G. Rebeiz, "A 108-114 GHz 4×4 wafer-scale phased array transmitter with high-efficiency on-chip antennas," *IEEE Journal of Solid-State Circuits*, vol. 48, no. 9, pp. 2041–2055, Sept. 2013.

[160] B. Khamaisi and E. Socher, "A 159-169 GHz frequency source with 1.26 mW peak output power in 65nm CMOS," in *European Microwave Integrated Circuits Conference*, Oct. 2013, pp. 536–539.

[161] M. Adnan and E. Afshari, "A 105-GHz VCO with 9.5% tuning range and 2.8-mW peak output power in a 65-nm bulk CMOS process," *IEEE Transactions on Microwave Theory and Techniques*, vol. 62, no. 4, pp. 753–762, April 2014.

[162] C. Cao and K. O, "Millimeter-wave voltage-controlled oscillators in 0.13um CMOS technology," *IEEE Journal of Solid-State Circuits*, vol. 41, no. 6, pp. 1297–1304, June 2006.

[163] W. Fei, H. Yu, W. M. Lim, and J. Ren, "A 53-to-73GHz power amplifier with 74.5mW/mm^2 output power density by 2D differential power combining in 65nm CMOS," in *IEEE Radio Frequency Integrated Circuits Symposium*, June 2013, pp. 271–274.

[164] A. Siligaris, O. Richard, B. Martineau, C. Mounet, F. Chaix, R. Ferragut, C. Dehos, J. Lanteri, L. Dussopt, S. Yamamoto, R. Pilard, P. Busson, A. Cathelin, D. Belot, and P. Vincent, "A 65-nm CMOS fully integrated transceiver module for 60-GHz wireless HD applications," *IEEE Journal of Solid-State Circuits*, vol. 46, no. 12, pp. 3005–3017, Dec. 2011.

[165] M. Adnan and E. Afshari, "A 105GHz VCO with 9.5% tuning range and 2.8mW peak output power using coupled Colpitts oscillators in 65nm bulk CMOS," in *IEEE Radio Frequency Integrated Circuits Symposium*, June 2013, pp. 239–242.

[166] E. Shamonina, V. A. Kalinin, K. H. Ringhofer, and L. Solymar, "Magnetoinductive waves in one, two, and three dimensions," *Journal of Applied Physics*, vol. 92, no. 10, pp. 6252–6261, 2002.

[167] M. J. Freire, R. Marqués, F. Medina, M. A. G. Laso, and F. Martén, "Planar magnetoinductive wave transducers: Theory and applications," *Applied Physics Letters*, vol. 85, no. 19, pp. 4439–4441, 2004.

[168] I. V. Shadrivov, A. N. Reznik, and Y. S. Kivshar, "Magnetoinductive waves in arrays of split-ring resonators," *Physica B: Condensed Matter*, vol. 394, no. 2, pp. 180 – 183, 2007.

[169] X. Shen, T. J. Cui, D. Martin-Cano, and F. J. Garcia-Vidal, "Conformal surface plasmons propagating on ultrathin and flexible films," *Proceedings of the National Academy of Sciences*, vol. 110, no. 1, pp. 40–45, 2013.

[170] S. Ma, W. Fei, H. Yu, and J. Ren, "A 75.7GHz to 102GHz rotary-traveling-wave VCO by tunable composite right /left hand T-line," in *IEEE Custom Integrated Circuits Conference*, Sept. 2013, pp. 1–4.

[171] E. Jones, "Coupled-strip-transmission-line filters and directional couplers," *IRE Transactions on Microwave Theory and Techniques*, vol. 4, no. 2, pp. 75–81, April 1956.

[172] R. Ludwig and P. Bretchko, *RF Circuit Design: Theory and Applications.* Prentice-Hall, 2000.

[173] P. Pieters, S. Brebels, E. Beyne, and R. Mertens, "Generalized analysis of coupled lines in multilayer microwave MCM-D technology-application: Integrated coplanar Lange couplers," *IEEE Transactions on Microwave Theory and Techniques*, vol. 47, no. 9, pp. 1863–1872, Sept. 1999.

[174] C.-Y. Yu, W.-Z. Chen, P. Chung-Yu Wu, and T.-Y. Lu, "A 60-GHz, 14% tuning range, multi-band VCO with a single variable inductor," in *IEEE Asian Solid-State Circuits Conference*, Nov. 2008, pp. 129–132.

[175] K.-F. Fuh, "Broadband continuous extraction of complex propagation constants in methods using two-line measurements," *IEEE Microwave and Wireless Components Letters*, vol. 23, no. 12, pp. 671–673, Dec. 2013.

[176] Y. Tousi, O. Momeni, and E. Afshari, "A 283-to-296GHz VCO with 0.76mW peak output power in 65nm CMOS," in *IEEE International Solid-State Circuits Conference*, Feb. 2012, pp. 258–260.

[177] A. Tang and M.-C. Chang, "A 294 GHz 0.47mW caterpillar amplifier based transmitter in 65nm CMOS for THz data-links," in *IEEE Topical Meeting on Silicon Monolithic Integrated Circuits in RF Systems*, Jan. 2013, pp. 27–29.

[178] J. Grzyb, Y. Zhao, and U. Pfeiffer, "A 288-GHz lens-integrated balanced triple-push source in a 65-nm CMOS technology," *IEEE Journal of Solid-State Circuits*, vol. 48, no. 7, pp. 1751–1761, July 2013.

[179] M. Adnan and E. Afshari, "A 247-to-263.5GHz VCO with 2.6mW peak output power and 1.14% DC-to-RF efficiency in 65nm bulk CMOS," in *IEEE International Solid-State Circuits Conference*, Feb. 2014, pp. 262–263.

[180] B. Kim, D. Helman, and P. Gray, "A 30-mhz hybrid analog/digital clock recovery circuit in 2- mu;m CMOS," *IEEE Journal of Solid-State Circuits*, vol. 25, no. 6, pp. 1385–1394, Dec 1990.

[181] S. Pellerano, S. Levantino, C. Samori, and A. Lacaita, "A 13.5-mw 5-ghz frequency synthesizer with dynamic-logic frequency divider," *IEEE Journal of Solid-State Circuits*, vol. 39, no. 2, pp. 378–383, Feb 2004.

[182] J. Lee and B. Razavi, "A 40-ghz frequency divider in 0.18- mu;m CMOS technology," *IEEE Journal of Solid-State Circuits*, vol. 39, no. 4, pp. 594–601, April 2004.

[183] M. Tabesh, J. Chen, C. Marcu, L. Kong, S. Kang, A. Niknejad, and E. Alon, "A 65 nm CMOS 4-element sub-34 mw/element 60 ghz phased-array transceiver," *IEEE Journal of Solid-State Circuits*, vol. 46, no. 12, pp. 3018–3032, Dec 2011.

[184] B. Razavi, "A study of injection locking and pulling in oscillators," *IEEE Journal of Solid-State Circuits*, vol. 39, no. 9, pp. 1415–1424, Sept 2004.

[185] M. Tiebout, "A CMOS direct injection-locked oscillator topology as high-frequency low-power frequency divider," *IEEE Journal of Solid-State Circuits*, vol. 39, no. 7, pp. 1170–1174, July 2004.

[186] C.-Y. Yu, W.-Z. Chen, P. Chung-Yu Wu, and T.-Y. Lu, "A 60-ghz, 14% tuning range, multi-band vco with a single variable inductor," in *IEEE Asian Solid-State Circuits Conference*, Nov 2008, pp. 129–132.

[187] N. Saito, T. Tsukizawa, N. Shirakata, T. Morita, K. Tanaka, J. Sato, Y. Morishita, M. Kanemaru, R. Kitamura, T. Shima, T. Nakatani, K. Miyanaga, T. Urushihara, H. Yoshikawa, T. Sakamoto, H. Motozuka, Y. Shirakawa, N. Yosoku, A. Yamamoto, R. Shiozaki, and K. Takinami, "A fully integrated 60-GHz CMOS transceiver chipset based on WiGig/IEEE 802.11ad with built-in self-calibration for mobile usage," *IEEE Journal of Solid-State Circuits*, vol. 48, no. 12, pp. 3146–3159, Dec 2013.

[188] H. Hoshino, R. Tachibana, T. Mitomo, N. Ono, Y. Yoshihara, and R. Fujimoto, "A 60-ghz phase-locked loop with inductor-less prescaler in 90-nm CMOS," in *IEEE European Solid State Circuits Conference*, Sept 2007, pp. 472–475.

[189] C. Lee and S.-I. Liu, "A 58-to-60.4ghz frequency synthesizer in 90nm CMOS," in *IEEE International Solid-State Circuits Conference*, Feb 2007, pp. 196–596.

[190] T. Mitomo, N. Ono, H. Hoshino, Y. Yoshihara, O. Watanabe, and I. Seto, "A 77 ghz 90 nm CMOS transceiver for FMCW radar applications," *IEEE Journal of Solid-State Circuits*, vol. 45, no. 4, pp. 928–937, April 2010.

[191] J. Lee, Y.-A. Li, M.-H. Hung, and S.-J. Huang, "A fully-integrated 77-ghz FMCW radar transceiver in 65-nm CMOS technology," *IEEE Journal of Solid-State Circuits*, vol. 45, no. 12, pp. 2746–2756, Dec 2010.

[192] B. Martineau, V. Knopik, A. Siligaris, F. Gianesello, and D. Belot, "A 53-to-68ghz 18dbm power amplifier with an 8-way combiner in standard 65nm CMOS," in *IEEE International Solid-State Circuits Conference*, Feb 2010, pp. 428–429.

[193] M. Bohsali and A. Niknejad, "Current combining 60ghz CMOS power amplifiers," in *IEEE Radio Frequency Integrated Circuits Symposium*, June 2009, pp. 31–34.

[194] C. Law and A.-V. Pham, "A high-gain 60ghz power amplifier with 20dbm output power in 90nm CMOS," in *IEEE International Solid-State Circuits Conference*, Feb 2010, pp. 426–427.

[195] J. Chen and A. Niknejad, "A compact 1v 18.6dbm 60ghz power amplifier in 65nm CMOS," in *IEEE International Solid-State Circuits Conference*, Feb 2011, pp. 432–433.

[196] Y. He, L. Li, and P. Reynaert, "60ghz power amplifier with distributed active transformer and local feedback," in *IEEE European Solid-State Circuits Conference*, Sept 2010, pp. 314–317.

[197] Q. Gu, Z. Xu, and M.-C. Chang, "Two-way current-combining w-band power amplifier in 65-nm CMOS," *IEEE Transactions on Microwave Theory and Techniques*, vol. 60, no. 5, pp. 1365–1374, May 2012.

[198] Y.-N. Jen, J.-H. Tsai, T.-W. Huang, and H. Wang, "Design and analysis of a 55-71ghz compact and broadband distributed active transformer power amplifier in 90-nm CMOS process," *IEEE Transactions on Microwave Theory and Techniques*, vol. 57, no. 7, pp. 1637–1646, July 2009.

[199] E. Afshari, H. Bhat, X. Li, and A. Hajimiri, "Electrical funnel: A broadband signal combining method," in *IEEE International Solid-State Circuits Conference*, Feb 2006, pp. 751–760.

[200] F. Ng-Molina, T. Martín-Guerrero, and C. Camacho-Peñalosa, "Power and gain considerations in distributed amplifiers based on composite right/left-handed transmission lines," *IET Microwaves, Antennas Propagation*, vol. 4, no. 8, pp. 1000–1006, Aug 2010.

[201] C.-T. Wu, Y. Dong, J. Sun, and T. Itoh, "Ring-resonator-inspired power recycling scheme for gain-enhanced distributed amplifier-based CRLH-transmission line leaky wave antennas," *IEEE Transactions on Microwave Theory and Techniques*, vol. 60, no. 4, pp. 1027–1037, April 2012.

[202] W. Fei, H. Yu, Y. Shang, D. Cai, and J. Ren, "A 96-GHz oscillator by high-Q differential transmission line loaded with complementary split ring resonator in 65nm CMOS," *IEEE Transactions on Circuits and Systems II*, vol. 60, no. 3, pp. 127–131, March 2013.

[203] K. Eccleston, "Multiband power amplifier for multiband wireless applications," in *International Conference on Microwave and Millimeter Wave Technology*, Aug 2002, pp. 1142–1145.

[204] D. Zhao, S. Kulkarni, and P. Reynaert, "A 60 ghz dual-mode power amplifier with 17.4 dbm output power and 29.3% pae in 40-nm CMOS," in *IEEE European Solid-State Circuits Conference*, Sept 2012, pp. 337–340.

[205] W. Chan and J. Long, "A 58–65 ghz neutralized CMOS power amplifier with pae above 10vol. 45, no. 3, pp. 554–564, March 2010.

[206] W. Chan, J. Long, M. Spirito, and J. Pekarik, "A 60ghz-band 1v 11.5dbm power amplifier with 11% pae in 65nm CMOS," in *IEEE International Solid-State Circuits Conference*, Feb 2009, pp. 380–381.

[207] D. Sandstrom, B. Martineau, M. Varonen, M. Karkkainen, A. Cathelin, and K. Halonen, "94ghz power-combining power amplifier with +13dbm saturated output power in 65nm CMOS," in *IEEE Radio Frequency Integrated Circuits Symposium*, June 2011, pp. 1–4.

[208] J. Essing, R. Mahmoudi, Y. Pei, and A. van Roermund, "A fully integrated 60ghz distributed transformer power amplifier in bulky CMOS 45nm," in *IEEE Radio Frequency Integrated Circuits Symposium*, June 2011, pp. 1–4.

[209] M. Abbasi, T. Kjellberg, A. de Graauw, E. van der Heijden, R. Roovers, and H. Zirath, "A broadband differential cascode power amplifier in 45 nm CMOS for high-speed 60 ghz system-on-chip," in *IEEE Radio Frequency Integrated Circuits Symposium*, May 2010, pp. 533–536.

[210] T. Kjellberg, M. Abbasi, M. Ferndahl, A. de Graauw, E. v.d.Heijden, and H. Zirath, "A compact cascode power amplifier in 45-nm CMOS for 60-ghz wireless systems," in *IEEE Compound Semiconductor Integrated Circuit Symposium*, Oct 2009, pp. 1–4.

[211] D. Chowdhury, P. Reynaert, and A. Niknejad, "A 60ghz 1v + 12.3dbm transformer-coupled wideband pa in 90nm CMOS," in *IEEE International Solid-State Circuits Conference*, Feb 2008, pp. 560–635.

[212] K. Raczkowski, S. Thijs, W. De Raedt, B. Nauwelaers, and P. Wambacq, "50-to-67ghz ESD-protected power amplifiers in digital 45nm LP CMOS," in *IEEE International Solid-State Circuits Conference*, Feb 2009, pp. 382–383,383a.

[213] J.-C. Liu, A. Tang, N.-Y. Wang, Q. Gu, R. Berenguer, H.-H. Hsieh, P.-Y. Wu, C. Jou, and M.-C. Chang, "A v-band self-healing power amplifier with adaptive feedback bias control in 65 nm CMOS," in *IEEE Radio Frequency Integrated Circuits Symposium*, June 2011, pp. 1–4.

[214] J.-F. Yeh, J.-H. Tsai, and T.-W. Huang, "A 60-ghz power amplifier design using dual-radial symmetric architecture in 90-nm low-power CMOS," *IEEE Transactions on Microwave Theory and Techniques*, vol. 61, no. 3, pp. 1280–1290, March 2013.

[215] D. Zhao, S. Kulkarni, and P. Reynaert, "A 60-ghz outphasing transmitter in 40-nm CMOS," *IEEE Journal of Solid-State Circuits*, vol. 47, no. 12, pp. 3172–3183, Dec 2012.

[216] K. Khalaf, V. Vidojkovic, K. Vaesen, B. Parvais, J. Long, and P. Wambacq, "60ghz transmitter front-end in 40nm LP-CMOS with

improved back-off efficiency," in *IEEE Topical Meeting on Silicon Monolithic Integrated Circuits in RF Systems*, Jan 2013, pp. 6–8.

[217] A. Scuderi, C. Santagati, M. Vaiana, F. Pidala, and M. Paparo, "Balanced sige pa module for multi-band and multi-mode cellular-phone applications," in *IEEE International Solid-State Circuits Conference*, Feb 2008, pp. 572–637.

[218] G. Liu, P. Haldi, T.-J. K. Liu, and A. Niknejad, "Fully integrated CMOS power amplifier with efficiency enhancement at power back-off," *IEEE Journal of Solid-State Circuits*, vol. 43, no. 3, pp. 600–609, March 2008.

[219] D. Chowdhury, C. Hull, O. Degani, Y. Wang, and A. Niknejad, "A fully integrated dual-mode highly linear 2.4 ghz CMOS power amplifier for 4g WIMAX applications," *IEEE Journal of Solid-State Circuits*, vol. 44, no. 12, pp. 3393–3402, Dec 2009.

[220] G. Hau and M. Singh, "Multi-mode WCDMA power amplifier module with improved low-power efficiency using stage-bypass," in *IEEE Radio Frequency Integrated Circuits Symposium*, May 2010, pp. 163–166.

[221] J. Kim, Y. Yoon, H. Kim, K. H. An, W. Kim, H.-W. Kim, C.-H. Lee, and K. Kornegay, "A linear multi-mode CMOS power amplifier with discrete resizing and concurrent power combining structure," *IEEE Journal of Solid-State Circuits*, vol. 46, no. 5, pp. 1034–1048, May 2011.

[222] B. Koo, T. Joo, Y. Na, and S. Hong, "A fully integrated dual-mode CMOS power amplifier for WCDMA applications," in *IEEE International Solid-State Circuits Conference*, Feb 2012, pp. 82–84.

[223] H. Jeon, Y. Park, Y.-Y. Huang, J. Kim, K.-S. Lee, C.-H. Lee, and J. Kenney, "A triple-mode balanced linear CMOS power amplifier using a switched-quadrature coupler," *IEEE Journal of Solid-State Circuits*, vol. 47, no. 9, pp. 2019–2032, Sept 2012.

[224] W. Fei, H. Yu, K. S. Yeo, X. Liu, and W. M. Lim, "A 44-to-60ghz, 9.7dbm p1db, 7.1% pae power amplifier with 2d distributed power combining by metamaterial-based zero-phase-shifter in 65nm CMOS," in *IEEE MTT-S International Microwave Symposium*, June 2012, pp. 1–3.

[225] W. Fei, H. Yu, W. M. Lim, and J. Ren, "A 53-to-73ghz power amplifier with 74.5mw/mm2 output power density by 2d differential power combining in 65nm CMOS," in *IEEE Radio Frequency Integrated Circuits Symposium*, June 2013, pp. 271–274.

[226] F. Shirinfar, M. Nariman, T. Sowlati, M. Rofougaran, R. Rofougaran, and S. Pamarti, "A fully integrated 22.6dbm mm-wave pa in 40nm CMOS," in *IEEE Radio Frequency Integrated Circuits Symposium*, June 2013, pp. 279–282.

[227] T. Quemerais, L. Moquillon, J. Fournier, P. Benech, and V. Huard, "Design-in-reliable millimeter-wave power amplifiers in a 65-nm CMOS process," *IEEE Transactions on Microwave Theory and Techniques*, vol. 60, no. 4, pp. 1079–1085, April 2012.

[228] S. Aloui, Y. Luque, N. Demirel, B. Leite, R. Plana, D. Belot, and E. Kerherve, "Optimized power combining technique to design a 20db gain, 13.5dbm ocp1 60ghz power amplifier using 65nm CMOS technology," in *IEEE Radio Frequency Integrated Circuits Symposium*, June 2012, pp. 53–56.

[229] I. A. Ibraheem, N. Krumbholz, D. Mittleman, and M. Koch, "Low-dispersive dielectric mirrors for future wireless terahertz communication systems," *IEEE Microwave and Wireless Components Letters*, vol. 18, no. 1, pp. 67–69, Jan. 2008.

[230] F. Schuster, H. Videlier, A. Dupret, D. Coquillat, M. Sakowicz, J. Rostaing, M. Tchagaspanian, B. Giffard, and W. Knap, "A broadband THz imager in a low-cost CMOS technology," in *IEEE International Solid-State Circuits Conference*, Feb. 2011, pp. 42–43.

[231] H. Tang, G. Yang, J. Chen, W. Hong, and K. Wu, "Millimeter-wave and terahertz transmission loss of CMOS process-based substrate integrated waveguide," in *IEEE MTT-S International Microwave Symposium*, June 2012, pp. 1–3.

[232] W. Fei, H. Yu, Y. Shang, and K. S. Yeo, "A 2D distributed power combining by metamaterial-based zero-phase-shifter for 60GHz power amplifier in 65nm CMOS," *IEEE Transactions on Microwave Theory and Techniques*, vol. 61, no. 1, pp. 505–516, Jan. 2013.

[233] G. Q. Luo, Z. F. Hu, Y. Liang, L. Y. Yu, and L. L. Sun, "Development of low profile cavity backed crossed slot antennas for planar integration," *IEEE Transactions on Antennas and Propagation*, vol. 57, no. 10, pp. 2972 –2979, Oct. 2009.

[234] S. Hu, Y.-Z. Xiong, B. Zhang, L. Wang, T.-G. Lim, M. Je, and M. Madihian, "A SiGe BiCMOS transmitter/receiver chipset with on-chip SIW antennas for terahertz applications," *IEEE Journal of Solid-State Circuits*, vol. 47, no. 11, pp. 2654–2664, 2012.

[235] H. Tang, G. Yang, J. Chen, W. Hong, and K. Wu, "Millimeter-wave and terahertz transmission loss of CMOS process-based substrate integrated waveguide," in *IEEE MTT-S International Microwave Symposium*, June 2012, pp. 1–3.

[236] F. Xu and K. Wu, "Guided-wave and leakage characteristics of substrate integrated waveguide," *IEEE Transactions on Microwave Theory and Techniques*, vol. 53, no. 1, pp. 66–73, 2005.

[237] J. George, M. Deepukumar, C. K. Aanandan, P. Mohanan, and K. Nair, "New compact microstrip antenna," *Electronics Letters*, vol. 32, no. 6, pp. 508–509, 1996.

[238] D. Kim, J. Kim, J.-O. Plouchart, C. Cho, D. Lim, W. Li, and R. Trzcinski, "A 75GHz PLL front-end integration in 65nm SOI CMOS technology," in *IEEE Symposium on VLSI Circuits*, June 2007, pp. 174–175.

[239] G. Liu, R. Berenguer, and Y. Xu, "A MM-wave configurable VCO using MCPW-based tunable inductor in 65-nm CMOS," *IEEE Transactions on Circuits and Systems II*, vol. 58, no. 12, pp. 842–846, Dec. 2011.

[240] C.-J. Lee, K. Leong, and T. Itoh, "Composite right/left-handed transmission line based compact resonant antennas for RF module integration," *IEEE Transactions on Antennas and Propagation*, vol. 54, no. 8, pp. 2283–2291, Aug. 2006.

[241] R. Liu, A. Degiron, J. J. Mock, and D. R. Smith, "Negative index material composed of electric and magnetic resonators," *Applied Physics Letters*, vol. 90, no. 26, pp. 263 504 1–3, June 2007.

[242] D. R. Smith, S. Schultz, P. Markoš, and C. M. Soukoulis, "Determination of effective permittivity and permeability of metamaterials from reflection and transmission coefficients," *Phys. Rev. B*, vol. 65, p. 195104, April 2002.

[243] X. Chen, T. M. Grzegorczyk, B.-I. Wu, J. Pacheco, and J. A. Kong, "Robust method to retrieve the constitutive effective parameters of metamaterials," *Phys. Rev. E*, vol. 70, p. 016608, July 2004.

[244] K.-H. Tsai and S.-I. Liu, "A 104-GHz phase-locked loop using a VCO at second pole frequency," *IEEE Transactions on VLSI Systems*, vol. 20, no. 1, pp. 80–88, Jan. 2012.

[245] A. M. Niknejad and H. Hashemi, *mm-Wave Silicon Technology 60 GHz and Beyond*, A. M. Niknejad and H. Hashemi, Eds. Springer, 2008.

[246] D. Kim, J. Kim, J.-O. Plouchart, C. Cho, W. Li, D. Lim, R. Trzcinski, M. Kumar, C. Norris, and D. Ahlgren, "A 70GHz manufacturable complementary LC-VCO with 6.14GHz tuning range in 65nm SOI CMOS," in *IEEE International Solid-State Circuits Conference*, Feb. 2007, pp. 540–620.

[247] O. Momeni and E. Afshari, "High power terahertz and millimeter-wave oscillator design: A systematic approach," *IEEE Journal of Solid-State Circuits*, vol. 46, no. 3, pp. 583–597, March 2011.

[248] B. Razavi, "A millimeter-wave circuit technique," *IEEE Journal of Solid-State Circuits*, vol. 43, no. 9, pp. 2090–2098, Sept. 2008.

[249] L. Franca-Neto, R. Bishop, and B. Bloechel, "64 GHz and 100 GHz VCOs in 90 nm CMOS using optimum pumping method," in *IEEE International Solid-State Circuits Conference*, Feb. 2004, pp. 444–538.

[250] E. Ojefors, U. Pfeiffer, A. Lisauskas, and H. Roskos, "A 0.65 THz focal-plane array in a quarter-micron CMOS process technology," *IEEE Journal of Solid-State Circuits*, vol. 44, no. 7, pp. 1968–1976, July 2009.

[251] M. Uzunkol and G. Rebeiz, "A low-noise 150-210 GHz detector in 45 nm CMOS SOI," *IEEE Microwave and Wireless Components Letters*, vol. 23, no. 6, pp. 309–311, June 2013.

[252] M. Uzunkol, O. Gurbuz, F. Golcuk, and G. Rebeiz, "A 0.32 THz SiGe 4×4 imaging array using high-efficiency on-chip antennas," *IEEE Journal of Solid-State Circuits*, vol. 48, no. 9, pp. 2056–2066, Sept. 2013.

[253] S.-W. Chu and C.-K. Wang, "An 80 GHz wide tuning range push-push VCO With -boosted full-wave rectification technique in 90 nm CMOS," *IEEE Microwave and Wireless Components Letters*, vol. 22, no. 4, pp. 203–205, April 2012.

[254] D. Cai, Y. Shang, H. Yu, and J. Ren, "An 80GHz on-chip metamaterial resonator by differential transmission line loaded with split ring resonator," *IET Electronics Letter*, vol. 48, no. 18, pp. 1128–1130, Aug. 2012.

[255] J. R. Whitehead, *Super-Regenerative Receivers*, 1st ed. U.K.:Cambridge Univ. Press, 1950.

[256] F. Moncunill-Geniz, P. Pala-Schonwalder, and O. Mas-Casals, "A generic approach to the theory of superregenerative reception," *IEEE Transactions on Circuits and Systems I*, vol. 52, no. 1, pp. 54–70, Jan. 2005.

[257] J. Bohorquez, A. Chandrakasan, and J. Dawson, "Frequency-domain analysis of super-regenerative amplifiers," *IEEE Transactions on Microwave Theory and Techniques*, vol. 57, no. 12, pp. 2882–2894, Dec. 2009.

[258] Y. Shang, H. Yu, D. Cai, J. Ren, and K. S. Yeo, "Design of high-Q millimeter-wave oscillator by differential transmission line loaded with metamaterial resonator in 65nm CMOS," *IEEE Transactions on Microwave Theory and Techniques*, vol. 61, no. 5, pp. 1892–1902, May 2013.

[259] F. Caster, L. Gilreath, S. Pan, Z. Wang, F. Capolino, and P. Heydari, "A 93-to-113GHz BiCMOS 9-element imaging array receiver utilizing spatial-overlapping pixels with wideband phase and amplitude control," in *IEEE International Solid-State Circuits Conference*, Feb. 2013, pp. 144–145.

[260] M. Tytgat, M. Steyaert, and P. Reynaert, "A 186 to 212GHz downconverter in 90nm CMOS," *Journal of Infrared, Millimeter, and Terahertz Waves*, vol. 33, no. 11, pp. 1085–1103, 2012. [Online]. Available: http://dx.doi.org/10.1007/s10762-012-9930-x

[261] M. C. Wanke, M. A. Mangan, and R. J. Foltynowicz, *Atmospheric Propagation of THz Radiation.* OSTI, Nov. 2005.

[262] T. Schneider, A. Wiatrek, S. Preussler, M. Grigat, and R.-P. Braun, "Link budget analysis for terahertz fixed wireless links," *IEEE Transactions on Terahertz Science and Technology*, vol. 2, no. 2, pp. 250–256, 2012.

[263] S. Hu, Y. Z. Xiong, L. Wang, D. Hou, and T. G. Lim, "A low-cost high-gain antenna array and its integration with active circuits," in *IEEE Electrical Design of Advanced Packaging Systems Symposium (EDAPS)*, Dec. 2010, pp. 1–4.

[264] F. Vecchi, S. Bozzola, M. Pozzoni, D. Guermandi, E. Temporiti, M. Repossi, U. Decanis, A. Mazzanti, and F. Svelto, "A 60GHz receiver with 13GHz bandwidth for Gbit/s wireless links in 65nm CMOS," in *IEEE International Conference on IC Design and Technology*, June 2010, pp. 228–231.

[265] B. Razavi, "A 300-GHz fundamental oscillator in 65-nm CMOS technology," in *IEEE Symposium on VLSI Circuits*, June 2010, pp. 113–114.

[266] T. Mitomo, R. Fujimoto, N. Ono, R. Tachibana, H. Hoshino, Y. Yoshihara, Y. Tsutsumi, and I. Seto, "A 60-GHz CMOS receiver front-end with frequency synthesizer," *IEEE Journal of Solid-State Circuits*, vol. 43, no. 4, pp. 1030–1037, April 2008.

[267] Y. Jin, J. Long, and M. Spirito, "A 7dB NF 60GHz-band millimeter-wave transconductance mixer," in *IEEE Radio Frequency Integrated Circuits Symposium*, June 2011, pp. 1–4.

[268] A. Tang, Q. Gu, Z. Xu, G. Virbila, and M.-C. F. Chang, "A Max 349 GHz 18.2mW/pixel CMOS inter-modulated regenerative receiver for tri-color mm-wave imaging," in *IEEE MTT-S International Microwave Symposium*, June 2012, pp. 1–3.

[269] R. Han and E. Afshari, "A 260GHz broadband source with 1.1mW continuous-wave radiated power and EIRP of 15.7dBm in 65nm CMOS," in *IEEE International Solid-State Circuits Conference*, Feb. 2013, pp. 138–139.

[270] R. C. Daniels and R. W. Heath, "60 ghz wireless communications: Emerging requirements and design recommendations," *IEEE Vehicular Technology Magazine*, vol. 2, no. 3, pp. 41–50, 2007.

[271] S. Cherry, "Edholm's law of bandwidth," *IEEE Spectrum*, vol. 41, no. 7, pp. 58–60, July 2004.

[272] K. Kang, F. Lin, D.-D. Pham, J. Brinkhoff, C.-H. Heng, Y. X. Guo, and X. Yuan, "A 60-ghz OOK receiver with an on-chip antenna in 90 nm CMOS," *IEEE Journal of Solid-State Circuits*, vol. 45, no. 9, pp. 1720–1731, 2010.

[273] J.-D. Park, S. Kang, and A. M. Niknejad, "A 0.38 thz fully integrated transceiver utilizing a quadrature push-push harmonic circuitry in sige BICMOS," *IEEE Journal of Solid-State Circuits*, vol. 47, no. 10, pp. 2344–2354, 2012.

[274] A. Natarajan, A. Komijani, X. Guan, A. Babakhani, and A. Hajimiri, "A 77-ghz phased-array transceiver with on-chip antennas in silicon: Transmitter and local lo-path phase shifting," *IEEE Journal of Solid-State Circuits*, vol. 41, no. 12, pp. 2807–2819, 2006.

[275] M. C. Wanke, M. Lee, C. D. Nordquist, M. J. Cich, M. Cavaliere, A. M. Rowen, J. R. Gillen, C. L. Arrington, A. D. Grine, C. T. Fuller *et al.*, "Integrated chip-scale thz technology," in *SPIE Defense, Security, and Sensing*. International Society for Optics and Photonics, 2011, pp. 80 310E–80 310E.

[276] Q. Wu and X.-C. Zhang, "Free-space electro-optic sampling of terahertz beams," *Applied Physics Letters*, vol. 67, no. 24, pp. 3523–3525, 1995.

[277] Y. Yan, Y. B. Karandikar, S. E. Gunnarsson, M. Urteaga, R. Pierson, and H. Zirath, "340 ghz integrated receiver in 250 nm InP DHBT technology," *IEEE Transactions on Terahertz Science and Technology*, vol. 2, no. 3, pp. 306–314, 2012.

[278] V. Radisic, W. R. Deal, K. M. Leong, X. Mei, W. Yoshida, P.-H. Liu, J. Uyeda, A. Fung, L. Samoska, T. Gaier et al., "A 10-mw submillimeter-wave solid-state power-amplifier module," *IEEE Transactions on Microwave Theory and Techniques*, vol. 58, no. 7, pp. 1903–1909, 2010.

[279] M. Abbasi, S. E. Gunnarsson, N. Wadefalk, R. Kozhuharov, J. Svedin, S. Cherednichenko, I. Angelov, I. Kallfass, P. Leuther, and H. Zirath, "Single-chip 220-ghz active heterodyne receiver and transmitter mmics with on-chip integrated antenna," *IEEE Transactions on Microwave Theory and Techniques*, vol. 59, no. 2, pp. 466–478, 2011.

[280] A. Hirata, R. Yamaguchi, T. Kosugi, H. Takahashi, K. Murata, T. Nagatsuma, N. Kukutsu, Y. Kado, N. Iai, S. Okabe *et al.*, "10-gbit/s wireless link using InP HEMT for generating 120-ghz-band millimeter-wave signal," *IEEE Transactions on Microwave Theory and Techniques*, vol. 57, no. 5, pp. 1102–1109, 2009.

[281] D. Tse and P. Viswanath, *Fundamentals of Wireless Communication.* Cambridge University Press, 2005.

[282] J.-D. Park, S. Kang, S. Thyagarajan, E. Alon, and A. Niknejad, "A 260 GHz fully integrated CMOS transceiver for wireless chip-to-chip communication," in *IEEE Symposium on VLSI Circuits*, June 2012, pp. 48–49.

[283] M. Nazari and A. Emami-Neyestanak, "A 15-Gb/s 0.5-mW/Gbps two-tap DFE receiver with far-end crosstalk cancellation," *IEEE Journal of Solid-State Circuits*, vol. 47, no. 10, pp. 2420–2432, Oct. 2012.

[284] G.-S. Byun, Y. Kim, J. Kim, S.-W. Tam, and M.-C. Chang, "An energy-efficient and high-speed mobile memory I/O interface using simultaneous bi-directional dual (Base+RF)-band signaling," *IEEE Journal of Solid-State Circuits*, vol. 47, no. 1, pp. 117–130, Jan. 2012.

[285] S. Palermo, A. Emami-Neyestanak, and M. Horowitz, "A 90nm CMOS 16Gb/s transceiver for optical interconnects," in *IEEE International Solid-State Circuits Conference*, Feb. 2007, pp. 44–586.

[286] I. Young, E. Mohammed, J. Liao, A. Kern, S. Palermo, B. Block, M. Reshotko, and P. Chang, "Optical I/O technology for tera-scale computing," *IEEE Journal of Solid-State Circuits*, vol. 45, no. 1, pp. 235–248, Jan. 2010.

[287] S. Ma, H. Yu, Y. Shang, W. M. Lim, and J. Ren, "A 131.5GHz, -84dBm sensitivity super-regenerative receiver by zero-phase-shifter coupled oscillator network in 65nm CMOS," in *IEEE European Solid State Circuits Conference*, Sept. 2014, pp. 187–190.

[288] J. B. Pendry, L. Mart-Moreno, and F. J. Garcia-Vidal, "Mimicking surface plasmons with structured surfaces," *Science*, vol. 305, no. 5685, pp. 847–848, 2004.

[289] F. J. García de Abajo and J. J. Sáenz, "Electromagnetic surface modes in structured perfect-conductor surfaces," *Phys. Rev. Lett.*, vol. 95, p. 233901, Nov. 2005.

[290] J. T. Shen, P. B. Catrysse, and S. Fan, "Mechanism for designing metallic metamaterials with a high index of refraction," *Phys. Rev. Lett.*, vol. 94, p. 197401, May 2005.

[291] D. Martin-Cano, M. Nesterov, A. Fernandez-Dominguez, F. J. Garcia-Vidal, L. Martin-Moreno, and E. Moreno, "Domino plasmons for subwavelength terahertz circuitry," *Optics express*, vol. 18, no. 2, pp. 754–764, 2010.

[292] M. Navarro-Cía, M. Beruete, S. Agrafiotis, F. Falcone, M. Sorolla, and S. A. Maier, "Broadband spoof plasmons and subwavelength electromagnetic energy confinement on ultrathin metafilms," *Optics express*, vol. 17, no. 20, pp. 18184–18195, 2009.

[293] J. G. Rivas, "Terahertz: The art of confinement," *Nature Photonics*, vol. 2, no. 3, pp. 137–138, 2008.

[294] H. F. Ma, X. Shen, Q. Cheng, W. X. Jiang, and T. J. Cui, "Broadband and high-efficiency conversion from guided waves to spoof surface plasmon polaritons," *Laser & Photonics Reviews*, vol. 8, no. 1, pp. 146–151, 2014.

[295] Y. J. Zhou, Q. Jiang, and T. J. Cui, "Bidirectional bending splitter of designer surface plasmons," *Applied Physics Letters*, vol. 99, no. 11, p. 111904, 2011.

[296] J. Wu, Y. Kao, H. Lin, T. Yang, D. Tsai, H. Chang, C. Li, I. Hsieh, L. Shen, and X. Zhang, "Crosstalk reduction between metal-strips with subwavelength periodically corrugated structure," *Electronics letters*, vol. 46, no. 18, pp. 1273–1274, 2010.

[297] J. Wu, D. Hou, J. Shen, H. Chiueh, T. Yang, and C.-J. Wu, "Differential transmission lines with surface plasmon polaritons at low frequencies," *Electronics Letters*, vol. 50, no. 5, pp. 379–381, 2014.

[298] H. E. Lin, T.-J. Yang, Y.-H. Kao, J.-J. Wu, C. Li, C.-J. Wu, and X. Zhang, "Experimental verification of the suppression of crosstalk between bended parallel microstrips via designer surface plasmon polaritons," in *PIERS Proceedings, 2013 IEEE*, Sept 2013, pp. 1–4.

[299] A. P. Hibbins, B. R. Evans, and J. R. Sambles, "Experimental verification of designer surface plasmons," *Science*, vol. 308, no. 5722, pp. 670–672, 2005.

[300] B. K. Juluri, S.-C. S. Lin, T. R. Walker, L. Jensen, and T. J. Huang, "Propagation of designer surface plasmons in structured conductor surfaces with parabolic gradient index," *Optics express*, vol. 17, no. 4, pp. 2997–3006, 2009.

[301] C. R. Williams, S. R. Andrews, S. Maier, A. Fernández-Domínguez, L. Martín-Moreno, and F. García-Vidal, "Highly confined guiding of terahertz surface plasmon polaritons on structured metal surfaces," *Nature Photonics*, vol. 2, no. 3, pp. 175–179, 2008.

[302] F. Garcia-Vidal, L. Martin-Moreno, and J. Pendry, "Surfaces with holes in them: New plasmonic metamaterials," *Journal of Optics A: Pure and Applied Optics*, vol. 7, no. 2, p. S97, 2005.

[303] U. Fano, "Effects of configuration interaction on intensities and phase shifts," *Physical Review*, vol. 124, no. 6, p. 1866, 1961.

[304] C. Pelard, E. Gebara, A. Kim, M. Vrazel, F. Bien, Y. Hur, M. Maeng, S. Chandramouli, C. Chun, S. Bajekal, S. Ralph, B. Schmukler, V. Hietala, and J. Laskar, "Realization of multigigabit channel equalization and crosstalk cancellation integrated circuits," *IEEE Journal of Solid-State Circuits*, vol. 39, no. 10, pp. 1659–1670, Oct. 2004.

[305] D. Schinkel, E. Mensink, E. Klumperink, E. van Tuijl, and B. Nauta, "A 3-Gb/s/ch transceiver for 10-mm uninterrupted RC-limited global on-chip interconnects," *IEEE Journal of Solid-State Circuits*, vol. 41, no. 1, pp. 297–306, Jan. 2006.

[306] J. Lee, W. Lee, and S. Cho, "A 2.5-Gb/s on-chip interconnect transceiver with crosstalk and ISI equalizer in 130 nm CMOS," *IEEE Transactions on Circuits and Systems I*, vol. 59, no. 1, pp. 124–136, Jan. 2012.

[307] B. Kim, Y. Liu, T. Dickson, J. Bulzacchelli, and D. Friedman, "A 10-Gb/s compact low-power serial I/O with DFE-IIR equalization in 65-nm CMOS," *IEEE Journal of Solid-State Circuits*, vol. 44, no. 12, pp. 3526–3538, Dec. 2009.

[308] J. Lee, M.-S. Chen, and H.-D. Wang, "Design and comparison of three 20-Gb/s backplane transceivers for duobinary, PAM4, and NRZ data," *IEEE Journal of Solid-State Circuits*, vol. 43, no. 9, pp. 2120–2133, Sept. 2008.

[309] H.-J. Song, J.-Y. Kim, K. Ajito, N. Kukutsu, and M. Yaita, "50-gb/s direct conversion QPSK modulator and demodulator mmics for terahertz communications at 300 ghz," *IEEE Transactions on Microwave Theory and Techniques*, vol. 62, no. 3, pp. 600–609, March 2014.

[310] Y. Shang, H. Yu, C. Yang, S. Hu, and M. Je, "A high-sensitivity 135GHz millimeter-wave imager by differential transmission-line loaded split-ring-resonator in 65nm CMOS," in *IEEE European Solid State Device Research Conference*, Sept. 2014, pp. 166–169.

[311] H.-Y. Chang, M.-F. Lei, C.-S. Lin, Y.-H. Cho, Z.-M. Tsai, and H. Wang, "A 46-GHz direct wide modulation bandwidth ASK modulator in 0.13-μm CMOS technology," *IEEE Microwave and Wireless Components Letters*, vol. 17, no. 9, pp. 691–693, Sept. 2007.

[312] H. Wu, L. Nan, S.-W. Tam, H.-H. Hsieh, C. Jou, G. Reinman, J. Cong, and M.-C. Chang, "A 60GHz on-chip RF-interconnect with $\lambda/4$ coupler for 5Gbps bi-directional communication and multi-drop arbitration," in *IEEE Custom Integrated Circuits Conference*, Sept 2012, pp. 1–4.

[313] J.-B. You, M. Park, J.-W. Park, and G. Kim, "12.5 GBPS optical modulation of silicon racetrack resonator based on carrier-depletion in asymmetric pn diode," *Optics express*, vol. 16, no. 22, pp. 18 340–18 344, 2008.

[314] T. Li, H. Liu, T. Li, S. Wang, J. Cao, Z. Zhu, Z. Dong, S. Zhu, and X. Zhang, "Suppression of radiation loss by hybridization effect in two coupled split-ring resonators," *Physical Review B*, vol. 80, no. 11, p. 115113, 2009.

[315] D. R. Smith, D. C. Vier, T. Koschny, and C. M. Soukoulis, "Electromagnetic parameter retrieval from inhomogeneous metamaterials," *Phys. Rev. E*, vol. 71, no. 3, p. 036617, Mar. 2005.

[316] H. C. Nguyen, Y. Sakai, M. Shinkawa, N. Ishikura, and T. Baba, "10 gb/s operation of photonic crystal silicon optical modulators," *Optics express*, vol. 19, no. 14, pp. 13 000–13 007, 2011.

[317] A. Oncu, K. Takano, and M. Fujishima, "8Gbps CMOS ASK modulator for 60GHz wireless communication," in *IEEE Asian Solid-State Circuits Conference*, 2008, pp. 125–128.

[318] K. Katayama, M. Motoyoshi, K. Takano, N. Ono, and M. Fujishima, "28mw 10gbps transmitter for 120ghz ask transceiver," in *IEEE MTT-S International Microwave Symposium*, June 2012, pp. 1–3.

[319] G. Rasigade, M. Ziebell, D. Marris-Morini, J.-M. Fédéli, F. Milesi, P. Grosse, D. Bouville, E. Cassan, and L. Vivien, "High extinction ratio 10 gbit/s silicon optical modulator," *Optics Express*, vol. 19, no. 7, pp. 5827–5832, 2011.

[320] I. Young, E. Mohammed, J. Liao, A. Kern, S. Palermo, B. Block, M. Reshotko, and P. Chang, "Optical I/O technology for tera-scale computing," *Solid-State Circuits, IEEE Journal of*, vol. 45, no. 1, pp. 235–248, Jan 2010.

[321] K.-S. Ha, L.-S. Kim, S.-J. Bae, K.-I. Park, J. S. Choi, Y.-H. Jun, and K. Kim, "A 6gb/s/pin pseudo-differential signaling using common-mode noise rejection techniques without reference signal for dram interfaces," in *Solid-State Circuits Conference-Digest of Technical Papers, 2009. ISSCC 2009. IEEE International*. IEEE, 2009, pp. 138–139.

[322] J. W. Poulton, W. J. Dally, X. Chen, J. G. Eyles, T. H. Greer, S. G. Tell, J. M. Wilson, and C. T. Gray, "A 0.54 pj/b 20 gb/s ground-referenced single-ended short-reach serial link in 28 nm CMOS for advanced packaging applications," *Solid-State Circuits, IEEE Journal of*, vol. 48, no. 12, pp. 3206–3218, 2013.

Index